I DEDICATE THIS BOOK FOR PEOPLE THAT ARE DIFFERENT. WITH THE LOVE OF GOD, I HOPE THAT YOU ARE INSPIRED IN ALL AREAS OF YOUR LIFE BY THE CONTENTS OF THIS BOOK.

Copyright © 2014 **Robbie Dee Ewens**
All rights reserved.

ISBN 10: 1514139146
ISBN 13: 978-1514139141
Library of Congress Control Number: 2015911896
LCCN Imprint Name: CreateSpace Independent Publishing Platform, North Charleston, SC

At Last! Free to be Me

CONTENTS

- Preface   Page 8

Chapter One – How it was in the Beginning

- Introduction   Page 11
- Childhood   Page 12
- Adolescence   Page 16
  (Some explicit sexual acts mentioned in this chapter so discretion needed to who should read this chapter)
- Getting Married   Page 20
- The Beginning and End of a Marriage Page 28
  (Some explicit sexual acts mentioned in this chapter so discretion needed to who should read this chapter)
- The Meaning of Life   Page 32
- My New Life in God   Page 42
- A Visit to Hell   Page 46
- The Power of God Experienced - Witchcraft Fare   Page 50
- Jehovah Witnesses   Page 52
- The Conversion and Salvation of Paul Medford   Page 54
- The First Prophesy   Page 58
- Closing the Business Down   Page 58

Chapter Two – This New Life in Christ

- The Visions   Page 63
- Interlude – Let me Explain Being a Christian   Page 70

Chapter Three – A Sent One

- Travels Around the UK – First Trip to Youth Hostelling in Scotland   Page 82
- Travels Around the UK – The Second Trip to Scotland: Isle of Mull   Page 91
- Travels Around the UK – Off to the South of England   Page 93
- First Trip to USA   Page 96
- Second Trip to USA   Page 111
- Third -Trip to USA – Meeting My Wife and the Second Prophecy   Page 112
- Trip to Nigeria and the Third Prophesy   Page 145
- Fourth Trip to USA

Chapter Four – Moving and Facing My Heart. Twenty Years of Refining Starts

- My Wife, Priscilla and the Wedding   Page 167
- And we Lasted Ten Weeks Together   Page 177
- Ice Skating and the Gypsies come to Christ!   Page 188
- The Miracle Return to the United States of America   Page 194
- The Ugly Heart Resurfaces with Vengeance   Page 203
- A Double Life Style and the Hypocrisy of it   Page 207
- The Never Ending Downward Spiral   Page 207

- ❖ Our Cry for Help Not Fulfilled. The Powerless Church　　　　　　　　　　　Page 216
- ❖ Starting to Break – A Retreat in Kentucky　　　　　　　　　　　　　　Page 218
- ❖ Who Am I? The Answer Profoundly Revealed　　　　　　　　　　　　　Page 226
- ❖ A Whole New Understanding of What This Life is About　　　　　　　　　Page 226
- ❖ Living Through the Pain of What I Did to Others　　　　　　　　　　　Page 227
- ❖ Final Steps of Recovery into God's Righteousness?　　　　　　　　　　Page 229
- ❖ A Prayer and Lives are Saved　　Page 232
- ❖ The House gets Destroyed　　　　Page 241
- ❖ The Old House and The US Coastguard Finds Me　　　　　　　　　　Page 252
- ❖ Why Can't I Overcome and get the Victory!?　　　　　　　　　　　　Page 256
- ❖ Selling the Old Home　　　　　　Page 257

Chapter Five – My Destiny in Life. Sanctified and Commissioned unto God for this Very Purpose

- ❖ I am Nearly Fifty: A Terrible Shock　Page 260
- ❖ I am Fifty: The Prophesized Start of Ministry　　　　　　　　　　　　　Page 264
- ❖ This Insanity Has to Stop!　　　　Page 265
- ❖ I am Fifty-One! Did I Miss God?　Page 265
- ❖ The Desire of my Heart: I am Transgender!!!　　　　　　　　　　　Page 270
- ❖ Transgender: Definitions　　　　　Page 270
- ❖ 'True' and 'False' Transgender people　　　　　　　　　　　　　　Page 290

5

- ❖ Changes to My Body — Page 294
- ❖ Changes in My Behavior — Page 297
- ❖ Pictures Before and During my Transition — Page 300
- ❖ Persecution against Being Transgender — Page 307
- ❖ Overcoming the Fear of Man — Page 315
- ❖ YMCA Experience — Page 324
- ❖ The Church, Religion Verses the Kingdom of God and Transgender People — Page 329
- ❖ A Hearts Cry — Page 329
- ❖ My Argument — Page 330
- ❖ Definition of a True Transgender Person — Page 335
- ❖ Definition of a False Transgender Person — Page 335
- ❖ A Legalistic Church Response to True and 'False' Transgender People — Page 336
- ❖ Scriptures: Introduction — Page 343
- ❖ Looking at the Scriptures — Page 343
- ❖ Looking at other Material — Page 360

Chapter Six – Moving Forward: The Present and the Future

- ❖ 2014: Refined, Set Free and Sent Out. What will it Look Like? — Page 382
- ❖ The Agony of a Pending Divorce — Page 384
- ❖ Divorce Mediation and Rejection — Page 386
- ❖ People Start to Turn Back to God — Page 391
- ❖ OYP — Page 392
- ❖ Accepted in a Bible Based Church — Page 393

- ❖ Salvation at Starbucks!   Page 396
- ❖ Art and the Horses   Page 399
- ❖ Translady Turns to Christ from Being Atheist
                                          Page 403
- ❖ First Divorce Related Court Session Page 404
- ❖ Time for Surgery!   Page 410
- ❖ Crossing the Gender Line   Page 419
- ❖ A Letter to My Wife Prisci   Page 422
- ❖ The Current End of this Book!   Page 423
- ❖ Appendix 1 – Online Documentaries and Articles
                                          Page 429
- ❖ Appendix 2 – Contact Information   Page 429
- ❖ Acknowledgements   Page 436

Preface

Okay, well, here goes. God told me to write a book (and people have been telling me to do so for a few years now), so here it is. But, if I missed God, then at least I hope my story and journey to the truth about my life and the truth about life will help you, a relative, or a friend that you may know.

Gee, I hardly ever even read books except my Bible! My grammar is not exactly of a high standard, and I will have to heavily rely upon good old Microsoft spell check (which has already found one error!). But, I do have a story to tell, quite an incredible story, and inside that story are many lessons to be learnt for everyone young or old. If this request is indeed from the Lord, then I state now that I hope that each lesson shines into your heart as clear as the sun shines at noon in a clear sky.

Please note that I will be graphic at times to the extent that I feel that you are getting a clear understanding of what I went through. Some behaviors like sex are all too often talked about in the third person, like that 'thing' some people do. Not here, so be forewarned. However, I do not go into graphic details, rather just label what went on so as to be as offensive as little as possible. We do, however need to get this stuff out into the open so we can be clear on what we are addressing, and therefore possibly help some folk out there get the real victory over it so that they may have a life that is real, true and gives inner peace.

Although I wrestled with sexually immoral practices, one could just as easily substitute, or add other forms of habitual behaviors such as alcoholism, drugs, violence, or compulsive lying. Also, what we consider perhaps more minor wrong habits are really just the same too: overeating, obesity, stealing, law breaking, continually being critical, angry, greedy, materialistic, or workaholic. If I have missed yours in here, then add it yourself.

I had many different possible titles for this book and I am going to list them here and explain why each would have been appropriate:

At Last! Freedom from the Bonds of Sexual Immorality

This title tells of my struggles to overcome lust, sexual lust that started during my adolescence and colored my whole life until I was fifty years old. Sexual lust motivates and drives a person to do things that otherwise they may not have ever done in their lives. Freedom from this is truly liberating indeed, like having to wear a darkened pair of sunglasses all your life then suddenly they are removed and you can see all these beautiful colors and everything is brighter. This was the original title of the book but I thought that plastering such a title on the cover might cause an issue with some people!

An Hispanic and an Englishman's Modern Day Pilgrimage
I was hoping that my darling wife Prisci would participate throughout this book to give her story and her point of view as she saw her life, my life, and our twenty plus years of married life. As of April 2014, when she had divorce papers served on me, dated April 2nd, our twentieth wedding anniversary date of all things, it does not look like she will be contributing. My heart is broken.

One Man's Walk with God
Jesus Christ revealed Himself to me, a nobody from a non-Christian, non-religious English family of whom most were claiming to be atheists. My truly miraculous conversion and how the Lord sent me over three continents and showed me great and marvelous things warrants this title. My life is a continual unfolding of the mercy of God.

Found to be Transgender in Christ Jesus!
Oh my! Now here is a confronting title and most challenging to the majority of Christian believers, especially to those who believe that all forms of 'transgenderism' is a sin to be overcome. I devote a large section later in this book to define exactly what being transgender is, and discuss and challenge current traditional doctrines in the church.

Born, born again, and born again again!
Getting saved by Jesus Christ is the most profound of all my experiences all put together and I desire so much for others to truly be born again of the Spirit of God. The life transformation that takes place and continues throughout one's life is better and more real than anything you can find in this world. If you have ever wondered if there is more to life than just being born, living and then dying, here is your answer. So I was born as a baby in the flesh, I was born again by the saving grace of Jesus Christ that saved my soul unto Him. And now I am being born again, as it were in my body to a new life and a new world of people. I pray and hope my wife will join me, or rejoin me to serve the Lord in this journey.

So, is God really alive today in the modern world? Yes He is…read this!
There are thousands, tens and hundreds of thousands of people out there on this planet that are questioning the very presence of God. There are many Christian believers who are wondering where the power and gifts and callings that the Bible clearly mentions about are. My life is a true

testimony that God is alive and there for all those who will abandon themselves to Him and are willing to pay the price.

Just a nobody that God can use as long as ~~he~~ she doesn't become a somebody

I put this possible title in as it shows two things. Firstly, we are all nobodies; we are all just people that stay on earth in our bodies for a short time and then depart. To live life to the fullest you need to be whole. Your spirit, soul and body need to be whole, complete. A person who humbles him or herself to God and that remains humble can, by God's grace, have a truly amazing life. All our lives wind a different pathway in life but to go it alone, stuck in yourself, is not fulfilling at all. May this book be inspiring to you to desire and seek the Lord for the rest of your life that you may be whole in all things like I am, finally. What a journey!

Being an English person, you will at times find me using English words like 'boot' of the car so I will endeavor to place the American word (in this case 'trunk') in parenthesis for you just to make sure you understand what I mean.

There are times during the writing of this book that something happened that relates to what I am writing at that moment. I have chosen to include these events in the book. They will appear as 'Interruptions' and should hopefully be easy to recognize and understand.

Ready to face yourself like I had to? Ready to discover the truth about transgender people? If so, buy this book if you are reading it at a book store to educate yourself on this ever increasing reality in our current society that was once so hidden in secret, but now is becoming more visible.

PURPOSE

I do want to make myself perfectly clear on the purpose of this book. Firstly, I want to let true transgender people know that God does not condemn you for who you are and that any judgments of man against you on this subject are in error.

    Secondly, to the church, the Christian church body I write this book to challenge any traditional doctrines that not only contradict reality but are also in error as they are reading into scriptures that which is not there specifically, and then judging others by it. I will put my life testimony and myself before you to help reveal this and make myself, as long as I have the breath of life in me, available to you.

Lastly, I write this book to the general public. You who are interested in this truth and may even know a transgender person, or know someone that might be transgender. You may be a Christian and wonder how transgender people should be viewed. Should you openly rebuke us? Should you secretly judge us? Should you do neither and accept us, accepting that God can make, or at least permit a wide range of people in His creation? What *is* the Godly way that transgender people should be related to? This book attempts to answer some of these questions in a way that I hope will lead you to true and honorable answers.

And finally, everything I have written in this book is true to the best of my recollection, other than changing names of people and some entities for privacy sake. I have been particularly very careful NOT to exaggerate anything that I have written. God does not need our exaggerations. I write it like it happened. Thank you.

Chapter One - Introduction

Completing the Preface was an achievement for me! Now comes the story part. I feel that it is important that I give you, the reader, some background, a picture of my past. That way you will be able to see what God can do in a life, the life of a nobody like me. My story, for sure, will be different from yours, and that is good. That is how it should be. Each person's life is different circumstantially and we all make different decisions about how we are going to act in each situation. We are given different talents and develop those talents differently. And, if we manage to find a true relationship with God on a personal level and if we avail ourselves to Him, our lives can be quite amazing, full of tests and trials and *life*! But, having said all that, we, that is we human's, all have some things in common. We are all born, and we will all die in the body we have. We all (though sometimes we for sure must question this) have God's moral law inside of us (somewhere!). And, because of this we all have some understanding of right and wrong. And of course, the people around us and the environment we are in influence us all throughout our lives. My story then will wind a different path to yours, but the solution regarding the meaning of our lives is the same.

Before I give you some background on my life, please do not fall into the trap of judging my experiences against yours (or visa versa). Let's be clear and establish that I may have gotten into stuff either more deeply, or less deeply than yourself or other people, and we may have got there by very different paths, or you may have not got into anything I did at all. If you see yourself as being in a mess, the important question is, "How the heck do I get out of this?" Mind you, if you are reading this book and the truth is "I really don't want to get out of this," I understand too, just keep on reading. And if you are reading this book just to help others and you have your life sorted out then let me be the first to rejoice with you and I pray you help others with all you have been given.

As for me, which 'category' of wrongful behaviors did I get myself into? In some ways it really doesn't matter, any or all but for the record up front, I became a lusting person (in all forms of media), a transvestite, homosexual and other related behaviors. I could possibly have gone on to being a transsexual person all wrapped up in lust and pride. However, by the grace of God you will read how God, in His infinite wisdom and mercy, orchestrated an amazing path for me to journey upon... remember, what you are about to read is ALL true...

Chapter One – My Story - Childhood

My story....*my* story... okay here we go:

My name, Robert David Ewens is a Scottish name (well the Ewens bit is anyway). I was born on June 25th 1962 in a county called Surrey in South England, a little south of the London area. I don't remember living there at all. My first name, which apparently was chosen randomly in that I was not named after anyone in the family line, means a bright shining light, able to lead and kingship!

My parents, Roy and Ellen Ewens moved down to the south coast due to my dad's work situation, and then, by the time I was around four years old, we had moved to Leicester which is located in the Midlands, the central part of England, about one hundred miles north of London. My first main memories come from here onwards.

I have an older brother, Roger who is four years older than myself. I also have an older sister, Susan, who is two years older. On the outside looking in (and still to this day I am sure my dad would say), we were a seemingly typical English household. My mother was a trained nursery nurse, and had gained additional training for children with special needs. My dad was a well-educated, upright kind of English gentleman who always promoted good morals and worked hard to provide well for his family.

Life went on in Leicester, my dad working, if I recall correctly, as a warehouse manager for Gents, the clock manufacturer. Later, he took a similar position for Firestone Tires as by this time we had moved to another house where my parents live to this day on the outskirts of the city in an area called Birstall (Addendum: My mother passed away late summer

2013). He then went on to be warehouse manager for Ladybird Books which publish books mainly for children.

It was here in Birstall where I spent most of my childhood days. I do not remember moving to Birstall, but I do recall my first days at school. The school, which had both the infants (four to five year olds) and primary (five to ten year olds) school buildings on the same grounds, was just down the road, literally! The entrance was less than one hundred yards from my front gate on the other side of the road. We always had our 'lollipop' lady (American is a crossing guard I think) to assist us across the road. I was an innocent boy just living life. After attending the infant school for maybe one year, I went up to the primary school. I was a typical young boy who liked school at that age, being sociable and performed probably average to just above average in my classes. I reviewed my old school reports and saw that the only common comment from my teachers was that I needed to work at concentrating more and become more consistent in my work. I liked playing soccer and as I was a tall and skinny kind of build, I would usually play out on the wing where I could run a lot. Either that, or I would end up as goalkeeper (I think some people liked to aim for me but I didn't care, at least I stopped the ball!).

With my dad at work from 7:00am and back at 5:30pm Monday to Fridays, my mum was able to earn money by running a before and after school daycare service for the younger school children. Because of her extra qualifications, she could have more children in at any one time compared to other similar services. All I can remember is little kids everywhere! The dining room became a play area, so did the hall or lobby area and when the weather was nice, the back garden (backyard). There were toys, games, dressing clothes and books. I was going to say that they were all over the place, but that would not be true. My mum really did a good job of keeping things in order considering that there seemed to be almost ten children there at times! This may not sound a lot for some people but middle class English houses are small compared to most American houses. We had a two story brick house and only the downstairs was used for the day care with the living room and kitchen out of bounds for the children. This left the dining room (playroom), and hall for them all to play in.

I am not sure why, but my sister and I did not get along with each other at all really. At best, she kept herself away, at worst she was up to some kind of trouble. Well, that is how it appeared to me at the time. Not that I was a perfect boy at the age of seven and eight either!

As I am writing this story of my past to you now, I can clearly recall two occasions that I need to let you know about. When I was an innocent young boy my sister persuaded me to join in a few dressing up sessions for 'fun'. There were lots of clothes to choose from but she wanted me to dress in a dress. It was all seemingly innocent fun. I mean, she even once took me out around the block dressed like that. I remember a friend from up the road seeing me and teasing me, but I quickly put an end to that by letting him know that I was a black belt in the martial arts (the clown believed me and never told anyone). I did the same dressing up at least once with Susan when I was close to ten (my age not too clear here). It kind of bothered me so I asked my dad about it who told me something like,

"That's okay, some people do that and you will probably grow out of it." Anyway, it bothered me so I didn't do it again (truth was I liked it which is why it bothered me).

At the age of ten everyone in the school had to take a music ear test. This was back in the days when the old gramophone records were around. A group of us were taken into a room, given a list of questions that we had to answer after each section was played from the record. Now the record, as I remember, was just played from beginning to end once. You gave your answers, and out the room you went. End of test.

It must have been either the next day or just a few days after the music test that both my parents and I were informed that I had scored 100%. Only very few children do this we were told. The school virtually insisted that I should learn an instrument. I was asked what I would like to learn and all I can remember saying straight away without hesitation was, "The violin."

Now why the violin, only God knows, because I didn't even know anyone that played one!

Within a couple of weeks the school loaned me a violin and there I was in a class of some twenty plus other children with a cantankerous looking Scottish violin teacher called Mr. Wilson. He was friendly but you could tell that you shouldn't mess with him either, if you know what I mean. Well, sure enough, Mr. Wilson only took a few weeks to whittle the numbers down to less than a dozen, and then a while after that, down to three of us. I loved playing, I thought I was so great! I saw myself playing as a soloist in front of thousands, and they were all mesmerized by my playing. Grandiose dreams for a ten-year-old! My dad has a recording on the old reel-to-reel four track player of one of my first attempts at playing, what a racket! Scratching and scraping something that sounded more like recorded sounds from outer space! Yet, to me, it was beautiful. What's more, my parents totally supported my endeavors.

So my childhood life continued. At the age of ten, or about then, I remember kissing my first girl on the cheek in the playground. I got told off for it too! At home, I had my older brother and sister to relate to. At ten years of age, my brother and I were still sharing a room together. My parents had their room and my sister hers. This all seemed to work fine but I never got close to either of them. I seemed to be more of a loner. I would love to just get on my bicycle and ride to the countryside and just walk and sit down by the brook (creek) and just be there, in creation as it were. There I was always at peace. We lived on the edge of what we call a 'green belt' which is an area dedicated to nature where no building is allowed. Today, it is all built up so I do not know what happened to that law!

My parents brought us up to be independent yet they also enjoyed family. Neither of them were religious nor knew the Lord in their lives. My brother to this day says he doesn't believe God exists; in other words, he is an atheist, but I do not know what his beliefs were at that time. My sister, Susan, I think, believes in God now, but again, at that time I do not know. As for my parents, my dad believes that there is a creator but that the Bible for example, is just a collection of mythical stories and that Christianity just falls into the same category of 'religion' where all the other religions of the world belong (Addendum: My dad now claims to be an atheist too). My mother, well she kept quiet, but she for sure was not saved and we never, I mean *never*, had the Bible read in our house. I don't even think we had one, why would we want to?

Of the three children in my family, I was considered the more 'sensitive' child, and they were probably correct. I was more emotional I guess and had a real sensitivity particularly towards animals for some reason. It took me years to feel confident to even pick up a cat without fearing I would hurt it! Sounds somewhat stupid recalling this now but that's how I was then.

I often went around to my next door neighbors who had three boys. We got up to all kinds of pranks. There was a disused railway line just a five minute walk away up my street. We did all the things boys would do from creating our own 'gang' and have stone wars with other gangs, nothing really serious, just kid stuff. We would set the embankments on fire, then put them out (most of the time!). Etc., etc., etc.

One thing worth mentioning here was that it was around the age of between ten and twelve I think that I would sometimes have a dream. It was the same dream each time. I would go to sleep and I would be taken on to an operating table where I would have a sex change. I never saw any operation and there were no bandages or scars, nor doctors or anyone else around. I would lie on that table and wake and get up as a girl of the same age. I could see my small breasts and I had a female body shape. I was *so* happy, I was wanting this to be real. I remember that I would try to want to stay in the dream even after I woke up and the next few nights I would want to go back to the dream again, hoping that when I would fall asleep I would be back there again. Well, I guess by the age of thirteen or so I stopped having that dream and stopped seeking it as male adolescence started.

By the time I had moved up to the High school, which was located a mile and a quarter away (a nice walk every day!) I was definitely into my violin playing. Having survived the Mr. Haggis, I mean Mr. Wilson's sifting process, I had my first lesson at my high school with....Mr. Wilson! So he continued to be my violin tutor through my teenage years. Arrr yes, my teenage years…

(Some explicit sexual acts mentioned so discretion needed as to who can read this chapter)

Chapter One – My Story - Adolescence

Now why, oh why did God make us go through adolescence! This really has me scratching my head! Anyway, it does exist and both boys and girls have to make their way through it. I have heard horror stories of how some ladies, and some men were never informed of this stage of their lives. More accurately, I would say how much they were miss-informed. I was not one of those. In high school, besides music classes, I liked mathematics and biology so in biology we covered all that stuff about how to make babies. I think I was about thirteen years old at that time. Sex was starting to draw my attention, and for sure, it was all the other classmates, boys and girls. This is the 'giggling' phase of finding out about sex. It seemed to me that some girls were very knowledgeable on the subject, especially when it came to the practicalities. Got me thinking that they had 'done it' with someone, and some had I discovered later. We were taken into the theatre room where movies etc. are shown at the school. Here I had my first eyeful of various men and women's sexual body parts and we all had a lesson on the importance and usage of different types of contraceptives and how our bodies change.

Some things in school didn't go too well. It seemed that both my brother and sister had got themselves not the best of reputations and, as the 'third of the Ewens family' I was already marked by a few teachers as a bad boy. I also got myself into trouble a few times for fighting. Actually, I had a few classic fights that were well talked about in school for some time after. I remember once my sister actually sticking up for me at school when some girls were unfairly picking on me. That was the one time that she touched my heart. She fought off the group of girls that had it in for me for some reason or other. As for my brother, Roger, being four years older than I, he was already up in the final year in another building so I did not see him at all. He got himself the reputation of not bothering at school (oh, except in mathematics which he liked). Up to the age of about thirteen I got on well with my brother.

Roger had taken up fishing with his friend, Andy, who lived a few streets away from us. I also showed great interest in fishing and finally persuaded my dad to let me go with him. It wasn't long until I was more successful than my brother. Seems like me and the fishes were in collaboration with each other (my wife today will probably tell you it is still that way!). My dad gave us all pocket money until we were eighteen years old so I would save most of mine for fishing gear.

At home Roger had friends around to play snooker on a three-quarter-size table (a parent game that pool came from). I joined in at times and got pretty good myself, but got humiliated on a few occasions as I would sometimes win some of the betting money through hard shots they all thought were 'flukes', just lucky shots. I quit playing with them after going upset to my mum and dad.

Something else was also happening in my home that was kept from me. My mother was having some mental health issues. What I mean is that she became diagnosed over a period of time as being manic depressive schizophrenic. Imagining that people were after her to drug her and do things to her. But, like I said this was kept from me, and the condition, as I understand it, developed over a period of time.

Where was I during that time? Good question. Well I was all wrapped up in my own self-discovery of what sex was about simply because neither my mum nor dad spent much time guiding me through this critical phase of my life. Because I was not having a close relationship with my parents, I 'adopted' a family, full of pretty girls. The eldest, Susan was a girl in my school form class that I really liked. Her other two sisters were also very pretty. I spent most of my after school time at their house. I was relaxed there. I never dated, nor kissed any of them. I always conducted myself properly and just enjoyed being with them, but it resulted in even more time out of my house. My parents didn't seem to be bothered about this. I was always much more at ease being with girls rather than boys.

So to date I had biology lessons at school, comments and suggestions from school pals and girls about sex, and now, at the age of around fourteen to fifteen with some of my friends, we somehow got hold of the porn magazines. It's amazing how Hustler and Penthouse and others can all of a sudden be found. We had them hidden up the disused railway line. We only gloated over them, we didn't get up to anything else. No sexual experiences came out of that, just typical young men "Oooing, arrring, and look at that pair of t..s" stuff. Then there were the few romantic novels that were kept in my room. I soon got to know which pages had the bed scenes in them. I had a great imagination and would use it a lot too.

Then there were the music trips. As I had become quite proficient at playing the violin, I got into the top senior county music orchestra at an early age of fifteen. This meant missing some other school activities to go on these trips, which was a little hard on me but there you go. Also, my parents sacrificed their time and money to really support me.

These trips involved staying in different schools in the county during some school holiday time where we (the whole orchestra) spent time together learning our pieces that we were going to perform both at home and abroad. Here was my first introduction to sexual activities.

Music courses lasted for usually a full week at a school. Boys slept in classrooms at one end of the school, the girls at the other end, with adult guards posted throughout the corridors to stop "boy meets girl" encounters. The posted guard idea worked for the corridors but not for boys (and some girls!) who would climb out of classroom windows (ground floor of course!) and run away from the school so as not to be caught in any flood lights, then run around the school field only to hop back into the girl's room and snuggle up with their girlfriend for a few hours in front of everyone in the room before returning. And no one said anything. As for me, only once did I join them and even then I had no girl waiting for me to the extent that I could jump into her sleeping bag!

But there was another event that repeated itself and really influenced me. There was another boy, we'll call him Nigel, who thought he was all that and more when it came to the art of sex. He always seemed to have some encounter to brag about with how he had sex with this or that girl. We would all listen and I would use my imagination as to what happened, I could not seem to switch it off. I would wake up in the mornings even on these courses, fully stimulated. Once, while on one of these courses my erection was spotted. Some made fun and told me to "wank off" (i.e. masturbate). A friend was more kind and said that it was normal to do that to oneself. The mean boy, Nigel, made fun and sometime during that day he masturbated all over my sleeping bag because he knew that I had never done it before. How sick. The next night I masturbated for the first time. I felt guilty and also relieved at the same time.

I continued to masturbate more and more from that time onwards. Using my imagination on what it would be like with a girl, and finding any stimulus I could to work with. I would stay up late at night at home to see if I could see any 'action' on the television. Back in the 1970's English television really did not offer much then, but anything would do me. I got confused about girls because I first saw them as something special to be with, to respect (even though I would not have used that word then). Now, more and more, they became a target for my sexual gratification. My eyes would wonder to the curves in their bodies and their breasts. Girls didn't help matters because they were forever finding ways to look sexy to the boys. Even at school girls would find a way it seemed to entice the boys they liked. Sex became a magnet and an increasing driving force in my life. Like a steam train fully stoked and starting off thundering down the track. It was taking a real grip on me even though I had no perspective on this, and no guidance from anyone. Porn movies also became available once or twice at a friend's house (he stole them from his dad) and this only added to my thirst.

At home I went looking for sexy lingerie like the stuff I saw in the porn magazines and videos. I found none so I would go downstairs and dress up in one of those dresses my sister made me wear once or twice when I was younger. I would find soft silky underwear to put on. The feeling stimulated me and I would relieve myself. Sometimes I watched myself in the mirror. Other times I would wear the clothes all night long, as by this time my brother had his own room up in the attic after my parents had a loft (attic) conversion done.

My sister, Susan, had very little to do with me by now. She left school to become a nanny in London after having a failed marriage relationship. Well with my dressing up to get stimulated, I guess I was somewhat having issues too! However, this activity did not last continually but rather seemed to come at random times, and it was all rooted in something deeper inside of me. I just did not have the insight nor wisdom to know that at the time.

At the age of eighteen I up and left home in disagreement with my parents; somehow I had convinced myself that they did not love me. My brother had already got in with the wrong crowd and had enlisted himself in the army.

I had auditioned and been accepted into a top music college in London on the violin performers course, and had taken a year off at the age of eighteen to 'live life' outside of my parents before going down to the Capital. That year was a year of working various jobs from gardening to paid music gigs. I paid for driving lessons, passed my test, and bought my first car (actually a small Ford Escort van). Somehow I managed to pass the driving test with only nine hours of experience, though I did have to take the test three times before I passed!

I was renting a room in a cottage out in the country, but managed to stay in touch with my closest school friends, Mark, Chris and Peter. We often went out to the pub together for a drink and just "hang out" as the saying goes.

I was still in the senior school orchestra at this time, and held the position of leader of the second violins, which gave me a certain status. People in my section looked up to me. I liked one girl in particular but was too shy to do anything about it. It was fear of rejection that really stopped me.

After another one of those away courses with the orchestra on site at a local school, one girl who was about eighteen came and kissed me after a drinking session at the local village pub. She was a little drunk but she told me outright that I had not ever had sex. I guess she knew from how I kissed. This really surprised her because I was also eighteen by now and she said everyone should have done it by now. I felt bad, that I was missing out, even failing, so I purposed in my heart to have sex as soon as I could. Well I hoped that it was to be with this young lady but no, instead I found out that a different girl in my violin section liked me, so here was my chance. I got to meet her and even had her dad drop her off near my accommodation to spend time together, alone in the evening! Crazy dad! I took her to my room and we had sex. After dropping her off to her dad again to take her home (she lived some distance away), I remember running down the street shouting,

"Yes! yes!" in victory.

I had done it, finally done it. The really dumb thing here though was what had I done? I was no Christian then and thought I had achieved some kind of manhood feat. And even more stupid, we used no contraception. About six weeks later the orchestra went on tour to Germany, my final tour with the orchestra before I would go to the music college in London. It was while on tour that some of her friends came to me to tell me that she had missed her period, and that she never had missed one before. My heart sank and I got scared, but somehow I managed to put that aside and I did enjoy the tour. At the end of the tour this young lady had her period, and boy, was I relieved!

    I have been sharing about my teenage life so that you can see that I was in many ways, just a lost soul looking for gratification in what life seemed to offer, and just went along with the 'norm' if only a little behind at times compared to others. There were a few other 'boy meets girl' encounters between the ages of nineteen and twenty while I was in college but I feel no need to go into any details about them.

    So what happened to me? How did I get from here to the mess I found myself in as a born again, spirit filled, called, and anointed Christian at that!? Read on…

Chapter One – My Story – Getting Married

From quite an early age, maybe nine or ten I had short intermittent times of wondering what life was really about but never got any answers that were permanent. By the time I was nineteen and at music college I revisited that question while living in London as a student. Being a major world city you can imagine that there is just about everything there that you can get involved in. In my search for the 'truth' about life I did just that to some extent. I did this course called 'EST Training' that was based on this man from the US who had this 'experience' through a mixture of Zen, Buddhism, New Age metaphysics, and probably a bunch of other stuff too. It was a two week course that ran over two very long weekends. Hosted in some hotel ballroom you were given tons of information about life, and did lots of mental and experiential exercises. Nothing was forced on you but the whole idea in the end was to 'Get It', whatever 'It' was. I took the course before leaving the music college as many people there had done it and said great things about it. It was costly but I used some of my grant money to pay for it. A very close friend from my growing up days, Peter, who was a really talented jazz musician had done the course and really encouraged me to do it.

So, doing this 'EST Training' did I 'Get It?' After two sets of long eighteen hour days and an openness to learn, I did get it. The 'revelation' was truly mind blowing and seemed to set my mind free to soar to new heights of experiencing life. I was so taken with the experience that I offered to help out as did my friend Peter. Over the next year we assisted setting up and 'guarding the doors' to make sure that there were no interruptions during the course program. It was during one of these door monitoring or guarding sessions that Peter and I had the same experience at the same time, and it scared the heck out of us both. We, by sheer coincidence, were standing at a door each and at one time we just looked over at each other and at the same time saw each other as demons! It really was a shock, quite horrifying for both of us to experience the same thing. Something inside of me told me to get out and leave this organization. However, this was not before I was to experience something quite unique in one of their other programs.

There was a two session 'Communication Workshop' that was offered and I, for some unknown reason to me, was asked to oversee the logistics of it from start to finish. I had been helping out for some months so I guessed that they were happy enough for me to take on this special role. My first job was to set up, to position exactly, all the stage and chairs. And when I mean exactly, that is what they wanted. Chairs had to be in exact lines, exactly the same distance apart from each other and each row exactly the same distance from the next row. The open alleys had to be some exact distance and the stage perfect to all set requirements. And, this had to be done at the beginning of every day, and after each meal break. I had a team of volunteers to work under me, all of us doing this voluntarily.

I believe that the purpose of this event was to show that real communication is conducted in the spirit realm, not in the natural where we think a thought, speak it out, the other person hears it, processes it, and does the same in response. During the first session nothing seemed to be happening as the facilitator gave out information as people listened, were allowed at times to ask questions and did those processes, or mental exercises that I recognized in part were what I did in the main 'Est Training' in order to 'Get It.' By the way, you had to have completed the main training before you were allowed to do the communication workshop.

So there was I sitting center back of the hotel ball room with my helpers either side of me ready to do something if requested. I too, of course, was paying attention to the whole event. I was as much participating in this as anyone else. During the second weekend, the second and final session, still it seemed heavy going and nothing, no breakthrough seemed to be happening. I had done my job and my helpers were great. All was in control. The facilitator at one time started to look at me, more than once, yet he never said or communicated anything to me. I looked inwardly at myself and suddenly I got it. As I was overseeing the whole logistics, I had to get it first! Then, bam! I had this revelation in the spirit and I seemed to bypass my mind and see things before they happened. It was a weird experience. Then, it was like the whole room erupted as people were being asked to talk in pairs to each other with one talking and the other having to quickly respond and then the first person doing the same and both continued back and forth non-stop. What happened was that people would start to say something and then the other person would start to know what their partner was going to say and would finish off their sentence, and then each would get to know what each other was even thinking before any words were spoken at all. The breakthrough had happened.

    Looking back over the events of that workshop, I find it interesting and it really helped me be more open to the truth that there is a higher world dimension, a spirit world that is very real, and maybe more real than all the physical, tangible world we are more used to operate in. Anyway, after that experience with my friend Peter, I quit and left for good.

    The next search for this thing called 'Truth' about life took me into something called 'Rebirthing'. Its purpose was for you to go back experientially in time and relive your moments of birth and get over the trauma of it. It was a long process that you did on your own, in the bath tub! What you did was to fill the tub with warm water that was to represent a similar sensation of being in your mother's womb and turn the lights off and be in darkness as you sank below the water line with everything except your nose in order to breath. Then you would let your mind take you backwards in time until you finally got to the moment of your birth. I think that the concept was that our mind does fully record everything that has gone on in our lives, yet we seem to be hindered from accessing that information from about four years and earlier with only a few exceptions where people may recall something as early as two years of age.

    So into the lukewarm bathtub I would go in darkness and let my mind wonder through my childhood. I was greatly surprised how much came back to me in little pieces. However, I never seemed to be able to get right back to my first few years of life, or to my birth so eventually, I just stopped doing it altogether.

    Yet, many, many months later when I was living in an apartment in London that I was sharing with Peter and Lance (another long-term violinist friend from my school days who was older than myself and was already at the music college that I was going to), I woke up one morning reliving my birth! Literally, I was wide awake but I could hear myself coming out of the womb. Sometime before that I could hear both my parents talking (maybe even many days before that I am not sure). I saw light for the first time and that is all I can recall about it other than it was very real to me. A weird and yet beautiful experience that was. All I remember was that I was fine about being born and it really was not that traumatic for me at all.

I also touched on transcendental meditation for a period of time but again I never stayed the course with that. It was if someone or something kept pulling me away from all these things I got into. Well, the final major deal that I got myself into was the Church of Scientology by founder Ron Hubbard. Boy, was this an experience to remember. Now, how does a person get into something like that? Not hard actually. They set up these shops in major cities such as London where people are always walking by and they offer free personality tests. So, one day there I was innocently walking down some main shopping street in London and as I passed by one of these places, not even noticing what it was, a man called to me offering this free personality test. I stopped and thought about it and kind of liked the idea, so, as I had time free I agreed.

The inside of the shop was nothing weird, just a few rooms with other people I guessed doing the test that I was about to do. The man explained that it was quite a long list of questions, but that it would be really worth doing as it was accurate. I was fine about that so he sat me at a table and gave me a large booklet and I started to go through it. It must have taken me almost an hour to complete the test, after which the same man thanked me and said to wait a short while and he would go over the results with me. After another twenty minutes or so I was sitting down with him looking together at my results. I have to say that it was very accurate indeed. It nailed my strengths and weaknesses really well, almost to the point of making me uncomfortable. Now that I was impressed, he started selling me on improving my weaknesses and told me that they have a way to do that here. He recommended that I read this book called 'Dynetics' by this Ron Hubbard man and come back and see him so that they could help me. No real sales pressure after all I thought. I bought the book for a few pounds and left thanking him for his time.

Back at my living accommodation I started to read the Dynetics book and soon really got into it. It was very logical and claimed to produce some amazing results. I also recognized many of the methods from the 'Est Training' that I had done. The basic idea in Dynetics is that right from birth we all experience bad things in one way or another and this pain gets locked up in us, in our souls and bodies so that over the years, as we get older and experience more bad things, our bodies get weaker and our lives get more dull with the burdens of carrying all this junk. Going back in time to 'relive' these experiences in a certain way with someone else there helping you get through it will release the 'life' inside of that event and give it back to you in the here and now. This process can take a long time to fully get through but the idea is to eventually become what they call 'Clear', that is totally clear from all bad life experiences. Then, (and they do not tell you this up front) you go on to various states of being and basically become god in your own life where you can make things happen in life. This was, by the way, the same end result that the 'Est Training' told you, that you were god in your own universe.

Well, I bought into it and even got a young lady from my music college to join me and together we did these 'reliving' processes to each other at this center once we had been trained to do so. Interestingly, they also had the 'patient' hold a metal tube in each hand that had a low voltage passing through it tied to a meter. The helper would use the readings on the meter to help guide the patient through things. When the patient was remembering an incident and there was some charge on their 'life stuff' in it then the meter would spike so they would spend some time 'reliving' that memory until the spike left altogether and they could then move on to another memory. Interesting concept don't you think? In many ways, just another form of basic psychology.

My friend and I continued to work on each other for some weeks but one day, when we were upstairs in this office as usual doing this, I heard this commanding voice inside of me say,
"Get out!"
It was so commanding and authoritative that it scared me and I knew we had to stop all this. I told this to my friend and she was also relieved as she was getting on edge about it too. We decided to leave it all, so we did, and never returned to it either.

Like I said earlier in any major city you can get into stuff real easy. I still though did not have the answer as to what life was really about, so my journey continued in life.

At the age of twenty I rebelled and left Music College after successfully completing one year. This was a shock, for people just didn't up and leave one of the elite London music colleges (unless they were kicked out of course). Its equivalent to leaving the Julliard School of Music in America. But I did quit, my reasoning was that my music was not going anywhere really. I could see myself ending up playing in some good orchestra and doing lots of tours, but this I had already experienced in my teenage years and did not really go for it as a lifestyle. But it was more than that really. I felt that there was more to music than all this. The problem was that I had no clue as to the answer to that question.

After leaving the music college, I remained in London working. I did a few different jobs, including a little playing for a while, but then sold my violin and my bow to a dealer in my home town of Leicester. I took a job selling insurance for a while, and then became, a cleaner of domestic houses and industrial buildings. Doesn't sound very glamorous, and it wasn't but I didn't care, at least I was earning money.

I also got involved in multi-level marketing with a well-known company, Amway, that sold mainly cleaning products. I would attend and sometimes lead meetings at people's homes to sell the products and get others involved. I did quite well at this in a short space of time, mainly in getting others involved. I did make some money from it, but not much. It was after one such trip into North London that I met my first wife.

I had already determined that I wanted to marry, and hey, what better time than the present. I was a horny (well I was) fit, but slim young man who had this 'available' sign printed on his forehead, if you know what I mean. There I was dressed up in a suit and returning on the last underground train (subway) on the Northern line, when I met Karen, a young lady about my age. Somehow we got talking and she gave me her phone number before she departed the train. I guessed she must have liked me, otherwise she wouldn't have given me her number right! I told my friends Lance and Peter, who I was sharing a flat with in south London. They asked if I was going to call her. Now this is where I have to be plain honest. I liked the idea of a female liking me; it really boosted my ego. My mind liked it and my emotions agreed, so I called her and we dated. Why did we date? Well, to me she was pretty enough to want to jump into bed with! It's the truth, and the evidence of the next few weeks proved it. She, a virgin, was gently led into my bed, with her full consent too, of course. We continued this for a few months, then came the visits to the parents and relatives, and within eighteen months I think I, in a roundabout way, asked her to marry me. She agreed, and in less than a year, when I was twenty-one, we got married in her home town of Chester, northwest England (not too far from Liverpool). Sadly, her dad had died only a few weeks before the wedding so he never got to see his eldest daughter marry.

While we were living together in London, I had managed to save up some money for a deposit on a house by having us both live in cheap accommodation, even in a squat (a derelict building that people break into, reconnect the power and then live there free). And yes, we lived together within a few months of meeting, but that was considered the norm as it is still to this day. Once we lived in a flat (apartment) over a massage business. I found out later that the place was a front for prostitution, not that I ever went in for services but it did get my attention. I bought Karen 'sexy' clothes and when she would wear them, gee was I turned on! It seemed though that most of my efforts were directed like that with her.

The problem with buying your own home was that the houses in London were way too expensive. So we looked further afield and decided to live in this new city called Milton Keynes which was located about fifty miles north. We bought a small two-bedroom house. Karen quit her job in

London (she was a head waitress in a large store restaurant) and I started a new job in real estate selling new houses.

On the outside, all seemed to be going well. Two young people starting off in life together, how romantic. Well, it might have been romantic if neither of us had any 'baggage', and what I mean by baggage is all those events, experiences, thoughts, decisions, and beliefs that we have accumulated in our lives up to that point. We are continually experiencing new things and making judgments and decisions based on what we experience. Some people, I think, confuse all these things that mold a person's behavior into what it has become, with who they really are underneath all that. Getting a bit deep I guess, but more on this later in the book.

Back to my baggage, and you can see here that my bag was pretty full on the subject of sex. No drugs, very little alcohol to excess, a little stealing, and much lying of course (couldn't tell my parents and other respectable folk what I have been up to!) Of course, at that time in my life I had no idea to view myself this way. I am sure if someone did try to point out the pitfalls of my past affecting my present and future I would probably agree with them, and walk away and leave it at that, not even spending five minutes seriously looking at myself. Like most young men, I was into ... myself! It's all about *me* really, and, of course, it is important to help others and try to do good. Yet still, even in all this, one seeks self-reward. Come on, if you are reading this and saying that's not fully true......get real with yourself. If you can't see it right now I could either spend the next few chapters going over all my 'good deeds' in life and be honest how there is a portion of something in each event for myself. Take my word for it, or at least accept the possibility of what I am saying is true, we are far more self-centered and selfish than we like to admit. Maybe you already know this to some extent and agree, and that's okay with you to be that way?

So what was my baggage? Let us have a look inside Rob's sack: Well, see here, we have Rob the 'sensitive' boy. We have Rob the, OOOOOOoooey, the cross-dresser and sexual fetish boy! We have Rob the porno magazine and video watching masturbating boy. We have Rob the prideful musician and violinist. And let us not forget the Rob the moral adviser to all! Full of answers I was about life. There's probably more, and I will add more if they come to mind. You only need to look back into your past yourself to find your own. Oh, and yes, ever been told that 'you will grow out of that' by someone? I tell you a truth, you may indeed stop the behavior either for a while, or maybe until you die, but the truth is that if you have indulged, then that thing is embedded in your heart and no attempts by *self-will* to *fully* remove it will work. You can try covering it up, try hiding it, try running from it, try pretending it is not there (denial), yet there you really know it is. Trouble is, we get too prideful to admit it, even to ourselves sometimes! I did all the above! The good news is that there is a permanent solution that you will read about later in this book.

Me and my backpack of 'goodies' entered into this marriage with Karen with the best and most honorable of intentions (I often wondered why the best of intentions rarely resulted in what was intended!). We had our good times and our times of arguing. We went on holidays, we visited relatives. We talked about having children, so I bought a big dog called 'Ben' instead. We talked again about having children and she got pregnant. She wanted to move near to her home town close to her mother, so we moved. I got a job working for Avco Trust (was later bought out by Beneficial Trust) who issue personal loans and related activities (debt collecting!). Rob the business man, excelling at finance and on an accelerated management training course. We bought a three-bedroom brick house in a village called Mickle Trafford on the outskirts of an old Roman city called Chester.

Here I worked hard to improve the house and do well at my job. Karen did some part time work once our first baby Charlotte was born. It was a life changing event and I was so proud to be a dad. I took care of the family finances and we were doing okay. We had some savings, and a few stocks and bonds. We were making equity on our house as prices were soaring in the current economy run by the Conservative Party, otherwise known as the Tory Party under the headship of our first female prime minister, Margaret Thatcher, the 'Iron lady' as she was called.

The house was looking fine with new double glazed windows throughout, new quality carpets, complete re-wiring, new built-ins in the girls bedroom, fresh wallpaper on the walls, and flowerbeds in the garden all looking good. Two cars (nothing special, but they were ours!) in the driveway, and good neighbors around us, what more could a man ask for! Another child, and yes, we wanted another, and 'pop!' in less than a twinkling of an eye it seemed we had two beautiful daughters, Charlotte and Jemma. I treasured them both (and still do).

You would think that from this point in my life I could have gone on to tell the perfect romance tale. I could, but that's all it would be, a tale. Things were starting to go wrong, small things at first…

(Some explicit sexual acts mentioned so discretion needed as to who can read this chapter)

Chapter One – My Story – The Beginning and End of a Marriage

Kind of an ugly sub-title this one isn't it. Well, a marriage breaking up is just that, ugly, especially when children are involved. Karen and I had been married for some six or seven years when things started to change. I had taken a change of direction in my career as a finance manager with the consumer finance company Avco Trust. I went back into music. I found a private music school where I first helped out with the administration, then I took a more overseeing role with regards to the other teachers and was given the position of head administrator. I got hold of a violin and started playing again, and teaching. I always knew that I would come back to the violin and had mentioned this to Karen. She never particularly seemed interested though and I don't think that she ever, not even once, heard me perform. Seemed she was too busy being the mother. I say it this way because, looking back on things, she ... I put myself in check here. It is always too easy to point the finger at the other person and not look at yourself first and as this book is about me I am going to focus on me. However, I do will say this, a wife can really make or break a man. She can grind him into the ground or help him soar up high into the clouds in life.

Here was I, Rob, trying to be the honorable man, while still carrying his backpack of 'goodies' from his past. People around us thought we were the ideal couple. Gentle on the whole, fun loving, with two dogs (we rescued a terrier which we called 'Lucky' and I still had Ben, my German Shepherd and Collie cross), two wonderful girls, two holidays a year, and the occasional arguments yet overall, normal. But what they did not see was two people moving away from each other. Or, if anyone did see it, they kept quiet.

You can only suppress a natural desire for so long, even if that natural desire has been, how should I say, corrupted. My sexual desires were just that, natural. It is natural for a man to want sex. What is questionable is how and where he goes about getting it. Eventually a man's sexual drive will burst out. Actually, what often happens is that he starts to look outside his marriage for gratification if it is not being met inside the marriage.

It was only a matter of time before something would happen and sure enough it did. There was this sexy college student who taught young children music in the private school I worked at. She had a reputation of being a horny (hot) thing. She was also the boss's, that is, my boss's younger sister. I am sure I must have had this huge invisible (to me) sign over my head "horny man available…now! Any offers grab me!" On the outside I was a respectable, upright married man but on the inside completely the opposite. Even today I cannot recall exactly how this girl and I got together but we did. We had our hot little 'touching, rubbing and pressing against each other' encounters every week, for weeks. Now, when that happened, at home my sexual appetite dropped. It seemed at first that life was in balance. Even my relationship with Karen seemed at first to improve. I was more than happy to go to work (of course! Money and a fondle!), and at peace more at home with the distant relationship married lifestyle that had become more and more established by myself through the years of being married with Karen.

One problem though, something inside of me knew I was doing wrong. Call it my conscience. And then, all of a sudden, that young lady moved away to college. I was back to square one. Work had also changed a little. I had come up with this idea to create a music course to help instruct young children in basic music skills, by mail! I designed a ten-month course that consisted of ten monthly packs of materials that included various musical games and activities all instructed from an audio cassette tape. I was going to launch this venture through the music school but the boss got greedy and wanted not only to be in control of the business, but also reap all the profits too! As I had worked on my idea almost completely outside of work hours and off the premises, I decided to leave the school and have a go at setting up my own company to launch this venture. I was excited and even though I knew I had very little capital myself, I would find a way, and I did. Just a few thousand pounds of our own money from refinancing our home, a small business bank loan, credit here and credit there with material suppliers and I was ready to go. I bridged the income gap of leaving the music school by pretending that I was serious about being a financial advisor, selling personal investments and insurance for a company based in Liverpool.

As for sex, I was too busy and excited to pay attention in that area as my energy was being channeled into this new business venture (now there's a lesson. How many of us just keep busy all the time until we crash and burn, when really all we are doing is avoiding facing the truth about what is inside of us that we don't want to face?). I rented a business unit, an office inside a converted warehouse where there were many other small businesses. I spent a lot of hours getting the finances, the business plan, the marketing strategy, the designers and artists, the recording studio, the printing company, and the legalities of starting a business together. Finally, about six months later I launched the product.

Going against the success of the business were two major obstacles. Firstly, there was the matter of the finances. I only had enough money to pay for the first pack (remember I said that there were ten monthly packs in all) and to get the master copies for pack number two. I also only had enough money for one marketing campaign over a six-week period. I had to get the minimum estimated number of responses through the advertising and public relations activities in order to continue. And guess what! The campaign failed, it fell well short. But I was determined, and I fought my way for the next year to gain every order that I could. I came up with ways to promote the business at no cost to myself through promotions and articles. The business even won entrepreneur of the year award for my region! It was hard going, it was long hours. I did continue to teach the violin privately and this, together with a small income from my business kept my family supported. So somehow I survived the first year and the creation of the whole ten-month course mainly, thanks to the printing company that went well out of their way extending me credit.

Pressure can do strange things to a man and I was no exception. Issues deep inside of us that we have (even unknowingly) buried there can rise to the surface. Again, I was no exception. At first I had a single helper in my office, a young lady that was sent to me for work experience. I always treated her well, but I sure wanted to get hold of her at times when the window blinds were down. I never did. When times got tough and I could not even afford a helper (my wife never came in to help out) I was there on my own. I am not sure of how this happened; nope that's not true, I remember… I started buying porn magazines from garages (gas stations) when I went on my trips to promote the business. I would masturbate to relieve myself as a kind of stress reliever. I took the magazines into my office. I had constructed a storage area at the back of my office to hold the course materials. It was concealed, very private there. I would read the magazines there sometimes and hide them high up on a shelf. Looking through the advertisements some advertised clothing, sexy clothing. I remembered my days as a teenager and it was like all of a sudden, this great urge to feel the soft silky sexy clothing and erotic sensation more than ever before. I ordered the catalogs. They were sent to my business post box in brown packaging so I assumed no one knew. Some catalogs came with a free sample of sexy underwear. I was fired up and driven. I would imagine being like those ladies all dressed up. I started to use the company credit card to go shopping for ladies' clothes that would fit me. I kept the clothes hidden at work. When Karen was out, I would look for old dresses of hers to wear (she seemed to quit dressing nice for some time now). I would prance about in the house. I got this elation of 'being free'. What it really was, was some way to escape from all the pressures around me as well as satisfying my sexual craving but it was all self-centered and selfish. What I had no idea about through all of these activities was that there was a real issue at hand relating to my female oriented actions that I was not to discover for many years to come. To make things go even deeper, I started to go to the massage parlors and pay for hand sex. Even though I did this quite a few times, I always felt bad afterwards. It didn't stop me though. Sex and work, work and sex were very closely related. I even bought a blow-up doll to have sex with (don't recommend them at all by the way). And in the mist of all of this Karen and I were just continuing being married, her being the mum, and I the dad.

All these things happened over a three-year period. Towards the end of this time I was so into dressing that not only did I have the full gear (wig and all), but I would go out dressed. My good friend Lance turned up on the scene and he not only helped me in my business on the computer but also went out with me fully dressed. He did not judge me at all and nor did he try to change me. A rare quality that I have found in few people. I attended get-togethers with other people like myself in Manchester City (which was about a forty-five-minute drive away). I was shown how to look more feminine. I loved it but deep down something was not right. I felt guilty because I could not be honest about myself to most other people, especially family. These other men, dressing like women were a mixed crowd. Some were doctors, others students, yet others manual workers, but most were office based people. Some even came with their wives! I seemed to be accepted but I knew for sure that Karen would freak out if she knew. I never desired to tell her, she would end the marriage. My very real frustration was that I knew I could not speak to her about this. Besides, I was being unfaithful to her, and I knew that was wrong, so I was in a losing position.

Another shift took place. I went from dressing as a fetish (i.e. for sexual arousal) to just wanting to be like a woman for pleasure. I grew my nails long and started to remove body hair. I saw my work wardrobe more as representing who I was than my wardrobe at home. Then came more bad news, my business was failing and I started to owe more and more money to people. I was getting late in paying the rent on the office, and late paying my suppliers. I did keep them informed as to my situation and they did bear with me. I was also getting late to pay a mortgage payment on my house but my dad in England was kind enough to send us the money for that payment.

At home the feeling of being separated from Karen grew, and we were arguing more and more. My daughters, ages about four and six by then were getting impacted. I didn't know what was going on in my life; I felt driven, out of control. I would go away and just cry sometimes about why things had to be so messed up. Why do things turn out bad when you have good intentions? Why? Why? Why? And what *is* the purpose of this screwed up thing we call life anyway? Lots of questions, no answers.

I finally got to the stage where I had to leave, or at least I felt I had to leave the home to get a break, to get some clarity on my life. Trouble was, Karen had always said that she would never take me back if I left her.

One day I called her to tell her. She knew it was coming and she made no fight to keep me. However, she did guess right about me dressing up. I don't know if someone saw me, or if she saw all the signs and said nothing, but she came out with it and I admitted it. She did agree at a later date to go with me to see a specialist about my 'condition' so she does have that to her credit.

We went to see the country's top specialist who was based in Leeds (Northeast England), over one hundred miles northeast of us. A bag of encouragement he was too. He told us both that there has never been a case where someone has completely overcome this desire in his or her lives, not one. He said that it would come and go throughout life. I left disappointed in one sense, happy in my current sense (after all, maybe Karen would accept me this way!). Unfortunately, Karen's response was the opposite. She thought the specialist told a load of bull and didn't believe him. I can only but imagine what kind of impact all this was having on her. I say imagine, because I really didn't know her. Sounds crazy, but it is possible to live and sleep with someone and not know them, even after ten years. Sure, we knew each other's reactions to things, and we knew that if one did this, then the other is likely to do that. If I met her needs in one way, she would soon meet mine in another. Yet, neither of us knew each other's hearts.

I left the home and rented a small room at a house in the same city so as to be close by. The house belonged to an English teacher. She had books everywhere you looked. It was a small brick town house, situated in the middle of a whole row of houses close to the street. I rented one room at the top of the stairs. A Spanish student rented another room up the stairs too, though I hardly ever saw him.

Karen filed for divorce on the grounds of irreparable damage (I think that was the reason). My lawyer accepted but placed a condition on it that would protect me to still see my girls. I didn't want a divorce and told her, but I felt it was my entire fault anyway so she had the say in the matter. I had left her the house and everything in it. All I had was the house debts, some clothing, my violin, and a seriously failing business.

What happened over the next few weeks as the divorce was being finalized can only be said to be a miracle…

Chapter One – My Story – The Meaning of Life

Did I write that title? Yes, I did. Let me continue…

It was really hard being away from my girls. Heart-wrenching, and then my whole life seemed so screwed up. My marriage was shipwrecked, I could only see my beautiful girls once a week, my business falling further and further into debt. I had no money, and no purpose to life. I got depressed (and I am a really positive kind of person). At one time I remember being in my rented room seriously contemplating suicide. It didn't seem a bad option but I still felt that there was more to life and if I did take my life, I would never find it. What *was* this big deal I had about life anyway? Why did it even bother me? But it did.

The struggle continued, the struggle to keep my business afloat and the struggle to try and understand what the heck was going on in my life. My business now was in debt (and this was a personal debt in my name) to the tune of around eighty thousand pounds plus (that was equivalent then to about one hundred and forty thousand dollars back in late 1980's). Talk about stress. You might think that my sexual activities would be at their most rampant at this point, being that it brought about some kind of relief. But strangely it did not. I think I was too depressed at that time anyway without even realizing it. I got mad at myself about all the porn magazines, catalogs and clothing, and one day I just got all of it and threw it all away. I wanted it no more. Well, that is what I told myself then.

To still help promote my music course, I would sometimes attend activities, you know, exhibitions and the like, where I could rent a table and promote directly to the public. One such event was an annual meeting of home school families from across the country. I cannot remember how I got hold of the details but I had gone ahead and rented a table for the first day of a two-day event that was being held some sixty miles or so away.

Loading up my car with all the display material I had, together with some samples of the course, I left early morning on a clear sunny day. Traffic was nonexistent and it did not take me long to get there. The event was taking place in what looked to be like an old converted school in some wonderful grounds in the middle of the countryside. Behind the school were other buildings that all seemed to belong on this large complex. I parked the car and went in. Finding someone to ask, I collected my display material and set it all up before the event was due to start. The displays were located in a room up some stairs. There were a few other people their setting up too and we chatted about what we were offering.

From around ten that morning people began to come by. I would talk to them and promote 'my business'. Some seemed quite interested and would stay and talk for a while. Others smiled politely and walked on. It was kind of a little weird as two things started to happen. Firstly, I noticed that I was getting all upset about my life even though I did my best to not show this. This was strange because usually I am focused on what I am doing, but I was not able to achieve this at that time. Secondly, these people all seemed to be particularly happy and that baffled me. By lunchtime someone had invited me to join them in the dining hall. I accepted, and entering the hall I again witnessed all these families from all over the country literally playing 'happy families' together. Some were helping fetch the food from the kitchen area, others were helping serve. Others were handing out plates and cutlery, and yet others would clean away used dishes. And the people, they were *so*, I mean *so* friendly. I sat down to eat, and enjoyed the conversations and the food.

After eating I said that I had better go back upstairs to my display. They didn't seem too concerned about that. An older man who had his wife and children there walked with me. He invited me to sit down when we were away from most of the crowd. He started to talk to be about Jesus. "Whosus" I thought, then okay, I got it "Jesus, the Jesus in the Bible Jesus", I am in here with a whole bunch of Christian folk. Then, I remembered, the conference was for Christian home schooling families.

The man was a really nice man so I politely listened to him. He started telling me about Jesus, and it all (so I thought) went in one ear and straight out the other. Even today, I cannot remember what he said. I do remember that it was sounding a little farfetched to me.

Going back up to my display, I felt empty. There was hardly anyone up there. The man had invited me to come and listen to a meeting they were going to have later that afternoon in the dining hall area once they had cleaned it all up. I thought about it but dismissed the idea. I started to feel lonely, it was as if all my troubles were being highlighted around all these 'happy' people. And that made me feel even worse. I ventured downstairs and stayed for a few minutes some distance away from where they were having a meeting of some kind, probably a service. I left and went back upstairs to be joined later by that same man who spoke to me earlier. He said that they, they being the organizers, would like to offer for me to stay the night and stay tomorrow too, at their expense. I said yes. They showed me nice clean beds in one of the back buildings where I was to sleep and they invited me to dinner that night, breakfast in the morning and then lunch before they all went home.

When evening came and I went to my bunk bed I noticed that there was a hardback book near each bed. Curious, I had a look to see what it was as they all looked exactly the same, all brown and the same size. Looking closer I saw the words 'Holy Bible' and I started to fear. Maybe that's too strong a word, more like I got nervous. I felt that I needed courage to pick one up and read some of it. I chickened out and left them alone.

I slept well that night and after I had got up and had taken a wash, I was back at the breakfast table playing 'happy families'. The tables were long, some twenty something feet in length each, so plenty of room for more than one family. At our table were about fifteen men, women and children. Across from me was this man with his wife and I think three children. To my left was a lady who I found out was a single lady with two children, one of which was still a baby. On my right, if I recall correctly was the man with his family, the man who tried the previous day to tell me about Jesus (poor guy, I hope I didn't hurt his feelings because I was not getting what he was trying to tell me). I was asked about my business, so I happily told the story of how I did this and did that, and won the entrepreneur of the year award, etc. I helped clean up a little and went back up to my display but only stayed there for a few minutes. I had lost the desire all of a sudden to be the business promoter. My display was no longer of any importance for some reason. I was confused as to my own state. I went back downstairs and was invited again to join them in a 'service' as they called it. I did, for a while, sitting right at the back for easy exit when I wanted to go. I did get up and leave and wandered around for a while not thinking much really. I did wonder what was going on here. Was there something here for me I pondered?

I was going to leave after lunch so around eleven I started packing away my music course materials into my car. At lunch, the same group of people were at the table. During the meal (which was very good by the way) I was asked again about my business and was more than happy to go on about it. Right in the middle of my story the man opposite where I was sitting, the man with his wife and three children, looked straight at me. I mean straight into my eyes, and he said (gee, he had the audacity, the nerve, and in a loud voice too!),
"You think very highly of yourself, don't you."
I was stunned, more like nailed to the wall. There was something about the way he said it that didn't make me get outwardly mad, or dismiss him as stupid. His eyes were, well, being kind. All went quiet for a minute. It was like I had the whole place staring at me. I had to admit it, it was true so I said something like,
"Well, yes I guess I do."
You would think that I would have run straight out of the place and never come back, but I didn't. People started talking again like nothing ever happened. The lady next to me asked where I came from. She had been to Chester and said that there was a church there near a roundabout that had a water fountain in the middle. I didn't really pay much attention to her, but felt sorry for her that she had children but no husband. Odd thing though, she seemed quite happy to me.

A short while later and I was driving back to my messed up life in Chester, back to seeing my children once a week, to a business that was failing, to a failed marriage, and to no close friends. I remember sitting in my office one day just staring at nothing for what seemed hours.

Even sex had become of no interest. I remember a lady photographer that had showed some interest in me in recent days. She came by again and one day she invited me to have dinner at her house. Her parents would be out she told me and she said that she had pictures in her bedroom to show me. Talk about a suggestive invite. I agreed to meet her, so that night I drove over to her parents' house located in a little village about fifteen miles away going towards Manchester.

She was all dressed up and so was I. She was a good cook too as the meal was really fine. With her at one end of this long teak table and myself at the other, wine was poured and we chatted a little. During the meal she indicated that more than a meal was on offer, and then she asked if I would like to view her pictures upstairs. Sex on a plate! But something hit me inside and I didn't want to go there. I didn't want sex. I could not believe myself as I turned her down and said that I needed to leave. She must have thought that there was something wrong with me! There was, something inside me was pulling me away from the very thing I had been seeking and had driving me for years. A few minutes later I found myself driving myself back to Chester wondering why I had done what I just did.

About a week or so later I had this weird thing happen to me. I had been at work in my office and left early in the afternoon to go back to my room that I was renting from the English teacher, Janet. I was not in any low emotional state or anything, and nothing unusual had happened that day. I opened the door to the house and went inside. At around three in the afternoon the house was empty. The landlady was not back from her day teaching English at school, and the Spanish student, well I had no idea what his schedule was at all. I started to walk up the stairs when, after I had placed my foot on the first step, I heard a voice, a loud voice speaking to me. It was a man's voice, gentle yet very firm and very close to me. The voice said,
"Rob, I want you to read the Bible."
Scared the hell out of me! I froze and thought,
"I am going crazy; I am now hearing voices!"
I went to take the next step and the voice came again,
"Rob, I want you to read the Bible."
I froze again, No, no doubt about it, this was not a voice inside my head, it was around me and loud. My stomach started churning over. My head was in a spin. It was as if someone had thrusted a farmer's pitchfork into my belly and was turning it around. Somewhat dazed, I made my way up to my room and sat down on my chair in front of my little desk. I just sat there for ages. Finally, I heard the front door open and close. Janet, the landlady must be home. I thought about that voice and about reading a Bible. I wondered if this was the answer to my question, what is life really about? I sat there for a little longer. I decided to go and ask Janet if I could borrow one of hers. I assumed she would have a least one Bible because of all the books she had everywhere. For some reason it took courage for me to go and ask her. After about twenty minutes I went downstairs to the living room and spoke to her,
"Janet, do you have a Bible that I could borrow?" came out of me in a cautious, somewhat nervous way.

You might have thought that I had just pointed a gun at her as she shook, made a little jump backwards exclaiming,
"Why do you want to read *that* thing for!?"
Then she seemed to calm down and explained to me that she didn't own a Bible. She thought again and said that her daughter had left some of her stuff with her and had one up in the loft (attic). We went and found it. I thanked Janet and went back into my room to my desk with book in hand.

Okay, now what? There I was at my desk with this book called the Bible. Gee, the most I knew about the Bible was from school, the story of David and Goliath, Noah and his ark, and the Christmas nativity play. Oh, and one of my school friends, Mark, had two brothers named Matthew and Luke and if they were to have another he would be called John, as Matthew, Mark, Luke and John were all about Jesus. That I remembered. I opened the Bible at the beginning. Genesis, Chapter One it was headed. And I read the words in my head "In the Beginning God created the heavens and the earth. Now the earth was without form and darkness was over the deep. The Spirit of God hovered over the darkness." I continued for a few more paragraphs and pulled a face and yawned. This was all a bit far-fetched and heavy reading it seemed to me. Then I again remembered my friend's name Mark, and Matthew and Luke. I flicked through the contents and found the chapters. I started to read Matthew. It was all about Jesus, his birth and events that took place. Then things got a bit supernatural, like water turning into wine and sick people suddenly getting healed, and a few loaves of bread to feed thousands. I stopped reading. I was having a real problem with some of this stuff. As much as I was having a problem accepting it, there was something inside of me urging me to read on, that my answer was to be found here. I read some more before giving up and falling asleep.

Life went on for a couple of weeks when one day I got this urge to go to church. I thought the thought to be quite weird. Why would *I* want to go to church? But the urge stayed with me. The next Sunday I went to this little church in a village. It was called St Peters Church. Kind of an old traditional church really, with an old organ, wooden church pews, about large enough to house maybe a hundred people. Of course, it was not full, maybe fifty people plus children there. I was given a hymnbook and followed along the best I could. Reminded me of my old school days in the school choir (all musicians had to be in the choir in my high school).

I cannot say that the service stimulated me. I cannot even recall what the preacher, or should I say vicar, said. After the service tea, coffee and biscuits (cookies) were served as people began to mingle and chat together. Some, actually many people welcomed me, and a few talked for a while. I found myself looking at all these people thinking that they were nice, good folk. My eyes scanned around as I said to myself,
"Nice people, but not what I am looking for." and I politely left.

Of course, there was a problem with my own thoughts too. I didn't know what it was that I *was* looking for anyway!

The next week the urge to go to church was still there. Once again I attended a church, a different one this time, but with the same outcome. I got a little down during the following week, feeling things were hopeless. I had my routine of trying to keep my business afloat, of going out and about teaching my violin students, and trying to keep busy and positive. As the following weekend came along I heard the single mothers voice in my head that was at that home education conference that I had gone to, as she told me about the church near a fountain in Chester. I wondered as I drove around one day where it was. Would you believe it, it was the closest church to where I was renting my room! I parked up and went up to the door to see what time the Sunday service was going to start. I noticed that the door was all locked up which I thought odd for a church. I mean, I thought that churches were supposed to always be open, like a refuge to run into? Maybe not in these days of vandalism. I departed and carried on with my day.

On Sunday I went to that church, it called itself a Restoration church; whatever that meant. I went inside after being greeted by some friendly person at the door. This church was set up very differently. It was modern, chairs instead of wooden pews, a large stage that housed a modern band. The band consisted of an electric keyboard player, a flautist, two guitar players, a full kit drummer, and singers. This would be interesting I thought. People were milling around and being friendly. A man in about his mid to late thirties came up to me and welcomed me and seemed genuinely interested in talking. He offered me a seat next to him and his family. I was unsure and declined and stayed at the back, close to the exit door. The service started and the music was good and even the words, which were displayed up on a projector screen, seemed to speak to me, have meaning. Then the preacher, pastor man, went up and started his thing, his preaching. But this was different from my other two experiences. The man was relating to real life in a way that I could relate too. I even found myself starting to cry at one point. What was going on with me? At the end of the service the man with his family that talked to me at the beginning came up and asked how I found the service. I said I did like it and thanked him, and left.

I went back to the same church the following week. In fact, I thought about it a few times during the week and even got a little excited about going. Now that *really* puzzled me. You have to understand, because I was never brought up knowing anything about church and what it was about, I thought that it had no value for me. All I saw were religious people following a bunch of 'do's' and 'don'ts', and then turning right around and being hypocritical fighting in wars against other religions that too seemed to think they knew the truth and were serving God. I knew that there was a

God, or creator, or whatever you want to call him or it. It is stupidity to me to think that all this world around us is a bunch of coincidence. We alone are made up of billions of parts yet amazingly they all have some kind of order. And what's more, there are no two things in the same place at exactly the same time! Amazing genius who calculated that! There is a beauty in the flowers that only a flower can give out and no man can copy. And, how big is the universe? If you go to the edge you have to asked the question, what is after the edge? And our brains cannot cope with the reality of understanding eternity, time and distance that goes on for ever and ever. And how small can we go? Once it was a particle, then a molecule, then an atom, next we broke down the atom and have neutrons and protons, and recently we have come across something new that is supposed to move so fast they exceed the speed of light. When will it ever stop? These are a collection of thoughts that I reflected on at various times in my life and were not far from me as I went through life now as a man who was now divorced and alone.

    On the third Sunday I had my two daughters with me. I told them that we were going to church and that they had a great children's church. Jemma was six and Charlotte almost eight. They were a little uncertain as they wanted to be with their dad and not this new thing. I understood but promised to take them out for the rest of the day. I went with them to where the children's church was being held. It was a large, colorful room and there seemed to be lots of adults helping out. I kissed the girls and made sure they were okay before I left. The eldest, Charlotte, seemed more unsure than her sister. I left and went into the main service, which had just started. Afterwards I mixed a little more with people and this sweet little old lady came up to me smiling and gave me a small book. She said, "God told me to give this to you."
A crazy statement if I ever heard one, God the one who made all this creation speaks to this little old lady?! Anyway, I politely received the book and stuffed it in my back pocket not wanting to offend her. I left to go find my two daughters who seemed to have had a good time but were nevertheless glad to see me. They had done colorings and had learnt a new song.

    All three of us went back to that church for the next few weeks and I started to make a few friends. An older couple, who referred to themselves as church elders invited me and my girls over for a Sunday lunch. We went over and I had the opportunity to ask some direct questions to the man. Although I cannot recall exactly the questions I asked, I do remember leaving that house with some questions answered and some not. The elder was very open and honest with me, and if he did not know the answer he would say so. I greatly respected him for that.

    Later that afternoon, after I had returned my daughters to their mother, I was back up in my room, alone in the house. I do not know where the landlady was that day, nor the Spanish student. Alone, and feeling a little lonely in my room I sat down on my chair with my wooden desk in front of me. I looked out of the window which was right in front of me. It was a cloudy day (typical of England!), and the rest of the view were some trees and brick houses. Dull, sad, and just plain miserable, I thought.

A few days later, I remembered that little book the old lady gave to me in the church. I had it in my room. After finding it, I sat down again and, for some weird reason, decided to make the commitment to only read from one page to the next *if* I could fully accept what the text was saying. I opened to the first page, then the next, and the next. Soon, I was three quarters the way through when I hit an obstacle. I had fully agreed with the book in that I was what they called a 'sinner'; that is, I have made mistakes in my life (durr!) and that because of these I was separated from God. It also said that I was born with a sin nature. In other words, sooner or later I was going to do wrong things, even if I had the very best of morals and intentions. This really helped explain my life patterns to me. The book also explained that Jesus Christ was God's only Son, and because he did not come with sin inside him (hence the story of the virgin birth through Mary), then this Jesus could offer himself up for all mankind's sin. The price of sin is death, that is separation from God and that is for sure what I had in my life, a separation from something that I knew was missing to make me complete. It was like I had gone through my life trying to find things that would satisfy me, but, like trying to place a round peg into a square hole, nothing would fit. Could it be that this is really what I was missing in my life? Could this be real? Could I have the very answer to my question about life right before me?

Truth is I got scared, and excited at the same time. The obstacle that I had come to was a prayer. I read the prayer in my head and asked myself if I could say this out aloud and mean it. The prayer took the whole one page but was fairly short. It went something like this:

"Dear Lord Jesus,

I come to you as I am, as a sinner. I have done many wrong things in my life, some big, some small. I now understand that it is because of my sin that I am separated from God.

Jesus, I believe that you are the Son of God. That you came to save man from his sin and return us back to God. I believe that you came to live here and that you died on the cross, shedding your blood for the price of my sin and rose again.

I understand Lord Jesus, that if I confess my sin before you and ask you to forgive me, you will do so, and if I ask you to be my Lord and Savior you will be.

Lord Jesus, I confess my sin to you and I repent and turn away from sin in my life. Please help me, come into my life and be my Lord and Savior.

Thank you Lord Jesus for saving my soul. Amen."

The trouble was, I really could not say this out aloud *and* fully mean it. As I went through it again and read it in my head I started to recall all the bad things I had done in my life. They became so numerous that I saw (and I mean *saw* with my eyes open) this large black ugly cloud form over me. It got so heavy that my head started to bow forward under the weight. I could see in that dark cloud times when I lied and did wrong things but also many other things were in there too that I had done but could not recognize what they were. I did not know what was going on. I looked at the prayer in the book again, and then, something happened. Something came into my room. It is really hard to put down in words but it was as if this light or presence came in and it gave me strength. At that very split second, I realized that I *could* say this prayer and *fully* mean it with everything inside of me. Still with my eyes open I read out the prayer aloud. I finished the prayer… and nothing happened. I read the prayer again out aloud all the way through, I said I was sorry for all the things in my life that I had done wrong. I looked at all the lies, and sexual wrongs I had done… and still nothing happened. I read the prayer out again and I saw myself about to dive off into darkness. I was at the very end of a plank like that of a diver's springboard but it was way up high and I was on the very end bouncing up and down, about to dive off into…into darkness it looked like and it was very scary. The question in the picture was really clear to me, could I jump off into the unknown, knowing that there was no way back? I could. I finished the prayer for a third time or maybe a fourth time, fully meaning and believing every word. Nothing happened and immediately with my eyes wide open, I cried out aloud,

"Jesus, come into my life,"

… and, still with my eyes open, I saw this plain looking wooden door appear slightly to the left of me and floating up in the air. I reached out and went to open the door and as I just got to the door knob the door opened (I still do not know to this day if I actually reached out with my arm or I just thought it). I saw Jesus' face before me, the door had disappeared and there to the left of my window, coming through the wall, was the face of Jesus down to His shoulders. As I just stared at Him in His eyes, He came closer and I saw His white robe with a light blue sash over it and there was some gold there too. Jesus had sandals on as he drifted towards me. The next thing I saw was that I had Jesus in my room standing right before me. His eyes were piercing yet so loving. All I could do was to stare into those eyes of His as He came right up to me and gently, ever so gently reached out with His index fingers on each hand and just lightly touched both my hands. All at once that heavy black cloud that had been hovering over my head blew up. I mean, it was like a star that turned into a supernova, POW! into millions of insignificant particles sent across the universe.

Jesus had disappeared, the visions had all gone but I was then experiencing a stillness in my mind that I had never, ever had before in my whole life. It was like I was not even thinking, I was just being, I was just there. Like time stood still. Then, I heard this small gentle voice inside of me. I immediately recognized the voice, it was the Lord's voice! I sat there for ages and ages, totally marveling at what had happened. I began to cry, weep, and sob my heart out. The answer to life I had found. The hole in my heart was gone. I had found God and was finally complete inside.

My New Life In God

I woke up the next day a different person. I physically felt lighter and I was at peace. At peace with what you may ask? At peace with myself, at peace with the answer to life, at peace with this sick world that I was in but no longer belonged to in some way. Now that last statement is a bit odd but that is exactly what became true for me and still is to this very day. Such a huge change had taken place inside of me that this presence inside of me I knew was not something I had come up with, it was a divine presence that had a purity, a holiness about it. It was far bigger than anything I could conjure up.

Life did not continue as usual. I started reading the Bible more and more. It had a new meaning to me. Those parts that I had previously struggled to even believe became crystal clear. One day, I was up in my bedroom and my Bible was on my bed closed. I looked at it and then the pages started to shine, brilliantly shine like the sun's rays. I understood that this book was God's divine book, it was holy and pure and I needed to get it inside of me.

I went to church and could not stop telling people what had happened. I got mixed reactions as I went into all the details. Some were really happy, others seemed skeptical. A few seemed put off. This puzzled me. I mean, I was saved!! Saved!! You know, SAVED!!!! No hell for me, I have the Kingdom of God as my reward for abandoning my life to Jesus. People are such odd things.

I would tell both my daughters, Charlotte and Jemma, about Jesus and the more I read in the Bible, the more I told them. It was not long that they, in the way young children understand, gave their hearts to Jesus. Both were still a little uncomfortable though about being left in children's church. They wanted to be with me. I, though, in my zeal for them to know God more didn't see that then.

Really, in my life, I was still in a daze. I really had not grasped what had happened to me. I followed this voice inside of me. Go here, wait here, do this, say this to this person. So I did, and it was not long until I had the church eldership in uproar. Let me explain, I started to see what was going on in people's lives and had this ability to see ahead of time. I saw warnings and areas where the church was stifling the Spirit of God, the same Spirit that was inside of me from the day Jesus came inside me. I was not afraid to tell people because I had this real yearning to help, a real drive of compassion to see the very best in people come out of them. Well, just going around telling people the truth can cause all kinds of issues and that is what happened, so I started to get a bit of a reputation by those who did not want to hear the truth, especially concerning their own lives. They don't want to be messed with, so it was easier for them to label me as something bad and to avoid me than to admit and face the truth in their own lives.

I heard about this thing called the baptism in the Holy Ghost or Holy Spirit. It seemed that people could babble away in some baby talk of a language that made no sense to me at all yet seemed very rewarding to the person who did it. I learnt that although the Spirit of God had come inside of me, there was still more. There was a way to release this Spirit to work through me more. I liked that idea! I quickly found out what it was that I needed to do. I had to ask God for the baptism of the Holy Spirit and God would give it to me. Then, I would be able to chatter away like all these other folk and this chatter was one way I could talk to God. Well, okay, if you all say so!

That afternoon, after going to church, I went up to my bedroom and sat on my bed with the Bible.
"Okay, God, please give me this baptism in the Holy Spirit please," I asked.
Nothing happened. Again,
"Okay God, I am ready now, I am receiving the Holy Ghost!"
Nothing. Then I remembered what someone at church had said on the subject. They said that you have to start talking and then God will take over, or something like that. So I opened my mouth and heard this voice in my head,
"Stupid, don't you start making a fool of yourself! Babbling away like some mental person, it's not going to happen!"
Whoa there! Where did *that* come from?! I stopped, then thought, that's not me, that voice is *not* me. I opened my mouth again and started to make up a few funky word sounds.
"You sound *so* dumb and it's fake, you're making it all up!"
I carried on only to receive more verbal abuse. Then it happened, like the breaking of a dam wall. I could not stop. For ages and ages I talked in this way. It was like a new language (actually I found out later that that was

exactly what it was, my heavenly language that bypassed my mind, kind of a bit hard to explain if you are not saved and have never experienced this).

    A member of the Restoration church, John, had introduced himself to me. He was a friendly character. Somewhat overweight but he didn't seem to care (well, he was an excellent chef too!). It was clear to me that Jesus was number one in his life. He owned his house in Chester and through a mutual friend, Jeff, I was offered a room there to rent. I took up the offer and moved out of the English teacher's house. The atmosphere in Johns house was more peaceful and the location was good too, backing on to the fields that went down to the river Dee. John was also much more knowledgeable than I in God's word, the Bible. He also had lots of Christian videos (as well as tons of American football tapes!) and he encouraged me to look at them which I did. John was a great friend to me, he never judged me; always encouraged me. I particularly remember looking at tapes by a man called Reinhard Bonnke, a German born Christian evangelist. Later in my Christian life I had the privilege of personally meeting the man in England.

    It was while I stayed at John's house that my divorce to Karen completed (decree Absolute). It had seemed to have gone through in record time according to what I was told to expect. I still saw Charlotte and Jemma once a week but Karen was putting up demands for me not to take them to church and to have them on Saturdays. Eventually I agreed.

    My business was still barely surviving and I was still giving private violin lessons in the students' homes in the late afternoons and evenings. Both my students and their parents noticed a great change in me, but only a couple of parents seemed to be really happy for me as they believed in Jesus too.

    It was also while I was at John's house renting a room that some other profound events happened. Actually, a bunch of events that I will now attempt to record in chronological order as best as I can.

    I had been recommended to buy an NIV, or New International Version of the Bible as it was supposedly easier to understand than some other versions. I bought the largest, full study edition that I could find (I still have it to this day although I much prefer the New King James as it is far more accurate). I got such a hunger to read it that I started to seclude myself up in my bedroom for hours at a time. This was so unusual for me firstly because I like to be around people, and also because I do not read much at all. I am just not the book reader kind of person. However, I determined in my heart that I would read, out aloud, the entire Bible. This turned into an incredible journey in itself. There would be times when my eyes would drop to want to go to sleep, and this would sometimes happen when I had no reason to be tired! I remember a time when I was reading out of the book of Psalms and just kept nodding off in the middle of reading. I made myself restart the Psalm from the beginning. This went on for four or five times when suddenly "Bang!" there was this really loud electric sounding explosion, in my head! It was wild. And I was wide, I mean wide awake! I went on for hours after that. Seeking an explanation later, the Lord told me (yes that same small voice inside of me that was outside of my own thoughts. Gee, that must sound crazy but I cannot explain it any other way), the Lord told me that he was reprogramming my mind to fall in line with His. Okay!

I completed reading out aloud the whole Bible in twelve weeks. During this time I would sometimes almost fall asleep I guess. More like into a trance and I would be like lifted out of my body and I was taken to see things, spiritual things that we human's cannot see through our natural senses. Many great and awful things too. I have recorded a few of those times in the chapter on Visions, but there are a few that I cannot tell yet.

For example, although I was attending my regular church at that time, I was also going to this small fellowship at someone's mansion type house in the hills of North Wales. One day, I was running late, and so I was driving perhaps a little too fast around this country lane that would continually twist and turn which is typical of the country roads in this country. Now, what I did not know at that time was that my friend, Jeff, had but some twenty minutes prior, on this very same section of road, been praying for me for some reason he knew not.

So there I was driving around the bends etc., and suddenly the thought of a question that I had asked of the Lord came strongly in my mind. The question was,
"Lord, what will it be like in the New Kingdom, what is it like there?"
Immediately everything in front of me vanished. I could not see my hands on the steering wheel, the road had disappeared as did the hedge rows, the trees, everything. Then, I was standing off to the side of a great congregation of…angels?! They looked like people, but they were semi-transparent and they wore long robes that were also transparent. Both the angels and the robes had light in them so that they were radiant. Aloud I exclaimed,
"The angels!" but the Lord who was with me said,
"No, these are the saints."
They were all facing this large throne that was seated up high, but the light coming out from it meant that you could not see who was sitting on the throne as it was so bright and intense. The music and continual worship was… was… well, I guess the only words that fit here is heavenly or divine. I marveled greatly.

Then, I was back driving my car along that twisty country road. However, I was further down the road, maybe a few miles from where I last remembered being. To this day, I have no memory of how I drove the car during my 'visitation'. When I finally got to the fellowship meeting, as

I walked into the room of some fifteen or so people, they turned and all looked at me. Someone said, rather exclaimed,
"What happened to you!?"
I told them and they said that my face was shining, radiant.

The Word of the Lord came to me at some time during my early days of being saved (early April 1992) and I am going to insert it here. Please make a careful mental note of this because as the years went by you will see that it is very accurate. The Lord said to me,

"For two years I will reveal Myself to you and on the third year I will deal with you."

Why did all these things happen to me at this time in my life? Simply because God, I believe, ordained it and because there were a group of Christians that had decided to band together and pray for my soul to be saved. I found this out a year later when I was invited back to that home-schooling Christian group of people. Those wonderful folk at the dining table had come together and continually prayed for me. God bless them for doing so, praying for little me who they only briefly met and may have never seen me ever again. Such is the power of unselfish prayers.

A Visit to Hell

Within a short space of time I got myself dismissed from my first church, the Restoration church in Chester, because the leadership said that God does not tell and send new converts to go on trips, as I was claiming that the Lord was sending me to America. If I did not basically obey them and submit to them they said, then I could not come back to that church. Well, you can guess what I did of course, so I could not return again. I was sad about it as that was the church body through which I came to know Jesus. I had also made a few good friends by then, but fortunately, they still remained good friends outside of the church. In actual fact they too were disappointed at what the leadership did. However, there was another reason though that the leadership did what they did.

I had been visiting with the pastor and this other pastor from a sister church at their request over recent weeks. They were concerned about something in me but they never let on to what it was. Then, a sequence of events happened. The first unusual thing that I noticed was with my new friend and 'landlord', John. One day he did something unusual. He had been in a time of prayer and fasting I believe and I had come back from working one day. I met him walking down the hall in his home and he said to me,

"You know, if you ever meet anyone that has a demon," as he raised his right hand up towards my face,
"You say, In the name of Jesus Christ I cast you out!" and with that done and said, he went by me to the kitchen to cook!
When he did that though, I felt weird. I said something like,
"I don't know if I could do that."
But the incident bothered me inside.
I had been told by the leadership that I could not attend services nor any bible classes while they were seeing me. They had also told the congregation to keep away from me so I was feeling really isolated and I could not work out what was going on. Then, out of the blue, the lead musician of the music group came to me and invited me to go to Manchester to a special music seminar that was to take place. As this man invited me I heard the Lord say,
"Go!" so I got the details and on the day drove myself over there.
The whole invite thing was weird in of itself. I play the violin but the church had never heard me play at all. I was not part of the music worship team, so why invite me at all? Not only that, but they had been told to have nothing to do with me.

    Well, after driving to the Manchester location, and parking my car, I went into this old red bricked building and followed the signs upstairs to the gathering. I sensed the Lord at work here and I knew that something was going to happen.

    There were about fifty or more people there. Apparently the Apostles of the Restoration church were leading this special event. David Hadden was the name of one, then there was another man who I cannot recall his name, possibly Peter. Lastly, there was this African American man that really looked familiar for some reason; a something Davis Junior was his name. He was a small, slim, an older man with big shining eyes and a huge mouth out of which not only came a big smile but an amazing singing voice. All three of these men were anointed of the Lord I sensed.

    The 'service' started and I just could not keep my eyes off Peter as he ministered the Word of God from the Bible. Towards the end he went up to me in front of everyone and complimented me on paying so much attention and he blessed me by shaking my hand as a thank you. When we touched together though, it was like a surge of electricity passed between us. So strong was it that we both, at the same time, were totally shocked for a moment. Neither of us said anything once we released but we both looked surprised indeed!

    Then we split up into groups and I was in this group of all musicians, some twenty or so people. Once we were all gathered together, two of these men started to go around us and pray for people. Immediately an amazing thing happened. The Spirit of God, His Holy Spirit manifested in that room in a very strong way. All of us, I mean all of us started to prophesy to each other, saying things to people that we did not know anything about, but were revealing things in their lives to them. It was amazing I tell you, dear reader, literally out of this world and into another dimension we were all transported at that time.

When one of the men, an apostle, came up to me to pray I was happy to let him do so. He placed his hand on my head and started to pray. I cannot remember what he said but I distinctly recall this anger inside of me start to boil up from deep down in my being. It bothered me and I told him what was going on with me. All he said was,
"Don't worry. It will come out." And he left to go to the next person.
That was the end of that visit but that older black man seemed so special to me. There was something very different about him. His deep singing voice was divine. It was to be many years later that I started trying to find out who this man was. I knew that he was familiar. With the use of the internet, I was sure that I had found him, Sammy Davis Jr. If it was not him then it was his identical twin! There is only one problem with this discovery though, I found out that he died in 1990! And it was in 1992 that I met him! I still to this day do not have the answer to this.

Back in Chester at the restoration church: During one of the visits to the two pastors in their office I was in the process of saying something to both of them, when I felt something wrong inside of me just for a few seconds. At the same time both pastors looked quickly at each other with that knowing look of 'we know what we have here.' I left that meeting with my head starting to spin. I thought of being evil, of my mother who was mentally ill and I heard this loud condemning voice in my head say,
"See, you are crazy just like your mother."
What was happening to me? My mind started to get bombarded with all these bad thoughts. I had to get back home to John I thought.

Once John had come back from his job I went to him and asked him if we could pray together. He said yes and for me to wait in the back living room and he would come in shortly, once he had started to prepare dinner. I sat down in this comfortable rocking chair while I waited. I was not at peace and my mind was in a turmoil. What was happening to me? John came in and sat down next to me on the couch. Like I have mentioned, he was a big man and he held out his large hands to me to hold as he started to pray. I held his hands as I closed my eyes and bowed my head, and then it all came out.

Immediately I found myself getting really angry and even though my eyes were closed I could see red, blood red. Then flames and fire. I opened my eyes and looked at John. I said to him,
"You are looking at the devil."
He gently but firmly said,
"In the name of Jesus, I command you to go."

My eyes closed and I felt my whole body wrench and contort. My toes started to curl over and claw the ground, my fingers did the same and I could feel myself clawing into John's hands. Then my back arched over and it seemed to me that my spine was about to literally pop out of my back. And then, I went screaming downwards, down, down and down faster and faster I rocketed down into the darkness of death. Blood red and flames all around me as I shot down and it was not going to stop…then… I thought,
"I am going to die."
The very next split second I released my grip on John's hands and I flung myself back into the rocking chair. Sweating like crazy the first thing I said was,
"Are your hands okay?"
He reassured me that they were fine and unharmed, whereupon he got up and went back to his cooking in the kitchen! I was exhausted and for some reason I moved the coffee table out of the way and lay on the floor on my back. I stretched out my arms on either side of me making a cross out of my body and just started praying in the Spirit. I had no idea how long I was doing that for. All I remember was that when I came out of that state, John was back sitting on the couch eating his food and watching the TV! When I got up, I felt so light I almost thought I was going to float away! I went and rested and fell into a good restful sleep. I was free.

    The next day I asked the Lord for some understanding on what had happened. He told me that I was attacked by the devil as He had permitted, and that the devil had legitimate claim against my soul because of many wrong beliefs and things that I had done in my life. Then the Lord proceeded to show these things to me, and on each one I renounced them as being lies. For example, doctors told my parents who then told me that there was a chance that I could end up like my mother, a manic depressive Schizophrenic. I renounced the lie. Another was a whole collection of lies that I picked up through participating in the Church of Scientology and the Est training. As I went through and renounced each one I felt my strength returning in my soul. Finally, I finished this time in the Lord and I saw Him smile at me.

    Then another thing happened that I did not expect. I could see Jesus at a distance from me up in the air and to my right like He was floating there. In His arms that He held close to His chest, was a glowing light. This went on for about two weeks and all through this time I was very weepy. I think that my violin students and parents must have thought it most odd but no one questioned me. I finally had to ask the Lord,
"What is that you are holding?"
And the Lord replied,
"It is your soul. Never again will it be taken from Me." I broke down and cried in thankfulness.

I went back to see the church leadership once more as the Lord had told me to go to the US soon. They were still not in agreement and gave me an ultimatum to not go and submit myself to them, or, if I did go then I was not welcome back in the church. My chapter about my first missionary trip to the US tells of what happened from here onwards.

The Power of God Experienced – The Witchcraft Fare

So after my first missionary trip to the US, I was attending a small Assembly of God church located on Queens St, in the city of Chester where I lived. What I did not know was that my 'reputation' had already gone ahead of me and the pastor here was wary of me. Anyway, I was faithful in going on Sundays, and on Wednesdays they would have a much smaller assembly in the back room. It was during one of these small midweek meetings the pastor announced that the hotel, which was nearby, was going to host a psychic fair starting this Friday and over the weekend. He wanted us to all pray against it but before we did pray the Lord said to me,
"Who will go to represent Me?"
As I thought it was a question for everyone I asked if anyone was going to go there for the Lord?
"You don't want to go in that kind of a place," was the kind of reply I got from the pastor.
So, we prayed against it and again the Lord asked me,
"Who will go to represent Me?"
I said,
"Lord, I will."

The fair was scheduled to start on the following Friday evening. The problem was that was my busy day for teaching violin students. But God had made all the arrangements. All my students cancelled which is a very rare thing to happen, for even one of them to do so.

So, taking my Bible as instructed by the Lord, I headed for the Hotel to represent Jesus. Going through large double glass doors I went up to the hotel staff that were at the reception desk. I had noticed the psychic fair sign in the foyer pointing to a flight of stairs so I guessed that it was happening up those stairs somewhere. The staff noticed my large Bible and asked me if they could help, upon which I explained that I was a Christian and that I believed that it was wrong to do what they do in these fairs. The three ladies agreed and they gave me full reign to do whatever I wanted to do there.

Well, I had arrived a little early so I went and sat at a small bar area that was just off to the side of the entrance foyer. It did not have doors

to the foyer, just open plan which was great because I could see anyone coming in. I sat there for a few minutes drinking a non-alcoholic drink and eating those free peanuts that they put out. I placed my Bible up on the bar top as two burly workmen came in and came up to the bar. It looked like their work day had just ended and they were there for a quick pint or two of beer before going home. One saw my Bible and asked me,
"Is that a Bible?"
I said yes and after a short conversation they knew why I was there. So, they said to me,
"You just stay sitting right there and we will grab anyone that comes in and bring them to you and you tell them what you just told us."
Okay! And that is what happened all that evening. Many did not even go upstairs; others did but they seemed to come back down pretty quick, from what I could tell.

    At the end of that evening session some of the people from the fair came down looking a little disappointed to me. I asked them,
"So, how's it going?" as if I didn't know!
Giving me a little bit of a downcast look as I would describe it, they said that it was disappointing, but they hoped it would be better over the weekend.

    The following day, Saturday, the Lord had me there again. If I recall correctly there were two sessions that day, an afternoon and an evening session. At late morning, just before it started I went up the stairs and met a boy, probably in his mid-teens, sitting at a table at the entrance to the fair. His job was to collect the entrance fee. I stopped and talked with him a while. He told me that it was his dad who ran the fair and that he did it not because he believed in any of it, but because he had to because of his dad. I told him about being born again as a Christian and following the one true God. He told me a story of his brother who was still incarcerated and how someone went to him and told him about Jesus and he got born again.

    I went back down the stairs, but once the session had started I went back up again. The Lord told me to pay the entrance fee. Now I really did not want to do this, as I did not want to support the event in any way at all, but after checking with the Lord I did so and went in. You then walked down this short hallway where you could hear the soft music playing. Walking into the event room you notice the dimmed lighting to try and create this mystical atmosphere (I am surprised that they didn't have a smoke machine there too! I mock). There were small tables placed near the windows, and at each table was a person with their stuff on their table whether it be a glass ball, tarot cards or whatever. There were rows of individual seats laid out facing these tables for the 'customers' to sit while I guess they waited for a turn to go up to one of the tables. Well, there must have been some one hundred to a hundred and fifty chairs there, but I only counted about six people sitting on them! I quietly sat down near the center back of the room. I got my Bible out, silently read a little then bowed my head and prayed quietly to the Lord.

After a few minutes I looked up and the lady at the table right in front of me, maybe some twenty feet away, was staring at me. Looked to me like she was shaking too. I went back to praying. The next thing I knew was that a man came up behind me and asked to speak with me. He asked me to step outside with him so I did. He told me that he was the organizer of the event (that teenager's dad) and that I was disrupting the event in there. I said that all I was doing was sitting there quietly at the back praying. He told me that if I wanted to do that then he would find me a room somewhere where I could do that, upon which I said that I was quite happy doing it right where I was, thank you. He started to get a little annoyed and went to his son and refunded my money and asked (told) me to leave. I checked with the Lord and I went back down the stairs.

Downstairs I did what I did the previous day, only those two workmen were not there of course, but the staff were fine with me talking to people as they came in. Again, some did go upstairs and others did not. That was the afternoon session done.

I was back for the evening session and the Lord had me just stay standing in the middle of the foyer. Some of the fair staff saw me there, including the dad, the organizer, and he did not look happy with me at all. I just smiled politely. It was different this time, inside me I felt the strong presence of the Lord. It was starting to get dusk outside but I could see the people parking their cars and walking towards the glass doors to the hotel so I would start to pray for these people not to come in. Nothing happened at first, but after a while I started to see people turn around. A few put their hands on the doors, like one couple who looked at each other, turned and left. Then the intensity of the Lord became so great that all I did was stand in the middle of the foyer and I could feel (for lack of a better word) this beam of energy blasting out from me through those doors. It was an awesome sensation. No one, I mean I cannot recall anyone coming in once that started. I even remember the hotel staff looking at me with 'bug' eyes as I stood there.

Once that experience subsided I went and sat down at the bar and rested. The evening psychic session was soon to end. The organizer and a couple of his staff came down and saw me. Glaring at me with anger they were mumbling between themselves.
"So, how did it go?" I teased them with a smile.
Oooo, you should have seen that man's face. I don't remember them replying to me. I do remember that they packed up and left the city without even having the Sunday sessions! Praise the Lord!

Jehovah's Witnesses

One day while I was at big John's house on my own, there was a knock at the door. I went and opened it and there stood two Jehovah's Witnesses (must have been a Saturday as they usually only go door knocking on Saturdays!). Now, I had been instructed by big John in the past not to accept these people in and to politely tell them that I was not interested and close the door on them. This is what I did. After doing so, however, my heart was grieved for them, so I got down and prayed for them. In the middle of my prayer the Lord told me to go to their meetings. I told this to John and he said that if God was telling me to do that, then I should obey and go.

A few weeks past and one day I was walking through a little village called Buckley where I had been visiting friends. I noticed two young men washing windows to business premises. There must have been something about them that told me they were Jehovah Witnesses but I cannot recall what it was. Anyway, I went over to talk to them and they seemed happy to stop their work and talk to me. I was right, they were both Jehovah's Witnesses. In fact one of them was the son of a 'pastor' of a congregation in an area of Chester called Blacon. He gave me the address and times and invited me to come along. I said I would do that, and that I would visit this Saturday evening for the next service.

I was not sure what to dress in to go to this meeting. I had heard that they wear business dress to some degree but the Lord had me in blue jeans and a big loose t-shirt that said something like "Jesus is Lord!" on it. I drove over to this Kingdom Hall as they referred to it and went in. Wow, was I going to stick out in appearance! All the men seemed to be dressed exactly the same way. Black suits, white long sleeved shirts and a tie. One of the two young men that I had previously met, the 'pastors' son came to me and invited me to sit down with him in the middle of one of the rows of wooden pews. It was a traditional set up there. Two adjacent rows of pews with a center isle leading to a few steps up to the stage, the platform where a black piano resided as well as a small preacher's podium.

A few (really dead) songs were played on the piano and people sang along without any real zeal I noticed. Then the pastor gave a whole lesson on how to overcome challenges when going out witnessing together. That was it. That was the 'service'. I had been quietly praying, just praying for, well I cannot remember but immediately after the service, before I could even get up from my pew seat, I was surrounded by the pastor and other 'elders' of the church. I was asked all kinds of questions by them regarding my faith in Jesus Christ. Afterwards the young pastor's son invited me to a Bible study that he went to, so I agreed.

At the Bible study I caused an upset in the group of about a dozen or less people. They wanted to start with prayer so they started praying and I found myself praying out aloud in the Spirit. I did not realize that once I started doing this they had all stopped and were staring at me. I had my eyes closed and was just flying around with Jesus somewhere! Then I came to, opening my eyes, and realized what was happening. I looked at them staring at me. One of them asked me what I was doing,
"Praying in the Holy Ghost, the Spirit of God language," I answered smiling at them.
They tried to tell me that the Holy Spirit was just a force of Jehovah's energy and that praying like that was of the devil himself! Well, these people are really mislead I thought. I went to a couple more Bible studies and then left them for good. The Lord had taught me what I needed to know. They have even mistranslated the scriptures and made up their own 'Bible' to try to show that God is not Father, Son and Holy Spirit all as one but that Jehovah is the only God and the deity of the Son, Jesus becomes subordinate, being worded in their book as son in lower case, and the Holy Spirit, becomes just a force of energy. They missed it. They are guilty of trying to put the understanding capacity of a man to explain the Bible, but the Truth of God is a revelation of God beyond man's comprehension. That's why it is a revelation, and why it requires faith to see and live in it.

The Salvation and Conversion of Paul Medford

Having just returned from one of my missionary trips to the US which I think was the first trip to that country, I settled down to earn some money. I was doing some work at a lumber yard that was located in Deeside right on the tidal river Dee in North Wales, less than ten miles from Chester. The place was a family run business that employed about a dozen people. They made privacy fences and all kinds of sheds. There was a full carpentry workshop that made anything from doors to custom furniture. The business location was a rough area, where there were many unemployed people around so break-ins and fights were not uncommon news. Drug dealing and use was probably the main evil going on.

I had the job of loading and unloading lumber deliveries using a large diesel side-loader. I also made deliveries using a mid-size commercial flatbed truck which was great fun to navigate around all those twisting country lanes. The owner, Phil, was a very outgoing person, so outgoing that you would think he was on the border of outrageous at times. He loved the Lord and really believed in putting himself out there when it came to talking and expressing his faith. So much so at times that it seemed driven and not real which concerned me. However, he was very, very good to me.

One day Phil saw a young man that he knew in the yard but rather than going to talk to him he asked me to do so. I went up to this rather shabby looking man in his early twenties. His eyes were all glossy and you could tell that he was doing drugs. I introduced myself and so did he. Well, at least he was coherent I thought. His name was Paul, Paul Medford, and as we walked slowly around the Lord told me to tell him about the Gospel of Jesus Christ. I suggested we sit down on the concrete jetty by the river Dee that used to be a dock loading area, now demolished except for a few large boulders of concrete here and there.

As I started to talk to Paul, I noticed that, in spite of his chemical condition, he was really paying attention and the Lord's presence was there with us. After clearly explaining the gospel, I asked Paul if he was ready to repent and he said he was. Following a prayer of repentance and believing in Jesus Christ was declared by Paul, his eyes just like woke up! His glossy drug induced deer in the headlight look went and he seemed to be fully in his right mind. After a short time he left and I, thanking the Lord for the honor of using me, went back to work after telling Phil.

Paul lived in a council area that is equivalent to the American projects and his neighborhood consisted of small two story brick built houses. He lived in the heart of a drug dealing and using community. His girlfriend was also a big addict. They had three children, all young. They had two boys aged about four and six, and a baby daughter maybe a year old. Because of their really poor living conditions and lifestyle the DHSS, Department of Health and Social Security, were often involved for the welfare of the children. I went to visit them once, as the older boy had decided that he wanted to see if he could fly and opened up the upstairs window of their two story house and promptly jumped straight out expecting to fly! A broken arm was the result.

Their house was filthy, un-kept and totally disorganized. I even saw needles lying around the floor that had been used for drugs. His girlfriend immediately took a real dislike to me on that first visit. She was high on drugs and was barely coherent. I left after helping Paul clean up a little. I also introduced Paul to a new church fellowship (my third church by now!) that was located just inside North Wales in a town called Mold. He was eager to learn and change his life around.

I had started going to this new church body in Mold through the Lord's instructions. After dismissing myself from my second church, the Assembly of God church, one day I was travelling through Mold for some reason and the Lord took me to the local public community center. He had me pray around the building, then I went about my business. Some weeks later I heard that there were to be some special guests that had been invited there for some open Christian event. It was promoted that healings and signs would happen. The Lord told me to go.

By the way, I had left that Assembly of God church because on one of their midweek services the pastor asked for committed people in the church to come up and pray for the sick and needy that had already been invited up to the front. As far as I was concerned, I was one of those committed people so I went up and I placed my hand on this young man's shoulder. He was in quite a lot of pain from having trapped nerves through excessive body building exercising, and the Lord instantly healed him on the spot. We both greatly rejoiced, praising the Lord! The following Sunday service the pastor was waiting for me at the church door and pulled me aside and scolded me for going up to pray as I was under a trial period with his church. What! I found out later that he and the pastor of my first church, the Restoration church knew each other well and were keeping an eye on me. I cried and left the church. Jesus never put people on trial periods.

So what a surprise I got when I walked into this community center meeting in Mold. There were both of the pastors from the first two churches that I had been dismissed from, and most of their congregations! I was polite but basically ignored them. Now I was confused because the Lord had told be about having a place to go worship regularly. No way could it be with these folk!? The 'special' guests came in and the meeting began. By the end I was not very impressed. The guests were glorifying themselves more than Christ Jesus, although I believe that the Lord still did honor some of the prayers for healing.

I was still a little confused about that whole incident but after a few weeks went by, my friend Jeff told me that there was this new fellowship that had just started and that the pastor was a man from a South Wales church and that God had called him here to preach. I bore witness in the Lord that this was the place for me for now. Pastor Idris Williams was the man's name and guess where the church was establishing itself? Yes, in the Mold community center!

The first time I went there with Jeff, he took me straight up to the pastor and introduced me. Then Jeff told him that I played the violin. Pastor looked at me and then said,
"Bring it and play with us starting next week."
No audition, no nothing. Just come! So I did, and this was to be the very first time that the Lord had me truly worship Him in a public setting. When I arrived for the pre-service practice session I was put up on the low platform with all the other musicians and a microphone was placed in front of me. But I had no music stand for the music so I asked the band leader, the keyboard player and she replied,
"You don't need music. Just play!" as she smiled at me.

I am classically trained. Trained to read and memorize and play, or just play with the music. Now, I had to 'just play!' Well, okay I guess. And that is how the Lord started to teach me how to play in the Spirit. This was the church that I introduced Paul Medford to.

Some many days later I was driving on behalf of the lumber yard to go to a customer's house who owed the business money. As I drove along the main highway the Lord spoke to me, telling me to go to Paul's house. Well, I had a commitment to try and collect this money so I did that first (unsuccessfully) and then drove straight to Paul's house. Knocking on the door his girlfriend answered looking a little scared.
"What happened" I asked with a concerning tone to my voice.
"Paul has been taken to hospital." She almost tearfully replied as she held what seemed to be a change of clothes for him.
"Can you take these to him?" She asked me looking down at the clothes. She had the children to look after so I agreed.
"So, what happened?" I asked again.
"Some men from Liverpool broke into the house and Paul was sleeping on the couch in the living room. They had metal bars and just kept hitting and beating him saying that he owed them like over ten thousand pounds." Thankfully none of the children nor herself were harmed. I got to find out later that these people were drug dealers from Liverpool that Paul had owed money to for years, yet they never had bothered to do this before. Maybe after just getting saved into the Kingdom of God stirred up a hornets nest!

On arriving at the emergency entrance to the hospital the Lord told me to take my Bible in with me. I went in up to the reception asking to see Paul Medford. The lady receptionist, looking at my Bible asked if I was his minister and I found myself saying yes. I was escorted straight away to a cubicle where Paul was lying unconscious. I was left there and they said a doctor would be around shortly before Paul goes in for x-rays. He had been there I think between one and two hours, so I guess he was not in a life threatening condition. Huge golf ball sized lumps where on his forehead, his arms and what little part of his legs that were visible.

I had to pray. Getting before the Lord I prayed that Paul's body would be fine, that none of his bones would be damaged or broken. An amazing thing happened. A bright light came into this small area where only a pull across curtain separated us from everyone else milling around the emergency area. The light stayed for about thirty seconds and then departed. Immediately after that the curtain was whisked back and the doctor together with other people were there. After asking me who I was they told me that Paul was now going to go for x-rays but because he, for sure has so many bones broken, he will be in there for about an hour or so, so that they could x-ray his entire body. I left and went back into the waiting area.

I believed that I stayed at the hospital just waiting, but I cannot for sure remember. I do remember being told that Paul was back out of the x-ray lab, that he was conscious and I could go see him which, of course, I did. He was heavily sedated and could barely talk so I prayed, talked to him, and read the Word of God to him. Quite some time later in comes the doctor again with all the x-rays in his hand. As he looked at them his face showed great surprise.

"Well, it's amazing," he finally said as he shook his head from side to side and continued,

"Not one bone in your body is broken. You just had some severe bruising and will need crutches for about two weeks," he said in amazement.

Praise the Lord! I tell you, the doctor really was amazed too, he could not comprehend finding nothing broken based the number and severity of the blows from the steel crow bars that were used. I mean, not even one fracture was found!

The following day I went back to visit Paul as they said that they were going to keep him there for a few days under observation. I met Paul walking towards me using crutches as I went in! He had discharged himself saying he was fine! I helped him a little into the car and took him home. That Sunday Paul was back in church… no crutches, and was there helping stack the chairs!

The First Prophesy

While at some event that one of my brothers in Christ had invited me to, I was lead to go up for a time of prayer. Although I cannot remember all about this particular meeting, I can recall that the preacher was a well-respected black man and that he carried some anointing on his ministry. Anyway, we were somewhere in England and there I was lining up to receive from the Lord as he worked his way down the prayer line. What was most interesting were the words that came out of this man's mouth as he knew nothing about me,

"The Lord is going to send you into dark and dangerous places." And that was it.

I did not quite know what to do with that statement, so I just pondered on it in my heart and put it away in my memory somewhere. Little was I to know that these very same words were to be spoken over me twice more on two different continents before they would come to fruition.

Closing the Business Down

The Lord instructed me to close down my music business, the correspondence course that I had created for young children. It was called the Carousel Music Company and, if you recall, it was a ten-month correspondence course to teach children basic music skills, all instructed from an audio cassette tape. The innovative course had won the regional Entrepreneur of the Year Award but it was well underfunded from the start so, together with the bad economy at that time in the country, it had been in a state of struggling financially. I had been instructed by the Lord to completely close down the company within four weeks. This meant that I had to contact all my customers to let them know and do some kind of special reduced offer so that at least they could get all of the music packs completed for their children. I felt doing that was the least I could do.

Due to the financial struggles of the business I was now in a situation where I was really in debt. By now I must have owed about (approximate figures here) in today's monetary value about $6,000 to the local advertising agent that was just across the way from my office, a $35,000 bank loan to the notoriously hard on small businesses Midland Bank, over $150,000 to the printing company that continued to extend credit to me way beyond any logical sense (but they believed in me and that I was doing my very best to make this all work), and about $8,000 or so to the Inland Revenue Service (IRS) on taxes past due. There were a few other minor debts too but I cannot recall the details. Overall, some $200,000 plus in today's terms.

I asked the Lord how I was supposed to do this in a responsible way. I had set up the company as a Limited company which is like the LLC in American businesses so it helps free the individual from any creditor trying to seize your personal assets but in my case there were a few different clauses in my terms of financing. The IRS could always claim on me directly, the bank loans I had to personally guarantee, and the printing company had me sign clauses to allow one of their directors on my board at Carousel, I had sold them shares in the business and in doing so I made myself personally liable to some degree.

The Lord directed me to a Proverb:

Prov 6:1-5
  My son, if you become surety for your friend,
  If you have shaken hands in pledge for a stranger,
  2 You are snared by the words of your mouth;
  You are taken by the words of your mouth.
  3 So do this, my son, and deliver yourself;
  For you have come into the hand of your friend:

Go and humble yourself;
Plead with your friend.

4 Give no sleep to your eyes,
Nor slumber to your eyelids.

5 Deliver yourself like a gazelle from the hand *of the hunter,*
And like a bird from the hand of the fowler.

NKJV

So that is was I did. I sat down in my office and started to write letters to all my creditors, that is except the bank manager at Midland Bank. I was a little scared as to what to do there. All my creditors knew that I had conducted my business as honestly as possible as I had always kept them informed. My bank manager even came to visit me once or twice but now it was different, I had to close the operation down and they were going to possibly lose their money or take action against me.

This all took place I believe towards the end of 1993 into early 1994, after my third trip to the US. And most people knew that I had got saved and that I was flying here and flying there as a missionary. It could have been construed that I was living it up a little rather than paying my creditors, but you will read in the chapters later about my travels that the Lord made the provision for me each time. It is hard to know quite where to place this story so I have jumped the gun just a little by inserting it here so please be patient with me on this.

Not only did I write to my creditors, but the Lord told me to visit them too. That is, all except the IRS as you don't visit them as far as I knew. So, I made arrangements and first on my list was my advertising agent across the way from my office. I sat down with him and told him the full story including how I got saved and the commission from the Lord on my life. After I had explained that I was closing down the business, he seemed to fully understand and made no attempt to recover any of his money but just shook my hand and wished me the very best.

The printing company was next. They had set up a full board meeting at their premises with the business owners and board members. I was nervous as I drove the ten miles or so northwards to them in my car. However, the Lord had me put on praise and worship music and I ended up getting carried away in His presence so by the time I arrived I was just loving the Lord and fear had gone. Walking into the board room I met with some eight or so people, most of who I already knew to some extent. They gave me a seat and I briefly explained that I was closing down the business and why. I said that I was sorry as I knew that I owed them quite a sum of money and had no way to pay them back right now. Their response touched my heart. The big boss man stood up and said,

"We have already been discussing you and your business together. We have seen how you have conducted yourself since we became involved at the very start of your venture. We believe that you have done your very best to make it work in hard times. We too would have liked it to work which is why we were happy to help fund you. You do not need to worry about the debt, we have already written it off on our books. We also would like to offer you a job here if you ever want one."

Everyone around the table was smiling and they all got up and came to me and shook my hand. I was so taken back at their amazing grace and kindness towards me that I got teary eyed. I left that building stunned and joyful.

A few days went by and the Lord reminded me, "You have not gone to see the bank manager."

My head dropped. I had definitely been procrastinating on that one. So, taking a big breath, I called the bank and made an appointment to see him. I had to give a reason so I just said that I was closing down my business. On the day of the meeting I have to say that I was definitely nervous. This bank had been in the news even recently as being noted for taking tough measures against small businesses, so I was preparing myself for a bit of an ordeal.

A secretary came to me and invited me into the manager's office. There he was sitting behind his impressive large desk looking down at some paperwork. His secretary announced me as I went in and walked up to his desk. Looking up from his paperwork he looked at me for a second and, with a serious facial expression he stood up and extended his hand towards me. I took it and he gave me a good firm hand shake like a friend gives another friend. I was a little taken back by it but then he talked to me saying,

"Mr. Ewens, I know how you have been conducting yourself since you launched this business of yours. I am sorry that it has not managed to be successful and get through this economy. I have seen you work hard and you have stayed in touch letting us know what was going on. Don't worry about the debt to the bank we are not going to claim anything off you for it." And he smiled at me.

I stood there, still holding his hand I think! I was yet again stunned. I could not thank him enough and he got that I was most grateful. I had signed my personal assets to the bank as security so he had all rights to claim some if he wanted to.

Last of all came the IRS and again they had a no-forgiveness government policy running (as usual) and would make people pay back by installments and slap on charges with it. Well days went by and I think after a couple of weeks or so, I received this formal letter from them. I remember sitting in my almost empty office space and opening it. With great joy I read that the overdue taxes were voided out for some reason I cannot even remember. All I remember was that I was debt free! Over $200,000 in today's terms was wiped clean by the Lord through people all being merciful to me. I even got a significant tax refund mailed to me from the IRS years later! I praised and thanked the Lord in my office and prayed that He would somehow bless these people for being so kind to me.

My final debt was the mortgage on the house where my now x-wife lived. On divorcing me I took all the debts and left her with everything in the house which was on the market and sold a few months later after she had moved to a nice rental house in the city for herself and the girls. I gave her the proceeds (which was not much) from the house sale. I wanted her to be as secure as was possible even though she was the one who divorced me.

Chapter Two – My New Life

The following visions occurred during various times after I got saved. I will also refer to some of them as I continue my life story, so please forgive me when I repeat myself…

The Visions

So what is a vision and how is a vision different from one's own imagination? A good question. For me, I have discovered that although I have mistaken a divine vision for my own imagination and visa versa, there is one phenomena that helps me distinguish one from the other. I find that when I recall a vision I cannot manipulate it by my will, nor can I change any part of it. Also, with a true vision there is what I call 'life' in it. What I mean is the vision is alive in some way. Hard to put into words. With things I imagine that is not so, I can alter both the sequence and content of what I 'see'. Listed below in this chapter are many visions that I have been blessed to see. They are not put down in any particular order, nor do I, on the whole, necessarily place any specific interpretation to them.

One of my earliest visions was personal and quite disturbing. I was actually sitting in the bathroom during the day when the Lord showed me a vision of something like the shape of a funnel or a curved vase you could say. The base of the funnel was like a vase with the bulge at the base and the narrowing funnel going up before it opened out. In the base were the majority of Christian believers. They were all crunched up together pretending to be contented in where they were, but really they were not. Some had ventured up the funnel but only a few would go. The Lord asked me if I would go, if I would leave the comfort of the many and venture forth up the funnel. I was about to say that I would when the Lord warned me of what I would face if I went. He said that I would be seriously questioned, especially by other Christians because I left the pack. He said that there would be times when I would even question myself and even think I was going crazy, and there would be great times when I had little understanding as to what was happening to me and would have very little support around me. I still chose to go up as the Lord said that He would always be with me.

Coming to the Lord I had seen Jesus face to face in my bedroom where He finally appeared to me in person and came up and touched me. This you have already read about earlier in this book.

I had seen the pages of my Bible on my bed shine brightly.

On another occasion after reading the Bible I went into this trance like state and I was taken somewhere and saw all the devils and demons or evil spirits in the air. They were getting squeezed together and time was running out for them and they were all very angry. And I saw the Spirit of God and the heavenly angels using the Name of the Lord to banish them away. Again I saw the children of God, like me, speaking out God's word and the angels beat back the demons who got even more angry.

Once I was driving my car along a motorway (interstate in the US) when I pondered in my heart how far away the Lord was. I heard Him say,
"This close",
and what my eyes saw became like an image projected on a screen and then suddenly the Lord turned off the projector of everyday life and the screen became brilliant white that you could not really look at and the Lord was standing there before me. Then once again I saw the road and traffic ahead of me. I praised God for showing me all this.

While married to Karen I had damaged my lower back through diving at the swimming baths and digging the garden. The local doctor had told me that I would have to put up with this for the rest of my life. Sometimes it would just be a dull ache. At other times it would have me laid up in bed for a while, especially if I pulled it again.
      Well, one morning, in the summer of 1992 I awoke finding myself speaking in tongues, that crazy nonsensical chatter that does nothing for one's own mind! Immediately I saw a vision of a transparent red-pinkish glass splinter wedged in-between two vertebrae in my lower back. I heard the voice of the Lord say,
"Don't move."
So I kept still, while still speaking in tongues. Wondering what was going to happen next, the Lord said,
"Pull out the splinter."
So I reached with my hand behind my back (I was lying sideways on my bed) and sure enough, I felt the splinter! More like a huge chunk of glass stuck in my back!
"Pull it out." The Lord commanded me.
So I started to pull the wedge out. I could feel my back pulling in resistance but the wedge started to come out. Somehow I understood that it was the devil who had put it there. As the final tip started to come out I felt my back muscles in that area all move, more like twinge. With the wedge out I threw it away and….. and I started laughing! I just laughed and laughed! I knew my back was healed!

Within a few days I went back to the doctor, who also confirmed that my back appeared to be fine. He asked me what happened so I told him,
"Jesus healed my back when I was in bed the other day."
He looked at me in disbelief but seemed please that I was happy my back was okay!

I had been pondering in recent past what it would be like in heaven, like how would we know and interact with each other? Driving around one day as I pulled up to a minor road junction, the Lord showed me what we would be like. I saw bright pure stars shining and dancing together. Each star was made of the same brightness, they were all the same yet each one was a saved person, a living soul that was safe in God and free from its earthly body. As I saw all this I was filled with such peace and joy far beyond anything I had experienced from things before I met Christ.

Later, actually some time later, maybe over a year or so, again while I was driving, I was taken up into the heavens and saw the city of God. It was some distance away at first as I was lifted up towards it. The city shone from a great distance and I remember my heart pounding with excitement. As I was taken close to it, it shone like the color of pearls from the sea. The next thing I remember I was standing in a street that was all aglow with that same pearl shine. Everything was solid yet transparent. Really hard to explain this. Angels were passing by and we seemed to communicate even without talking. There was a heavenly (only word I can use to explain this) 'music' in the air yet it wasn't music as we know it, more like an atmosphere. I also saw twelve great doors or gates with each gate highly decorated with all kinds of bright precious stones. Next, I was back on planet earth! I was so grateful to God that He had shown me these things. I felt (and still do) highly honored.

I had decided one year, I think it was in early 1994 to do a charity swim. I had to swim one mile and had been practicing in the city swimming baths. I think it was about 70 lengths in a 25-yard pool to cover that distance. I found that concept not too exciting so after taking this matter to the Lord, I decided that I would swim a mile across a lake instead! The trouble was, I had to do the swim by early April, and English waters are still really cold at that time of year! Fearing not, I sought the Lord again and decided to swim a mile across one of the Welsh natural lakes, Lake Bala. As I lived on the border of North Wales, it was only about an hour's drive away.

When the day came I took my canoe, an orange lake kayak with the idea that I would get someone to be with me as I swam. All I was going to wear were a pair of speedos! I had checked the map and found a good starting point on one side of the lake and would swim over towards a campsite which was just over a mile away across the water. I drove first to this campsite and found a willing teenager who would canoe alongside me. He thought I was crazy! I think it was he who pointed out that the lake is fed directly from the melting ice waters of the surrounding mountains!

I was starting to wonder what I had gotten myself into as he jumped into my car and we drove around to the launch area. I unloaded the canoe off the top of the car and got the teenager into the water. I stripped down to my swimming trunks. Gee, it was cold! I put my toes into the edge of the water, yeek! I must be crazy! I didn't even have any vaseline to insulate myself with! Nevertheless, I had committed myself to do this so taking a big breath I waded in. Yep, sure was cold! The water was also very clear. It is a trout lake and they do not even allow powerboats on the lake in order to keep the water as pure as possible. The lake is also very deep, the deepest I believe in North Wales.

I swam the breast stroke as this way I could at least keep my head above the water most of the time. I swam for a minute I guess when I did what one should never do… I looked back. I had gone only about twenty meters! I had barely left the shoreline and already my skin was turning from white to blue! This also made my arms ache (I guess the blood was not reaching my muscles properly or something!). The teenager had gone a little distance ahead of me, I guess enjoying his free kayaking session!

All I remember doing was offering up a prayer to God to help me. He did in a most marvelous way. After that prayer, I remember thinking how wonderfully clean the water was, even drank a little as I swam. The next thing I remember was my knee scraping against a rock on the far side! I don't remember getting there but I must have done so as the teenager was there with my canoe. I got out, thanked the boy and ran about two miles around the shore to get my car, drove back to the campsite to load the canoe and went home really thanking God for being there when I needed Him! I still cannot recall how I got across that lake.

Heaven opened and I saw Jesus looking down. I was attending a Sunday service at a church in Atlanta, Georgia, USA. The Lord had sent me to a church called Word Changing Ministries (made up name). In the middle of worship, I looked up and the top of the church vanished. I saw heaven looking in and the Lord Himself smiled down at us all.

Gray USA. While in England staying at a friend's house in about 1995 I went downstairs for breakfast. I sat at the bar table about to pour some cereal when I suddenly saw the sea of China. Out of the sea came horrible creatures that seemed to crawl out from the beach. They were demonic and they took to the air and flew hard and fast over the top of the earth and down over Alaska then northern Canada. Millions of them, a whole swarm and as they flew south all the land that they went over turned gray. A gray death and destruction for nothing lived where they flew over. They flew down passed Canada and into America destroying all the ground that they went over.

I heard the loud beating of like a million angels wings; it was the final time of harvest for souls on the earth. A darkness had covered the whole earth and to the east and to the west were what looked like tornados that reached up into the heavens. They both roared thunderously. I stood in the midst of destruction as I heard the wailings of men as the two whirlwinds moved. The West moved eastwards and the East moved westwards, each eating up all life as they covered the earth. I trembled in great fear for I did not know at this great time of tribulation if I would survive, if the winds would take me away or if I would make it into His Kingdom. They passed behind me then came back again, and again, each time getting closer. Then, they headed straight for me. My heart pounded and I was gone. I was in this corridor with lots of others. We all seemed to know each other and we were all happy. We had made it.

Once, while on my first missionary trip to the US, the Lord had me ride my borrowed bike (bicycle) out into the countryside and then into a small housing development. Coming to a dead end the Lord had me get off my bike and sit down on the curb. Wondering if I was really even hearing God I looked around for maybe someone to talk to. Maybe God was going to bring me someone? But no one came. I waited. There came a short light gust of wind in the trees around me. A leaf was falling in front of me and I caught it before it touched the ground. It was a green leaf. Nothing special about it really. It was shiny on one side and it was complete, no bits missing. I noticed how the veins branched out from the main stem where the leaf was once attached to the tree. It was then that I heard the voice of the Lord say,
"Tear it up but keep the veins intact."
So, I gradually, and carefully removed all the 'flesh' part of the leaf so that all was left was the veins, just the skeleton. The Lord said,
"This is what I am going to do with you."

I saw a vision of two hoops, the kind kids play hoopla with. At first they were apart from each other. Then the Lord brought them closer together so that one slightly overlapped the other. Then He slowly moved them more and more over each other until finally they were exactly on top of one another. He told me that He was showing me that once we were totally separate from each other. Both existed, yet totally separate. On being saved (born again), we overlapped a little. Now, as He refines us more and more, we will eventually become one. Again He showed me that this also was the natural (man) taking on board the supernatural God. The two shall indeed eventually become one.

I had a vision of Africa and the Lord said He was sending me there. I asked,

"Where?" meaning where in Africa and He again showed me the vision, the shape of Africa and a spot where there was a bright white light. I had to go there. Looking at a map later, it was located inland in Nigeria to the east a little.

While on my first visit to Tulsa, Oklahoma I awoke one morning while staying at a new friend's apartment (Drew, who became my best man at my wedding), I opened my eyes to see a huge angel of the Lord. He was so big that he towered in front of me. His robe was taller than the room, it went through the ceiling, through the roof and way up into the sky, yet I could also see his whole majesty. I was scared by his mighty presence. He just looked down at me. He was formidable. I asked him (funny, not out aloud I believe, but in my head),
"Who are you?"
He replied,
"I am Michael, placed to war and protect the souls of men."
I realized that he was an Archangel.

    I have seen the Archangel Michael a few times since. I feel strongly that there is a reason why I see him and that there is something I have to do that also has something to do with him. The interesting thing is that he has never moved and has always the same stance, for years right up to late November 2013. His stance was tall, formidable and very serious. His mighty sword was always in his hand and held down with the point touching the ground. No movement at all, time and time again. Then, in 2013 when the Lord had commissioned me into the ministry He has for me and I was over fifty years old, Michaels' stance changed. Still no movement but he now held his mighty sword up high to the heavens and his face victorious and ready to do battle.

When visiting a well-known church in Orlando, Florida (Pastor Benny Hinn's church), I was going to take a short swim to cool myself down in the lake by the church, but as I started to walk towards it, I had a vision of me standing in the middle of the lake and my feet and legs were being bitten. I turned around and went back to the church. Later I was told that there were alligators in there! Having never been to Florida before and seeing no signs and there was no fencing up, how was I to know!

(I typed this one up before 2013): In mid-2004 I was given a vision concerning myself as I was battling for my freedom from the sexual immorality of cross dressing and all the other sins it can lead to. The Lord showed me two different ways that I could come before Him at the ends of days. I would either be a strong healthy young man whole and well-tanned, with bright eyes and good teeth with a great smile unto Him. I also had a full pair of female breasts (?!). Or, I could come before Him as an old man, gray looking, very drawn and skinny with wrinkled skin. No breasts, but no eyes at all! Just black holes. This vision scared me (still does) and I am battling for its meaning. I shared it with a lady in church who has what is called a prophetic based ministry. She said that the first man with breasts represented feeding the church as that is what breasts were for, feeding. I think that there is more to it than that still to be revealed.

Once while at home in the USA, I saw a room before me in the house of God which I was in, in the Spirit. I had not been in this room before and as I walked to the door, it opened but it had a flame of fire all around the entrance on the top, sides and bottom. It would take great courage to enter in this room that was divine health and healing. I saw but did not enter. And then, days later, I was about to walk up on stage at church to play my violin on stage with the praise and worship group at Fathers House church in Tulsa when I saw the door of flames again and I walked through it as I walked up on the stage. That was an amazing service that morning but the pastor cut it all short for some reason which I sensed grieved the Holy Spirit.

Shortly after meeting with Jesus when I first got saved, I found myself asleep. I was awakened and I rose and left my body. I could see my body there sleeping peacefully. I knew all was well as I was lifted up off the earth and the Lord was with me. We travelled far across space passing most wonderful and marvelous galaxies filled with amazing and awesome colors and shapes too marvelous to be able to describe. We went to the most high mountain where we could see all of creation from the beginning to the end of time all in one go. And I marveled. We then travelled down to a dark valley and I saw the angels of God taking demons bound in chains, those evil spirits that rebelled they were, and there were two angels of God taking one demon spirit. The Lord showed me where they were to be taken and we stopped just before a high, dark yet burning with flames, bottomless chasm. And the angels of God took their captive spirit over the chasm where they were not able to return and the evil spirit was bound in chains awaiting final judgment. Again I marveled at this sight. This is the place for the evils spirits to reside and it happens when a believer truly discerns correctly and binds that spirit, and the Lord said that people of man on earth need to bind the evil spirit and tell them to be bound and cast into darkness to await their judgment. That way they cannot return to create havoc on the earth.

I quite often see angels around when I am traveling either in the car I am driving, or on a plane. They are not inside with me, they are around the vehicle helping guide it along.

The road of Glory. For the past few years, maybe about four years or more now, I have had this repeated vision that I maybe get once a month or as often as a few times a week. I am on this path, a road really, but I am the only one that I can see on it. It is made of a clear illuminant almost crystal like material, transparent yet solid. I am always facing one direction and am heading to this brighter and brighter light which I know is the Glory of God. At first the road was a dull golden color but as I have been travelling on it for some time now it is getting more intense in shine and looks more yellow and I can see further up the road and it starts to get even more white. I have seen myself in all different kind of body positions while on this road. I have been walking tall and upright a few times, I have been downcast and sluggish and wanting to stop and give up. I have been on my knees and have placed my violin down on the ground and I have even seen myself curled up on the road wanting to vanish away. I have heard the Lord speaking to me, encouraging me to get up and continue so I have but often it is hard. Right now it is March 27, 2014, and for once I am tall and upright and walking slowly yet decisively forwards with the light of God shining onto my face. I am not ashamed of who I am.

Chapter Two – Interlude – Let me Explain Being a Christian

I have discovered that there are both good and bad things about being a Christian. Firstly, please let me clarify what I mean by the saying 'being a Christian'. A Christian is someone who has realized not only that there is a God, the creator, but also that we are separated from Him because we are ourselves are not worthy to be with Him, because we are not perfect (who needs to be told that!). When this person (and I guess I may be talking about you right now), when you hear the story about Jesus, are willing by your own free choice to accept Jesus as the Son of God, and you are willing to ask Jesus to forgive you of all the times you messed up in your life (Bible calls that sin, which literally means missing the mark, missing perfection), and accept Jesus as your personal (yes, that is your very own private) Savior and Lord (boss) of your life, and you choose (and put this into action) to follow your new boss for the rest of your life…. then this is what I am referring to as a Christian, both a believer *and* a follower of Jesus Christ. This gift of God is free, but it will cost you everything as you have to give up your life completely and hand it over to God.

The bad things first. The bad things about being a Christian. You cannot plead ignorance anymore when it comes to knowing what is good and what is evil. Even if we have not studied the Bible, we still know the difference. Even if we play the denial game, we still usually know what we are doing. How can this be? Simply because from the time we allowed the Spirit of God to enter us when we repented and accepted Jesus into our lives, God's light entered in too and that light is the Spirit of truth, the Holy Spirit of God. The light exposes all, yes all, that is dark inside us whether we like it or not. We can fight against it, we can pretend it is not there, we can try to walk away and not address it, but the light of truth changes not, so we know that which is not good inside of us as that light shines. We may try, but we cannot con ourselves anymore. What should we do then? Face the truth about those things in us as that the light of truth has revealed and allow God to deal with them. Note that it is the Spirit of God that shines His light in us as and when He desires to so that we can overcome what we need to overcome. How? Well that is revealed as we go through this book.

Another 'bad' thing about being a Christian. People see us differently. Old 'friends' tend to fall away that do not know or want to know the Lord. We can get labeled 'weird' because we are empowered in a new way by the Spirit of God and we start to see people, situations and even life differently. We start to understand that there is a spirit world that really does exist, and actually this spirit world is just as real as the physical world. Not only that, but we now have the rights in Christ Jesus to impact both the physical and the spiritual worlds in ways that were completely closed to us before. It is like we have been living our lives under a blanket and we never got to see what life really is all about, like a cloud of deception. All this can freak folks out sometimes! I mean, you try telling a person who has not entered the Kingdom of God about eternal truths and things of the Spirit, and that the Holy Spirit of God has come inside of you! They will think you crazy. Hey, if you are reading this right now and have not given up your life to Jesus as I mentioned at the top of this chapter, you probably think so too! But please hang in here okay. Stay with me on this even if you do not understand, agree or believe.

We are often not prepared for what is to come after we become a Christian (by the way, the Bible calls it being born again, not reborn physically, but born anew in your inner spirit man by the Spirit, the Holy Spirit of God). The truth is, is that after you accept Jesus and are 'born again' by the Spirit of God, you have entered not only a new world but also a battlefield. And, anyone who enters into battle should have prepared him or herself for what is to come. To walk on to a battlefield with no armor and no weapons is foolish. Sadly, many people do just that as a Christian. Now, this is NOT the fault of the new believer at all. This is the fault of the church, the body of Christ to whom it has been given the responsibility to nurture new believers to maturity. Which brings me to another point. The church of believers is made up of people, and we are NOT perfect (but hopefully we are getting better!). Therefore, it really is not hard to go into any church and pick faults. In fact, hopefully as a mature Christian now, I could probably write a whole book on the faults of the modern Christian church. Even my own church has many faults, after all, I am in it! However, the organized churches of today, on the whole have lost their way, fallen into apostasy and become powerless. More on that later too.

Now to the good points about being a Christian. I would not trade anything; I mean *anything* to go through the first thirty years of my life before I was born again. As I mentioned in the first chapter, I was married, had a nice house, two daughters and a good job until it all came crashing down around me. Now, with my eyes open to the truth once I got saved I find that I can do some things that I could never do before. First and foremost, I have a great, a really great gift. I have been forgiven and I can forgive others to a depth far beyond what my 'forgiveness' level was before. Do you know, I mean do you have any idea what it is like to carry burdens on your shoulder your whole life or to carry the burden of guilt? You probably do, and it's not nice is it. It saps your energy away from you like a drain hole in a bath tub that you can't shut off so the water continually leaks away. The more you fill the tub up with life zeal and energy, the more it seems to drain faster. And as for innocence? Lost it. Who of us can still claim that we are truly innocent in all areas of our lives? Me neither. Yet, and here is the good news, the burden of my wrong ways (which includes wrong thoughts, words and actions) is gone. Yes, I mean GONE! I can wake up every morning at peace and with a positive attitude without being in any state of conscious denial. And what's more, I can and do this every day even if there are a bunch of bad situations happening around me. I must add here though that there is one condition to this. I do take the time to look at myself and ask the Lord to reveal if there is anything I have done wrong so that I can ask for forgiveness.

Carrying no burdens is not just a once only event when you accept Jesus into your life, once saved you need stay in that place of true humility before God that His grace may cover you and your sins are forgiven as you go. So this is Christian benefit number one, to carry no burdens that have come into your life whether by your actions or the actions of others, by nature or some other means.

Next, knowing the truth about life. Many a person asks that question at some time in their life. I did as early as a teenager. Life did not make sense to me. We are born, we experience good and bad things. We do good and bad things. We get some of the things we want, some things we don't want and never seem to get all the things we do want. And then…we die! Blackness, Ka-put! It all comes to an end. So what's the point of it all? It did not make sense.

As a boy, young and innocent to some degree, full of energy I just 'lived life' under the direction and support from my parents. As a teenager in adolescence striving to understand, this compelling drive called sex and sexual attraction seemed to consume most of my thoughts and motives. In my twenties, life was to be met head on, get to be a winning player, succeed and conquer, earn money and make a name for myself. Get married, support a family and settle down to embrace the joys and trials for raising children. We can sure make ourselves keep very busy doing all these things. Yet, it seems to be at very few times in life through all this that we stop and ask ourselves that really important question. Actually there are two:
"What is life really about?" and, "When I die, what happens to me, if anything?"
If you have not allowed yourself to ponder these things or if you are so full of pride and arrogance that you make some stupid reason not to ask yourself (in which case put this book down and pick it up again when you get off your high horse and start to act like you have a brain and a heart), then take time out here and do so. Go somewhere that is away from any personal, electronic gadget or distraction and ask,
"What *is* life about?" and, "When I die, what happens to me?"
I asked these questions a few times in my life before I found Jesus. I *really* asked myself these questions after losing my first marriage, lost my job, money etc. Maybe we need to be stripped down of all those things we like to accumulate in life to help us feel secure and that gives us some kind of purposeful meaning to life. I mean, the truth is, is that we don't take any of our 'stuff' with us when we die, so again, what is the point of it all!

In my twenties in London I tried a bunch of approaches to find the answers. As you know, I did the EST training which was a course that mixed all kinds of religious and philosophical teachings from meditation to Zen and Buddhism. I tried the Church of Scientology, re-birthing and transcendental meditation. I have even read most of the Koran (in English). Yet, I never found a deep answer to my questions that lasted with me. Sure, they all have some kind of explanation and some brought me some good but with each one I left because they seemed to have something to some degree but not everything, not this ultimate, absolute thing called 'the truth' that I seemed to want so much at times. Looking back on each experience now, they all seemed to have some aspect of truth but then it would get all mixed up in other teachings that seemed to end up getting you 'hooked' and you would end up with more burdens inside then when you first started. Nope, these were not the answer. The answer did come the day I invited Jesus Christ into my life to reign and rule.

The truth because even now, thirteen years later (I guess I wrote this back in 2005. It is 2014 and still true for me), I carry no added burdens and all my wrongs have been released off from me. Truth because I discovered that I was right, there really is more to life than just being born, experiencing life and dying. Truth because I saw a much larger picture about life that no longer has me in the center of life, with everything about me. This truth sees a picture that spans right from before the creation of the physical universe through to its re-creation in our future. No longer is time a restrictor in this picture but an eternal purpose, and with this purpose I found a purpose for my existence. Truth because I discovered that I am not an accident, nor an evolved amoeba, and no more a wondering soul. Truth, because now my eyes have been opened and I see God before me and after me because I came from Him as a breath of life and one day will return to Him as that same breath of life having hopefully passed the test that this life is all about.

Hey, hold on a minute! What's this 'passing the test of life business?' Good question my reader. When you see the bigger picture about life, one's stay on this planet we call earth takes on a new meaning. You become born for a purpose, you have to find what that purpose is, then you have to live that purpose against all odds! Sounds fun? Sounds more like it sucks eh!? Sounds more like a sick joke. If God was all that great and wise, why would He set things up this way? He sounds more mean than good. Well, I have to admit, looking it that way I would have to agree (had the same thoughts myself) but to gain an answer to this I have to tell you some of the truths about this set up (Christian Bible readers can find this in the old testament, Genesis to Ezekiel). Sitting comfortably? (OOOee, I can just hear some traditional theologians with pen and paper right here ready to make their arguments against this!) Here we go…
(Warning: This is kind of deep stuff, so if you want a quick, simple version we could say that God created you to do good to others and He will reward you for them. So, if you want to skip this detailed explanation, go to the a few pages on.)

God existed and exists in Spirit and He had everything all set up fine. In His wisdom he had created other celestial beings called angels, angelic beings. There were chief angels, called Archangels, and lower ranking angels (think I am crazy and making this story up? Just hang in there okay). God gave His life, His light to each of these beings. God also gave them His knowledge, including knowing good and evil. To know whether something is good and not evil, you have to have both right? If only good existed then there would be no such thing as good and evil. Same for black and white. In fact, the whole of creation is set up with opposites; up and down, in and out, Yin and Yang, positive and negative etc. etc. If everything was black how would you know what white was?

Come to think about it, how would you know that the black even existed!? Okay, heavy mind stuff, let me continue.

God also has the power to choose and this too was given to all the angelic beings. Now, all of this is out of our understanding and our perception of time, for this was an eternal setup. God created the heavenly hosts to reflect His light and to worship Him in purity and for eternity. There was, however one potential problem that God both knew about and foresaw. The angelic beings could choose to not worship their creator and this is what happened eternally. An Archangel called Lucifer (in English) was given to be the head of praise and worship. He was even made with musical instruments inside of him. He was allowed to get very close to God, even to walk at the very feet of God (at His footstool) his creator. So what happened?

At one time in eternity (now there's an oxymoronic statement!) he chose to desire to take the place of God. Rather than being fully satisfied worshipping and serving his creator, he rebelled and chose to try and exalt himself to be equal to God. That was an eternal error for God could see without delay (as time was not) the rebellion and had the Archangel cast out of His presence. At the same moment out of time Lucifer, being such a powerful angel and as head over legions of angels, deceived and persuaded a third of the entire angelic beings to follow him. It was at this moment that time as we know it began, like a sentence. It was at this moment that Lucifer was stripped of his name and became Satan, the devil, the deceiver and accuser of all that is good. And where did Satan go? Well, God is light and (per my comments previously), you have to have darkness in order to know light. Satan and the other fallen angels were cast into the darkness. And then? God had a plan that you and I are now living, whether we like it or not. This is what God did: He created a physical realm in the darkness (Genesis chapter one), the universe that we have today. God created it and set laws to it that all of creation has to follow. Physical laws such as time and gravity, that we have to physically abide by.

In the beginning God first set up things perfectly as He is only perfect, and in His infinite wisdom He even created a place before time for those who would rebel such as for the fallen angels including Satan. That's where the story of Adam and Eve came in. I am not going to give a Bible study here but if you have never read the story in the Bible I would recommend doing so in the first book of Genesis. If you have read it, you may want to check out what I am about to declare.

God created Adam, the first man and breathed His life into this man that He had created a body for from out of the dust of the earth. This breath of life was the same that God had given his angelic beings. Man became a living soul through the breath of this life of God. God then created Eve out from Adam to be his helper and life companion. They were given a garden to live in that have every fruit and seed to eat that they

needed. They were to come together and multiply and eventually populate the whole earth. Okay, STOP! Time out here! Lots of story and it raises the question,
"Err, what's the purpose behind all of this?"
Coming to that, just hold on… God, being all knowing, knew however, that this was not going to come to pass that way. Traditional church doctrine usually says that God wanted Adam and Eve to not sin and therefore we would have a heavenly earth with no evil in it. Not so. God knew two things with this set up. He knew that in this same realm where earth was, was Satan and his fallen angels. God knew that Satan was going to get Adam and Eve to follow him by deceiving them some way. The earth was formed out of the darkness, in the dark realm where Satan had been cast down to out of the presence of God. The Devil (Satan) was also allowed into this 'paradise' garden where Adam and Eve were.

Because God knew that Adam and Eve were going to fall and rebel, He did not give them eternal life, nor the knowledge of good and evil. Unlike God, in the beginning they did not know good and evil (Genesis 3:22-24). God told Adam (Genesis 2:15-17) that when he would go and disobey Him, that he would die. This was not an "if" statement by God, it was a "when you" statement. Now let's think for a moment about this. Why would a God, the loving God that us Christians claim is His nature to love as He is love, set Adam, the first man to fail? You see, after Adam and Eve did sin (miss the mark, disobeyed) due to the Devil deceiving them (Genesis 3:6-7), they were cast out of the garden of paradise without eternal life in them (Genesis 3:22-24). They had sinned by partaking in the tree of the knowledge of good and evil. Up to that time they did not know good and evil. And why were they cast out? Because also in the garden was the tree of life that gave eternal life. So God cast them out and guarded the entrance with an angel so that neither Adam nor Eve could reenter, otherwise if they ate from the tree of life they would live forever in that fallen state. Well, wasn't God so cleaver that He did not give them both eternal life when He created them, or maybe He revealed the truth in His Word (the scripture) that said that Adam was going to sin and fall from God so, knowing this He made a way for man to die. And ever since, man has been born and dies with a nature that is 'fallen' as it were. Well that is, until Jesus came but more of that maybe later.

Okay, we need to answer the question as to why did God place man in a situation where He knew was going to end up in failure and rebellion to God? Now we have Adam and Eve as sinners (both missed the mark and disobeyed) having babies etc., and the earth gets populated. The bible gets somewhat messy here because Genesis talks about Nephilim, celestial beings (fallen angels) that came and had sex with women and they gave birth to giants of the land and man continued in all kinds of wickedness so God eventually flooded the whole earth except a few in

Noah's household. And the story goes on, and on with man getting more and more wicked as time goes on (no different from today really).

So back to the question as to why this was set up by God in this way? God allowed the manifestation of evil on earth in this dark realm (John 1:5; 3:19; 8:12; 12:46) together with corrupted fallen man where the devil now ruled and reigned (Ephesians 2:2) so as to place man with the opportunity to qualify himself or herself into His Kingdom. From darkness into light. In order to get out of the darkness or dark realm, you have to put off all darkness before you can rise into the light of truth, into God's Kingdom. But, as usual, there is a catch that the Bible spends books and books and chapters and chapters covering in all the Old Testament (Old Testament is all the books before Jesus came). These books tell story after story of man's continued rebellion to God and God's laws. No one seemed to pass the test. Even when men or women of God were sent to the people to tell them to get their act together, they killed these very same people because they did not want to hear the truth, nor be exposed to it. Man was sick in the heart and didn't want their darkness to be visible for fear that the truth about them would be exposed for all to see. Satan has been both blinding mankind and deceiving us right to the present day! And one of Satan's biggest lies is that he does not even exist and that it is all one big made up story by man. Now that's an easy one to follow isn't it, really tempting to believe that too! Heck, many a Christian has entertained doubts like that too, including myself at first. Now, I wonder who could be speaking into my mind for those thoughts to come?

If we only realized how closely our minds are spiritually attached, we would start to make sense of how and why we think certain things and then act accordingly. I could go into this really deeply but this is not the time to, as I still need to answer the question of why God set this all up. Simply put, God set up Adam to fail and all future generations to fail for hundreds of years so that a pathway between the truth, the true light could be made into this darkness (earth) so that man might have a way to legally (that is without breaking any of God's laws) enter God's Kingdom and live eternally with Him. And God could only do this through the free choice of man to obey Him just as the angelic beings had free choice, including Lucifer as he was called back then, but they chose to rebel. Gradually, individuals on earth followed God.

One main person was a man called Abraham as God later called him. Abraham obeyed God by even pre-acting out on earth, to sacrifice his only son that he loved, in the natural, what God later did on earth with the true light, that is Jesus Christ. Again, this is a long story but it is all there in scripture in the Old Testament and even is explained in the New Testament. What an incredible plan! God creates a bad situation to get even worse in a place where those which were supposed to follow Him now were in rebellion (Satan and then all of mankind). Then God uses the free choice of sinful man to create a way for sinless Jesus Christ (Jesus means God with us and Christ means the anointed One of God) to enter into the earth. And we know how popular Jesus was. In spite of Jesus' miracles over and over again, many could not see that the truth was in Him and that He brought pure light into the world because He was that pure light. Man had become so sinful, and his heart hardened and darkened that he was missing the truth right there before him. Blinded by… yes, you guessed it, by Satan. Satan used people to try and have Jesus killed even just after he was born. In fact, Jesus had a death sentence around his neck from the moment he was born, but His time did not come until he had matured as a man and declared that there was an alternative to this sick life. Jesus said over and over again that there was another Kingdom, another life to be had. He even ascended and descended after He was crucified to and from that Kingdom (John 1:51; 3:13; 20:17). He came to earth to show us the way home into God's house so that we could still live here on earth until the last breath in our bodies and then we would take on a new celestial (an incorruptible) body and live in eternity with Him in the true light. Jesus made a path for us to follow. This path was not made by any other person from earth, it couldn't be because each of us has sin and a sin nature. How can that which has sin find a way into a perfect sinless Kingdom. God demonstrated that with Satan that God cannot allow darkness of any kind into His Kingdom. If He did then the light would no longer be true, it too would be corrupted. That is why you get the story of the virgin mother who became pregnant before she had sex (Matthew 1:23). Jesus Christ was born seeded not by corruptible man but by the Spirit of God coming upon Mary so the chain of sinful bloodline was stopped right there.

    The sin nature is carried in the life of a man, in his blood. A woman who becomes pregnant keeps her blood separate from that of her baby. This is medically proven to be so. Mary became pregnant due her believing God's angel that she was so, and she was. So, Jesus was born with pure blood. In all ways Jesus was a man with that one exception, He had no sinful nature. Now, was He tempted in all ways like we are even to this day by the devil? For sure, and some! The devil wanted Jesus to make an error and sin, but through discipline and suffering, even unto death on a cross, Jesus did not sin. Jesus simply told us over and over again of His Kingdom, that is God's Kingdom and demonstrated acts of that Kingdom while He was here on earth. Wow! This is why He is called the Son of God, God's Son.

    This is one long explanation to get to saying that the truth is that we are living in a sick, corrupted, fallen world ruled by the devil, Satan who goes continually telling lies upon lies to deceive all of mankind in any way that he can to stop us finding out about the truth about God. Satan hates God and wants God to fail because he (Satan) wanted to be in control and exalt himself as God which was the start of his own downfall. God set laws into place and through the obedience of some men over histories of time, Jesus Christ came and left, leaving you and me with a story and a pathway to follow if we want to really escape all this corruption and lies, find and live in the truth with true inner joy and peace no matter what is going on around us.

Then, if we do accept Jesus and follow Him, we need to be prepared for one mighty battle while we are still here on earth because Satan and his forces will now be all out to get us, for he knows something else. Satan knows that this is all going to come to an end one day, and that there will be a final judgment upon all beings dead or alive. Satan fell and took a third of the angels with him. God is rebuilding His Kingdom (Psalm 147:2) with faithful souls. Do you get it? Did you miss that? God is looking for faithful souls for His Kingdom that will be eternally faithful. And where do you think God will find these faithful souls? Yes, here on earth! We are literally earning our way into a specific place in the Kingdom of God. Even Jesus Himself said that He was going to the Father to prepare a place for us (John 14:2-3). Now, before any Christian gets all flustered by what I just wrote here, let me clarify my words. You cannot earn your way through your own purity and right standing before God and get a place in the Kingdom of heaven. You still have a sinful nature that disqualifies you at the start. And if you could then there would have been no reason for Jesus to come! No, one has to change one's nature *first* which is done by truly accepting Jesus Christ and committing your life to Him from your heart. In doing so, God gives you the Spirit of truth (John 14:15-17) and your nature changes (2 Peter 1:4) as God Himself enters you. You are cloaked in Jesus and Jesus' blood is upon you and that is what God sees, not guilt blood but pure sinless blood. Now you qualify.

Next, you are commanded in this sick world to do good, to love all and to do good to all, living your life even unto death (Revelation 12:11). Why? Because you no longer belong here (Ephesians 2:6), you belong in the Kingdom of God. However, while you are here attached to your earthly body you have to remain faithful and true through all the trials and tests of life. Think that by accepting Jesus and then carry on conducting your life doing evil will get you into the Kingdom of God? Oh no it won't for not even those who may think that they are for sure going into the Kingdom on the day of judgment may not make it (Matthew 7:13-22). You have to accept Jesus Christ *and* follow Him *and* do good as lead by His Spirit to get your full reward (Matthew 6:1; 10:42; 16:27) no matter what it looks like. That is the calling we are all called to. Want your reward to be great, then do all you can to promote truth in love without judgment, but rather giving mercy, and promote God's Kingdom in every (yes every) situation you find yourself in.

Here is a real doozy of a truth. When we are born again of the Spirit of God, saved by Jesus Christ, our hearts and souls still need to be worked on. Yes, the Spirit of Truth came and resided in us to shine light in us. Now starts the process of God revealing the darkness that we all have inside of us and He will bring it into the light, it will manifest, show (Ephesians 5:13) and we have the choice to be convicted of this darkness and repent and allow Him to remove it from us, or we can stubbornly harden our hearts and refuse to repent. This is how God works; He works from the inside out to purify our hearts. It is our hearts that He is after, to make them pure, without sin, with no darkness, and in doing so His light shines brighter out of us and we move closer to Him resulting in more of His Will being done and not ours.

To summarize your life dear reader, you are in a battle whether you like it or not. If you have not accepted Jesus Christ and are trying to do good, you still cannot make it into the Kingdom of God. If you have accepted Jesus Christ you are commanded to do good. You accept Jesus by faith and live by that same truth that you believed when you got born again and through this you eventually become faithful as God purges out evil desires in your heart that we all have due to our past sinful nature whether you have acted on them or not. However, you are in a fierce battle against Satan and his forces while you are here on earth, but you do have the promise of the next life in eternity with God. The more the Lord purifies your heart, the less the devil can tempt you into sin because the deeds of your flesh have been put to death (Roman's 8:13). Read the Bible for there are many, many ways you can not only protect yourself but also go around destroying the lies and works of the devil which is your calling because as you do so, you are demonstrating God's Kingdom in the face to the devil and deceived mankind. This is the greatest, most fantastic challenge one could ever have and God has equipped you both with His Spirit and His Word (the Bible) to succeed. Now that really is good news! Do you have what it takes? Are you willing to give it all up for Jesus and the promise of eternal life?

Are you getting the picture, the story, the vision? God, His celestial kingdom, it falls, God creates a new realm, the physical world in the darkness, making it subject to laws so that it is not eternal but temporary. He puts man there to fail, puts man to the test to show he cannot make it on his own, makes a way for God to reenter the darkness through Jesus Christ, relies upon each person's choice to accept or reject Jesus and to follow Him. Those who do accept and follow have their eyes opened and gain eternal life through believing in Jesus and doing their best to follow Him, fighting the fight and faithfully doing right while still in their earthly body. The body dies yet the soul rises to be given a new heavenly body and a place prepared in God's eternal Kingdom which is where God intended us to be! Bam! Passed the test of life and God is rebuilding His Heavenly Kingdom in eternity with faithful souls to fill the void of the eternal fall of Lucifer and the third of the angels who were all unfaithful! Once the numbers are all in then comes the end and God re-creates a new heaven and a new earth free from sin and the effects of sin (read the whole book of Revelation).

Before I end this chapter, what of the person who rejects Jesus? Then the opposite of the previous paragraph is true. This *is* the judgment of God (John 3:18-21). If you reject Jesus then you have condemned *yourself* from God. Eternal separation from God. Separation from God right here now on earth before you die in this temporary world which is what you have right now if you have not accepted Jesus and follow Him. So nothing new there if you are not saved but, when you die you also will face God and His judgment. All that you have thought, said and done will be judged and you will be found guilty of being less than perfect in your life. You will not be able to, you cannot pass into God's Kingdom with any imperfection. Your soul will be cast away forever into darkness and into torment, out of the presence of God Almighty. Sorry, but that's just the way it is. Want to argue the point, go ahead, and argue away, it won't change God and the way He has set this all up. Hey, I would love to make things easier for all of us to be saved and go into God's Kingdom but since when can that which is created go to the Creator and tell Him what to do and how it should be?! So, go ahead and reject this Jesus stuff as nonsense, as just a story full of fantasies but remember this, what if you are wrong? Your whole life is ruined… forever.

Chapter Three – Being an Apostle, a Sent one…

My First Trip: Youth Hostelling in Scotland

My very first trip out with the Lord was to Scotland. This happened shortly after I got saved and had already experienced rejection from my first two churches by that time. The Lord told me to go to Scotland back packing, staying in youth hostels for about a week. I knew that it was to be a break for me from the stresses I had experienced. What I did not know was that it was to be a learning experience with the Lord too.

All excited to go, I packed my fishing gear for sea fishing, loaded up my flat bottomed lake kayak and checked that my white Ford Orion was worthy of a long drive. I didn't want to go on my own even though I knew that the Lord did. Of course the Lord won in the end. All my possible buddies could not come for one reason or another (I even offered them a free ride and hostel accommodation!). So I left on my own.

I had planned to stay in two different hostels. One was close to Loch Ness and the other located close to Loch Morar (Loch is pronounced "Lock"). The drive would take me up through the beautiful English Lake District, then through the graphic and very picturesque Peak District. From there I would head north into the Scottish lowlands that had rolling hills that were almost small mountains in some cases. Once past Glasgow the rolling hills start to disappear and the more rugged Highlands take over. Peaks get taller and roads get fewer and more snake-like as you start to climb to higher altitudes. You can sense the air getting less polluted and a feeling of free isolation starts to take over you. Soon you are totally enveloped in mountains, peaks and valleys, with houses few and far between.

I cannot recall much more of the trip up there but once I got to my first YHA (Youth Hostelling Association) hostel near to Loch Ness I was ready for a break from driving. I went inside to check in. The atmosphere in these hostels is usually very relaxed and this one was no exception. Most of the time the in-house 'managers' are volunteers who have a few responsibilities to keep things in order and take the payments etc. I met a really nice couple that took care of my booking. What was unusual was that rather than putting me in the general men's dormitory, I was given a private single room at no extra charge or explanation. All I could assume was that the Lord wanted me to have it so I could spend some time with Him without interruption.

On the first full day I had breakfast (you bring and cook your own food in a communal kitchen and have to clean up after yourself) and purposed to go on to Loch Ness with my kayak. I remember that it was a sunny day and almost warm for Scotland! I think it was around June time when I was there. The first day was quite uneventful. Nice and relaxing on the waters of Loch Ness (and no, I did not meet with 'Nessie'!).

Day two: I decided that I was going to go back packing up over behind the hostel and cross two peaks separated by a valley of sorts (a rather steep one). Then I would circle back towards the hostel to arrive early evening if possible. I had brought all my survival gear and appropriate food, and of course, my well-worn but excellent hiking boots. I planned my trip on the map and informed the hostel managers of my intention for safety reasons in case I should not return by nightfall. This is especially a good thing to do if, like I was going to do, you go on your own. The weather in Scotland can turn nasty real fast. The forecast was sunny with clouds and reasonably warm but up on the peaks somewhat cooler.

Double checking all my gear and supplies, off I went. As I was, and thankfully have always been, a fairly fit person I could cover quite a lot of ground with my long legs and light body, weighing in at around 140lb without my backpack. Up to the first peak I went.

There had been a lot of rain recently and much of the peaty ground was somewhat 'squishy' and at other times real boggy so that you had to be careful where you trod otherwise you would be in danger of filling ones boots with this black colored peat water. The air smelled clean and the fresh scent of the shrubs that covered parts of the ground just added to the joy of being out in God's creation.

I was progressing well and had just about reached the first peak when I saw quite an unusual sight. Only some fifty feet or so from the very peak was a natural spring. Nothing too odd about that, they are to be found in many places like this. However, this one was different simply because of the large quantity of water that it was producing. It seemed an unnaturally large volume compared to the amount of ground that was above it. I was puzzled and heard nothing from the Lord concerning it. I guessed that maybe some different pressures under the ground moved water to come out in this location. One thing I did know, it was clean water so I washed my face and took a drink.

Now, the next portion of my trip was to descend down a steep slope just at a certain point where the map contours were not too close together, which indicated a gentler slope that I felt I could negotiate. Then, I would cross a small stream of rain runoff water and scramble up the other side to the second peak before descending down back to the hostel. A good plan, but the surprise and first lesson was just about to come.

Going down the slope was okay but boy oh boy when I got down to cross the small stream it was not there. Oh no, the stream was a raging torrent of bubbling, gurgling black peat water from the recent rains, plus debris that flew down the river at a fast pace. The stream should have only been a few feet wide according to my map so that I could have jumped it quite easily. Now it was some twenty plus feet wide and Lord knows how deep! I stopped and reasoned that I should turn around and go back up the slope from where I had come and return safely that way to the hostel. Then, after hearing nothing from the Lord all day, *now* He wants to speak to me,

"Cross the river."

Hmmm, okay now is that you Lord? Maybe He is not meaning that I cross it here. Maybe there is a narrow section further upstream.

"Throw your back pack over to the other side right here."

Okay, now you have got to be joking, Lord. All my food and survival gear is in that! The Lord went silent on me. I thought and thought, and finally thought it best to trust in the Lord (it better be His voice that I am hearing!). So, making me some room near the water's edge I selected a landing location for the back pack so that it would not roll back down into the water and be lost forever! Taking a few practice swings and swinging again to build up some momentum I launched my pack with my trust in God, over the raging waters. Boom, it landed solid just a few feet from the water's edge on the other side and did not move an inch from that spot. Great, now that is done and I am all isolated here Lord, what next? I inquired.

"Make yourself a strong staff and cross the water."

So I looked around and soon found a good strong and straight portion of a branch about seven feet long. After testing its strength, I decided it would work for me. Well there was only one thing left to do, cross the rapids! I took off my boots and two layers of socks, tying my boots together and, wrapping them over my shoulders, took my first step into the murky waters. It was only about two feet deep but the current was very strong due to the steep descent. Step two and I could now feel the power of the water pushing against my legs. I started to use the staff as a third leg, praying for the Lord to guide me. Step three and the water got deeper. Three feet deep and now the force of the water would easily push my leg downstream when I lifted it up to take a step. Taking a few more steps got harder and I had to lean in against the current. I was not scared I don't think, just intensely concentrating on what I was doing. I was half way across, balancing mainly on the staff as that had the least resistance to the current being thinner than my legs. The water got shallower now and it became easier, then I was finally out on dry land. Phew! Made it!

      And the Lord said…

"Trust Me."

Yes Lord! I rejoiced in making it. Drying myself as best as I could I put on my socks, my boots, had a snack and, while keeping my trustful staff, made my way up the other side. I got back to the youth hostel just as the sun was going down as originally planned.

The next event and lesson from the Lord came at the second location, a hostel near to Loch Morar. I do not know why I chose this place but I guess why not. After checking in, I was given a small family dorm, all on my own again though which is again strange as the hostels get busy in the summer time. I looked on my map and decided that the following day I was going to venture out to this Loch, Loch Morar and I found a bay at the tail end of the Loch where the river runs out. The road went very close to the water's edge so I thought that I could launch my kayak there, and then paddle past two large bays on the same side of the Loch to a parking area a couple of miles north. I would drop off my kayak, drive my car north to the parking area, run back, get in my kayak and paddle my way around the two bays back to the car. Sounded like a plan! Lesson number two from the Lord about to unveil itself!

It must have been around nine in the morning by the time I pulled up to unload my kayak. I met no other people at all. It was a beautiful day. The sun, the clouds and a moderate wind. I got out, thanked the Lord, and started unloading my kayak, my oars and, well that was about it really. The next thing I knew was a white Range Rover pulled up in front of my car and a man got out. After greeting me he asked me what I was doing (I thought that to be rather obvious!). I told him my plans upon which he said that the Loch was private! What! I thought, this is God's land. Looking blankly at him he explained that some rich Arab had bought the entire Loch! He said that this was the deepest Loch in Scotland, actually the deepest natural inland body of water in Europe, over a mile deep and has treacherous currents. Oh great! I silently checked in my heart that the Lord wanted me to still do this. I got the green light. Smiling, I reassured this warden that I was a very strong swimmer and knew what I was doing. He took a look at my skinny yet somewhat muscular body.
"Okay." He said,
"But I have to get your personal details down and go through a safety check list with you."
"Okay." I replied as he went back to his vehicle and came back with a clip-board and a list of questions for me. I gave him my name, address and the hostel address I think together with other general personal information. Then came the safety check list:
"Spare paddle?"
"No." I replied. He looks up at me.
"Spare helmet?"
"No."
"Do you have a helmet?" He inquired.
"Err... No." I smiled. All I had on was a pair of swim shorts, a loose t-shirt, and water shoes.
"Additional buoyancy aids for your kayak?" I think he asked.
"No."

"Life jacket?" He asked questioningly.
Smiling with a big smile, "I told you I was a very good swimmer. No."
I thought that he would try to stop me from going but to my surprise he just had me sign the liability waver, gave me a final warning to be careful and off he went.

    I placed my canoe by the water on dry land together with my paddle and went back up to my car. Oh, yes, I did have a spray deck skirt for the kayak. That is one of those deals that you step into then fasten it around your waste so that you are water tight and then fasten the bottom edge of the skirt around the rim of the kayaks opening. That way the idea is that water cannot get inside the boat as long as the skirt is in place. Of course, it also means that you are attached to the kayak whether you like it or not! Again the idea is that if you capsize, you can use your paddle under water to upright yourself before you drown without water flooding in making it virtually impossible to do that maneuver. Sounds all well and good yes? Rolling the kayak they call it. Trouble was, I had never learnt how to roll a kayak! I had no idea which way to twist my body and how to use my paddle while upside down!

    After driving about two miles I parked my car up in the car park and proceeded to jog back to my starting point. At arriving back at my kayak, I prayed and got in. Securing my spray skirt, I pushed off from the bank. The sun was up and there was a fresh breeze. I gently paddled my way across the first large bay. The small three to four inch waves gently buffering against me were nothing for this kayak that was designed for still waters and the ocean, having more of a flat bottom than the river versions. I remember smiling and just leaning back and taking in the beauty of all God's creation around me. That was to be the last of my smiles for a while…

    Approaching the point of the first bay revealed some of the sheer size of the Loch. It also unleashed a surprise for me. That nice little glide that my kayak was doing through the small ripples on the water's surface disappeared all of a sudden. It was not really noticeable until you got there but the wind was howling down the Loch and, being at the bottom end and now moving out of the protected bay area, it hit strong. I was launched into swirling waters. Waves were suddenly three to four feet high and coming at me from the front left and right for some reason. I quickly woke up from out of my peaceful trance of God's creation!

    With all effort I sat upright, strengthened myself and did my very best to just keep upright and move forward. It was really hard and at times the first two feet or so of the front end of my kayak would be completely submerged with my tail end sticking right out of the water (I guess. I never made time to look behind me. Can't blame me for that!). Somewhere in the midst of all this effort and commotion I managed to round the point and head to the far shore of the next bay (which technically was my first of the two full bays I had planned to go around). Heading in towards the edge there were no calm waters and there were dangerous rocks on the shore line so no getting out unless I paddled all the way in the bay towards the road. I stayed near the rocks and turned my kayak around and just rode the two foot swell. My arms were aching and I was totally saturated above the spray deck.

I stayed there to recover myself and after a few more moments I thought it best to head in to dry land in this bay rather than go around the next point. It was just far too dangerous. Of course, God had other plans. "Are you not going to complete what you started?" He inquired of me. "What! I nearly drowned Lord!" I exclaimed out aloud while still being buffeted and sprayed with water. I complained some more and again he said,
"Are you not going to complete what you started?"
Maybe God was a little deaf;
"I nearly drowned Lord and was only by Your grace that I did not."
His reply,
"But you didn't drown."
I calmed down a little and backed out to the next point. It was rough out there. I contemplated for a while what the Lord had said to me, to finish what I had started.

[Interruption: Dear reader, I have to tell you this. It is March 16, 2014 and I am typing this on my laptop in my old 1987 Sundancer cabin cruiser boat. It is docked on an outside dock on the north end of Burnt Cabin Marina at Lake Tenkiller near Tahlequah, Oklahoma. I have been here from yesterday, Saturday. I often try to get down here most weekends. A great way to relax after a week's work and concentrate on writing this book. With security cameras all over the dock and a locked entrance, it is a safe place to go to. Yesterday was nice and sunny with no rain and little wind. I was croppy fishing from the dock until about eleven last night. All was peaceful. After adding some more to this story, I went to bed in my cabin and fell asleep.

I Woke up with it raining and the wind had picked up a little. But now, as I am writing about this incident at the Loch, God seems to be wanting to remind me of what it was like! The wind and waves have never, ever been like this while I have been in this boat. My goodness, I am bouncing around all over the place and some stuff is falling off the shelves! Coincidence? I think not! Let's hope my tie downs all hold out! As I look outside it is daybreak and there are hundreds of sea gulls fighting against the wind and for the first time I see large white pelicans in the water! It's like I have been transported to somewhere else!]

Back to the Loch in Scotland. I chose to follow the voice of the Lord and to complete what I had started and trust in Him that He would safely see me through. So with my forearms still aching a little, I once more ventured out.

It was different this time, very different. A peace came over me that totally removed all fear. My arms stopped aching and I put less effort in it seemed. Yet the waters were just as violent. As I headed around the point this huge fishing trawler came by. I guess it was trolling for salmon. I was close enough to see the workers on board all staring at me! I smiled, waved briefly and shouted,
"Hello!"
They just stared back a little amazed I guess at what was before their eyes. They probably thought I was stupid.

Rounding the final point I could finally appreciate the huge size of the Loch. Gee, no wonder these waves were so big! This Loch is enormous! Now, here is the funny part of what happened. Here I am coming into calmer waters of the bay where my car is parked. I have on this red t-shirt that is now totally bedraggled, sagging due to water saturation. My hair is soaked, heck all of me is just plain soaked! But I am happy, I finished what I planned to do and the Lord was my helper. As I approached the gentle sloping end of my journey to land my kayak, two obviously 'professional kayakers' were getting ready to launch out. They had all the gear. Life jackets, spare buoyancy aids, spare paddles attached to the sides of their kayaks, helmets, the gambit. They paused in what they were doing and looked at me as I came ashore and after releasing the spray skirt from around the rim of my kayak, I stepped out. They obviously looked a little surprised at seeing me, but were polite enough not to comment on that. Instead one of them asked me how it was out there today.
"Oh," I replied,
"It isn't too bad. Just a little bumpy in the waves!"
I gave them a big smile. They launched out. I got myself dry using a towel I had in my car, loaded everything up and praised the Lord for teaching and showing me that He was truly with me at all times.

On my second to last day, I wanted to go fishing so I noted a small bay on the coast that was not too far away to drive to. Scotland has many of these small bays. Usually they have small sandy beaches and rocky outcrops at either point. You can, even in summer time, find one and be the only person on that beach. If you catch good weather it is beautiful, but many people prefer to travel to south England to places like Cornwall and Devon towards Lands End as warmer waters and weather are usually a priority for a holiday.

I had two fishing rods and tackle with me and, after packing a lunch at the hostel, I set out in my car for a fun days fishing. After a short drive around those twisting country roads followed by a short walk from where I had to park my car to trek over a small bluff and there she was, my little bay. Unknowingly, lesson number three from the Lord was about to commence.

Now there was one solitary house made of brick that had been built I guess many years ago. A dark red brick had been used in its construction and, from a distance, it looked like it had been vandalized. The rest of the bay was just typical as I have just described. Two rocky outcrops were about three hundred yards apart from each other made of dark, almost black granite at either end of the bay, with a pretty sandy beach linking them together. As you looked up towards the house a rough tall grass grew in patches in the sand then dirt. It was a little breezy but the sun was again out and you could just smell the wonderfully refreshing salt in the air.

I took all my tackle and went to the nearest rocky point. Setting my stuff in a safe place so that the waves of the sea that hit the rocks would not wash my gear away, I proceeded to take my hunting knife and find some bait for my hooks. I was after large limpets, those rounded pyramid shaped mollusks that tightly grip to the rocks. I was also looking for muscles but I did not find any. So limpets were the order of the day and there were plenty to be found. I was not sure if the tide was going in or coming out, but it seemed to be half way at the time so I kept an eye on the water level. I did not want to get myself stuck out on this rocky point with the water coming in behind me. Not that the point was too long anyway, it probably extended out about a hundred feet or so at low tide.

Fishing was simple. I take a heavy weight, about a four once lead and tie it to the bottom of my line using a length of weaker line than my main line. I do this because this weight can sometimes get stuck in the rocks and you want it to break off there so that you do not lose the rest of the setup, the booms and hooks that I place up from the weight. Off from the wire booms that were about twelve inches long and stretched away from the main line, I attached a small length of fishing line and a large enough sea hook to hold a limpet. I used four booms so I had four hooks with bait on them. The idea then is to cast it all out and place your rod against the rocks so that the tip is pointing up in the air. You then tighten your line until you have enough tension from your weight to your rod tip so that the tip is just a little bent into the line. I did this with both fishing poles and, watching the rod tips, sat down and waited. And waited…

I noticed that a family had arrived and were going in and out of the house. Shortly after, the two children, teenagers by all accounts, started walking towards me. They asked the usual question,
"Have you caught anything yet?"
"No." was my polite reply.
We got into a little discussion and I found out that they were from the south of England, that their father was a head school teacher, and that they

had bought this house as their dream holiday home that one day they could come and fully live in. Unfortunately, they said, vandals had broken in and done some damage. The house was not furnished except with a few basics and they did not mention about anything getting stolen. They left and went back to their 'dream' home. Sadly, vandalism is not uncommon in the UK together with graffiti. Anyway my heart went out to them.

Back to my fishing, time went by and I tried casting to different places with no sign of a fish. I found myself in this funny conversation with God. As my heart was for that family I said to the Lord,
"Please would you give me a fish and I will give it to that family as a gift. It needs to be large enough to feed them all."
No response so I repeated my request to the Lord,
"Lord, please give me a good sized fish and I promise you I will give it to them."
Nothing. I stared at my rod tips expecting to see one bounce into action but nothing happened, The rods were nicely propped up against the rocks about eight feet away from where I was sitting. Still nothing happened. I had been fishing for hours with not a bite. I said to the Lord,
"I believe You so much that I am going to go over there are pick up that rod and reel in a fish."
So, I got up went over to my shorter fishing rod and, just as my hand gripped the rod and reel the tip suddenly bent right over! I struck and the fish was on! It was a good one too whatever it was. After a few minutes I could see it nearing the surface. It was a bright orange color. I had no idea what it was. The fish tired and I brought it ashore, lifting it out with my hands. It was a wrasse, I think they call it a rock wrasse. It was a good size too, about six or seven pounds in weight. Sure looked tasty I thought. I bet it tastes good. I have never eaten wrasse before and this baby had lots of meat on it. But I had promised the Lord that I would give it to that family. Trouble was, I was also fishing for my dinner. Back at the hostel, all I had for dinner were some potatoes and vegetables. I needed a main dish!

After removing the hook, I bonked the fish hard on the head with a rock to kill it and walked over to the house holding my prize fish. Knocking on the door they welcomed me in and told me their names etc. (sorry cannot remember their names). I presented the fish to them which they seemed very grateful for. I stayed there, oh, for about half an hour I guess and had the opportunity of sharing my faith in Christ Jesus. Afterwards, I went back to my fishing after wishing them well on the house and they thanked me again for the fish.

Time went by again and I really needed to leave soon and still had not caught my dinner. As I was just thinking about that fact, my rod tip started to twitch forward. I sprang up into action and grabbed the rod and struck home. It was a lively fish for sure as it darted here and there. Very

different from the wrasse I caught earlier. Landing it I saw that it was a Pollock and not a bad size Pollack at that. Perfect for my dinner!
"Thank you Lord," I said out aloud.
I packed up and went back to the hostel. You probably think that my fish story ends here but there's more…

On my last day at the hostel, and my last day in Scotland I packed all my gear up except my fishing tackle. For some reason I just could not get that orange wrasse out of my mind! I kept wondering what it tasted like. I had just enough time to get to that same bay that I was at the previous day and fish for just a couple of hours before I had to head home, back south to Chester.

I decided to fish the far point so I stretched out my long legs and set off at a pace. Quickly I found some limpets and cast out just one rod this time. The morning sun was up and it was yet another beautiful day. After, I don't know, maybe an hour of not catching anything and no bites my mind drifted off. More like day dreaming really, and I was dreaming of the orange wrasse. I was holding my fishing pole this time and I was snapped out of my delirium with a tug on my line that almost jerked the rod out of my hand! Striking, I hooked the fish and started playing it and yes, guess what, it was a bright orange wrasse of similar size to the one I caught the previous day! God had honored my actions and given me my desire. Thanking the Lord profoundly, I packed up and went home, licking my lips in readiness for a delicious meal of orange wrasse!

So my trip ended up being lessons in trusting the Lord my God in dangerous situations, trusting Him for me to complete what I started out to do, and that He will provide when I do what is right first and keep my word. Wow!

The Second Trip to Scotland: Isle of Mull, Scotland

I am not fully sure why I went on this short trip to the Midwest side of Scotland. I cannot even fully remember if indeed this was before or after my trip mentioned above but I don't think it really matters. All I can remember was that for some reason, almost by a sheer fluke (but I know God either orchestrated or at least permitted it) I wanted to find my old school sweet heart (that I never once dated as I was too shy!). Susan was her name. She was the eldest of my surrogate 'family' that I would visit a lot when I was a teenager growing up. We were also in the same school form class so I got to know her really well.

Susan now lived in Scotland in a town called Oban. After hopefully seeing her I was planning to catch the ferry over to the isle of Mull. It was quite a long drive up and I had not contacted Susan at all.

Indeed, all I knew was that she was working up in this town for some newspaper of some kind. That was all I had.

When I arrived the first thing I noticed was that it was a large town. Where would I start? I parked up and started walking in the town center area. Down this street, up that one and finally after walking for some time around I stopped and leaned against the wall of a building to rest a moment thinking I was getting nowhere, and why was I even doing this.

I looked up at the sign on the building that I was leaning against, and yes, you guessed it, I was leaning against the local newspaper offices! I went in through the door and up the stairs to the reception where I asked the lady if a Susan xxxxxx worked there. Of course, she could be married, so her last name may be different. And there she was, I could see her working in the office behind the reception area. We made eye contact and we were both just staring, shocked to see each other. She obviously recognized me straight away as did I her. She came over asking how and why I am here. I told her to see her. She got a little well, she blushed I guess, and grabbing her coat she said she would take a break and we could go out in her car for a short time. She was a tiny lady, really short and next to me accentuated that feature.

I am not sure if I was hoping for something to happen here or maybe I was just needing some kind of closure in my heart. We drove around a little in her small car as we remembered some of our past lives. We talked about her family and her other two sisters. She was married with children and lived nearby and was happy. At the end of the drive we ended back at her work, said our goodbyes, and I wished her all the best in her life. That was the last time I saw Susan and I could move on.

I decided to end the trip with a visit to the Isle of Mull where Christianity was believed to have first entered the country. Catching the ferry later that day I pondered over our meeting. I still could not make full sense of it. The weather was turning bad and the ferry company said that this was to be the last crossing of the day out of Oban due to rough seas. The ferry was small and bounced around in the rough waters.

Part way across we passed by a small island that I noticed was different. It had rock pillars that rose out of the sea and they were slightly separated from each other yet at times almost seemed to touch. The dark charcoal black rock glistened as the sun reflected the salt water that crashed and pounded against them. The most unusual feature of these pillars was that they were hexagonal, no idea why, but they were. I soaked in the whole scene. Years later I was to discover that the Jewish composer Felix Bartholomew Mendelsohn who composed my favorite violin concerto saw this sight too and was inspired to compose the famous (that is to us classical folk) Fingals Cave overture.

Well, I did make it to the island and found one of the early built churches. I quietly got down and prayed to the Lord for His mercy for people. As far as I can recall that was that trip done.

Off to the South of England

Before I tell you of this adventure in the Lord I have remembered something that happened at about this time in the city of Chester where I was living.

The Lord, through my prayer times had kept saying a couple of sentences over and over again to me. You would think that I should be able to recall what He said but for some reason I just cannot right now. Anyway, I knew that they were not in my Bible. Finally the Lord told me to go to the Chester central city library reference section so I obeyed and took the local bus public transport into town, which a lot of people use in England to avoid spending money on petrol (gas) and parking fees. The whole city center area (downtown) had been pedestrianized over recent years which seemed to work well in this rather pretty city. Lots of history here too. It even has an old Roman wall that the city has long outgrown but you can take a walk on top of most of it still to this day.

Over to the main library I go and up the stairs to the reference department. Looking around I cannot find the Bibles so I ask one of the attendants there to help me. I was taken to a book shelf against the far wall and a whole bunch of Bibles were there. I thanked her for her help and just stared at them all. The Lord simply said,
"The big one."
There was this really large hard backed, gold leafed Bible on the bottom shelf that was very old looking indeed. Carefully I picked it up and took it over to an available spot on one of the long tables that they provide. The front indicated that it was a Roman Catholic Bible, I think a King James translation. I just opened the Bible up and laid it fully open in front of me. Looking straight down on the left page there it was, that exact same scripture that the Lord had been speaking to me many times. It came out of the book of Second Esdras the prophet. No wonder I could not find it in the usual Christian canonic Bible! First and Second Esdras was excluded a long time ago and is only listed as Apocryphal literature now.

I really only read the Bible, but occasionally the Lord will tell me to buy a book. This happened when I was still living in Chester. There was a Christian book store there and the Lord told me to go there and get a book. I went in and there, of course, were books everywhere, but the Lord took me to one shelf and showed me 'Good morning Holy Spirit' by a man called Benny Hinn. I purchased and read that book and it was most excellent. The Lord also lead me to a book that was about this man Smith Wigglesworth and He had me place the book for many days on my bedside table without opening it. Then He would have me read certain parts and it would directly relate to what I had just been reading in the Bible.

Soon afterwards the Lord told me to travel south in England. Now I had lent the Smith Wigglesworth book to a good friend, another prophet of the Lord called Keith Winson. I had met Keith under quite strange circumstances. While still in Chester one night I was driving my car along a country road and I saw a man walking in the dark towards me. Now usually I would not make anything of it but the Lord told me to stop and pick him up so I did. He was a short and slightly rugged man of maybe thirty something years old. He seemed a little not really quite with it and well, basically, he was drunk. However, for some reason the Lord impressed me to take him to a local pub! So I did and we sat down and I got (I think) some nonalcoholic drink for each of us. Straight away I was speaking to him of the Lord and I sensed the Spirit of the Lord present. Keith confessed that he had wondered away from the Lord and had become a drunkard and his life was a mess. He repented there and then in the pub and the Lord immediately sobered him up. That was the start of a good long relationship that only ended a few years later when I was back in the US, and I thought something had happened to him.

I later discovered that he had been taken into hospital and his whole body and all of his organs had cancer. A man of God was sent to him while he was there and asked him if he wanted to stay or go. The very next day Keith was found dead in his bed with a big smile on his face. He had decided to go. Keith, in the few years since I first met him, had established a ministry to South Africa and made numerous other Godly connections. His life had purpose and was not wasted. Since then, during a few really hard challenging times in my life, I have 'seen' Keith and seen him offering up prayers on my behalf.

So getting back to the story, I had given Keith my only book on Smith Wigglesworth. Also rather amazingly the church, the Assembly of God church on Queens Street in Chester, had invited a special guest to speak one day and the Lord told me to pay attention (this all happened before I left that church). The guest was an older man and he testified that he had had the privilege of being mentored by the one and only Smith Wigglesworth!

Now the Lord kept saying Smith Wigglesworth to me but how ever hard I tried to locate Keith and get the book back from him I failed so ended up leaving for my trip to south England without the book. The Lord had somehow put me in touch with a ministry called the Francis Schaeffer ministry. They had a live-in program for younger people down in the southern part of the country and I was invited to come and visit.

It was a two-day journey and I had not planned anything. All I had determined was that I wanted to take a fresh bowl of fruit to the ministry as a gift. So after packing my bags I set off heading south. As I drove I still kept thinking about the Smith Wigglesworth book that I had not brought with me.

Late in the afternoon I was heading into the Sussex Downs (I think!). Beautiful countryside full of open wild fields, nature's smells, butterflies and colorful flora. The lord had me drive up to a remote area (of which there are many in that area) as dusk came. It was warm, being summertime and I remember looking up into the sky at all of the stars of heaven. It was so peaceful. In fact so peaceful, that I just fell asleep in my car.

I awoke feeling very refreshed as the sun arose up over the horizon. I continued my journey south passing through a few towns and villages. Only a few miles or so before my destination the Lord had me stop in this small town where I could by some fresh fruit as a gift for this ministry. There seemed to be only one grocery shop there once I had asked someone for directions (grocery in England means a shop that basically only sells fresh fruit and vegetables, produce). It was located on their one main street that was on a hill.

As I walked down the hill towards the grocery shop an unusual thing happened that I have never experienced before. A lady, a late middle aged lady who I soon discovered worked in the grocery store was outside and looked like she was waiting for me. As I got within earshot, she started waving to me, encouraging me to come into her store. She seemed excited for some weird reason. Anyway I bought my fruit and on paying the Lord told me to ask her about there being a Christian book store here in town. Now, you have to understand in England it is often hard to find a Christian book store in a city, least of all a small town?! That's pushing your luck a little. Anyway this really sweet little lady took me outside her shop and carefully pointed down the hill across the other side of the street. She said there was a small side road there and I needed to go down that and I would see a big warehouse on my left and to go in there. With a big smile she left me as I started walking once I had dropped off the groceries in my car. The Lord again reminded me,
"Smith Wigglesworth."
Taking the little side street as instructed it looked like I was in a residential area but, as I rounded a corner, there was the warehouse set back off the road on the left hand side just as the lady had told me. No indication of what went on there though. Only one sign, 'Private. authorized access only.' Great! But the Lord said I was authorized to go in. So I did! Entering through a small side door of some kind into a small reception area, a man came up to me asking if he could help. I asked him what this place was and to my amazement he said that this was the main distribution

center of Christian books across the country! I excitedly asked him if he had books on Smith Wigglesworth and he took me into the warehouse and showed me all the publications about the man. Awesome God! I bought the same book that I had lent Keith and a few more besides.

It only took me a couple of hours or so to complete my journey to the ministry house. It was one of those large Victorian properties that had been converted into small dorms and rooms for ministry purposes. I was made welcome and they showed me where I could spend the night as they gave me a tour of the facility. Meals were communal, held in a large dining area that looked out on the back of the main house. There was a mixture of people staying there and it seemed that they had all had some sort of troubled background at home, and that this was a place where they could recover. The people running the place seemed very at peace with me being there and allowed me to mix with everyone as the Lord led. I was never asked for references or asked anything about myself at all, they just had peace for me to be there.

Now the only really significant event, and I think the only purpose (but what do I know) for me to be there happened on my second day. We were all having a meal, dinner I think and some were asking me questions about my faith in Christ Jesus and I found that all I could speak was scripture. It got so embarrassing that they started laughing at me a little like I was this religious nut of some kind. Great! There goes my credibility. However, I also sensed that something was about to happen.

After the meal I went into the back garden. There were a few others out there also walking and talking or just hanging around. The Lord led me to go to a young lady, maybe in her early twenties. She looked at me scared as I came up to her. She was scared. I asked her,
"If the Lord could give you anything right now, what would it be?"
I cannot accurately recall the words she said but it amounted to,
"To be free of this" upon which I immediately said,
"Be free in Jesus' name!"
She shook violently but only for a brief moment like she got a bad case of the chills and then her whole complexion softened and she quietly wept. She was free.

First Trip to USA

While I was in the process of closing down my small company in England the Lord told me that He was going to send me to America. I had been having a really hard time since I got saved in England. My then x-wife thought I was nuts and I was causing no little stir in the church. This is how it all happened (please excuse a little brief repetition)…

After my miraculous experienced of getting saved (see chapter One – The meaning of life) I could hear the Lord's voice so clearly. The trouble was, I was also too eager and open to speak out what I heard the Lord say. One Sunday morning service at the Restoration church in Chester while there was a time where you could go up to the microphone and share something, I did, and to the surprise of many as I was so new there. It all seemed to happen in an instance. One minute I was sitting down; the next I was up there with the microphone (which is not like me because I really am somewhat nervous in public), telling the whole church that I knew what was holding them all back and it was staring at them right in the face. I said other things too that I cannot even remember to this day, but I remember saying something about stifling the Holy Spirit.

I was asked to visit the pastor and associate pastor shortly after that speaking session. When I went to see them, I found myself accusing them of heavy shepherding, which is where the church leaders hold too tight a control over the congregation. Well, you can image their response! They for sure did not like it and over a couple of other meetings where I also told them that the Lord was sending me to America, they told me to basically be quiet, sit down in church and behave. As for the Lord sending me to America, they said that the Lord does not send new believers out and that I was not hearing from God. However, they kind of covered themselves in that by saying that it would be better for me to not to go anyway. But I knew that I had to go, the urge of the Spirit of God inside me was too strong so when I told them they gave me an ultimatum: I could either stay and follow their guidelines, or leave to America but not come back into the church; I would be expelled.

I wrestled with God over this situation of whether to go or not. The idea did seem crazy because the Lord had told me to go to this place called Mobile and fly into Atlanta. I did not even know where this place Mobile was until an older man who had a business at the same location where I did, walked into my office and started talking about that very place. I found out it was in the state of Alabama on the Gulf coast. How I was supposed to get there I had no idea.

In the mean time I had caused another stir in the 'new believers' class that the church held. A really nice mature couple had been talking to us about finances and prosperity when they asked the small group of about ten of us to put our hands up if we wanted to be millionaires, as they said that God wanted us to prosper. All raised their hands up excluding myself. I had an issue with this. By this time I had read the Bible cover to cover and not once did I find where it said God wanted us to be millionaires. Meet all our needs abundantly, yes. I was asked why I did not put my hand up as some giggled or looked at me like I was stupid or something. I explained by scripture my answer and then pointed out to this lovely couple that they had been Christians for well over twenty years and have not got even close to this level of income! I was asked to leave the class by the pastors.

Not only was I told to behave and be quiet, but now the church was being told to have nothing to do with me. I felt so isolated. I thought church was supposed to be a warm friendly place? However, God did bring around me four individuals. First was big John as I would always think of him. He was a really wonderful man who was single, a great chef, and if you recall, I was renting a room in his house in Chester. Both he and his parents attended the Restoration church. It was John that first encouraged me to raise my hands to praise the Lord. Though it may sound odd, I was so reserved that it really was embarrassing to me at first to do so.

The other three believers were around my age, which would be around thirty. There was Paul, Tony, and a young lady, Sharon. The two men hung around together all the time as a team, and we would all get together at times. Sharon had a real heart for the Jewish people and it would not surprise me if today she was in Israel probably married to a Messianic Jew.

It was Sharon that gave me something special to hang on to only a few days before I was to depart for Atlanta. If I recall correctly, it was November 1992. The Lord had told me to take no money at all and to book the flight to Atlanta and return four weeks later. He said that I was to meet a lady who would, quote,
"Stick out like a sore thumb to me," and that I was to tell her everything that the Lord had showed me so far.
That was it, He gave me nothing more other than He was going to reveal Himself and His power to me.

Sharon called me while I was at my office a few days before my departure. I told her that I had no idea as to what I was to do or where I was to go. She said,
"Don't worry, I believe an angel will take you exactly where you need to go Rob."
I believed her. Big John was kind enough to drop me off at the Manchester International airport. My first big journey into the unknown was about to begin and it would start with… with an angel taking me to where I needed to go! Okay!

Many hours later the plane landed on the runway at Atlanta, United States of America. After collecting my one suitcase I headed for the main exit to the outside. The Lord told me to go to the side and pray before I went out, so as inconspicuously as possible I did just that before I went through the glass doors to the outside.

The outside area was elevated, not at ground level. There was a big car lot on the other side of the road and a line of taxis close by with their drivers hanging around or in their vehicles. Straight away a man came up to me and asked if I wanted a ride 'downtown' as they called it. I thought him to be a little pushy so I said no thank you. He came back a second time and asked me again. Getting a little annoyed for some reason, I told him again,

"No, I am waiting for a lift (a ride)."

He went away and I felt bad because I had just told a lie to get rid of him. I repented to the Lord. A short while later the Lord told me to cross the street and start walking so I did. I was walking downwards towards the street level with the car park (parking lot) to my left, the side of the street that I was now walking on. As I rounded the bend I noticed this big car, a limousine being loaded with luggage by a small black man and another man was there too, looked like he was from India. The black man saw me and asked me if I would like a ride. Well, the next thing I knew was that I said yes, I had hopped over the low concrete wall, handed him my luggage and was in the back seat of this limo sitting next to this man from India! The limo drove off out of the multi-story parking lot.

    I realized that the black man was also a taxi driver. His ID card was hanging up in the front and he had all the radio equipment taxis carry. He told me the Indian man's name and I introduced myself, and said I was a born again Christian missionary. The taxi driver wanted to know where I wanted to go and, of course, I had no idea! So I told him that. He said that he would take care of this other man who was a new student at the university downtown. The Indian man was very interested in what I had just said to him. He had heard of being a Christian of course, but never heard of being 'Born again.' He wanted to know more so I explained the gospel to him and what it meant. Now the taxi driver could hear the whole conversation but he said nothing.

    We arrived at the university where the man from India had to register his arrival and do paperwork. The taxi driver was so helpful to the man. He went to find where he needed to go, walked him there and waited for maybe an hour for him to get the paperwork all done. Then, back to the limo where I was still waiting and we drove off to the man's new student accommodation location. Finally we both said goodbye to the man from India after he had paid the taxi driver. Yeek, I thought. I had no money.

    The taxi driver got back in the car and turned around to me and asked me where I wanted to go. I had no idea what to say other than could he just drive around a little please. It was as we were driving around that the Lord reminded me of what Sharon had said to me, that an angel would take me to where I was to go. I was thinking of this big white angel with wings, not a short black taxi driver! But the Lord indicated it was this man at the wheel. Okay, so I said to the man,

"Just take me to wherever you want to and drop me off please."

Immediately he said,

    "I know a church that is open on Thursdays that my cousin goes to. It is back past the airport. I will take you there for no charge at all."

Praise the Lord! I relaxed and he started, or maybe it was me that started the conversation about being saved into the Kingdom of God. He had some reservations about it, so I asked him what they were and I addressed those concerns of his. During this discourse he asked me, "By the way, why did you turn me down twice for a ride from the airport?" It was him that first came to me once I had exited the airport! I was supposed to have gone with him all the time! As I failed to do that, the Lord blinded me so that I did not recognize him the third time, when I hopped over the wall and got into his limo!

As we pulled around the back of this huge church building that was called 'Word Changing Ministries' (made up name) and the pastor was a Reginald Cent, the Lord spoke to me and said that the taxi driver was ready to receive Him and repent. We stopped in the back parking area and there were people making their way into the building, though not a lot of people compared to the size of the structure. I got out and the taxi driver got my luggage out of the boot (trunk). After thanking him very sincerely, I started to walk off towards the church entrance when the Lord arrested me and reminded me to ask the driver if he wanted to be saved. Turning around I got his attention and asked him. I was surprised for some reason as he came to me and said yes. Not quite sure exactly what to do here, I asked him to close his eyes and raise his hands to heaven, and I lead him through a prayer of repentance. People that were still making their way into the church stopped and watched me. The taxi driver opened up his eyes after the prayer and said to me,
"Nothing happened."
I replied,
"Did you mean what you said with all your heart?"
He replied,
"Yes."
"Then it is done. It is not about what you sense or feel. It is done."
I gave him a hug and turned and went in to the church, wondering a little if anything really did happen, but God knows.

Inside the huge auditorium was a gathering of maybe a hundred people. I was welcomed and was asked to join in with the group. I noticed that everyone but myself were black folk, not that it bothered me in the slightest. We all gathered together below the stage in the center rather than being scattered all over the place. I discovered that this was a mid-week meeting for new believers and some other pastor here other than this Reginald Cent was taking the meeting. He preached, actually he taught but I cannot remember on what but I was impressed, that I do remember. We had times where a microphone was passed around to those who wanted to say something (now where have I seen this picture before!) and of course, I just had to raise up my hand for it didn't I! Standing up with the microphone to my mouth I proceeded to thank the pastor there for all he said. It really encouraged me. I explained that I had just stepped out of the airport in faith and God had brought me right here and if I had to get on the next plane back to England it would have been worth the trip.

After the service we all started to leave. In the foyer just before you go out some people asked me a few things that I cannot recall and then the pastor that ministered came up to me and asked me what my plans were. I said that I did not know and on hearing that he said that the church is going to put me up in a hotel for a couple of days then they will find me a member's home for me to stay in. I was quite taken back by this generosity. I must have looked shocked and I really did not expect this nor wanted to put them out and I said so. He smiled and said that it really was fine and he arranged for someone to take me and my luggage to a hotel not a mile down the main road that this church was close to.

After checking in and the church paying for me I went to my room and prayed to the Lord for His goodness and to bless those who did this good deed to me. I fell asleep only to be woken up by the Lord in the middle of the night to turn on the television. Dave Robison was talking about the children in Haiti needing sponsorship for health care and education. It touched my heart and I decided that should do that one day (I did a so few years later). I went back to sleep.

I really cannot recall what happened the next day but the next event I do remember was walking to the church for a Saturday service. While walking in the hot November sun that they seem to endure there (England would already have had its first frosts and would be cold by now!), the Lord impressed me to go into a small store that I was approaching, so I went in and started just walking around, having no money there was not much else I could do anyway! I noticed a worker up a ladder stocking the shelves. He looked down at me and asked me if that was a Bible that I was carrying under my arm. I said it was whereupon he decided to inform me that it was inaccurate and misguided.
"Really?" I said as he got down from his step ladder.
He came up to me, a black man probably in his mid-twenties. I looked him straight in the eye and he just froze there right in front of me. After a couple of seconds he said,
"You are anointed aren't you." I replied,
"Yes" and he quickly turned and ran back up his ladder begging me to leave him alone!
I did manage to get his name and said I would pray for him. I left the store and went to church.

At this church service for some reason that I do not know unless it is their policy with visitors, I was escorted by some ushers right to the very front center row and shown a seat. I followed along. This time the church was pretty full and there were musicians and a whole choir up on the platform. Quite a big performance really. So the music started and the choir was instructed to stand, and there she was. Just as the Lord had said to me,

"Stand out like a sore thumb."

There was this short and very white young lady about my age in the choir. The only white lady in the choir. I am sure we both made eye contact which I guess is also not surprising as I think I was the only white man in the congregation at that time! After the service I was once again in the foyer hoping really to meet this lady when she appeared, looking for me! We introduced ourselves, her name was Sharon and I got some of her basic information written down.

I was to be taken that day to some residential home to stay with a couple from the church and a man came up to me and told me he was to take me to this home as they were expecting me. I told this lady Sharon what was happening and how the Lord had brought me here to tell her all the He has told me so far. She was excited to hear about it and said that she would arrange for us to get together with her best friend as well. I was to be at church the next day too, for Sunday services. I was so thirsty for the Word of God.

The church man helped me load up my luggage and we drove off after the service. While on the road I guess the Lord must have redirected him because he told me that he was not going to take me to this arranged persons house but two a different couple's home in some suburb somewhere. Their names were Don and Janice and this is what happened…

As we pulled in to Don and Janice's driveway they apparently were at the back of their home, down in their den room when the Lord told them that a visitor was coming to stay with them and that He had sent me to them for my entire stay in Atlanta. My chauffer (if I may use that word here) knocked on the door and the couple shortly answered and welcomed us in. The man explained what the Lord had said to him and they said that they already knew because the Lord had just spoken to them both.

Don and Janice were wonderful people. A couple that really loved the Lord and had dedicated their home for His purpose. All of us, including the man that was so kind to drive me there, sat down and I started talking. I recounted to them some of my walk with the Lord including getting kicked out of church and how the Lord had brought me to America. I am not quite sure now how it all happened but I ended up praying for them. Laying my hands on them and blowing in the Holy Spirit into their bodies soon they were are spread out across the floor consumed by the Holy Ghost. I was acting like a drunk man and could barely stand myself. We all stayed in this condition for about an hour and if I recall correctly I think it was Ms. Janice that was out cold for hours!

The couple were great hosts and I tried to be as little bother as possible. Janice was a school teacher and Mr. Don was a janitor. One evening when I went out with Sharon from the church to her mobile home in an area called Fayetteville to meet with her and her best friend, the Spirit of the Lord was present. At the mobile home I started sharing the Word of the Lord and just started straight away to speak into these two friend's lives. A neighbor drove by and called them. He was a believer too and was concerned that something was going on there. Sharon assured the man that all was well so he never called in. Soon the Lord again touched them and gave Sharon's friend, I think, a real revelation as to her life calling.

Sharon dropped me off back at Don and Janice's house. They were down in the den watching some revival or healing meeting of some kind on the television. As soon as I went down to join them, they both stood up and said that they would leave the program on for me and promptly both went off to bed! Okay, so I went to sit down on the couch but the Lord told me to sit right in front of the screen, literally in front of it so I did. Then the Lord said,
"Watch my faithful servant." and as I watched this man called Benny Hinn take this service in Toronto, Canada, I felt like I was right there too.
I just sat there and soaked it all in. Afterwards, I too went straight to bed.

I slept well and when I finally got up only Janice was there. Mr. Don had gone to work. I had some breakfast then Ms. Janice said she too had to go out, so shortly I was the only one in the house for a few hours. Mr. Don had said to help myself to the music and television in the den so I went down there which is only a few steps down from the kitchen. I decided to put some worship music on and as it played I danced around the couch and coffee table praising the Lord my God. Part way through one song I decided to go up to the music player and change the song for some reason. As I went up to the machine I felt this buffer, an invisible barrier so, quickly dismissing it I pushed forward more. I was suddenly lifted up and carried around the coffee table and placed (kind of thrown really) into the couch! I was stunned, shocked. What the heck was that?!
"That is me" said the audible voice of the Lord and somehow I knew that this had something to do watching that television program last night.
"This is a little taste of Me" said the Lord and I understood that no flesh and blood can come into His presence and I am of flesh and blood.
I stayed on the couch for some time motionless and in awe.

When Mr. Don and Janice came home later in the day I did not mention anything about what had happened in the den. Mr. Don said that at his work they had a small bible study group and I was invited to come that week. The Lord said for me to go so I said yes to Mr. Don. The meeting was for the next day, if I correctly recall, and he was to take me in and back afterwards. He kept apologizing that there was only about four of them in the group but that didn't matter to me.

On arriving at his work, I was shocked, we were at the CNN World Head Quarters! Through the janitor's entrance we went and all the way up to the top executive floors and to the CEO's office area. There we met this wonderful lady who was the CEO's personal assistant I believe. She ran the Bible group and had permission to use the executive board room for the meeting. She took us there through these large solid wooden double doors to a table that could easily sit forty people I am sure. She invited me to sit down but I could not, I was a little agitated, unsettled, so I paced up and down the room seeking the Lord. She sat down with Mr. Don and a fourth person came in that they obviously knew and was a regular. Then one more person arrived and it was suggested that we close the doors and start, but I, rather abruptly said to leave them open. I actually thought that my attitude was a little on the rude side. She started then to pray out aloud for the Holy Spirit to come and again I interrupted her and said,

"He is already here but let's just wait a moment please" (or something like that).

Two more people turned up, and then another. Then another and more so that within a few more minutes we had a room of about twenty-five people or so. Most had no idea why they were there! The Lord had just drawn them in. They knew about the Bible study as the CEO's assistant would always send out a communication but she told me afterwards that my presence was not advertised at all.

We started the meeting and I was asked all kinds of questions regarding the scriptures and things like why do innocent children get killed and what happens to them? I was struggling with the direction of this meeting and then I heard the Lord tell me to get everyone up and into a circle and to lay my hands on them. I suggested this and all were fine about the idea so I went around laying my hands and praying for people and the Lord was present. You could even see some visible signs that the people were getting touched by the Spirit of the Lord Jesus Christ. Well, what truly happened there I do not know, all I do know was that God for sure did something! What an amazing story though, how a janitor brought the Spirit of God to the CNN World Head Office!

It was soon time for me to depart I told Mr. Don and Janice as I needed to go to a place called Mobile in Alabama. Now, they had no idea that I had no money but they were happy to agree to drop me off at the Greyhound bus station in downtown Atlanta and insisted on picking me up and stay with them on my return about two weeks later. I packed my few belongings after Ms. Janice was kind enough to have all my clothes washed for me, and just before we left they gave me the money for the round trip! Mr. Don had to go to work so we said goodbye to each other for now and Ms. Janice took me to the bus station. As I got out of the car she called over to me asking,

"Who are you going to meet there? Do you have any idea?"
I smiled and said,

"You call someone and arrange for them to meet me!" and I turned and departed into the bus terminal!

The bus journey was a little crowded and hot. We also had to change buses. It was fun though as I got to meet some interesting people to say the least. One such person was a mature Hispanic lady who was a devout Roman Catholic. We sat next to each other for many hours so I had plenty of time to tell her all about the Holy Spirit, and asked her if she had received Him? She had not and agreed for me to pray for her to receive Him. I prayed for her and her whole complexion softened. She smiled and, and went to sleep!

Another time I ended sitting next to a younger lady who had overcome being paralyzed in her legs. I cannot remember if that happened due to an accident or if she was born that way. Anyway, she was all about herself. It was *her* own determination and effort that resulted in her gaining her legs back. She was adamant about it too, so you can imagine her reaction when I said that it was the mercy of God that enabled her to overcome! She started to hate that we were next to each other. Unfortunately for her though, all the seats on the bus were taken so she had to endure me for a few more hours! ☺

The trip went through Birmingham, which is located in central Alabama. We got there in the middle of the night and we had time enough to stop off and eat. Don and Janice had given me a little extra money so I got a bite to eat. As we boarded another bus we continued our journey south towards Mobile. Most of us were tired and I was for sure, so I napped most of the time for the rest of the way.

We arrived at the Mobile bus terminal in the morning on the following day, and because I had rested, I was wide awake but my body was a little tired from being cramped up for most of the journey. I got my luggage and wondered what was going to happen next as I waited near the public telephones. Had Janice contacted someone, and if so, were they here and how would they find me with all these people milling around? Then I heard a man very close to me using the public phone. He was describing, or repeating what he was hearing from the other person on the line. He was describing…me! I looked at him and he at me and, while he was still on the phone, he asked me,
"Are you Robert?" With a big grin I answered,
"Yes!"
"Found him," he said to the person on the phone and hung up.
Shaking my hand warmly he introduced himself as LeRoy and he gave me a story of how this lady had called his church and he had ended up coming here because something about me playing a violin and he has one at his house or something like that. Anyway, here he was and he was most kind and friendly.
"You must be hungry?" he asked, and I was too!

"Yes, I am a little" I replied.
He took me to a McDonalds and as we were just about to go in he asked again,
"You are hungry?"
"Yes" I replied again.
"I will get you a biscuit then." He proudly announced.
Well, to an Englishman, a biscuit is what Americans call a cookie, and English 'cookies' are small, like two bites! However, being the polite Englishman that I am, I said nothing. Inside McDonalds the server then asked me a weird question I thought,
"Would you like jelly on your biscuit sir?" What!
Now Jelly is what you Americans call Jell-O. Okay, this is a crazy country with the weirdest of eating habits indeed, Jell-O on a cookie to fill me up! Of course, I was soon to learn that we had different meanings and I was grateful for the food. I told LeRoy and we both laughed.

    LeRoy was a musician and lived close to the waterways in the city. Together with his wife and two daughters they lived in a pleasant house that had water access too. They were all very welcoming and said that I was to stay with them while I was visiting. LeRoy's wife Brenda was Roman Catholic and the girls all went to a Roman Catholic school. LeRoy soon told me that he was concerned that his wife was not saved and I could tell he wanted me to speak to her sometime about that.

    I got on really well with LeRoy. He took me to his church. It was an old red brick church a little away from the city center (downtown). As we walked in we were met by a few of the voluntary staff. Immediately we got into a prayer circle for some reason and as we all prayed the Spirit of God moved on us all. Some people got very 'drunk' in the Spirit I guess you could say. I was then introduced to the pastor, a big solid man who was kind and also protective of his sheepies, which is a good thing to some degree of course. He was very kind and I found out that his church was on a monthly rental deal, and how they really went out of their way to help the needy. I got to witness this too as the local Social Security office would send people down to the church if they could not help them. People that didn't have the money to pay their electricity bill and were going to, or had been cut off. People with children that were short of food. I found out that all too often this church body would even give away their next month's church rent to help others out. They were literally living month to month and sometimes week to week. This was a good church and the more I saw the more I knew that the Lord was pleased with them.

    LeRoy asked if I would attend a meeting of a group of men that were part of the Business Men's Gospel Club or something like that. I did and we all met in a board room with some fifteen or so business men. They asked me to pray for one particular man who had to make a hard decision so I did. While I was there, one man in particular was brought to my attention so after the meeting I mentioned him to LeRoy, and I said that I would like to meet him as soon as possible. LeRoy said that he would arrange it and told me nothing about this man other than his name.

LeRoy took me to this man's work place a couple of days or so later. The business was a large lumber yard. I waited outside his office while LeRoy went in. I had absolutely no idea why I was there or what I was going to say. After a few minutes I was invited in to join them. I found out that this man was the owner of a growing and very successful lumber business that expanded across that section of the country. He had a lot of responsibilities but was most humble too, fully acknowledging that it was the Lord who had promoted him and that all he was, was a steward of the Lord's blessings. He had a good heart indeed. He then looked at me and asked why I was there. I immediately got a vision and as it was being revealed to me I described it to him and LeRoy,

"I see churches coming together in what looked like the middle of the town or city where there was green grass and a big organized platform with genuine praise and worship to the Lord, exclaiming Him as Lord of Lord and King of Kings, and many came."

Now, I don't think that I used those exact words but I can see the vision even right now as I type this. This big man sitting behind his desk started to weep. He looked at LeRoy, and LeRoy said,

"I have told him absolutely nothing."

I had no idea what they were talking about. As the man got himself together he explained that the Lord had put it on his heart to do just what I had described and to do it in the Mobile Square downtown. Well, praise the Lord! I found out many months later that he funded it and they organized a multi church outreach and were praising and worshiping the Lord as the Lord had told him.

LeRoy wanted me to spend an afternoon out shopping with his wife Brenda. It was his way of asking me to try and get her 'saved' i.e. Born Again as it were. So we went out and did a little shopping and we did not really talk much about the things of the Christian faith. When we got back to her house I asked her the fundamentals of Christianity. Did she believe that Jesus the Christ, only Son of God suffered, was crucified and rose again by the power of God so that all that should believe in Him will be saved? Brenda said that this was true for her. So I double checked that this was still very real for her and that it was a very personal, heart belief. It clearly was. I explained that beyond the basics of believing who Christ is and confessing and turning from our sins, that one can go down many roads. One Christian movement believes that; another does not but believes this, etc. And they all think that they are right too! She had accepted Jesus the real Jesus and it was real and true for her. Anything that is added to that will be tested in the final day so that that which is not of the Kingdom of

God will be burnt up, but that which is true, the person will receive his or her reward.

Just because she was brought up in the Roman Catholic faith that many believers in the charismatic church are certain is full of ungodliness, does not negate that truth that Jesus Christ is the Son of God and He died and rose from the dead so that whosoever will call on Him will be saved. Charismatic churches are also so full of ungodly practices too! But I am not here to bash all the churches, I am just pointing out that if the fundamentals of Jesus and the gospel have been truly believed and confessed then that is the door into the Kingdom of God. Leroy's wife was saved and it was very real to her. So when he returned from work that day I pulled him aside and explained it that way. He was overjoyed that his wife was not going to hell but was saved! Yuk, I hate the doctrines of man that so entangle people and promote them to be judgmental.

One day I went for a walk as instructed by the Lord. I was close to the water's edge and at one place there were boats moored up. A lady was sitting at the edge on one of the boats and she looked sad so I went up to her. I asked her what was wrong and she explained the she had lost her children to the father, but he was lying and did it deceitfully. The Lord told me to tell her to go get her children as He has made a way. I think she thought I was an angel or something and when she looked away from me after I said those words the Lord had me run away quickly. I don't think she saw me disappear.

On another day I was to meet a young couple who diligently sought the Lord. He was from the military I think but out of it now working full time in a different job. He knew the Bible chapter by chapter and verse by verse and they both loved the Lord. They were members of this same church that LeRoy attended. I was invited to their house for some small believers gathering. I was made very welcome and at one time I started talking to both of them when we were all three in their large kitchen. Right there and then they agreed for me to pray for them so I laid my hands and blew on both of them and they both collapsed onto that hard kitchen floor.

When they did arise, they were fine. Now, I am not into theatricals at all but I let God be God and I will just stay a man. But I do know that every encounter with the Lord results in some changes and noticeable fruit of some kind, and for me that is the acid test that it is the Lord touching people. The gathering ended and I was taken back to LeRoy's house. The next morning I was at the church early with LeRoy. There was excited talking going on with some people in the pastors office. Leroy I think needed to speak to the pastor but we had to wait patiently. Soon the door opened and it was this couple from last night. They were beaming and later I found out that last night, right in the middle of the night when they were both asleep, they both woke up at the same time praying fervently in the Holy Ghost!

On another day LeRoy wanted me to meet someone that he thought was demon possessed. We went searching for this person in the town and kept just missing him wherever we went, so eventually we gave up.

On yet another day, I was invited to minister to a group of believers one evening at someone's house. It was a group of about twenty people and the Lord had me lay my hands upon them and the Spirit of God turned up and people were blessed by His presence. This kind of thing kept on happening and I think that it is appropriate that I emphasize something here to you, reader of this book.

Just because the Spirit of God creates some kind of manifestation with people is of itself nothing more than showing that something happened to that person right then. Some may question that it was just for show, or some may even question if it was of God, depending on their understanding and level of acceptance of what God does or does not do with people. I have never witnessed being used of God where people had started acting outrageously in some weird way at all. I have witnessed the reverse, where the person manifested some unusual behavior and was set free from it and calmed down. Often people seem to 'fall out' in His power and I am okay with that, providing it is real and not acted. Having said all this, the fruit or results afterwards is what validates any Spiritual Godly experience. For example, after I laid my hands and God showed up to those people in Atlanta, Don and Nancy and the other man. The results were increased physical blessing to them and for the other young man, he was promoted in his church and started singing solos in the Spirit which was always a heart desire of his. People started to see God profoundly at work in this man's life. You see, what resulted from meeting with the Lord is what is important, not the incident.

My memory recall fails me towards the end of this time in Mobile, but I do remember the pastor calling me up to him at my last church service to pray. With his big strong arm around me and the other grasping the microphone tightly, he allowed me to pray. He, I think liked me and recognized that I was from God but nevertheless he felt that he was responsible before God to be protective and I guess that this was one way to show me this. Maybe not, I don't really know.

I caught the Greyhound bus back to Atlanta and Don and Janice picked me up. They took me back to their home as they had insisted that whenever I came to Atlanta, I was to stay with them. They are such good people. I wonder what they are doing with their lives now?

It didn't seem long until I was flying back to England but not before the Lord had me attend a couple of more services at the Word Changing Ministries under Pastor Reginald Cent (made up church name and pastor here). I remember purchasing his teachings on the blood covenant which is excellent. The Lord, however, also had me write a note to Reginald Cent to rebuke him for separating himself away from the people. You see, he had body guards and at the end of the services, because he was 'so anointed' his body guards would be there to protect him and even escort him and drive him away in his big black limo. He was exalting himself, and using the excuse that people would, or might want to bother him or even hurt him. In the nicest way that I could, I put this into words in a letter, clearly saying who I was, so that he knew that I took full responsibility for my words. Well, all past services, I had been escorted to front seats but on this particular mid-week service I sat on the very, very back row and it was good that I did. For out came Reginald Cent and all but named me and rebuked me saying things like,

"I do not need someone to come from overseas to tell me how to run my church."

He was ticked off, angry. I just kept silent and Don, who was sitting next to me briefly turned and looked at me. Thankfully, Don was a mature believer and knew that it was the Lord that had instructed me, that I was just a vessel to try bring some correction to this man of God.

    So my trip ended and I was on my way home full of stories of how God revealed Himself and worked in many people's lives.

I received this letter from LeRoy later:

New Song Community Church

310 Dauphin Street
Mobile, Alabama
36602

(205) 438-LOVE

Rob,

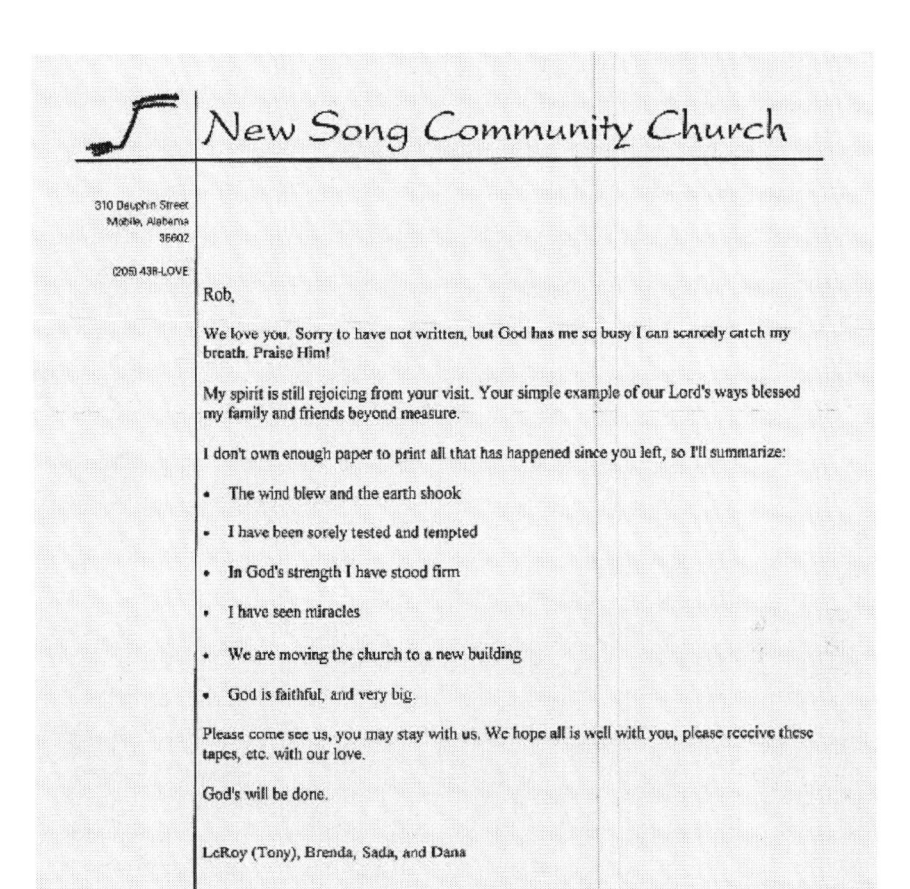

We love you. Sorry to have not written, but God has me so busy I can scarcely catch my breath. Praise Him!

My spirit is still rejoicing from your visit. Your simple example of our Lord's ways blessed my family and friends beyond measure.

I don't own enough paper to print all that has happened since you left, so I'll summarize:

- The wind blew and the earth shook
- I have been sorely tested and tempted
- In God's strength I have stood firm
- I have seen miracles
- We are moving the church to a new building
- God is faithful, and very big.

Please come see us, you may stay with us. We hope all is well with you, please receive these tapes, etc. with our love.

God's will be done.

LeRoy (Tony), Brenda, Sada, and Dana

Second Trip to USA

For some reason I cannot recall too well the short second trip to the US. I do remember arranging to visit Sharon, the white lady from the church in Atlanta. To cut a long story short, we just did not hit it off together and she was, in spite of my efforts, not the person that the Lord had for me to be with as a marriage partner which was the immature direction I wanted to take. The Lord never told me it was to be a relationship at all. All He said was to go share with her all that He had shown me and that part I did. Anything more was my handiwork! That mess up by me rather clouded that trip and I really cannot recall anything else at all! (Better end this chapter quick!).

Third Trip to USA – Meeting my Wife and the Second Prophesy

Summer 1993 and the Lord had told me to cancel all my violin student private lessons for two months during June and July that year. He was sending me back to the US. He told me to take no money, to fly out to Orlando Florida and to go to Pastor Benny Hinns' church. I had heard very little in England about this man other than he blows down a microphone and lots of people fall in the power of the Holy Spirit, or something like that, but I had seen him on television when in Atlanta at Don's house that one time and had read his book 'Good Morning Holy Spirit'. I was to return via Minneapolis/St Paul in Minnesota eight weeks later. That was it, and one day while driving my car in North Wales He gave me the specific date in June to go.

  I did not (surprise, surprise) have the money for the flight. At that time the English economy was hard. My little music business (the correspondence course for young children to learn basic music skills) was struggling to keep even afloat. But God, being God, brought a young Christian man to me to help me and I trained him to run the logistics while I was to be away. Also at that time, for no apparent reason sales suddenly increased enough and I had funds to pay for my flight, and even some over. Calling the same travel agent as last time for a cheap flight the man reminded me that for the cheap flights I have to book well in advance and I was asking for something very soon. Still I persuaded him to go search. Guess what? He came back on the phone to me and announced with surprise that there was a single seat left on the cheap flight scheduled for when I wanted to go to Orlando. I booked the flight and the return via Minneapolis/St Paul eight weeks later.

  The Lord told me to take just a backpack of clothes and a portable cassette and CD player that would run on batteries. It was summer time so I took clothes for that season. Other than that, there was not much more for me to do other than go. So there I was ready once more to go and my friend Jeff (I had moved out of big John's house by this time), the owner of the house that I was now renting a room from kindly took me to the International airport in Manchester.

  I had no idea what was going to happen on this trip but the Lord had told me that my English friend Lance was caught up in a cult; being married to his wife. He had shown me this after Lance had mailed me a photo of himself and his wife, and when I looked at her that is what the Lord told me was going on. I knew Lance was living in Minneapolis and I had his contact phone number. I cannot recall if I told him that I was coming to see him. I think I probably did.

While sitting in the airport departure lounge in Manchester after passing through security checks, I started to observe the other passengers that were also on the same flight as myself. Two young ladies, probably in their early twenties kept getting my attention for some reason but I could not work out why. I knew it was not lust or anything like that.

We started to board the flight and it was to be a packed flight. I finally found my seat and, yes you probably guessed it, of a three row seat I had the aisle seat right next to these two girls! Once on the runway, and as those wheels left the ground I knew that this flight was going to be interesting with these young ladies next to me.

They were quite sociable so we talked quite a lot on the seven hour flight between the movies that are played and meal times. I sensed that they were more than friends and that they were in a lesbian relationship. I did not judge them but the Lord gave me compassion. One lived in Manchester, the other in Orlando in an area called Orange County. The American girl had been visiting her English friend for a few weeks and now the English girl was to visit the US for the first time. It sounded a little more than this though, as if they were only telling me part of the story. They did notice that I had my Bible with me but I cannot recall any conversations around that subject at all with them.

Once our flight had landed and taxied to the terminal we all waited for that seatbelt light to go off so we could get up and depart. It always takes a good twenty minutes to get off a large flight and ours was no exception. It was while waiting in the narrow and crowded aisle that the American girl asked about my place of residence while I was to be there. I replied that I did not know as yet.

Before collecting any checked in luggage (of which I had none) we all had to line up for passport control. I noticed that the two girls were not together but in different lines for some reason, which I thought rather odd. The American girl called across from her line to me and said that I could stay with them if I would like to. I said that was very kind of her and, under the Lord's prompting, I said yes, please.

As it came to be my turn to pass over the line that they had you wait behind before they call you up, the Lord told me to tell the officer that I was a Christian missionary and that I was here to preach the Gospel. Well, okay! As I walked up to this lady officer she took my passport and looked straight at me and asked,
"Why are you here?" and my reply was,
"I am a missionary and I am here to preach the Gospel!"
Well, I tell you, I might as well have said that I was a terrorist! She went all bright red in the face and started pounding on her keyboard. Then, looking rather angry to say the least she commanded me to take a seat to the side where there were a few chairs. Keeping my passport, she made a call. Next thing I knew a big, burly officer came up to me and took me

around to some rooms in the back. Gee, thank you God! Now, what have You got me into!

Well, there was a small waiting area in the back and guess who was sitting there? The American girl, and looking very worried too. The officer escorting me had me sit down and went off somewhere. You could hear different voices coming from some of the rooms, even shouting at times. Seemed more like an interrogation area to me! The girl told me that she and her friend had been pulled aside for questioning. They had shared the same checked in luggage and the officers were suspicious so they were pulling it and searching its contents for some reason. As we were in mid conversation that same officer came back and told me to go into one of the rooms.

On entering the room I said hello to the officer behind the desk. He had a different demeanor, not so mean looking. He went through a list of questions then wanted me to empty out my backpack. The first thing that came out was my Bible which I placed out in front of him. Once empty he checked the pack and had me place everything back. Formalities over, he softened more and said that he was also a believer in Christ. He then started to give me some advice on where not to go in Orlando and he mentioned in particular an area called Orange County (just my luck!). Well, then he said that I could go and wished me well.

After finally passing through security I waited for either of the two girls to show up. I waited, and waited, and waited but no sign of either of them. Finally, the American girl came through looking really upset. Coming up to me she said that her friend was not going to be allowed into the US as they said she admitted that she was going to stay to live here with her. She was to be put on the next plane back to Manchester, England. She was so upset and I did my best to comfort her. I don't think that she even could have her checked in luggage yet as some of the contents were the English girl's.

A friend of hers came to pick us up after she made a phone call and off to Orange County we went. It was a short journey and soon we were going up some stairs in this big apartment block. There was a small group of young adults living in the apartment and they gave me the couch to crash out in which was fine by me. I remember my first night sleeping on that couch. This was to be my first introduction to the non-rent paying residents that I later found out were all over that state. Cockroaches!

I was tired after all that travelling so I quickly went to sleep. However, in the middle of the night I awoke. I could see a little as the white glow of the moon shone into the room through the partially covered window. And there they all were, cockroaches and big ones too! Now, I do not really mind insects but not if they are going to crawl over me, especially in my sleep! However, I was really tired and did not fully wake up. I just remember thinking that I hate cockroaches, and then fell straight back to sleep.

I was awakened in the morning by one of the young men in the apartment. Standing in front of me he said something like,
"What happened?"
I woke up sluggishly and said "What?"
"Around you, look" he pointed to a ring of dead cockroaches all about two to three feet away from where I had been sleeping!
I think I said something like "I don't like cockroaches."
There must have been over twenty dead roaches there. I didn't think anything more of it at the time.

I had the opportunity to share the gospel to the apartment inhabitants and soon news must have spread. We ended up there having a service and a prayer time. There was one young lady who clearly was having issues in her life. She had recently been released from a rehab house, for drugs, and she was now clean but having serious boyfriend troubles. Apparently there had been some kind of court order to keep him away but he still kept coming around and was threatening to beat her like he used to on a regular basis. I laid my hands on her for divine protection in the name of the Lord Jesus.

The very next day her so called boyfriend turned up at her apartment, but I had also asked to see this young lady again and happened to call on her just a few minutes before the 'boyfriend' turned up. He went berserk on seeing me there. Really, he was not happy at all, even more so when he found out that I was a minister. Arguments between them started then he left. After checking that she was okay, I also left.

The next day the 'boyfriend' returned wanting to beat her up straight away but, according to the young lady's story later, all he did was hit her once on the forehead. She fell to the ground but did not feel the blow. She said that she slowly got up and, looking at him straight in the eyes, calmly told him to leave and he did! She called the police and they later arrested him.

Now the girl from the plane flight, let's call her Kate, she went back to the airport the following day. I knew this because I was out for a walk in Orange County (you know the place that the police officer at my interrogation told me to avoid!) and I saw her waiting at the bus stop. We talked a little and I told her of the love of God and what Jesus did for her. She broke down and cried but I did not sense that she was ready to truly repent and be saved yet, so I did not take it there in our conversation.

I was on the way to go to the Benny Hinn's church that the Lord told me to go visit on that particular day when I was driving in North Wales. I think that I walked to get there as I cannot remember getting a ride nor a bus. The church was set back across a large parking lot and there was a small lake next to the main church building. As I walked across the empty lot I noticed that there was no one around. I knew that this was the right place from the sign and I had just asked someone directions just shortly before I got here, yet there was no one around. Strange, now why would God have me be here all the way from the UK when it was closed?

I was hot so I went towards the lake. Thought I would take my shoes and socks off and take a paddle and cool off a little. But when I got close to the water's edge I got a vision of me standing in the middle of the lake getting my legs bitten! I stopped and decided not to go in. Instead, I went to the main entrance of the church. It was all locked up but while I was peering in through the glass doors a man in a golf cart drove up to me. He was a very pleasant man and he said that he was Elijah, named after the prophet in the Bible. He asked about me so I told him about the Lord's word to me to be here on this day. Then the Lord spoke to me concerning his relatives, specifically his brother up in New York and so I told Elijah and he burst into tears and told me all about his brother. Afterwards he decided to call one of the pastors, for them to open the door. They came and welcomed me inside. They wanted to feed me then take me to see the senior pastor, Pastor Benny Hinn.

I got all excited that I was to visit directly with this man that I had only seen on television until this time. However, the Lord had different plans for me and told me that I needed to leave and go back outside as there were some people coming across the parking lot that I was to meet. I politely excused myself and went outside. Sure enough, just starting to come walking across the parking lot was a big black lady and two little boys, each one holding her hand. I went over to them, and as we met in the middle of this empty lot she told me this story of how these two boys were her grandkids and that she had taken them from their parents who were heavily into witchcraft down in south Florida. She wanted Benny Hinn to free them from any witchcraft. I smiled at her and said to her,
"Benny Hinn cannot deliver them at all ma'am. It is Jesus Christ alone that delivers. Do you believe this?"
She said that she did and I offered right there and then to make sure these children were free. So we all got together and sought the Lord and pronounced liberty in Christ Jesus to these boys and prayed for their parents. Afterwards, she was most grateful and said that she would come to some of the services while she was here. I said that I was going too. They left and then I also, not being directed by the Lord to go back into the church again.

The next services were on the following day, Sunday and I was there in the morning. I cannot recall what time I got there, but there were people all sitting around on the lawn area near the lake. I asked a few what was going on and they said that there was a short break between services and they were soon to go back inside. I was invited to join a lady and her friend so I sat with them. I asked about the lake and told them of my vision. They laughed and said that it was a good thing I did not go in there as there are alligators in the lake! Yeek, I had not even thought about alligators! We don't get them in England you know!

Somehow we got to the subject of music and that I played the violin. The lady asked me if I had heard of Maurice Xxxxx. I had not but she said that there were some tapes of his in the shop. I had no money but did not tell her this as she suddenly got up and told me to wait for her to return. She came back with a cassette tape of Maurice Xxxxx playing the violin. The black and white picture on the front of the tape box was of this man and it indicated that it had piano accompaniment that he played along with. I took a quick look at the titles recorded, "Jehovah Jireh", "In the garden with God", and others. Immediately I felt jealousy rise up in my heart. I wanted to be able to do this I said to myself inside. I put the tape in my pocket and warmly thanked the lady for her gift. It was to be a seed sown that would come alive years later in the US.

I think that it was the next day we had another meeting in the apartment and would you believe it, the 'boyfriend' turned up to the meeting! Not sure how that happened. Anyway the young girl was there and was somewhat nervous but I reassured her. At time for prayer I almost jumped on the man as I forcefully prayed for him and his soul and bound and loosed as guided by the Spirit. He fell back into a chair and his whole complexion seemed to change, to soften before us all. After a few minutes though, he seemed to regress somewhat and stormed out. He was not seen again while I was there.

Kate's mother was going to come and visit, pick up her daughter, and take her to her house which was located in the Tampa Bay area. The Lord told me to go to Tampa Bay. When Kate's mother arrived I was asked to help her up the stairs to the apartment. She was without sensation in the lower half of her body so was in a wheel chair. It was easier for me to pick her up and carry her up rather than helping her in the wheelchair. She was light and was pleasant to me, but I sensed ungodliness in her but said nothing.

After a little conversation I found out that she was also a lesbian and in a lesbian relationship with someone. I was asked if I would like to also go to Tampa Bay to stay with them. I gladly accepted the ride but did not commit myself to the hospitality offered.

The drive did not take too long and soon we were in Tampa. Lots of houses seemed to back onto the inland salt waterways, lagoons or whatever they are called there. Quite pretty really. Kate's mother decided to show me around the area a little, but as we drove around the Lord told me that I was to get off the car soon. We were in some residential neighborhood when the Lord said for me to get out. Being as polite and as thankful as I could be I made my request. They both thought that I was being rather odd and I guess I was. They stopped and I got my music stuff and backpack. And off they went.

I walked for a little while just enjoying the scenery and the presence of the Lord. Resting on a public bench near to the edge of the lagoon a lady, walking her dogs came up to me. We talked and it did not take long for her to tell me about her son who was not doing well (I cannot remember what was wrong with him) and she wanted to take me to meet and pray for him. She was an older and very respectable lady so I agreed and we went to her car and she drove us to see her son. All I remember about this event was that the son had a ferret that crawled all over him. I did pray and then his mother took me back.

As I walked the Lord started to give me some directions. Turn down that street, up this one and then count thirty-two houses down on the left and sit down (may have been a different number than thirty-two). So I did as He said. His instructions took me well into a residential neighborhood of medium sized single story homes. Most were well kept. On counting to house number thirty-two I sat down on the lawn. The house was for sale and on looking at it, seemed unoccupied. It was the only house like that in the street that I could see. So I sat and waited, and waited. Soon found out that, as I was sitting under the shade of a large tree, large red ants seemed to like it there too! Flicking off the little biters, I sat a little further away from that tree.

Well nothing seemed to happen. A local boy and a girl came by a couple of times on their bicycles. On the next pass the boy stopped, looked at me, and asked me a wonderful question,
"Are you a bum?"
Great! I wonder if the police will be called next?!
"No, I replied. God told me to come here."
Hmm, that must have sounded even wackier to him.
"No, you're a bum." He declared and peddled off.

Only a few cars ever came pass me but while one was passing, it slowed down then turned straight into the driveway where I was. Three men got out and went inside the house without even a word to me. They saw me but did nothing. After a short while they all came outside and over to me. They were helping remodel the house for someone and guess what? They were all Christian brothers and they, discovering that I was too, invited me in as they were about to pray together. I gladly joined them as I was tired of those ants and sitting on the grass.

One of the men was from Liverpool, near to Chester where I used to live in England. One of the other men was the church pastor and after we prayed he invited me to pray over their new church building project to help people in need. I agreed, and he also invited me to stay with them a few days. I was just about to be very happy and say yes when the Lord got my attention. The Lord said to me,

"You can go with them, but if you want a greater blessing then stay on the lawn."

I must say I wrestled with that one for a few minutes! Lawn plus ants verses a cozy bed and food. I turned down their generous offer but agreed to go and call them soon to pray with them over their building. The pastor gave me his number (well, I think it was the pastors number, if not it was probably the man from Liverpool). So I went back out and sat down on the lawn by the curb and the three men said their goodbyes and left together.

Hours went by and again, nothing happened! I was back to square one and had turned down a good bed and food for the night! I got ticked off at myself, and at the Lord. It was dark now but thankfully warm as it was summertime (it must have been early June). I got restless and picked up my stuff, got up, complaining something about wasting time and headed off towards the main road that I knew was about a ten minute walk away. A car or two passed by me so I tried thumbing it with no joy.

Finally, I made it to this kind of main road where I thought I would have a better chance to get a ride or something. I crossed over and stood under one of the few street lights. Really, the whole area was rather dimly lit. It was after eleven o'clock at night by now and very few cars came by. I crossed back over to the head of the street from where I had been lawn sitting. On that corner was a wooden public bench. I argued with the Lord, "So, this is the better blessing hey Lord, an old wooden bench for me. Well, I am going to count five vehicles to pass by and if none stop, then we will see what kind of God You are, because You said a better blessing to me!"

I sat down on the bench. It took some time for cars to even show and when they did I made no attempt to indicate that I was looking for anything from them. First car came and went by. Then the second. It must be well after midnight by now I thought. Car number three and four.

"One car left Lord and I am going to sleep on this hard bench!" I retorted at the Lord."

Car number five came and turned down the side road. A Jaguar if I recall correctly. It drove straight by. Right that's it! As I watched its tail lights start to disappear. And then! Its brake lights went on and it did a U-turn. It was coming back! I stood and watched as it passed slowly by me and did another U-turn at the main road and came back and stopped by me. A well-dressed man, obviously successful business man wound down his electric window and asked me who I was and what was I doing. He had a caring manner about him and seemed genuine. I told him that I was a Christian missionary from the UK. He checked that I did not have any living arrangements and when he found out not, he said that I could stay with him a few days. I got in the car and we drove off... right past the house where I was supposed to be waiting! I heard the Lord scold me and I quietly repented for my lack of faith and wrong attitude.

We drove to a nice neighborhood and his house was, well huge to say the least. It must have been over four thousand square feet. Had a huge full size indoor swimming pool too. Definitely a million dollar plus home. His family were away, the children visiting with their mother and they would not be back for a few days so he said that I could stay just for that short duration if I wanted to. He was a devout Roman Catholic and we talked for some time while he kindly fed me. Boy, was I starving!

He was having some uncertainty in his faith and he also had a business partner who had gone sour on him. His business 'partner' was trying to rip him off a large sum of money and he did not know quite how to handle it. He supported his family selling real estate and had been quite successful too. We prayed and I felt no more need than to do that. I hope, but do not know, that the Lord helped him and his family out. I stayed only for a couple of days there before the Lord moved me on. I asked the man if he could just drop me off in the town which he did. I called the person from the renovation house where I sat on the lawn for ages, and arranged to be picked up (I think! Recollection gone a little weak here!). I remember being taken up to a town called Clearwater and praying with them.

They invited me to a Sunday service in the morning on Father's Day. It was a small room but packed with about fifty plus people. It was a different kind of service for them as they had a guest messianic Rabbi ministering. As it was Father's Day they had a gift prize for whomever had a red dot on their program. Yep, that was me and I got a prayer book for fathers to pray for their children. Puzzled on this, I was sad as I had lost my children from my first marriage to Karen.

At the end of the service a short lady amongst others came to talk to me. I called her a prophetess from the start of the conversation and she was politely amused that I had discerned correctly and replied,
"In this case, it takes one to know one."
We had a good little conversation. I cannot recall if, or where I ate any lunch, but I do remember asking for a ride towards the interstate ten (I-10) as the Lord was sending me west towards Mobile, Alabama. They dropped me off at this huge intersection where I was positioned just above the intersection on the right side of the road so that I could get a ride from either the traffic coming straight down the main road or by the traffic turning onto the main road. Two major streets converging all controlled by traffic lights (signals). My ride blessed me and off he went.

The converging road had four, maybe five lanes to it and it was a very busy intersection at the time I was there. I tried thumbing a ride for a few minutes but nothing happened. Then, and maybe it was because of the heat but I kind of spaced out somewhat. I don't think that I was even sticking my hand out for a ride, but I remember looking at this corvette stingray sports car, one of the old style that has the big front wheel arches. I had always wanted to have one if I was to be given a choice. It was at the front of the turning traffic right over on the far lane some hundred or so feet away from me. Lights were red for the other traffic to move but when their lights went green this corvette driver put his foot down and crossed all of the other lanes in a second and came to a sudden holt just in front of me. Reversing back to me, the driver offered me a ride. Great, in a corvette!

Actually, the corvette's ride was really poor. Maybe because it was an older version and only in average condition. It was low to the ground and road noise was bad. Still, it was fun and I chatted to the middle aged almost hippy-looking driver. He took me as far as he could and dropped me off still some miles from the Interstate.

Next was the man in a little red car. He was kind enough to stop and give me a ride. He was troubled I sensed but after a little chit chat he started to open up just a little. He was married it seemed but was on his way to see his mistress! By the time he had to drop me off to turn into a housing edition where his mistress was, he was looking even worse about it! Anyway, he kindly said that if I was still there waiting for a ride when he came out, then he would give me another ride, as he was going further in the direction I was.

Sure enough, within an hour, out pops that little red car and on seeing me he stops and opens the door for me. We continued our little conversation. Apparently, his time with his adulterous lover did not go well (what a shame, huh!), and he seemed even more convicted. I didn't comfort him but I think I just told him some truths of the Kingdom of God and about the marriage covenant. I was never led to tell him anymore than I did. After a while he had to turn off so I thanked him for the ride.

Another ride that I can recall was your typical countryman who was used to living in the boonies somewhere. Tobacco chewing, spitting, dust ridden clothes and a car to match! Still, he was good to me and I thanked him as I departed.

[Interruption: Okay, I am once again on my little 1987 25ft cabin cruiser boat typing all this stuff up. It is April 19th 2014, Easter Weekend! At Lake Tenkiller the weather is really great. Sunny, a little light breeze and in the mid-seventies. Now the Lord told me to spend time on my laptop this Sabbath (Friday sundown to Saturday sundown) working on this book. I got here Friday evening about 11pm so went straight to bed. I was excited at the thought of getting up early to try catch some fish, croppy, for breakfast. I did not hear the Lord tell me *not* to fish so I was soon out there with some of the other regular fisherman at 6am. They were all catching, but was I? Nope. After a couple of hours I complained to the Lord and asked Him to please give me a fish for breakfast. And within a few minutes He did! Perfect size for me. Then He told me to stop, go cook and eat it and so back to working on this book. I thought I had plenty of food supplies here at the boat but messed up on that one. I was just about empty so ended up just eating the fish on its own. Knowing that I would need to go grocery shopping at Walmart in the afternoon, I got busy on this book. But, I kept thinking about the croppy! Often I would stick my head out from the cabin to see how the others were catching. And they all were too! But the Lord said to continue working on the book.

Twice I went out on my own accord to fish for a few minutes just to catch, you know, one or two for dinner maybe, or to give away to friends. But *no*, nothing, and the Lord wanted me back on the laptop working on this book. So I did. I then got well involved in doing this that it was soon mid-day and the Lord told me to go shopping, Off I went and came back with a bunch of groceries. Now, I needed to take the boat out and around to the marina shop to fill up with water, empty the waste and get a little gas as I was well under half a tank. The really nice marina lady, the mother of the family run business, Ms Karen, suggested I take the boat out for a run as it was so nice out. I thought I was to go back to the dock but the Lord agreed with her so I went out and took the boat about a mile to this little cove area just out of the gentle downwind. As I approached the cove the Lord was very specific on where He wanted me to anchor down and I obeyed. It was very close to the shore. So close that I had to throw the anchor on the land and snag it to a bush to hold the boat in place!

The lake water was very clear and I was only floating in a few feet, but my one and a half ton, twenty-five foot boat did not hit bottom at all. I did a little fishing with absolutely no results. Tried jigging, bass and sand bass lures, and float fished and bottom fished worm. Nothing and the Lord said,
"Go work on the book." Well I wasn't catching anything and I was really getting into this book now so I happily did so for a couple of hours I guess. Then, later in the evening the Lord said,
"Go fishing now."
That was an easy command to follow! Up I went to the deck and opened up the canvas back. I had left one fishing rod baited with a worm out there all this time and when I reeled it in the worm was gone. Probably one of those small perch I thought. So I got another worm and also a worm for the float rig and cast them out and sat down with my cold green tea drink. Off goes the pole tip that has worm on the bottom in about eight feet of water. Acted like an aggressive perch, I struck and missed. The worm was still on and I just dropped the bait back down. And again straight away and I missed it again and repeated the process. Gee, some fisher person I am! Third time and I hooked it, Hmmm, large perch I thought but when I saw it, it was a bass! Yes! Safely landed though I had left my landing net back at the dock. To cut a long story short, I only had a few worms in a tub in

the refrigerator and with them I caught these four big bass, and a big drum fish that I threw back as they are not good to eat:

Moral of the story…Obey the voice of the Lord! End of interruption!]

If I have the order of my rides correct, my trip then took me towards the town of Tallahassee in Florida near the start of the Florida panhandle. It was getting dark and following my last ride I decided to walk, and walk, and walk along this one long road. On each side of the road were trees upon trees. I was clearly in some forestry area. No street lights at all so as it got dark on this warm evening I could look up into the sky and see the Milky Way starting to show itself. As darkness fell, the Milky Way seemed to light up. It was awesome, so awesome that I laid down in the grassy verge on my back and just stared up in the Lord's wonderful creation. I praised Him and thanked Him. I watched shooting stars transverse the night sky and just got a little bit of reality on the enormity of God's handiwork. Awesome.

    I carried on a little further in the dark after finding some kind of rest area but there were no toilets and no one else was there. I stayed for maybe an hour at the most to rest but there was nothing comfortable for me to really rest on, besides I really was not tired for some reason. After a while I saw a dim light in the distance so I aimed to walk and stay under the light to see if I could get a ride. Very few cars were passing in the direction I was going, actually very few cars at all anywhere! When I got to the light I realized that it lit up a small gravel parking area behind which was the entrance to a mobile home park although it was a little hard to tell as there was very little lighting back there.

So I positioned myself under that light and waited for a vehicle to pass. It must have been well past midnight by now and although I could see for miles back down the road from where I had come, I saw no vehicle lights at all. Time went by, and some more. Finally some headlights in the distance. I hoped I could get a ride from someone nice at this time of the night. I had no idea where I was at all. Well, as hope answered, it was to be a safe ride at least. The car pulled over in front of me with its lights fully on. Standing there in its full beam I shielded my eyes with my hand enough to see the word 'Sheriff' on the side of the car. Out steps this big sheriff, hand on his gun holster and ready to take action if he needed to. However, once I had introduced myself to him and told him my cause, he, after checking my passport out, came back and was very friendly. Apparently they were out and about looking for some armed robbers that had just committed a crime in Tallahassee. I found out that Tallahassee was just a few more miles up the street.

The sheriff was the boss man, in charge of his night crew. He told me that Tallahassee was definitely not a good place for me to go through at night and he said that a lot of violent crimes take place then. So, he decided to give me a ride into the town to a hotel and restaurant area that would be well lit.

Sitting in his front passenger seat was a little scary at first. All I could see were guns and a rifle. Oh, and this loaded (he said) sawn off shot gun that was in some specially designed holster so that he could just grab it and fire if needed. The only trouble was that it was pointing right down at my left foot!

Once in Tallahassee the sheriff had me stand outside the hotel in a well-lit area so that I could hopefully continue my hitchhiking adventure. He also called one of his officers to park a little distance away on the other side of the road to watch me, to make sure I was safe until I got a ride. The Sheriff apologized that he could not take me further but he had to get back to hunting down those armed robbers. I was very grateful.

Still wide awake for some reason and having not eaten now for many hours, I was fine, doing well. A couple of cars passed by me and ignored my plea for a ride. It must have been 3am in the morning or around about that time. Another car went past, then, as I watched it go by, it did a U-turn about a quarter of a mile past me. Turning around again to pull up in front of me I could not believe who was the driver. A young and pretty girl, probably in her early twenties at most. She wound down the passenger window as I peered in. I said to her,
"You are the last kind of person that I thought would stop for me."
She looked a little unsure herself so I comforted her by showing her my Bible and telling her who I was. She said to put my stuff on the back seat and sit in the front passenger seat which I did. I sensed that the Lord was going to do something here but I had no clue what that was.

We drove a little and after I had shared the gospel with her she revealed her miserable life of torment and bondage to drugs and that her boyfriend was cruel and that he had gotten her pregnant now and he told her the she was going to have the devils baby. I listened and could not talk. After she finished I asked her to pull over, which she did, in the middle of nowhere! I told her again about Jesus and did she want to accept Him into her life. Her sister was one of those 'born again' people she said, and she was thinking about it and was actually on the way to see her. She wanted Jesus, she wanted to be free from all this.

We prayed and then I prayed and I cast out that demon of perverse lust. She screamed really loudly as her head wrenched back. I saw this dark shadow depart from her and vanish away. She calmed down. I waited patiently as she came to her right mind. She declared that she was free and free from drugs too. Well, praise the Lord I say! Then, she got a little uncomfortable being out there in the darkness with someone she did not know. Not wanting to offend her I departed and thanked her for the ride, encouraging her to go straight to her sister's and tell her what had just happened. Once again I was in the darkness on my own with the Lord!

I started walking and soon it was daylight. I found an open area where cars passed by frequently, and stood there to thumb another ride. And then I saw it, this hippy looking Volkes Wagon van that looked like it had been hand painted in multi colors. And all that I could tell while it was still a long way off! It was also swerving, not badly, but enough to notice. I really, really tried to put my hand down but for some reason it would not go down. And then it was too late. They had seen me, and in came this van as it swerved across the lane towards me and stopped rather abruptly. Windows down and the side sliding door gliding open, both the man and lady in the front seats told me to jump in. I did, well try to anyway. He had tiles and tools for tiling work piled up there. These people were your fun loving, living it up in good old free America folk. Kind of flower power people. They traveled through the country just living together and he earns the money doing tile jobs. Well, okay I guess! Each to his and her own. They took me as far as they could and dropped me off. Interesting experience that one was. What was to come next?

Well next got a little worse. It was a car full of young adults who, after I got in, wanted me to smoke dope with them and then go to some house and hang and do drugs there. Needless to say I politely said no and they too dropped me off before they had to turn off.

My next ride was with a rancher, an American cowboy in a blue rugged pickup truck that had round metal bars welded to the front, back and front sides. A really pleasant man the cowboy was and he was more than happy to help this English missionary on his journey, even took me out of his way a little to drop me off at the Interstate. As we approached the interstate he insisted on feeding me at the restaurant there. What a good man, may the Lord bless him for his kindness. After thanking him deeply there I was once again on my own with the Lord.

The on ramp to the Interstate was from a small road really so very little traffic went down it. With my backpack and music player in hand, I decided to walk further down onto the freeway. I walked down for about fifty yards just on to the emergency lane. Now there was road works there and traffic was reduced to a single lane. There was obviously a problem though. The workmen had put those large orange drums too close from one side of the lane to the other. Cars and small vehicles were fine at passing through but large trucks, unless they drove real careful, were in danger of clipping them. And that is exactly what I started to see happen. So, being the helpful person I like to think I can be sometimes, as there were no workman around at all, I started widening the drums just a little and reposition those that had been hit and moved. I totally forgot about getting a ride and before I realized it, I was some distance from my backpack that I had left by the side of the lane.

A big flatbed truck came by and pulled over on to the emergency lane just ahead of me. I went up to the driver and he asked me if I wanted a ride. He said that he was a Christian man and was delivering Baptist steeples around the country. He had a good spirit about him so I agreed, ran back to pick up my stuff, and back to the truck to experience a short stint of being an American trucker!

Traveling west on a big American Interstate is, well, never ending! I remember seeing a team of tractors all mowing the verges at one time on one side. I bet they all work for miles and miles up one side and then the same down the other side, only to repeat the process over and over again as the grass has already grown by the time they get back to where they started!

The truck driver had some issue with the engine and had to stop at one time, but he seemed to get it sorted quickly. He said he was hungry and wanted to buy me some food at this trucker's stop coming up. I was fine with that! Pulling into a cleaning bay we went inside while his cab was cleaned I guess (I never looked to check when we came out). Big trucks and big, mostly overweight truck drivers everywhere. They had showers that you could rent too. After lunching we were back on the road. It was not too long, however, that we made it to Gulf Shores where he dropped me off. I thanked him for his kindness.

I knew that this was where I was to be for a while. As I walked along a main shopping street I was just quietly praising the Lord and at peace when I noticed a car pull up close to me as I walked and it kept pace with me for a moment, long enough for me to notice, so I stopped and looked at the driver. He had just wound the window down, and stopping, asked me a few questions that I cannot remember. Anyway, he invited me to join him. He was going to a Christian leadership meeting of some kind. I took the ride and soon we were at this meeting with about fifteen people present. Not much seemed to happen there but the man, let's call him Terry, offered to put me up while I was there. I thanked him and said that would be great.

He was a godly man and his apartment was in very good order and was located fairly close to the beach too! However, the Lord had other things for me to do than play on the beach at the seaside. In actual fact, I never did go on the beach!

I think it was the very next day that I went with Mr. Terry to visit some people. We went to a house or maybe it was an apartment, where a lady and her twenty-something year old daughter were living. The mother was very welcoming but the daughter not so. She went off to her room once we came inside. The mother was very sweet and a Christian believer. She was really concerned for her daughter as she was getting involved with the wrong crowd and the mother thought she was doing drugs now too. I asked to see the daughter, let's call her Jennifer. Jennifer reluctantly came out and flopped herself down on a seat near us. I looked at her and it looked like she was waiting to be talked to, corrected etc. But the Lord gave me a song to sing so I just started singing it.
"Our God is an Awesome God, He reigns from heaven above..."
Wow, what a reaction I got (I am not a really good singer, just mediocre at best). Jennifer started looking sad, then started crying, then heavily she cried as she got up and ran into her room. I stopped singing. Her mother was looking at me with big eyes as if to say,
"Do you know what you just did?" Of course, I had no idea at all what I did.
What did I do? Jennifer's mother explained that that was the one song that she used to sing to Jennifer throughout her childhood and it pierced her heart to hear it again. Wow, awesome God you are.

I am not sure what happened to Jennifer after that but Mr. Terry informed me that she went missing, thought to have gone with her boyfriend to the boat casinos in a place called Biloxi, Mississippi. The Lord told me to go and try find her. I got directions with regards to which road I needed to walk out of Gulf Shores on and reconnect with the Interstate once more. I had not walked far when a man (let's call him Tom) called over to me to see if I wanted a ride. That was kind of odd too, as I was walking in an area of shops and other people were all around me, shopping. I told him where I was going and he said he was going there too. I discerned that this was to be my ride so I went with him.

On the way along the interstate heading west, we talked about my purpose to find this young lady if possible and talked about her doing drugs. Tom started to open up to me and said that he used to be heavily into drugs and drug dealing, but now, and for a few years now he was an FBI informant to help reduce that type of crime in the area.

Now, the Lord told me straight away as Tom was talking, that he was indeed an informant but he was lying about the drugs. The Lord said to me,
"He still is" that is, doing drugs.
I kept quiet and when he noticed I was quiet I guess the Lord convicted him. Tom started crying while driving. He confessed that he was hooked back on drugs and that he was on his way to see his pastor to extort more money out from him on a lie to feed his addiction. He cried more and said that we could both go to the pastor and he would confess and repent so that is what we did.

The pastor was a mature man and had understanding and compassion as confessions were made and things got worked out between them. The pastor also gave me some advice on where to look for Jennifer if she was here. There was this one particular floating casino that was a good place to look and I got a ride to the shoreline from the pastor. What a big boat! It was huge and well docked like it was permanently to be there. The state law did not allow casinos to be built in land, but a boat escapes that law. As I went in, I could just pick up the ungodly atmosphere of the place. Walking around the bottom deck I got a sense that she was not here, and not here at all. I left and after going back to the pastor's house Tom and I drove back to Gulf Shores.

Back relaxing with Terry for a short while. He was arranging for me to go out in the Gulf with a few friends for some deep sea fishing. What a fantastic idea! But the Lord moved me on to get to Mobile so I had to turn that down ☹. Dropping me off once more Terry and I said our goodbyes and blessed each other in the Lord.

Once in Mobile I called my friend, LeRoy, that I had come to know when on my first trip to the US. I called and asked him to come and pick me up and I was looking forward to seeing a familiar face.

LeRoy was a very kind man and it was a joy to see him. He talked to me excitedly about the prophesying I did on my first trip, especially to the lumber owner. The owner had taken what I said as a confirmation and had financed a large mixed church gathering in the city center to praise and worship the Lord. Then, he went ahead and purchased an empty store right in the city square block and the church had moved there. The Lord was moving. I really loved this church because they really did go out of their way to help people in need.

On Sunday I went with LeRoy to the new church location. The service was great, and it was wonderful meeting some of the people that I met from my first trip. One amazing testimony that took place in this service was a black lady probably in her thirties who had been on the streets and had got saved through the love that this church had extended to her. She had been a prostitute and had contracted AIDS which had been confirmed by the local hospital. However, here she was looking great and she told everyone of how she was prayed for and that she later went back to the hospital for her regular checkup, and they found no AIDS, and no HIV! She was free and healed from it all! The hospital checked her three times and eventually could only explain it as an original error that she never had it in the first place! Whatever! Praise the Lord!

After the service LeRoy wanted me to meet a friend, a Christian brother from Iran. Now, prior to this the Lord had told me to go to Tulsa, Oklahoma to meet someone special that same week. I knew of Tulsa from my friend from the UK, Lance, as he had met his wife there although they were now living in Minneapolis/St. Paul.

We were to meet this Iranian man at a diner so we drove there which only took a short while. The man, let's call him Hussein, was a dark skinned man, typical of people from that part of the world. He had lived a long time in the US and his speech was perfect American. As I walked into the diner the Lord had told me to ask Hussein about Tulsa, as the Lord was moving me on, starting this Wednesday, but I never got a chance to. This man just started talking and saying that he was packing and going to move in with one of his cousins, that his cousin lived, you guessed it, in Tulsa, Oklahoma. Once he had finished I asked him when he planned to move. "Wednesday morning."
Yes! So I asked him for a ride up there and I offered to help him pack etc. He said he would take me.

Now, the total sum of money in my pocket was but ten dollars, that's it, but I never told anyone how much I did or did not have. Interestingly, by the time this whole trip concluded I was given hundreds of dollars and gave away hundreds of dollars.

Wednesday came and LeRoy kindly took me to meet Hussein who had already fully packed up this yellow Ryder rental truck and had his small car hooked up behind. After saying goodbye and thank you again to LeRoy, Hussein and I started our journey north. The route would take us up the side of the Mississippi river and it would be a two day journey he informed me. I was fine, I was grateful I could give him some company and that he was kind enough to help me.

It was summer, late June 1993 and the Mississippi was huge. It was a chocolate brown, bubbling rage of a river when I first set my eyes on it. Hussein explained that there had been very heavy rains that year and the river had burst its banks and destroyed lots of crops. Most of the water had subsided by now, but the crops were ruined and the river was still high. We did indeed see thousands of acres of arable farm land wasted.

Hussein said that we were heading first to another one of his cousins in Arkansas where we would stay the night and continue on the following day. The total two-day trip was about eight hundred and fifty miles. As we journeyed he asked me if I minded him smoking. Now, we were in a small cab together and if there is one thing I do not like, it's

cigarette and cigar smoke. I had to ask him not to as I really could not stand cigarette smoke. His reply?
"Not cigarettes, dope."
Yeek! I abruptly looked at him and I think he got the message! I was thinking, and you call yourself a Christian?! (See how judgmental I was!). Anyway, he didn't smoke at all in the cab for the whole two-day journey.

When we arrived in Arkansas it was like stepping back in time. We were at a place called Pine Bluff, in Little Rock. Where we were was full of these large wooden huts, all wood no brick or stone to be seen. They were houses! As we passed through we went straight to the cousin's place of business. He owned a pizza restaurant. After introductions we sat down and ate all the pizza we could! Later we went back to his cousins home.

His home was one of those little wooden houses, a single story and there was not much room there but he was kind enough to put us up. We crashed out in the living room as the other bedrooms were full for his family. Well, the Lord woke me up early which surprised me as I was tired from all that traveling. However, I was quite refreshed and quietly, so as not to disturb Hussein, I got dressed and went out through the front door as instructed by the Lord. It was already daybreak and it was warm too, nothing like the UK! The Lord told me to go for a walk so I did. Up this road and down the next, it all looked the same in this residential area. Then I heard this squeaking sound and looked and saw this older lady just a little further down the street where I was walking. She was sitting on her front porch deck in a wooden rocking chair slowly moving backwards and forwards making that wooden creaking sound as she did so. As I walked towards her I noticed that she was looking straight at me. She had white hair and was probably close to being in her eighties. As I approached she extended out her hand and, with a shaking finger pointed at me saying in a clear but shaky voice,
"Ah, a man of God!"
I smiled and thanked her but did not feel like I was any more than just a man really.

She was a very kind lady and we talked about her missionary daughter in South America somewhere. Then, totally out of context she again pointed her figure at me and said,
"You're about to meet your wife real soon!"
Well, okay, if you say so I thought. And that was it. We blessed each other in the Lord and back to the cousin's home I went.

After breakfast, left over pizza I think it was, Hussein and I continued our journey towards Tulsa. As we approached the city he acted like he knew where to go. He had no cell phone so he had no way to call his cousin from the vehicle. Into the city we went, going northwards up I-75. He got lost, and we ended up stopping at a gas station somewhere east bound on I-244. He contacted his cousin there and got fresh directions.

Confident now, we continued east on I-244 and then we were to head south on I-169. I started to inquire to the Lord what I was supposed to do. He said that I was to get off at the very next place we stopped. I waited to see what was to happen as I guessed that the next place was Hussein's cousin's home. However, as we progressed southwards Hussein made this weird comment,
"I am going to take a short cut."
Upon which he signaled and pulled off onto 71st street. A short cut! I thought, you have never been to Tulsa, just got lost, and now taking a short cut? Oh, well. And sure enough, pulling on to 71st street he realized yet again, that he was lost and mumbled something about finding another phone box.

Hussein pulled up his van and car to a gas station, a Texaco station, if I recall correctly (it has gone now). After he had made his phone call I told him that this was where I was supposed to get off. He was genuinely concerned for me and gave me his cousin's phone number to call if I needed somewhere to stay. I thanked him warmly for his kindness as I watched him drive off.
"Well, Lord," I said, "Here I am again. I have but ten dollars in my pocket and no one but You and Hussein know I am here!"
I heard the Lord say to me,
"You are hungry aren't you."
Yes, I was! And the Lord said to me,
"Go and walk on this side of the street and stop and eat at the first place you can sit down and eat."
Well, I could see a place called Sonic, so I went there, but there was no place to sit. It was one of those American drive-in deals. They did give me a cup of cold iced water though when I asked them. It was early afternoon and hot, very hot for me though they all seemed quite used to it.

I crossed a small side street by some apartments (the QuikTrip gas station is on that corner now, but I cannot remember if it was there back then. I think it was). All I could see for eating places were on the other side of the main street, on this side seemed to be all apartments. I carried on walking (I am heading west) and then, just set back away from the road was a restaurant called Outback, a steak house place. It looked new and had empty plots of land on either side of it at that time. I knew that this was where I was to go in and eat.

On entering, I do not know quite why, but I left my music player at the entrance on the floor and only took my small backpack in. It all looked very new and I found out later that it had only been open a short while. I was taken to a seat and given a menu. Trouble was, all I had was ten dollars! The cost of the food here would go way beyond that if I was to eat a meal. And I was sure hungry! The Lord said for me to get a piece of

paper from my backpack and write on it 'Jesus is Lord' and place it up on my table. I thought that rather odd but I did it. The waitress came to me to take my order. On seeing my sign, she sat down and chatted about being a Christian. The whole place was virtually empty at that time of day so I guess she had plenty of time to kill. As we talked I said,
"There is someone who should have been here at noon but he did not turn up. When he comes, please send him to me."
Where did that come from! She said, looking a little surprised at me, that she would go and check with her manager. A couple of minutes later she returned exclaiming that I was correct and if he comes in she would send him to me. She went off to get me an iced tea and hot bread roll. Then a young man, another waiter, probably a college or university student earning himself some money came up to me. Looking straight at me he said,
"This is all I have in cash; please take it and do not refuse me." (or something just like that). I was shocked and looked at him. He was most sincere, so I gratefully accepted his notes and coins. He went off happy and I had more than enough for a good meal!

The restaurant was virtually empty when I arrived at about 3pm. Soon however, the place was busy, very busy. The man who should have clocked in at noon had arrived according to the waitress but he refused to come over to me. There was a couple with family members or friends with them to the table next to me. The two young adults were talking about whether to get married. A little while later the Lord had me speak to the young man and what I said apparently was most significant in helping him make the choice to marry. I just cannot remember what I said! After returning back to my seat and had finished my meal, I thanked the waitress and what staff I saw and left the restaurant, fully satisfied.
"Okay, now what Lord?" I asked Him,
"Go, stand on that street corner by the small side road that you crossed. Put on praise music as loud as you can and sing to Me!" was the Lord's reply. Well, uh, I am a rather reserved Englishman and we just don't do things like that in public! Okay, here goes so I went to the corner, selected some praise music from the collection I had and put it on the loudest volume and set the machine on the street corner. Thankfully I had brought along plenty of replacement batteries for the machine if needed. I stood by it and sang along as inconspicuously as I could, yet in obedience to the Lord.

Minutes, then half an hour went by and nothing happened. More music went on and still nothing and it was then that I noticed something, Americans do not walk anywhere, they ride! Just cars and pickup trucks everywhere! I was the only person on foot as far as my eyes could see. Still nothing happened and I got restless. I made another sign 'Christian missionary, place to stay!' and I held it out for about another half hour or so. Still nothing and I don't think God was too impressed with my attempt to make something happen. I put the sign away and as I did so the Lord said,

"Look."

I looked up as I was facing away from the main street and looking down the side road.

"See those apartments?"

I was looking at these brick and blue-gray colored apartments.

"Yes Lord." I answered.

"That's where you will be staying."

I went back to standing next to the street corner with the music still playing. More time went by and it was getting dark. I had been there for hours! Looking down 71st Street at the traffic coming towards me I could see that people had no interest in me. Many seemed too scared to even look my way. Maybe they thought I was a street person, a bum as they are called! Then, I heard a car horn blasting behind me over the noise of the traffic and my music. I turned around and there was this young couple in a convertible waiting to pull out of the small side street. The young man waved me over so I went over to him. He asked me,

"What are you doing?" A good question! Well here goes for the truth again…

"I am a Christian missionary and the Lord told me to stand here, put the music on full blast and praise Him!" I smiled at them. They smiled too and he replied,

"We heard the music and it sounded like praise music. That's why I called you over." (God is so good isn't He!)

"Where are you staying?" He asked me,

"Nowhere, I have just arrived in Tulsa." I replied.

"Great, we live in those apartments behind us. You can stay with us. We are off to a gathering, come and join us." He offered and I gladly accepted. I got my stuff and got into the back seat. His name was Andrew but he was known as Drew and his wife was Jamie.

And sure enough, after the gathering and barbeque food at some person's house we returned to the very same apartments that the Lord had shown me. Drew was to become a good friend and best man at my future wedding (of that later!).

The apartment was nice, clean and compact. They gave me a floor mattress and blankets etc. to sleep on. They had some kittens that loved to play in the blankets and on me! On the second day when I awoke the Lord put it on my heart to go to a Christian University of some kind. I asked Drew once he was up if there were any here in Tulsa? He said that there were two large ones in particular, Oral Robert University and Rhema Bible College. The first one registered with me so I asked if it was far and how could I get there.

"I need to meet someone special" I said.
And Drew's immediate reply was,
"Like your wife," he said grinning at me.
Said more as a declaration than a question, I blew it off. Anyway, Drew said that he was going there anyway today as he had enrolled in summer school classes and needed to pay his tuition fee. He said that he could drop me off but had to go to work and would not be able to pick me up until later in the afternoon. I said that that was fine. Drew wrote down his phone number for me.

After a quick breakfast we left the apartment and headed towards the Oral Roberts Christian University! I was excited as I imagined seeing hundreds, even thousands of Spirit filled Christian believers. What a great atmosphere that must be! We have nothing in the UK like that at all.

As Drew pulled into one of many car parking areas I was disappointed. The place looked virtually empty! I asked Drew about this and he said that spring term had finished and summer school not started so there would only be a few people around. I could still go to the book store and the prayer tower he told me as he pointed to this tower thing that had a live flame burning out of its top. Then he said that there was this 'Journey through the Bible' across the street. He went to pay his tuition but came back disappointed too. He said that the administration offices were closed so he could not pay. He double checked that I still wanted to stay and I did, I knew I had to. So Drew went off to work leaving me in this big empty parking area.

As I walked towards the buildings I saw some people milling around further up where there was this tall round building. I went up the steps to go in, wondering what it was for. A lady immediately called to me and asked me what I was doing. I explained, upon which she was quick to say I could not go in. This was the girls-only dormitory! Oops! Turning around, after apologizing, I decided that the prayer tower thing was a better choice!

To get into the prayer tower you first have to descend a little through a garden area. Then you come to these double glass doors and as I did so I knew that I knew that this was the place where I was going to meet this person I was supposed to meet. Maybe I was to impart to them or they to me, or both? As I opened the door and walked in my eyes first went to the nearest people that were behind this large reception counter. These were two girls, late teens I guessed. One was white American, the other Mexican looking to me as best as I could describe. They were playing some card game and looked at me when I came in. The Mexican girl stared at me with these big round eyes. As I looked at her for a second or two I saw this bright neon green sign in my mind. It flashed on and off displaying the word 'marriage', 'marriage', 'marriage.' I must have looked puzzled and I looked away thinking that she was only old enough to be my daughter!

There were two other ladies and a man also behind the counter and they were very polite to me. One lady, she introduced herself as Priscilla, talked to me and as she did so I literally felt the hand of God shove my right shoulder a few times, each time saying,
"That is your wife."
I really did my best to keep myself together and tried not to listen. She was far too pretty for me. She really was gorgeous and seemed very intelligent too. She asked me how I got saved and she had to listen to about an hour's story. I was mesmerized with her. She introduced the two girls and the Mexican teenage was in fact Hispanic like Priscilla was, and she was Priscilla's daughter! Bianca was her name. A great name.

Time seemed to fly by and after I went up and did the tourist walkabout thing I went back down to see this Priscilla lady. She had the job at the end of the day to secure and lock up the building so we walked and talked together as I followed her. We chatted some more and I felt even more magnetized towards her. The Lord said that I was going to go and meet her family that evening but I tried not to listen to Him. Sure enough in the midst of our conversation that's exactly what ended up happening. She had to run a couple of errands first as we, together with her daughter, ran around in this little red Ford Fiesta car of hers.

When we got to her parents' house, a duplex that they were renting, they were very welcoming. Now I have had the honor of visiting in many different homes as a missionary but the atmosphere here was different. There seemed to be some expectation in the air which would involve me somehow. It was like they all knew about me before I even turned up! I was invited to stay for dinner, a traditional Hispanic meal. I accepted gratefully as I was introduced to Priscilla's children. Bianca was the eldest and she was a teenager, much older than her two brothers Jeremy and Jacob. Jeremy I think back then was eight and Jacob six. I took to all of them straight away and I saw myself as their parent right there and then as I still do to this day.

Bianca was more like a second mom to the two boys as she was much older and Priscilla had to work multiple jobs to support them following her graduation from Oral Robert University with a double major in Spanish and political science. Jeremy was a very active child that seemed to get into everything and anything. Jacob seemed to just be a happy boy to me.

At the meal table I discovered that Hispanics love to talk and that eating is a social event. Priscilla's mother started saying a few things regarding the Lord and I don't think to this day she was aware fully of what she was saying as it directly related to things that the Lord had revealed to me in secret. After the meal somehow we got into a time of personal ministry and I laid my hands on and prayed I think for most of the family. The last person was Priscilla and as I approached her I stopped and laughed. This seemed to annoy her a little but I just knew that the moment I touched her there would be a spiritual connection that would confirm that she was to be my wife somehow. I went forward and touched her and prayed.

Priscilla and I talked together some more before she kindly took me back to Drew's apartment where I was staying. I was overjoyed to tell Drew and his wife Jamie about what had happened. All that night all I could think about was this gorgeous, hot blooded, hardworking, intelligent and loveable lady.

The next morning I awoke because those kittens were playing on my bed again! After getting up and getting dressed the Lord put it on my heart to go to a park. I asked Drew if there were any parks in Tulsa and he laughed and said that there were lots of them. I asked him to name a few. The second I think on his list was La Fortune and right away I said that was the one I needed to go to. He said that he could drop me off there but I would have to wait a few hours until he could return. That was fine with me.

All I took was my Bible and, once again I had no idea what I was supposed to do once I got there. As Drew drove me he kept on talking about having pizza for breakfast. I thought that rather odd but presumed that Americans maybe sometimes ate pizza for their breakfasts?! Drew dropped me off at the main entrance parking lot where the swimming pool and golf course entrances are located. And off he went to do some work.

I started walking along this track that went between some trees and a children's play area. It was a nice sunny morning and not too hot as yet though there was not much wind blowing at all. I communed with the Lord as I walked, just enjoying the park.

There were a few people milling around including some walkers and joggers using the rough track for their exercise. I stopped at a small concrete bridge of sorts that a small creek ran under. I noticed a man, a black man by the looks of it lying on one of the concrete picnic table seats. What was strange about it was that he looked like he was wearing a two-piece suit and had this nice hat over his face as he slept or rested. The Lord said to me,
"Go and speak to him."
Now, for some stupid reason I started to be rational with the Lord!
"Lord, but what if he is asleep. He may get mean or he may think I am going to cause trouble, or.."
"Are you going to go and talk to him?" Said the Lord in a much sterner voice.
I submitted straight away and started walking over to the man. As I approached him he did not stir so I did my throat clearing noise,

"uhaaa, Uuuummm," and he started to stir. Raising his hat with his hand just enough to look at me with one eye I spoke to him (and yes, this is exactly what I said),
"I am a missionary from England, and ... do you know anything about pizzas?"
Yep! That's what came out of my mouth, but it was too late to recoil my words, I had already spoken them out! I looked down at him waiting to see if he thought I was crazy or something but instead he sat up and said something that totally shocked me,
"I am a pizza salesman for a company that was founded in England."
I think we were both shocked at that moment! He invited me to sit and talk with him. God sure knows how to get a person's attention! He should have been at work he told me, that is why he was dressed that way. However, his relatively new girlfriend had been telling him about Jesus and he was resting on this seat chewing it all over in his mind.

We talked for about half an hour or so about the Lord and I was never instructed by the Lord to ask if he was ready to be saved and pray and repent so I did not go there. I thanked him for his time and left, probably still leaving him rather amazed at the whole incident! Later that afternoon, Drew returned and picked me up.

The following morning I knew that this was the day to go see Priscilla again, but this time to propose to her in marriage. I was scared and nervous but at the same time excited as I knew this was of the Lord. Drew kindly dropped me off again before he went to work. I remember him smiling at me as he drove off. Okay for you to smile at me friend, I thought, you are not the one who might get rejected here! It's odd that I should even be feeling that way as I knew that the Lord accepts me and that I will always be loved by Him. To feel scared that a person, even a very, very special person like my future wife might reject me seemed strange. But maybe not so, as this would be a most important change in my life and maybe hers too if she accepted me.

I should have gone straight to the Oral Roberts University prayer tower as that is where she worked, but still being overtaken by nerves, I stopped at another building that has a live gas flame at ground level in a fire pit of some kind. I sat down there just staring at the flame for a few minutes until I heard the Lord speak to me,
"Well, are you going to go down and see her?"
I mumbled something under my breath,
"If you do not get up and go now, will I have to lift you up Myself and take you?!" The Lord's voice had that slight sternness to it.
"*Okay!*" I announced to Him.
I got up and started walking towards the prayer tower, my mind galloping as to what I will do and say. At arriving back down those few steps into the

prayer gardens and through the glass doors, I still had no idea what I was going to do.

Priscilla and her daughter Bianca were in the back gift shop at the register. As I walked in I got excited to see her again. We greeted and I started to get nervous so I walked around pretending to be interested in what was on sale in the gift shop. I cannot even remember what I was looking at! Then, I saw a picture hanging on the back wall. It was a picture of a flute and a violin laid over each other. Priscilla had told me that she used to play the flute and there was my violin. I called over to her to come and look at something, so she and her daughter who was like a shadow to her then, came over. I said,
"Look, my violin and your flute!"
Now what happened next I did not find out until much later but Bianca tugged on her mother's clothing and whispered into her ear,
"Mom, I think this is the man God has for you."
Prisci almost but passed out on the floor. You see, the Lord, in the middle of the previous night had been telling Prisci that very same thing but Prisci, when we first met two days prior had no particular thoughts that way. Actually, she was thinking that she would introduce me to some of her friends! *She* had a particular man at the university that she *really* liked and he liked her too, but she had not done anything about it as the Lord had not released her to do so. Finally, in the middle of the night and still very tired she quit fighting the Lord and said,
"Well, *all* right, I guess" or something like that.
But the Lord did not stop there. He then made it clear to her that there were to be things that we would go through together and that it would not be easy but in the end things would work out very well. The Lord wanted her to go into this marriage if she agreed to it, with her eyes wide open so to speak.
I asked Priscilla if we could go outside into the gardens and talk a little. She agreed so we both went outside, leaving Bianca in charge of the gift shop for a moment. Dread came over me, fear of rejection but I took a deep breath and said something like,
"You have been on my mind ever since I met you the other day."
She replied,
"It's your fault that I got no sleep last night."
Ouch! Firey thing she is all right!
"Well" I said, taking another deep breath,
"The Lord has showed me that we are, err, are, err, like supposed to be together... like for life." We looked straight at each other.
"I know" She replied.
"Well if I am going to have a wife." I continued "then she has to be thus, thus and thus, as the Lord has a calling on me to do His will." Or something very close to that.

Priscilla's reply? Looking straight at me she boldly declared,
"Well, if I am going to have a husband then he has to be thus, thus, and thus!"
Unfortunately, to this day, I cannot recall what either of our 'thus' statements were! At that time we, no, she was on a roll...
"Besides, you haven't even asked me yet."
Oh, Lord, here it comes. At the peak of feeling rejected I got before her and asked her to marry me. Her reply was simply,
"Yes, okay," and with that she turned and walked off a little, leaving me with my mouth so wide open I am sure my bottom lip almost touched the ground!
She had not rejected me! Boy was I happy! So happy that I cannot remember even what happened after that.
Priscilla, Prisci as I started to call her, needed the confirmation of her family before she would agree to go ahead with this marriage so she spoke to her children and parents. She later told me that talking to her mother was the hardest. She went outside in the back yard with her mother and had to take a deep breath and swallow hard before she came out and said something close to,
"Mom, I think that man that came over is supposed to be my husband."
Her mom looked at her and simply replied,
"I know."
Prisci was amazed at her mother being so agreeable due to what they had all gone through in the past. Prisci has quite a story to tell herself. Time and time again she had gone through some tough times in her own life, but her family always came through for her as best as they could. She now had the family's support to marry me, even though she also knew that we were going to go through stuff together. She also knew that the cross-dressing behavior I had engaged in in the past was going to be revisited even though I had insisted that it was all over, which at that time I believed it was as I had been walking strongly in the Lord for two years and I had not seen one squeak of it at all. I saw no reason why that should not continue that way.

  Prisci had a duplex just a couple of miles or so away that she rented. Over the next few days before the Lord sent me on to Minneapolis we met there and did tons of talking. In fact, we pretty much went through everything in our lives. We also started to get rather passionate together and it was all we could do to restrain ourselves from jumping the gun and consummating our marriage before we were married if you get my meaning! We definitely had a very strong connection there all right! However, I was soon to find out that I seriously lacked in the area of understanding and relationship building.

  At one family mealtime that is with Prisci's parents, brother and sister and all the children, while having dinner in the parents' home, I mentioned that I was to go to Minneapolis St. Paul in a few days. The Lord had placed it on my heart to visit an old friend, Lance from England, who I believed was caught up in some kind of cult. I had no money to fund the trip when they asked me and they kindly put together my Greyhound bus fare between them. It was from this final location that I was to fly back to the UK.

So there I was, just met and proposed to, and now leaving, my future wife to continue my journey with the Lord. What a trip! I cannot even remember that bus journey I was so excited that the Lord had presented my wife to me.

I had Lance's phone number from when I was back in England so I had called him and made arrangements for him to pick me up when I arrived. It was good seeing him but at the same time I knew I had a purpose that he may not be too happy about. Still, on that subject I kept quiet. As he drove us towards the house where he and his wife were lodging, he noticed my concerns about his spiritual condition. He tried to say that all was well, but it wasn't. He decided to show me the 'church' that they all went to (the home owners were also involved in this cult) so we went there first (I may have this a little out of order here but the events did happen). On arriving we discovered that there was a service in session and I could hear what sounded like chanting, yes, repetitive chanting going on. As we walked down this well-carpeted wide hallway Lance took me into the bookstore. There was no one around but he started looking through the books at the titles. There was the 'Lost years of Jesus' and a whole mixture of what to me seemed more like New Age and Buddhist works. Gee, all kinds of books, but no Bibles. I said to Lance,
"Where are the Bibles?"
He looked, scanning the shelves to point them out to me and… he never found any. Nope, this place was evil to its core and somehow it managed to attract and entice intellectual types especially, I later observed. 'Church of the Elizabeth Clare (False) Prophet' it was called (my word addition in parenthesis). Seems like they believed that Jesus was just one of twelve Christ's and each would take their turn as the head of the order. Interesting concept… but a lie.

Lance then walked me further down the hallway past a few offices. I noticed that the door was open at one of these rooms and as I slowly walked by I looked in. There was a man behind his desk and when he saw me it looked to me like he was scared, like really scared. I just looked at him and walked on. As the chanting got louder, Lance followed by myself entered into the back of the 'sanctuary'. First I saw a statue at the back wall of Buddha. Then, I noticed that the room was quite full of people but they had all stopped with many looking straight at me. Not at Lance, at me, like I had two heads on my shoulders or something. I said to Lance something like,

"Let's go. We don't need to be here." Whereupon we turned and left the building.

Before arriving at his lodgings Lance pulled out some pictures of his daughter to show me, that is his wife's teenage daughter. By accident he pulled out the wrong packet from his car glove compartment and gave it to me. I opened it up and there were photos that someone took of this girl together with another teenage girl, undressing and dressing each other in witches' clothes. When I showed them to Lance he got all embarrassed and took them back saying that he meant to give me the other packet. I think he was starting to get the message that things were not well here.

    Lance pulled up into the driveway of this well-kept, and fairly large home where Lance and his wife were lodging. The Lord told me just to take my Bible in so I did. Carrying it under my arm we both went in. The husband and wife owners were both there and had set the main dining table ready for a meal for us all to have together. Lance's wife was also there but I do not recall her daughter being present. His wife did not seem too pleased to see me for some reason. In fact, there was a really strong awkwardness overall in me being there though everyone was most polite.

    Shortly, we were all invited to come and sit at the table to dine. I ended up right next to Lance's wife but I cannot remember who was on the other side of me. I still had my Bible with me. I put it down and then for some unknown reason I asked,

"May I pray and bless the food?" or something to that nature.

The man nodded his head and said that I could. Then, and I so rarely do this even to this day, I said to all,

"Let's hold hands while we pray" as I extended my hands out either side of me.

And that was the trigger. Lances wife suddenly got all angry and said,

"I'm NOT going to hold *his* hand."

She gets up all mad and storms off down the stairs towards the basement where apparently her and Lance were living. Off goes Lance after her leaving me with the owners just silent and looking at each other. Next we hear shouting and items getting thrown around. More shouting, a little silence, then off it went again. Finally, after maybe about ten or fifteen minutes Lance appears to us with his belongings all packed up in a green army pack and wanting to get out of the house. I, as politely as possible, excused myself as I picked up my Bible and followed Lance to his car. Moments later we were driving to a friend's house of his.

And that is how the Lord rescued my good friend Lance out of deception and lies. He stayed at this friend's house for a while but my return flight was coming up within a couple of days I think, so I could not stay with him to help him further.

If I recall correctly (and if I have this out of order I am sorry but again the incident is true), at one time he took me to another very nice house and I ended up down in the basement talking to the wife as she did laundry. I was talking to her about Jesus, the real Jesus Christ. The next thing I knew, she was crying her heart out at what I said as I kept re-emphasizing her need to meet and stay with Him, not anything false.

(Please forgive me but I am going to add in here three other separate incidences that I know took place in the Minneapolis and the surrounding area. I know that it was summertime and the events are true. I just cannot remember how they came to pass, or even if it was on this same trip! But, anyway here they are):

At one time I was in a café and got together with a church pastor. I think that maybe Lance may have put me together with this man. Anyway, we got talking about Bible matters and I ended up being invited to a gathering of believers that were using a school for their services. The gathering was of genuine believers in Christ. The Lord started to give me many words of knowledge (one of the spiritual gifts that the Holy Spirit can give us as He so desires) and through these words I was able to pray and minister to some of the people. One person I remember in particular was this really sweet girl who must have been about eleven or twelve years old. She let me hug her and I held her head close to me and prayed for her brain to function correctly. Later I found out that this was most accurate so I do hope that the Lord did something for her. I attended a follow on service on a more passive basis where the leaders were most complimentary of what had happened a few nights before.

  I was staying at this pastor's house where they were most kind to me. He had two teenage sons and they took me turtle fishing on this river. That was a blast! Never done that before. Before I left them I was asked to meet a godly man who happened to also be an airline pilot of commercial aircraft. I met him together with his adult friend, another mature Christian brother. We went up to the living room area and sat and talked about the things of the Lord while sitting on nice comfortable couches around this glass coffee table. Then, we all suddenly came to the same realization that the Lord wanted us to wash each other's feet just like Jesus did to his disciples as an example for us to do for each other. So, the pilot went and got a bowl of warm water, a towel and we proceeded almost silently to wash each other's feet.

  Afterwards they wanted me to pray over them so they stood up by the coffee table and all I did was barely touch both of them and BAM! Both went crashing down to the floor with the pilot ending up in the couch and the other man lying chest up right over the glass coffee table. I was so shocked at what just happened that I just stood there and watched. I wondered if the man on the coffee table got hurt? But he, actually both of them were out of it, I mean totally knocked out. After about ten minutes they came around and, thankfully neither were hurt in any way. We all prayed and hugged and I was taken back to the pastor's house. I hope something in their lives brought them closer to Christ through that event.

One incident that I have to mention happened when the pastor took me to another church that he would sometimes attend himself as they were fervent in prayer he said. Well, no denying that as we entered about an hour before the service. This was an old church building, all whitewashed on the outside and had the typical wooden pews and carved wood décor on the inside. An old traditional church that holds a maximum of about two hundred people. There were only about a dozen or so people there when we went in but oh boy were they into their prayers. Shouting and wailing all over the place at times. I sat down quietly and sought the Lord wondering why on earth I was here. No answer.

As the service was about to start the church pews soon got filled. Most of the people were black folk and so was the choir. Wow, I thought, I am caught up in one of those lively dancing, shouting outrageous singing gospel churches! You know, like the ones you sometimes see on television. And I was too, to the fullness thereof! Doing my best to fit in I just could not get into it however hard I tried. Everyone swayed and danced in their pews together. I tell you what, black folk sure know how to move their bodies to the beat!

I was most curious to hear the message once the preacher came out. And what a shock that was when he turned up on stage. He was a long haired, hippy looking white man! And the really crazy thing was, was that he was acting just like a black preacher too! I am sure that in some places he would get himself jumped on for acting that way, thinking he was mocking black people, but he was fully accepted here. Oh well, okay!

The whole service was just outrageous, it really was, with the typical drum cadenzas and bass guitar strums after every point the preacher made. Finally, the preacher made an alter call for people to get saved then also for some other reason and I heard the Lord speak to me,
"Go up and get prayed for."
What! You have *got* to be kidding me Lord, but the Lord only repeated Himself. I did nothing, I really was having a hard time as I watched this preacher want everyone to fall on the ground in 'the power of the Holy Spirit' as he laid his hands on them. If they didn't, then he was for sure going to get them down there! I stayed glued to my pew seat watching, disobeying the Lord.

Then, oh yes then, he, the preacher decided that he wanted to lay his hands on everyone, yes everyone in the building. I was near the front and I looked back at the rear doors. There was no way I could make an

excuse and get out through this tightly packed mob. I was trapped so as one row at a time went up I was shunted forwards towards the crazy preacher. I could almost see the Lord grinning at me! Soon I found myself in this line and that white man who was acting all black was getting closer to me. I could see him forcing those that would not go down by bending their heads so far back they had to loose balance. Whatever! I thought to the Lord as the preacher came to me. Then, he looked at me rather than just laying his hands on me like he seemed to be doing to everyone else. He backed off for a moment as the Lord spoke to me,
"Listen to what he is about to say."
I went still and quiet. The preacher moved towards me in all sensitivity and, gently laying his hands on me said,
"The Lord is going to take you into dark and dangerous places."
He prayed a little more, I think in the Spirit over me then moved on. The Lord had once again spoken out to me through another person, even using this crazy preacher.

At another time, Lance wanted me to meet this lady. He was really insistent about it and she called around to where he was staying at the time (this was well after leaving his wife so I am sure happened at a different time). He had arranged for us to go to an Ethiopian restaurant in the city for lunch. It was supposed to be quite an experience eating there. This lady was dressed for business and she was quite pretty and intelligent it seemed but there was something stressing her I could tell. She had to go off to her job afterwards so we took two cars but Lance said that I should travel with her so she agreed. As she drove I found that I could hardly talk to her. While going into the older part of the city she started to talk that she was worried, but then just started to cry a little. I asked her to pull over so she did and Lance just pulled in behind us. Her boyfriend was an alcoholic and kept imposing himself on her and she felt all messed up inside she said. I knew what to do and I said that I would pray for her right now. I touched her gently on the arm as I cast out the devil from her. With my eyes wide open and her shaking almost violently in her seat, I saw this black image come out of her, pass through the windshield of her car and away. She breathed a big breath and then just like deflated her body. She was free.

After a moment and after I checked that she was okay, we continued on to the restaurant. We all went in and sat down at this place as she tried to come to grips with what had just happened. I have to tell you about this restaurant though. It was an amazing place to go to. Firstly, there were the very simple wooden chairs and tables set on a wooden floor. The servers were all Ethiopians from what I could tell. They came and covered the table with a big piece of brown paper and gave us a menu from which we selected various meat and vegetable dishes, all traditional from their country. The drink menu was too, and I chose this hot spicy tea. I noticed that there were no cutlery offered to us at all, not even when the drinks came. My drink was given to me in a clear tall glass. It was warm and just looked like diluted milk! Really, it did not look like it was going to taste very good at all. However, when I took a sip of it my whole expression just lit up. It was fabulous! The best tasting hot tea I have ever had, I can almost taste it now as I am writing this down.

The meal came next and I soon got to find out why there was no cutlery, and also no plates! First they placed this really large dough looking pancake in the middle of our table on the brown paper. It must have been well over two feet in diameter. Then they proceeded to use a ladle to plonk piles of what we had ordered on it. Mounds of food scattered around. They then gave each of us a pile of smaller versions of the dough type pancakes and left us smiling to enjoy our meal. The food was great as we would tear off a piece of our 'bread' and use it to pick up from one of the piles and eat. Fun too!

Lance's friend was a little quiet, which was understandable from what had just happened to her. She ate though and kindly, without telling us, went and paid for the whole meal and thanked me and said she had to leave to go to work. She still looked a little out of it. I have always tried to find an Ethiopian Restaurant wherever I travel from then onwards but not found one yet.

Like I said above, I am not sure exactly where in the correct sequence of events these stories fit in but at least I have mentioned them.

So back to England from Minneapolis I flew.

Trip to Nigeria and the Third Prophesy

I believe that it was in 1993 that the Lord showed me a vision of Africa when I was in my small office unit in Chester from where I ran the correspondence music course for children. The vision was quite simple and it came with an instruction. I saw Africa and to the center and south a little, just above where the land starts to narrow heading southwards, I saw a bright glow, white in color, and the Lord said,
"I am sending you there."
I got hold of a world map (I had no internet access in my office back then) and saw that the country was Nigeria and the glow was in the eastern part and inland a little way. I did get excited that the Lord would send me that far away, but I had no idea why, nor when. I started telling my Christian friends and got a mixed response. Questions like,

"Who are you going to stay with? Who is your support group? When are you going? Exactly what are you going to do there? Which church are you going to join up with?" all came at me and all I could reply was,
"I have no idea, but I know God is sending me there."
Well, days, weeks and months went by and nothing happened. Life just went on. I carried on running my little music business. I also started up a bible study group in the business complex where I was located, in Chester. The building was an old railway station that had been funded by the local government to be converted to small and medium size business units that could be rented at a very reasonable price.

I also continued teaching my violin students that I taught in their homes located in both the Chester and the Wirral (an area on the west side of the river Mersey where Liverpool is located). I was very strict with my students with regards to their discipline for practicing and it was most rare to skip lessons at all. However, one particular week, on my busiest teaching day, Friday, parents were calling me or leaving messages on the answering machine to cancel the Friday lesson for that week. It was most unusual and I had no idea what to make of it until I played another message shortly afterwards on the answering machine. My friend Jeff (in whose house I was now lodging after leaving big Johns house) had left me a message telling me that the Sunday afternoon fellowship that we had been attending in this mansion house in the North Wales countryside had arranged a special event this Friday evening and would I like to go? The Lord said,
"Go," so I did.
The Lord also told me to ask the speaker about Africa. I got a little excited!

Thinking that the speaker was probably from Africa, or maybe was a missionary to that country, I drove expectantly to the meeting that Friday evening. This was a small fellowship of some twenty people and most seemed to be there. I got a little surprised, however, when I saw the special guest, a small white Welsh man, so I was a little puzzled about asking him about Africa. Anyway the meeting was good and the presence of the Lord was clearly there and you could see that this man loved the Lord Jesus Christ much. Afterwards I went up to him and simply asked him if he knew anything about Africa. Immediately he said,
"Victor. You need to contact him. I do not have his number with me but here is my number and call me for it."
And that was that. Meeting over, I left.

For a few weeks I held on to that man's telephone number and did nothing. Then one day the Lord told me to call him. He answered the phone and said that he did not have Victor's address, but that there was a big church in Belfast, Northern Ireland, that Victor would often go to and minister. He gave me the name of the senior pastor there and the phone number. This was a very well-known church and had done much to help reconcile the Catholic and Protestant people which had caused so much division in the country's past. I called and the senior pastor answered. I explained who I was and what the Lord had told me to do and to go to Africa. He gave me Victor Onuibo's phone number and address to write to. And where did this Victor man live in Africa? Yes, Nigeria! Not only that, when I looked up his address on the map it was exactly at the same spot in eastern inland Nigeria that the Lord had shown me! The Anambra State I think it was called near Enugu. I got excited about the trip even though I still had no other details about it. At some time after that the Lord told me that the purpose of the trip was for this man to lay his hands on me and pray and impart something spiritual into me. I was not quite sure at that time what that all meant.

Now, I had also at this time been instructed by the Lord to go on my third trip to America (previous chapter) and this time I was to fly in to Orlando, back from Minneapolis/St. Paul some two months later. Oh, and to take no money! I didn't have any money anyway!

Being excited about this third trip to the US, I was busy preparing for it when the Lord reminded me about Africa and that I needed to go up to my bedroom, seek His face, and write a letter to this Victor man. I did, and I wrote a two or three-page letter to him telling him what the Lord had told me. I mailed the letter and carried on preparing for my US trip.

So many exciting things happened on my trip to the US that time including meeting my beautiful wife to be, Prisci, that I totally forgot about Africa. Arriving home to Jeff's house from the airport I told him all that happened on that trip, how the Lord had presented my wife to me and how on the second day we met I proposed and she said yes! Then Jeff remembered and said to me that there was a letter waiting for me upstairs from Africa! I quickly went up to my room, and there it was. I remember just looking down at this envelope addressed to myself. The envelope was of embossed paper and had a red wax seal over the opening flap. It looked like something of royal origin. I carefully opened it and there was a short but clear letter to me from... the right honorable Arch Bishop Victor Onuibo! He was an Arch bishop! I had no idea. Who am I to go and be with such a man of God, I thought. He personally invited me to go over and minister in his churches and to get my visa and come over. He would arrange everything else for me. Here is a copy of his letter:

Victory Christian Mission Inc.

SECRETARIAT HEADQUARTERS (Victory Cathedral)
Nzekwe Close
Asata—Enugu
P.M.B. 1058
ENUGU ANAMBRA STATE

☎ 042-257686

VCM/HQE/23/

1ST JUNE, 1993

Robert Ewens,
13, Wirnal View,
Hawaroen,
Deeside,
CLWYD,
North Wales,
U.K.,
CH5 3ET

Dear Robert,

LETTER OF INVITATION:

Victory greetings in the most wonderful name of Jesus Christ of Nazareth.

I bless the name of Jesus who spoke to you and connected us together. Brother, I love you with the love of Jesus and I have a witness that you are Christ's candidate. I believe the Lord wants you in Nigeria.

With all my heart, I officially invite you to be our Guest in Nigeria this August. I will take care of all your immigration responsibilities while you are here in Nigeria. I have made adequate arrangements for your accommodation and feedings while you are in Nigeria.

Enugu is about 45minutes from Lagos Airport and it costs below £40 (forty pounds) to buy your ticket from Lagos to Enugu. As soon as you come into Lagos, my staff will welcome you and put you in the next Plane to Enugu. And we will be in Enugu Airport to pick you up.

Nigerian Airways, KLM and British Airways are one of the airlines that do Nigeria with other airlines. See any good travelling agent for good offer.

Nigeria is in the tropical climate. Experience good amount of rainfall and sun shine. Come with light dresses and raincoat.

Write me as soon as you settled the date of your coming and airline, so that we can be there to welcome you. You can telephone my office Monday thru Friday by 9.00a.m. to 3.00p.m.

We love you and it is my prayers that God will keep on blessing you. It is my prayers also that God will keep on supplying all your needs by His riches in glory in Christ Jesus.

Remain blessed.

Rev. Victor C. Onuigbo

I needed a visa to go to Nigeria, so I completed the necessary forms and sent my payment along with my UK passport and mailed them to the Nigerian Embassy in London. Weeks went by, months went by and I was getting a little anxious as I had heard nothing from that embassy. I was temporarily working at a lumber yard and the Christian owner, Phil gave me permission to use his work phone to call Nigeria when I wanted to. This was quite a deal as the cost to Nigeria from the UK is expensive. I tried calling the Arch Bishop so many times, maybe twenty or thirty times over the next couple of weeks. I soon discovered that the Nigerian telecommunications system was somewhat antiquated. I had to call the capital, Lagos, and the operator there would then manually connect me to the operator in Enugu (I think that's right) and then that operator would connect me to the church, to the number I wanted. This process kept breaking down. Sometimes Lagos never answered, sometimes the inland operator never answered. Sometimes there was no answer at the church when I did get through! Other times the operators seemed to just hang up on me.

Then, finally in the middle of one day when I was at the lumber yard, the Lord told me to call. I went straight away and did so. I dialed the number and expected to get the operator in Lagos first but nothing at all. Then the phone rang and after a couple of rings a man's deep voice answered. It was the Arch Bishop himself! Somehow I had totally bypassed both operators and the Arch Bishop was right by his phone! I explained to him the delay in the passport. He said that they had had revival meetings in August and had hoped that I would be there for that event. Anyway he understood the delay with the Nigerian Embassy and he said that he was going to London and would go into the Embassy and get my visa mailed to me quickly. And that is exactly what he did! Within two weeks I had my approved visa. While still in the middle of the phone conversation with this man of God, I paused and asked him a most peculiar question,
"Arch Bishop, did you die?"
Not quite believing what I just asked him, there was silence between us on the phone for a few seconds. Then I heard this deep chuckling on the other end.
"Yes" he said and continued,
"I was dead for about two hours in hospital and Jesus asked me if I would return to serve him."(These are not the exact words but amount to the same).
I felt most privileged that I was going to be with this man for a few weeks. By now it was October time and I sought the Lord on when to go.
"As soon as I can." was my answer.
Telling my close friends in Christ I got myself organized. Now, I had no money for the flight but the Lord impressed on me to go to the fellowship

that I was attending on Sunday afternoons before I went on my third US trip. I called them and spoke to the wife who invited me up to visit. Jeff, my Christian brother in the house I lodged told me of some bad news though. The fellowship had disbanded. The wife apparently had started to have an affair with one of the regular attendees, some detective, and it had come out into the open and everything fell apart from there. I was sad at the news. Still, I went up, met the lady and told her of my trip to Nigeria upon which she opened up the fellowship check book and wrote me a check, a blank check for me to fill in to cover the round trip flight! Praise the Lord! I blessed her for her kindness.

Now prior to this visit to the fellowship I had contacted my usual travel agent in Manchester who had the delight of putting up with my travel antics. This call was no exception. I told him that God was sending me to Nigeria as soon as possible, within a week or so please, and I needed the cheapest flight possible. He laughed once more at me and reminded me, yet again, that to get the cheap flights abroad I needed to book at least six weeks in advance. Once again I insisted that he looked for a cheap seat so off he went into his database and came back laughing as he found one seat for me on Air France for a good cheap price! I would change at Charles Da Gaul international airport in Paris, France, then fly over the Sahara Desert to Lagos. I left within two weeks.

I was excited and soon there I was flying Air France towards the Sahara Desert. Now the Lord for the first time had told me to take my violin so I had that as hand luggage at all times, knowing how rough checked in bags are handled, my violin would otherwise probably arrive in pieces! It was too large really to be accepted as hand luggage but the flight attendants understood so they found a special place for it near first class to keep it safe. The air hostess then came back to me and said that there was also a spare seat up in first class and she offered it to me! My first time flying first class and it was definitely a lot more comfortable.

I had no idea at all what to expect as I landed at Lagos airport, Nigeria. The Lord had specifically told me to take no money but I disobeyed (again!) thinking that I could be a blessing to someone at some time, so I had a between two and three hundred dollars cash in my wallet (I was told that US currency was the best to take). I had got ready so quickly that I did not even know what the weather was like! It was hot and humid I was soon to discover and the start of the rainy season. Now the Arch Bishop had said that he had arranged for me to be met by his local church in Lagos and he had given me the name of that church. They were to put me up for the night I think and then take me to the local airport and see me off on a plane to Enugu where the Arch Bishop would have pastors waiting for me.

The first thing that I noticed in Lagos airport as I was going through departure, was that I seemed to be the only white man around! As it was hot I went and bought a bottle of coke (it's all in bottles there, not cans). They charged me a lot just for that one drink and I got the idea that they charge as much as they think that they can get away with. I found out that there had been riots outside everywhere as gasoline had gone up to five point something cents a liter! Wish we had it so cheap in Europe! I was also told that you cannot trust the police, they are all corrupt. Interesting country the Lord has brought me to I thought! I got up and left with my one suitcase and my violin to go through the final security check.

    I could see lots of people, all black of course, waiting just past the security check point and one of the uniformed officers asked me if I had someone to pick me up. I said yes, that a local church was going to do so. So I was allowed to pass through. I was facing a whole crowd of people who all seemed to be speaking to me at the same time. The whole church is here I thought to meet me! Then, the security officer again came to me and asked if the church was here for me. I think that he was heard by the crowd as they started to say that they were from the church. Now, apparently there was a yellow line across the floor and these people were not allowed to pass it, but that did not seem to stop them this time and within seconds they rushed forward. The security officer pulled me back as other officers ran past me, truncheons in hand and started beating the people back. Once safely behind security again a lady officer explained that those people were not from the church at all but were touting taxi drivers that could not be trusted. They were more likely to take me into the desert, beat me or worse and rob me! Okay! Not a good idea!

    She asked me which church was supposed to meet me and after I named it she said that she went to that same church and that she would clock off early from her shift and personally take me there. She also told me what was going on in the country and that there was much chaos at present. Nigeria I discovered is not a poor country at all but the Muslim controlled government is not investing funds back into the country even to build a good infrastructure, but is using the finances for their own religious causes. Basically, you can trust no one but she seemed honest to me. We drove in her car a short distance to a church building of some kind. She took me to the pastor who was most apologetic and said that he was not expecting me at all. He had received a voice message on their answering machine from the Arch Bishop but he could not understand it as it was too broken up. He played me the message and it was so. He invited me to the evening service and then he said that they would have to put me up in a hotel for the night and then pick me up the next day to fly me to the Arch Bishop (I found out once I had returned from this country that Nigeria and in particular the city of Lagos had been listed internationally as No-Go places for all foreigners to travel to!).

    The service was loud with everyone dancing it seemed all the time to this weird three-two beat music that I just could not seem to grasp. Then they took me a short distance to the hotel, the Holiday Inn! Yes, something familiar! Well, not quite. More like a good motel in the US! Still I was most grateful. They paid a cash deposit on my room and I went up to rest after being told by the church strictly NOT to go out of the hotel as it was not safe to do so. I was most thankful that the room had an air conditioner. It was so humid!

After a short while, little before it got dusk, the Lord told me to, "Go take a walk."
"But I have been told not to do so Lord." I said.
His reply?
"Go for a walk." So I did.
I went up the hill, down a few streets and found myself heading the way back to the church that I had been to. At that point the Lord told me to just turn around and go back to the hotel. I did so and nothing happened and I was at a loss why I even needed to do all that. I had the evening meal and went up to my room and went to sleep.

In the morning I went down for breakfast. There seemed to be very few people staying at this hotel and at breakfast there seemed to be more staff than guests! I sat close to a table where this man was telling a story of how he was a salesman and had just been robbed of all his money and most of his belongings. I listened without making it obvious. My heart went out to this man and I got up and went to him saying that I heard what had happened to him and I hoped that this would help as I gave him I think $80 cash. He was overwhelmed (I later discovered that $80 back then was like over six months' salary!). I felt good that I could help and that I had money to do so. I went back upstairs and rested and waited for the church to come which was supposed to happen at noon.

At almost exactly noon I got a call from the hotel operator saying that my ride was there for me. I had already packed my stuff up so I took it all down to the reception area where I found a couple, no three smartly dressed young men who said to me that they were from the church to take me to the airport. Now for some reason unknown to me right then I decided to ask one of the men which church they were from. He answered correctly but I wondered just for an instant why I even asked that question. Anyway, I checked out of the hotel and gave one of the men from the church their deposit back. They helped me carry my bags and put them all in the boot (trunk) as I got into the front passenger side of this Mercedes. I noticed that there was also another car, a smaller blue car with us, following on behind with I think four men in it. Our driver of the Mercedes said that we were going to stop off at the church first, and this is where it all started to happen…

We were not travelling towards the church at all. I knew this from the walk I did the evening before. Now they had been talking to me about the corruption especially the police and that it was better while I was in the

car for them to take care of my papers and also they asked me if I had brought any foreign currency in, rather than exchanging it at the airport. I said I had a little and they said that I must have a completed green form which you get from the airport to give you permission to bring it in. Did I have the green form? No I did not. So basically they had my luggage in the trunk together with my unique violin and they had my passport and money in the back seat with them. Then fear came over me as a realized more and more that not only were we not heading towards the church but that these people were not from the church at all! Then the Holy Spirit comforted me with these words,
"And no harm shall befall you," which is what Jesus said to His disciples when he sent them out.
I got peace inside of me and asked them a couple of questions about the Arch Bishop that they, I felt, should know the answers to. And they fumbled and lied, and straight away after that as we just turned into some small residential area, the Mercedes radiator blew! I mean it blew, steam was gushing out and the men jumped out and quickly lifted the hood to try fix it I guess. The men in the car behind us all got out and I also got out, everything all happening so quickly. I remember demanding my passport, my wallet, my luggage and violin back. A yellow taxi cab came around the corner and one of the men (not sure why) stopped it and I got in and told the driver to take me to the hotel. And I was out of there. Ten minutes later I was back in the hotel using their phone many times to call the church who apparently never turned up for me. When I finally got through to the pastor he was most shocked and said that there was a delay and he had called the hotel only to find that I had already gone. He asked me if the car was a Mercedes with a cracked windshield and I confirmed that it was whereupon he exclaimed that I was very lucky to get away (I found out later that this syndicate group take and rob people and sometimes the people are never found). Delightful! The pastor told me to stay put until he personally arrived.

    Twenty minutes later the pastor, with two of his men, turned up and we safely made our way to the local airport where I was to fly inland to the Arch Bishop's church. The pastor insisted that I take the money he wanted to give me so I did. I tell you what, reader, God sure knows how to get you out of your comfort zone! However, the truth was, is that God did tell me NOT to take any money and I disobeyed Him. It was His mercy upon me that He saved me, out of what could have been the end of my days here on earth. I repented to the Lord for my disobedience.

    I still do not know to this day exactly how all that came to pass. Were the hotel staff involved? Was the local church involved? Were those waiters and waitresses at the breakfast a part of it as they saw I had money when I gave it to the man that was robbed? Was it all a set up and the robbed man was in on it too? What do you think? I guess one day I will know the truth on that. The moral of the story? Obey God. If He says take no money then TAKE NO MONEY, ROB! The money was the only thing missing once I got everything back.

Well, at arriving at the local airport, if that is what you can call it, we unload and walked into one large room where luggage was thrown to the side for anyone to pick up it seemed once it had been checked into a flight, and people were just everywhere. One of the men with the pastor went to buy my ticket and I saw him haggling over it. Finally it all seemed to be done and they wanted to take my violin and dump it on that pile of luggage. Sorry, isn't going to happen, my friends, so they gave up in the end reassuring me that my suitcase would be on the same flight as myself.

After waiting around for only a few minutes I had to say my goodbyes and thanked them all for their help as I was shuffled along with a line of other locals out into the open area outside near the runway. Err, where is the lounge or the boarding waiting area? There was none. Six feet tall and white skinned, I stuck out amongst the much shorter black locals for sure. We were asked to line up like we were going to do a military drill of some kind, then about twenty or so of us were marched right out on to the black tarmac runway that was so hot I am sure I was going to start to boil! Gee, great fun being a sent one by God!

We headed to one of the light blue colored Nigerian Airline jet planes that was being refueled. We were lined up a short distance from the mobile steps that airport staff had rolled into place so we could get up into the plane. Then, all of a sudden there was a big BANG! as a huge fireball exploded out the back of one of the engines of our plane! Everyone I think jumped back and there were some screams to go along with it. But the airport men just kept on fueling up as if nothing had happened so I guess all was okay. One worker, covering up his badge that I caught read 'cleaner' on it pulled me aside and placed me under the shadow of the airplane wing to wait out of the sun. Although I really didn't like the idea of being specially treated, the Lord impressed me to let it be, so I did.

Finally, the doors of the plane opened and we were asked to board but this man who was 'looking after me' insisted on moving me to the very front of the line. No one seemed to complain for some reason. I said thank you to the man, turned and started to go up the stairs when the man called to me and put his hand out to me. I turned around to him and the whole line of people waiting to get on the plane. You have to picture this in your mind. Only white man there, tall and standing on about step number five looking down at the airport cleaner who wants…I had a puzzled look on my face I guess because a few of the people said to me that he wants money. I do not know why this came into my head to do this but I stood there with both my hands up (my violin has a shoulder strap which is how I carry it). In my left hand was some of the money that the pastor of the

church had given me at the hotel. I raised up my left hand with the cash and my empty right hand whereupon I said out aloud for all to hear,
"What do you want, the money or a blessing from God?"
I could hardly believe what I was doing and what I had just said! Surely, all these people just want to get on the plane out of the heat and get going. But to my surprise they all started joining in. Some shouted out,
"Take the money!" while others shouted,
"No, take the blessing!"
This went on for a couple of minutes and I looked down at the worker and he took the money. I shrugged my shoulders and we all boarded.

Finally arriving at the Enugu airport (I think that is what it is called) two pastors found me from the Arch Bishop's church. They had been waiting there two days for me would you believe. Oddly, people including some airport staff would come up to me and ask me to lay my hands on them and pray for them. I did of course but wondered why they asked.

Travelling to the Arch Bishop's house involved passing through run down regions and one could tell that most people had very little in the way of belongings, totally opposite to Europe and America. We live like kings and queens compared to most of these folk. The Arch Bishop's house was also a bit of a surprise. It was walled in with a tall, maybe nine foot stone wall that had a lot of broken glass fixed at the top. Two large thick solid iron gates opened to let us in. The house however was quite moderate, somewhat luxurious in size compared to the locals, but nothing compared to our usual standards. The courtyard was compact and there was nothing fancy inside or outside about the house, just practical. The Arch Bishop's wife greeted me and I was shown my guest room and bathroom. She explained that her husband was away, actually ministering in Scotland at the time but he would be back in a few days. She was going to take me out to eat at a restaurant where the food was more European she said.

We got to the restaurant and after ordering she hit me with the news,
"You are taking the service in our main church on Sunday."
Then she politely went back to eating her meal. Yeek! I am?! Err, well if you say so. I had absolutely no idea what I was going to do and my stomach started to turn upside down at the thought of me standing in front of all these people and have nothing to say or do.

When I got back to my room to unpack I discovered that all my stuff had already been very neatly unpacked and put away. I needed a bath from my long sweaty journey and a young man who I gathered was a helper of some kind to the family explained that it was common for the water to go off here and that at present it was off. Then, when it is on it can come out muddy. Can't imagine us at home handling that very well! But it was normal for these folk. I found out later that most houses in the area got their water supply from the local creek and they carried it up to their homes on their heads. Yes, women carrying a five gallon container on their heads! No wonder they were short in height. So, anyway, the helper disappeared and came back and placed a bucket in the bath tub and then… well he never came back. I looked in the gallon bucket that was about three quarters full of water. I had to wash my whole body, clean my teeth go to the bathroom and flush the toilet all with this water. Making sure I got it in the right order I just managed the task. I was for sure ready for a good night's sleep.

    The next day Mrs. Onuibo showed me around the house and introduced her children to me. They were older teenagers if I recall correctly. They had a basement in the house but at the top of the stairs that lead down to it was a heavy duty solid iron door. I asked about this and the protective wall around the house. She explained that they live in a primarily Muslim area and also right on the edge of the savannah desert. Raids on Christians were not uncommon. She also told me that I was never to go into the savannah desert. Different tribes were out there and anything could happen.

    Interestingly I did not pack any shorts at all and I remember the Lord discouraging me from doing this but with no understanding. It was not until a few days into this trip when I was travelling around with the Arch Bishop that I found out that for a man to wear shorts means that he is a prostitute! Good reason not to bring them!

    It was Saturday, I was scheduled to take the main service on Sunday morning, and I still had no idea what to do or say. In this situation I find only one solution, fast and pray. So I did so I think for all of Saturday through until after the service on Sunday. The Lord started to show me what to say and do. In fact throughout the day and into the night He had me go through the entire service message over and over again, even out aloud. I was like an actor having to learn his lines and role through repetition. By the time Sunday morning arrived I was at peace yet a little nervous. We drove to the church, a large building by Nigerian standards and most of it comprised of the main auditorium. I was introduced to other staff members including pastors and teachers. I also met a Scottish man who was well on in age and his slightly younger wife. I was surprised to find out that they helped run a Rhema Bible College right there on the campus. I also found out that they had a connection to the Victory Christian Center in Tulsa, Oklahoma, where the now late pastor Billy Joe Daughtery was the senior pastor, under whose ministry I was later to be a part of for a few years as a member of the praise and worship group! I even got to meet the Scotsman's wife there in Tulsa a year or two later (her husband had gone to be with the Lord by then). It's a small world!

I was taken up on to the stage with these people and given a seat with them that faced the congregation (I hate that set up as it is like you are being exalted over them). They worshiped much and praised the Lord. I still could not get that funky three-two beat music. As for me the Lord did not instruct me to play the violin so I did not even have it there with me. The place was packed out, probably about two to three thousand people in all, not that I was counting. All the old wooden pews were full, so were the extra seats in front and back, the balcony was full and people had to stand at the back packed in like sardines! I found out later (thankfully, not before as I would have gotten really nervous!) that the church had been told that this great man of God from the USA was coming which is why it was so packed out. If only they knew, it was just little me from England with no great in my name at all!

It was my time to share and so, as per instructed by the Lord, I began acting out what He had had me rehearse all the previous day. I was given a cordless microphone and I had a pastor shadow me to translate into their local tongue. As it happened, most of the people I found out later fully understood English.

At one time in the service I took their very large Bible off the podium and jumped on it in demonstration of standing on the Word of God. People gasped as I did so. I talked about the devil's schemes and how to stand against them. I realized that every time I talked the people were very still and quiet, even more so when I was reading from the Bible. They had great respect for the Word of God.

Then, at one point the Lord had me go down one of the isles and look to my left and point and cast out the spirit of witchcraft. Then I found myself saying all kinds of Words and prayers, I was on fire in the Holy Ghost. I was not myself at all, the Holy Spirit had taken over me. Back up at the front I gave an alter call and hundreds of people came and crowded the front area. The additional chairs had to be pushed aside or removed and I looked down and said inside of me,
"Lord, what do I do now with all these people!"
The Lord instructed me to go down and pray for one at a time at first and lay my hands on their feet blessing them. That's how it started anyway because the presence of the Lord came in power and some people cried, others praised God, others kept backing away from me until some of them just fell over. With one or two people the Lord had me spend much longer time with, one I remember praying for him as he continually backed off unintentionally I think. I prayed for him through rows of people! Again, with one or two I saw in the spirit objects like spears and such sticking in them so I would reach in and pull them out in the name of the Lord.

How long that time lasted for I have no idea as it was as if time stood still. Afterwards, actually I cannot remember what happened afterwards! I do remember going back at some time to the Onuibo home and I do remember going to bed that evening thanking the Lord that He would see fit to use me that way. I was so grateful to God. That night I fell asleep just with a light sheet over me which was all you needed there anyway in that heat, though thankfully it got a little cooler at night.

In the middle of the night however, something awful happened to me. I was awakened out of a deep sleep as I could not breathe at all. There was something strangling me around my neck. As I awoke and became more alert I first thought that I had somehow got the sheet wrapped around me and I needed to unravel it but that was not so. In fact I could not move my body at all. I was paralyzed. I could not even talk or cry out to God! In a panic as I really needed to take a breath, I thought out as loudly as I could in my head,

"Jesus help me!!!" and my tongue was loosened.

I got Holy Ghost mad and rebuked the evil spirits and as I did so I saw a group of witches close by sending spells over to me. With much boldness I sent them back into the witches. I went back to sleep peacefully.

Arch Bishop Victor returned on the Wednesday if I recall correctly. He was a short, slightly rugged very dark black man. You could tell immediately that he was a godly man and was anointed. There was an atmosphere of authority about him that he did not manufacture himself, it was that given by our Lord Jesus Christ. He himself was most polite, caring and humble but also a very determined man of purpose. I was to travel around with him for the next two weeks and the Lord then told me very specifically to submit to him and support him and learn from him. So that is what I did my best to do.

It started with a most humbling of experiences for me. News had got around now that this man of God, actually an Englishman, was here so the very next time that I was to speak was at this healing revival meeting at the same main church that Friday evening. Actually I think that it was not me that gathered the crowds at all but the Arch Bishop as he had been away for a couple of weeks or so and had now returned. The event was supposed to start at 7pm if I recall correctly and I was kind of wondering about that as the Arch Bishop and I were out seeing some small church pastor and 7pm had come and gone. The Arch Bishop did not seem too bothered. I think we finally arrived at the church about 9pm. I soon learnt that being a few hours late is usual if not expected in this part of the world. I was to talk at some time but as of then I had nothing to say.

It all started with the Arch Bishop taking the microphone and pounding the praises of God and exclaiming His goodness, then, without hesitation calling on the deaf and mute there to come forward. About a dozen people lined up and one person that I remember specifically was an older man probably in his sixties and they said he was born deaf. Boom! The Arch Bishop covered the man's ears, commanded the deaf spirit out and the man was healed from that moment. Relatives testified that it was true that he had been deaf from birth. Other healings took place and some Words of Knowledge for healings of which one I also can recall. The Arch Bishop told of a lady with a tumor that was so big it was going to cost a lot to have it removed. He commanded it out.

Now, little known to us at the time (she came forward and testified a week later after going to the hospital to be checked out) but there was a girl, a teenager who loved to come to this church. Her mother, a very large lady, shall we say, hated for her to go so she would often beat her daughter when she asked or tried to go and she would lock up her daughter in her room. This had been going on for some time. The mother also had an extremely large tumor somewhere around her waist region. She did not have the money to have it operated on, there is no national health service at all in Nigeria and it would be over one year's pay for her to get the operation.

Ritually, she would feel her tumor before bedtime wishing it would go away. Well, I cannot remember exactly how this happened, but the daughter managed to persuade her mother to go to that healing meeting, probably suggesting that her tumor may get healed, I don't know. They went together but stayed right at the very back near the exit doors. After the meeting they left and as far as they knew nothing had happened but when the mother checked her huge lump just before going to bed, it was gone! She checked again and again then all you could hear in that house was this high pitch screaming! Her family came rushing around and they insisted she go to the hospital to be checked. The tumor had vanished, totally gone and that is why, crying and weeping and rejoicing and giving her life to Jesus, she testified holding her medical report in her hand the following week!

It was about 2am in the morning when I was introduced to speak. I had nothing to say but foolishly I took the podium and started to rabble on about hearing the voice of the Holy Spirit. After about fifteen minutes one of the pastors came up to me and passed me a note from the Arch Bishop. It simply read 'Please finish up now.' Feeling totally embarrassed, I quickly ended, went and sat back in my chair and at the first opportunity silently left the stage and ran to a quiet room, got on my knees and repented. I felt so bad. However, no one anywhere ever made a comment to me over it. They were all very graceful. After that, all the Lord wanted me to do was to go along with the Arch Bishop as he went to some of his one hundred plus satellite churches of varying sizes. A few occasions are worthy of mentioning here.

A couple of days after Arch Bishop Victor had returned he was away at his office doing work and I was in his house. In the afternoon, midafternoon the Lord told me to get up and go for a walk. I had my long pants on and a t-shirt even though it was so hot and humid. A man without at least a t-shirt on his upper half is considered indecent there and, as I have already mentioned, a man in shorts is a male prostitute. So off I went out of the Arch Bishop's compound, as it were. The first thing I came across just as I rounded the corner of the first 'street' which was really a dried mud track, were four vultures tearing into some dead animal. They are big birds! I never realized that they were so large. They were not afraid of me either and I ended up walking around them, those beaks looked mean.

I walked towards the small stream (creek) and saw ladies filling their containers with water. I also noticed that they used the same water to wash their clothes too. Surprisingly, when at the edge of the water I saw how clear and clean it looked. It even had fish swimming around in it quite happily. People looked at me but I never got into any conversation much with anyone. I walked some more and found myself heading towards the edge of the village development which was just a small way from my hosts' house. I was heading straight towards the Savannah Desert area.

It was then, while at the edge of the desert that I heard them. In the distance was the distinctive sound of drums beating out a consistent rhythm. I listened some more and then the Lord interrupted me,
"Go to them."
"Now hold on a minute, Lord," I argued,
"That is the one place that the Arch Bishop's wife said strictly for me NOT to go and you are telling me TO go?!" The Lord was silent.
I paused and still nothing. Now this land that is referred to as the desert is part sand, dust and dirt. There are many areas where these tall grasses that seem to grow over six feet in height are to be seen. There are shrub areas and even small clusters of trees dotted around the place, so I don't want you to get the impression that it is just sand dunes or something like that. The drums continued and they seem to be drawing me to them. Well, the Lord did say go… so off I went just as dusk was approaching.

The first sign of life that I noticed was when some shrubs started to rustle unnaturally. Looking closer I could see a few pairs of eyes staring at me. People were in the shrubs. I carried on, walking along this well-trodden track. It was starting to get dark, but dusk seems to linger a long time there, so I could still see where I was going. Obviously, there are no electrics and therefore no general lighting! The track took me straight towards a little incline through those tall grasses and into a small tree line. The beating of the drums got louder and louder. I saw no one at all.

Although I was being somewhat cautious I was at peace as the Lord had instructed me to go. Making my way through and out of the grasses the ground started to descend through the trees and then, there I was, standing in some kind of open play area or maybe a village open square of some kind. There were huts on the far side made from sticks and grasses and some people dressed in very simple but somewhat western style clothing mixed with I guess their traditional and very colorful cloths.

When they saw me, they seemed to disappear down one 'road' or should I say dust track. I followed in that same direction and found myself in the village on their market day. People had small tables out and were looking to sell very simple things like a piece of fish, some plates or rags etc. I walked down with other people keeping their distance from me and talking to each other. They all spoke in some native dialect of some kind so I had no idea what they were saying. Finally, I was led to go to one table where a young man was trying to sell pieces of fish.

"Hello, and how are you today?" He questioned me with a smile and in perfect English with a strong African twang to it.

I smiled back and got into this whole conversation with him after being introduced to his wife and family. I was so focused on what we were saying that I did not realize that almost the whole village had turned up there together with the village elders that help give advice and run the community. The young man gestured towards the huge group behind me and said that they wanted to hear about Jesus. I guess that somewhere along our conversation they got that I was a follower of Jesus Christ. The next thing I knew was that people gently got hold of my hands and arms and walked me together with them back to the open square area. Next, they placed a wooden chair on the ground in front of me and asked, no, told me to stand up on it. Then they gave me a bottle of chilled water (now how did they manage to get that here?!) as they all gathered around wanting to hear about Jesus.

Wow, I thought, if only people in Europe were so eager to hear about Jesus like these people were. At first I was at a loss as to what to say as I surely did not come prepared for this. The Lord was good to me though as I started to recount some of His parables and explain them. After about twenty minutes though I was done and I thanked them so much for being so nice to me (and not eating me ☺). I stayed with them a little longer wondering if there were any sick there that needed healing but nothing like that happened so I blessed them and left them and went back to the Arch Bishop's place in the dark.

Mrs. Onuibo was not happy that I had ventured out on my own into the savannah and as she was letting me know this her husband came to my rescue saying that if the Lord told him to go, then he had to obey, and look, he is fine!

On another day we were to travel a fair distance for a full gospel men's business meeting that the Arch Bishop had been invited to minister at. The roads were bad, I mean really poor quality, often just dirt. Heavy sudden rains had gouged deep ravines across the whole road in places so you had to follow everyone else and go into the farmers' fields then get back on the road again. Oh, yes, the Nigerian solution to traffic hold ups by the way is to simply create a new lane, even if there is no room for one!

It took us hours to get maybe forty miles and it was late afternoon when we got to the destination in a suburb of some town somewhere. It was an outside location on the second floor overlooking a street. About eighty people were there and there was a large long table waiting for all of the Arch Bishop's team to sit at, including myself. The Arch Bishop started to talk and minister, and the microphone stopped working. Didn't bother him, he just bellowed louder! The electrics went off, then on, then off again. Didn't bother him still. A brass band of some kind came down the street playing so loudly you could barely hear the Arch Bishop's booming voice and still he carried on not moved. Finally, the electrics were restored and the Arch Bishop told all of us at his table to go lay our hands on the people and pray for them. So we all did and the Spirit of Prophecy filled us all.

On another day we had to go somewhere else to minister at one of his churches. His Mercedes got stuck in some ruts (I encouraged him to get a four-wheel Land Rover!) and we could not get it out. We were in the middle of, nowhere really with just a few houses around us. But would you believe it, some people came out to help and they all seemed to know the Arch Bishop. We got the car unstuck and continued our journey.

We had to stay the night in a hotel but for some reason the three of us travelling together had to all share one room that had one king bed and one couch. I had to share one side of the king bed and the Arch Bishop had the other side! I found that amusing anyway!

The next day we went and arrived early to our location, so I went for a walk. That's where I learnt what 'white man' sounded like in the local dialect. "En-noocha" it sounds like, not sure on the correct spelling. I went to this building that had people milling around, some kind of shopping area I guess. I was just innocently looking at people when a voice spoke to me from up on the balcony,
"You should not be looking at the women," said a man smiling down at me.
I assured him that I had no sinful intent! He told me to come up and join them. They were about to have a church leadership meeting. I went around the back as instructed and was taken into a room with about a dozen people. They all looked to me, asked me to pray which I did and then the Lord gave me some words of wisdom (I hope!) to share with them. I was about to leave when the man who first invited me insisted that I came back to his home to meet his family and dine with them. I did not want to impose but he really insisted so I went off with him.

His home was likened to an apartment but was of a very basic clay wall construction. His wife was very pretty and cheerful and they had I think four children. After a little talking we all sat down to eat around a wooden table on wooden chairs over a bare floor. We were each given an empty bowl and a little side plate. No utensils at all. Hmm, I thought, this could be interesting. In walks the mother with this one bowl of.... of... white dough? Then she goes away and comes back with a larger bowl of some kind of soup broth with a big ladle. The father prayed and then the wife started to serve me some soup. Taking my bowl she was most careful to fish around for something that was in there. Finally, she found whatever it was and passed the bowl back to me. Everyone else was then served far more quickly. She explained that the white dough was pounded yam, a very common starch that they eat there. You take a piece and put it on your plate. Then you take a smaller piece just a little smaller than a golf ball, I guess, and make a short spoon shape out of it by sticking your thumb in the middle. Cool idea I guess and saves on washing spoons! You used your 'spoon' as long as it held up then you would eat it and make another.

Well, they all seemed to be waiting to start once I had started. I assumed that was being courteous. So I made my little spoon and scooped up some of the broth and drank it. It was good and I smiled and told them so. They smiled back but still would not start. I must have given them a blank look so the husband came to the rescue and said that they were waiting for me to eat the meat as they have given me the piece especially for me. Oh, my Lord, I just got it there and then. They were poor and this was probably the only piece of meat in the whole bowl. I was their special guest and they wanted to honor me with it. With tears in my eyes I fished around and found this chunk. On to my 'spoon' it went and... Ewe! it was awful! It was ninety percent gristle and slimy fat. That is the one concoction that makes me want to just throw up! But they were all looking intently at me. Forcing a smile, I did my best to 'chew' and position the food to slide it down my throat and somehow by the grace of God I managed it. With a big smile, I said it was great and thank you so very much! We all got eating.

The service was good and short and I played my violin a little and evangelized a little. Shortly afterwards we left to go home.

On the final day of my stay the Word of the Lord came true for me. In front of the whole church after much praise and worship including me playing a very, very different style of music on my violin than they were used to, the Arch Bishop called me up to him on the platform. He said, laughingly, that there were many very pretty Africans out there looking for a husband! Everyone laughed and I smiled for the Arch Bishop knew that I was engaged to be married to Priscilla in the spring. (Now the Lord had given me the date April 2nd 1994 as a wedding date while in Nigeria and, when I told the Arch Bishop he looked at his schedule and told me that he was scheduled to be in Tulsa, Oklahoma that very time to minister at the Victory Christian church!) The Arch Bishop continued, "But he has a woman waiting for him in America and I have a witness that this is the right woman for him," or something that amounted to that.

Upon which he came over to me and, laying his hands on me made a Spiritual impartation. All I can remember of what he said was that I had divine health. Somewhere else he had said to me that,
"The Lord was going to take me into dark and dangerous places," then he was encouraging to me about it.

So back to the local airport, then to Lagos, over the Sahara Desert, the Mediterranean Sea, and change planes at Paris as I did on the outgoing flight. Over the English Channel and over London in the night, to land at Manchester Airport the following day if I remember correctly. A ride home and I was tired! But God was so good to me.

It was good to be back, I still had my big dog Ben waiting for me. But Ben was starting to show signs of aging, weakening. He was a rescue dog that I had had since the days of my first marriage to Karen. His back legs had started to give out when I was living at 'big Johns' house before moving to Jeff's. Ben was the first creature I ever prayed healing for. His back legs were really bad so one day I laid my hands on him and asked the Lord to heal them and they fully recovered and I never saw him again with that issue!

Well, once I got back from my trip I decided that it was time to take Ben to the vets to be put down. That was a very emotional experience. Ben was a large dog, well over eighty pounds in his youth but probably about fifty now. When the vet had me place Ben on his table, he examined him all over, then he gave me a surprised look. He told me that he had no idea how this dog was still alive let alone able walk and run around. The vet said that all of his vital organs were shot. A bad heart, failing kidneys and liver etc. He did recommend putting Ben down now, and I agreed. I talked one last time to my faithful dog of many years. The vet prepared a large syringe full of whatever they use and cut the fir away from a small section on Bens front paw. I remember looking into Bens eyes as he fully trusted me. I stroked him but, as the vet just started to inject him, he went. Just like that and the vet was so surprised as he had barely started to inject. He checked that Ben was dead and he was but for some reason he injected all the rest of the chemical too. I thanked the vet, paid, and left crying but knowing I had done the right thing.

Fourth Trip to USA

This trip was not so much a missionary trip but more of a time to get to know my future wife a little more. Being as we had only met for but a few days in the summer of 1993 I thought that a return trip prior to us actually getting married would be prudent! So, after I returned from Nigeria, I booked to go to Tulsa Oklahoma. I also arranged to meet once more with Lance who was still up in Minneapolis-St. Paul area. My flight from Manchester, England was to land in Chicago on both the inbound and outbound flight, so I arranged a delay of a few days on my return flight home. That way, Lance said he would drive across state lines and pick me up and take me back so we could spend a short time together.

(Again, I have to apologize as I am fitting this Lance story in here and it may have happened at a different time. Nevertheless, again, it is all true.)

The weather was bad and snow storms had been hitting north eastern US when I flew out from the UK. Some flights were getting delayed but I was fortunate that mine was on time, so I landed in Chicago with plenty of time to get my connecting flight to Tulsa. It was December but Tulsa was still experiencing warm weather to some degree. Quite a dramatic change from Chicago that was having snow blizzards!

It was great to see Prisci again. I was so excited about us and we stayed attached to each other as much as possible during those three weeks. Prisci wanted us to get married, you know, do all the legal marriage stuff while I was there but I really felt a hold from the Lord not to do that for some reason so, even though she disagreed with me, we did not do that. We talked about the wedding arrangements a lot and we had a good time together, and some funny times too. Like one time we, together with the whole extended family, were eating at her mother and father's house. Prisci and I were arranging to meet up in the morning. I was staying at her sister Kathy's apartment just a short walk away. The apartment was superb, really well decorated, very clean and just really nice. Anyway we were just talking together at the meal table and I said that I would be over in the morning to get her up. This is what I said,
"I will come over at eight and knock you up."

Silence fell all of a sudden and Prisci's dad's glasses dropped part way down his nose and he just stared at me.
"What, what?" I said in my innocence as I continued,
"What did I say?"
"Did I say something wrong?"
Prisci tried to bail me out and make a joke by saying,
"Well, why wait until then!"
I found out that the term 'knocking you up' means in the US that you are getting someone pregnant! OOOps, my bad! I think they got it that I did not mean that!

So, by the end of the three weeks we did get to know each other more and I got to interact a little more with the lively three children who I just naturally took to. They were all unique, all so very different and all had their issues and challenges due to what life had dished out to them so far. For me though, it was a joy and no burden to marry into a readymade family. More challenging yes for sure, but something I was more than willing to do. I just had no idea how to do it! I really did not know the first thing about forming and building relationships. I would have to learn.

Happily, I returned to the UK after three weeks with Prisci and her whole family. All went well but there were some very different values that they had compared to English folk. Firstly, they have no concept of personal space at all. I mean, if they have something to say to you they have no qualms about being about three inches from your face if needed in order for them to feel that they are getting their point of view across.

A lot of the Hispanic life revolves around food and spicy, spicy it is too. And that is fine with me. I really liked most of their food with one exception and that is this thing called 'minoodle' (and I have no idea how you spell it), all I know is that it has tripe in it which is the cows, pigs or whatever's stomach lining! I tried it but not again, thank you. English food from that trip onwards all seemed very bland.

Another dynamic that I noticed was that the traditional Hispanic household, or should I say extended household has the senior mother more in charge than the man. I should have paid more attention to this earlier but that is always easier to say on reflection. Anyway, Prisci's mother seemed to run the show, not only between who was living in her home but also out to her children even though they were full grown and even if they were, or had been married. I got the feeling that I was going to be marrying the mother as well as Prisci to some extent. At least I did realize that I would need to be patient to allow the Lord to put things more in their Biblical order. One thing I did know for sure and that is a wife can make or break a husband. Having said that, the husband can also correct the wife so if he doesn't then he will bear the consequences of that.

The wedding date was set for April 2nd as instructed by the Lord as life went on in an atmosphere of excited anticipation for myself. Prisci and I had this amusing conversation regarding the date to be married. It was one of those,
"You go first."
"No, you go first."
"No, you go." So I did and then Prisci got her Bible and she had already written the first week in April for 1994 to get married. It was a confirmation for each of us.

Chapter Four – Moving and facing my heart. Twenty Years of Refining Starts

Moving to the US

My Wife Priscilla and the Wedding

So how did I get from North Wales to Oklahoma? Another amazing story that spans about three years in all. As you have read, I met my future wife Priscilla while on my third missionary trip to the US and also how the Lord went out of His way for both of us to confirm that He wanted us to be together if we so chose. Now the Lord had timed it perfectly, so that the date we married was either extremely close to, or was, to the day two years from the date of my salvation in April 1992.

    I think that I was far more excited about going to marry my wife than she was. Prisci is a real loving and compassionate Hispanic lady, very intelligent and full of Hispanic hot blood! She had rededicated her life to the Lord and followed His voice to move away from her home town, El Paso, Texas, and attend the Oral Roberts University in Tulsa Oklahoma.

    To briefly recap, Prisci had been in Tulsa for about four years I think before I met her. She had graduated successfully through the University with a double major, one in political science and the other in Spanish. She had worked hard, very hard indeed as a single mom bringing up four children and working two to three part time jobs and studying. That's no small achievement! So, by the time I arrived on the scene Prisci was very tired. She had asked the Lord to select her a husband as she still desired to be married and have a father for her children.

    Even on those first few days when Prisci and I first met, we would talk for ages about our lives. I do not recall anything that I did not tell her about myself, even all the ugly things that I had done sexually (although I did not go into graphic details). It was like we shared with each other what could take a couple a lifetime to share yet we did it in a few days before I was to leave to go to Minneapolis to see my friend Lance. If you haven't already done so, you can read the whole story in a previous chapter about my third trip to the US.

    So, Prisci and I had met on that third trip for about ten days before I departed to Minneapolis. Then, I visited her again after my Nigerian trip, this time for about three weeks at the end of 1993 where we had set the wedding date for April 2nd 1994 as instructed by the Lord to both of us (previous chapter). Prisci wanted us to technically get married before I left to go back to England while visiting her for those three weeks but the Lord put a check on me not to do that. That caused a little ruffling of her feathers but I was certain even though I had no idea why. Boy, was I to find out over the next two years!

After I left my new fiancé, flew back to the UK, and I think that it was on this particular flight that I flew to London and then up to Manchester before returning home. It was a connecting flight and I had just enough time from when we got off the plane at Heathrow to get to my second flight. We boarded shortly after I arrived in the waiting area.

The plane was much smaller of course than the transatlantic one and we soon all got packed in. I had a seat close to the front right side the exit so I could have more leg room for my long legs! I had booked this seat before I left on my journey. Next to me was a respectable businessman and he was very open to talking on the flight. So we chatted much about living in the UK, the cost of living, taxation etc. He then asked about me and he got most interested to find out that I was a missionary and he started asking questions about the Christian faith and as I answered him I noticed my voice getting somewhat louder. I sensed a silence around us and I am sure that there were many others listing in to our conversation.

We started to talk more about salvation and this time the Lord prompted me to ask this man if he was saved and upon saying that he wasn't I offered to pray with him to repent of his sins and to give his heart and life over to God through Jesus Christ. You could have heard a pin drop in that plane. He was a serious man and looked inside of himself for a few moments then said, yes, he wanted salvation for his soul. I prayed, then he prayed and then he just broke down and cried. This well-dressed businessman, an English man at that, openly crying and all those around baring witness of a man getting saved into the Kingdom of God. Praise the Lord!

Back home in Deeside, North Wales, at Jeff's house, I did what I needed to do with regards to my violin students tuition. I had to gradually get them all at a place where a new teacher could take over. They had all been doing extremely well, especially after the Lord had given me a profound revelation as to the purpose of music after I got saved. In fact, my students started to get the top places in their local schools orchestras and their exam results were very good indeed. This all happened as I taught them to play to the Lord and not to themselves, parents or anyone else.

I moved out of the room I was renting in Jeff's house as he was about to marry Lisa, a really nice, godly Christian policewoman. I was put in touch with this lady who was a travelling minister to missionaries and leaders in the church. She owned a small two-bedroom cottage in the Welsh countryside near a town called Mold. The cottage was on the outskirts of a small village called LLanarmon-yn-Ial (Pronounced "Klin-yarmon-yin-I-al") and the name of her house was Cherry Cottage. She was looking for someone to take care of her garden and lawn while she was away. So, I moved in there on that basis.

Cherry Cottage was hundreds of years old, had a white washed outside with those thick black wooden beams through it for structural support. Of solid stone construction, it was hard to keep warm but there was this large open fireplace in the living room that worked well as long as the wind was not in a certain direction. If it was blowing in that direction then you would be inhaling thick fire smoke at times!

I had one immediate neighbor, a small farm holding that was below my back garden (yard). Someone had built a single gate at the bottom of the back yard so that we could visit each other which I thought was a great idea. I got to know these people quite well. The husband worked in construction and left early and was often back late. They had three girls if I recall accurately. They were all in school and ranged from about ten to fifteen years of age. The wife, Janet, I think was her name, was a great caring person. Sometimes I would go down during the day and buy free range eggs from her. During these times we talked just a little not about anything in particular. Once, she did not have eggs so she said she would bring them up to me. The day that she did, the Lord got a hold of me so when I answered the door to her I could feel the love of God flowing out of me. I took and paid for the eggs and then I said to her,
"God is calling you Janet."
She just looked at me with big eyes and really took in those few simple words.

A day or too later I went down and talked with Janet about Jesus Christ and what she would need to do in order to get saved. Again, a few days later I revisited her, I think for more eggs. As I was invited into her large kitchen to sit down there was a light in the whole room, and it was coming out of her. She was radiant! Not a physical light as such, just a sense of lightness and brightness about her. Beaming with a smile she announced quietly to me that she had prayed. No kidding! I was so happy for her.

Although I was not paying rent to the cottage owner, she still had to pay the mortgage and one day she called me and asked for prayer to meet the payment for the next month. She was away in, in the US I think, in Houston. It was just a little while after that call when I was able to help her out.

Now, the cottage had a garage, not that I used it for my white Ford Orion car. Both doors swung open directly out onto the winding country lane. Rather dangerous to say the least, especially as we were on a blind corner! Anyway, she had this door stop that she used to pin back one of the doors to the road side, that is back to the hedge row. It was a marble looking figurine of a naked woman posing with her hands lifted outwards. One of the fingers was broken off and there was a little chip there too. For some reason I looked at it and wondered if it was worth anything. Switching it out for a common large rock I took the broken statue into the city of Chester to Sotheby's, the auctioneers. I left it with them for evaluation. A few days later I got a call from them saying that they should be able to sell it for about seven hundred and fifty pounds! I agreed and it did sell for about that price. I sent the money to the house owner who was made up that the Lord had answered her prayer!

Late March 1994 I travelled back to the US using the usual European green waiver card as it is referred to. Basically it avoids the need to get your passport stamped with a visa from the American embassy. You complete the green waiver card usually on the flight over. It allows a person to visit the US for up to 90 days as a visitor. However, by doing it this easier way you are also waving goodbye to your rights which basically means that the US authorities can do what they want with you according to their current laws.

Our wedding was a small affair and we all tried to keep the cost down. The venue was free, an Oral Roberts University wedding and function room of some kind. Free, because Prisci had graduated and worked there. Tables for about fifty people I guess were neatly laid out by Priscilla, her family and friends. I had met a couple there on a previous trip and the wife was gifted in worship on the piano, so I was going to play something on the violin along with her. There was also a friend of the family who was going to sing.

I gave a small talk about the gospel message and it included this small demonstration of the three corded rope that is hard to break. I had three lengths of cord and attached to one was a dollar bill that represented me working and providing, the second was a mug that represented Prisci the home maker and support, and the third was a cross, to show that it was the Lord who is in the midst of this marriage. I held up all three cords and platted them together to show that it was the Lord who binds us together and that it would be Him who would uphold His covenant between us. Whatever the Lord wanted us to do afterward, after this message resulted in a time of personal ministry involving praying for others. My best man was Drew, from the young couple that picked me up on the street corner and invited me to stay with them when I first got to Tulsa before I met Prisci. Here is a picture of us both from that wedding day:

The wedding, I thought, went well. I was overjoyed. I could not say the same for Prisci though. It looked like she had to be almost carried down the aisle! She smiled but was serious at the same time for she knew what was in the future for her to some degree.

One interesting point about the wedding service was that the Lord had me change one of the traditional marriage vows. Rather than declaring to each other, to the witnesses, and to God that we would stay married "through sickness and health till death us do part," I had it changed to "through all situations and circumstances, till death us do part." I was to find out twenty years to the day why this was changed.

As we did not have much money I had booked the wedding night in this simple hotel in Tulsa on a street called Admiral Place. Nothing exotic at all but it was a start. Someone had blessed us with a bottle of wine and we went to buy a Chinese takeout to eat in the hotel room. Prisci had purchased a white track suit, jogging pants, if you will, and a white tank top, otherwise known in the US as a muscle shirt for me to wear. I am not going to go into the events of that night but to say the Lord blessed our time together would be an understatement! We did pray before we did anything and committed ourselves to the Lord.

I had arranged for the honeymoon to be in Spain, via England. The plan was for us to fly to England together and spend a week or so at Cherry Cottage where we could also see my children from my first marriage, Charlotte and Jemma. Then, I had arranged to pick up someone on the way to the airport so that they could use the car and I did not need to pay high parking fees in order to leave it there.

We were going to fly to a part of Spain where Prisci's ancestry came from, an area called Catalonia which was on the south coast near Barcelona. After almost two weeks there we would go back to England for another week or so before I was to see Prisci off back to the US. I had things to wrap up here in the UK still before I could emigrate. We also had all that immigration paperwork to complete and process.

So, a very excited Rob and a tired yet mostly happy Prisci departed to the United Kingdom once more to land some eight hours later in Manchester. After passing through passport control and into the front of the airport I somehow messed up on transportation and I had us wait there for some hours which did not impress Prisci one little bit. Our approaches to finances and what we are willing to endure in order to save or stay in a budget were very different and we were to continually clash over this issue for some time to come. English people are most frugal and will scrimp and save in order to get something. For example, although Prisci is not the kind of person that just wants lavish things, she did want a really nice wedding ring and so I wanted to get all that I could afford. In order to do this I had to basically live off beans on toast and the like for many weeks, being really careful as to when I used my car in order to reduce spending on petrol (gas). Many things I had to happily change and it was all worthwhile. Prisci does not know until she reads this book (if she ever does) as to the joyful sacrifices I made that represents the ring on her finger. It took me months to get that money together but I did it by the grace of God and I do not regret one moment either. You see, when I would ever see it on her hand it always reminds me of how worth it she is for me to do things for her. I have always enjoyed doing things for her. It's like my love language to her. It would be that way for years to come too.

Eventually we got out of the airport and made it to Cherry Cottage. It was 1994, early April so the weather can still be a little chilly there, and more so for Prisci who being Hispanic I assumed was more used to hot climates. However, she seemed to do very well even though an old stone cottage can be cold even if it is warm outside as it takes weeks for the thick stonework to lose its winter coldness. I lit the fire a few times and I think we even slept by the fireplace once or twice… very romantic I thought.

Prisci was tired but she also had this great sense of humor. Hispanic humor usually revolves around some body part or other. It's true, it really does and Prisci was a great one for that. For example, even though this actually happened when we were in the US, the following is a perfect illustration. One day we were getting on so well and she just comes up to me and slaps me on the cheek, for no reason at all! I was stunned! Staring at her with a look to say "how dare you do that!" she stepped back and observed me for a moment then burst out into laughter! I had to join in eventually with her. She was such a darling. On another occasion, later when in Spain when I was driving around the mountains in a rental car with her she did something that nearly caused me to drive completely off the road! What a blast she was.

Prisci and I got to spend a few times with my children Charlotte and Jemma. I only can find one picture of that at present. Here it is when we were going off to an inside water park that was located right on the North Wales shore line:

That is Charlotte on the left with her eyes closed! She was about nine years old and Jemma, on the right would be about seven. And, of course, that is my darling wife, Prisci in the middle. She loved those two children from the first moment she met them.

After our week at Cherry Cottage we were to pack up our suitcase and prepare to leave fairly early the next day to pick up a man, a pastor of a small church by the name of Terry in a village that was on our way to the airport. Plans were good but Prisci and I were, after all, on our honeymoon, and staying up late had not fully packed and were both crashed, fast asleep as the sun rose the next morning. It was a telephone call that woke us up. Mr. Terry had been waiting for us for an hour on the street corner as arranged and had walked back to his house to call, wondering what was going on. I jumped up and immediately realized that we could be late for our flight! We both rushed to finish packing and within minutes we were on the road to pick up Mr. Terry (which I must say I was impressed with how fast Prisci got her stuff together and was in the car, quite amazing for an Hispanic!). After picking him up I had to make up some lost time.

We had to get all the way through these villages, through Chester and on to the motorway (Freeway) all the way to Manchester airport. I had to floor it a little on the old gas pedal. I was gentle on the country roads but when we hit the motorway I ignored the speed limits and hit over a hundred miles an hour. It was just at this high speed that I warned Terry, who was to drive the car back for us, that the brakes were a little faulty! You should have seen his face and how quickly he started praying!

Well, the good news was that we did arrive safely to the airport and, after saying a quick goodbye to Terry, we were rushed through the check in and moments later we were in the boarding line for the plane. Up we go and away we fly over the southern part of England, across the English Channel to France, then over the almost desert style part of central Spain to the built up touristic southern Mediterranean coastline to land at Barcelona. Before we even realized it we were on this shuttle bus that was taking us to our hotel for our sunny honeymoon in Priscilla's ancestral past.

We did have a great time there in Spain together. It was fun just being together, something that I have always been at peace with, I just love us being around each other. Whether she is mad at me or besotted with me and all lovey-dovey, I just love her presence right from the start to this present day.

Now I was the event coordinator for sure on this part of our honeymoon and I think Prisci was really more interested with just getting some rest.. Unfortunately for her, my zeal and excitement at us being together didn't come along with much wisdom and understanding on my part, but she was gracious enough to go along with my plans for us.

Man, was Prisci so, SO beautiful. I remember her one day after taking a shower, how she came out all wrapped up carrying a candle in her hands and just smiling at me, what a gorgeous being she was. I can see that moment right now.

I also remember us having a romantic evening meal at a local restaurant together. So peaceful, so surreal, when in the middle of chit chat she just came out and asked me,
"So, how are your colonies doing?"
We burst out into laughter together. She was referring to the English colonies around the world that were diminishing every year but it was just so funny how she put it.

We rented a side-by-side twin bicycle that had a canopy over the top of it to shade you from the hot sun. I had her pedal here, there and all over that part of the town we were in. Then we rented a tiny neon pink colored Fiat car and took off into the mountain regions to get out of the tourist areas and see Spain in its more natural setting. Twisting roads wound their way across acres of cacti plants, lime, orange, lemon and other fruit trees. We bought some kiwi fruit and Prisci showed me the art of how to eat one. And all over the place Prisci kept seeing women that looked just like her mother, a reminder of her Spanish descent.

One day we went to the beach. Now, it was still April time and that is still early in the year, the tourist season had not yet started so overall the town was fairly empty as was the beach. Still, it wasn't going to stop me going for a swim, even when the water was still cold! In I plunged showing off my manliness to Prisci. Off I swim leaving her sitting on the sand on a blanket reading a book. Out I go and when far enough out to think I am impressing her I turn and call her, waving to her. And, err, and she is paying absolutely no attention to me at all! Oh, well, I blew that one I guess as I swam back shivering and with my teeth chattering. Off to our favorite lunch place we went which was a small liver and onion bar style place run by a couple of English people. The food was really tasty and we loved it.

Prisci, I discovered also had the personality where it was not too hard to tick her off, to get her mad and upset and I was fumbling my way through this and all too often would tread on a sensitive area that got her going. Consequently, we also had times where she just wanted to be away from me to calm herself down. It was a sign of the firey dynamics that we were to experience throughout our lives together but back then I was the all-conquering Christian man that would be able to help this lovely woman overcome all, and help her to be this soft and gentle image of how I thought a Christian wife should be. Give me a break; what a dork I was. All she needed was to be loved, not changed. And I really did love her too and still do. Even though I had many issues buried away in my own heart, I truly loved her from the moment I saw her.

Prisci was so tired from all her life at Oral Roberts University, working multiple jobs and trying to be a good mom in Tulsa that she just often crashed out in the apartment. I would just spend time looking at her as she peacefully slept. Sometimes I would just sit by her and stroke her hair. I would wonder to myself, what kind of person have I married here? I really had no idea at all, we barely knew each other still. I knew one thing though for sure, It was not going to be dull marriage in the slightest!

What I have not mentioned to you, dear reader of this book, is that after my divorce from Karen in England in 1992, when the Lord brought back my desire to have a wife again, He asked me,
"What kind of a wife do you want?"
"Lord," I said "I want a hot, passionate, fun loving, very intelligent and gorgeous wife that I will never get bored with and will be a challenge for me," was my enthusiastic response.
I think the Lord had met my request in much abundance indeed! This was sure proven true over the next twenty years as you will get to find out.

Mr. Terry picked us up at Manchester airport once we had flown back from Spain. So back to Cherry Cottage we went for a few more days until Prisci had to fly back to the US. We travelled to see my parents in central England who loved Prisci. I had the most amazing thing said about her from my mum and dad (we say 'mum' not 'mom' in England). They came to me and said that Prisci was wonderful and that they both believed and hoped that this marriage would work, unlike the first marriage where they both quietly had doubts about it and were not surprised that it ended the way that it did. My parents never once let on that they thought and felt those things about my first marriage, but now that they had met Prisci it was a big thing for them to say so, being so impressed with my new wife.

We also went to the local pub in Llanarmon-yn-Ial. There was only one pub in that small village so all the locals would regularly turn up there. You should have seen some of their faces as Prisci walked in with me. They stared at her as discretely as they could, not only because she was new to the pub, but because she was pretty too! After a couple of times in the pub we just seemed to fit in.

Pubs in the UK are different to American bars. Pubs are a social meeting place for not only adults but whole families. Generally speaking there are two main sections, one is the bar area which is usually a small room located separately, often to the left or right side of the building as you walk in. This is for people over the age of eighteen and most of them are smoking rooms. Louder music is played here and maybe a game of darts or American pool too. Mostly for beer drinkers that might get a little lively at times!

On the other side of the pub would be the much larger area, the lounge as it is usually referred to. It is a strictly nonsmoking area and there is a bar too. The atmosphere is always friendly and whole families are allowed in this section. The only stipulation of law is that you have to be eighteen to drink alcohol but there are a range of nonalcoholic drinks available for children and minors. The seating is always cozy and you can find a nice little nook, maybe by the open fireplace and enjoy your drink and spend time together. Mind you Prisci raised a few eyebrows when I ordered the drink for her at the bar. She was with me as I ordered a Kahlua and cream. The bar man looked at me then at Prisci, then back at me with raised eyebrows. You could almost hear him thinking the question, "Is she pregnant or something?"

English, or Welsh folk for that matter, are not familiar with that drink combination. The bars don't even usually carry cream. This bar man ended up going upstairs to his home (often the pub owners live above the pub) and brought down some full milk for her. I remember Prisci laughing about it.

The final day arrived. Prisci was all packed and I remember silence as I loaded up the car. Neither of us wanted to part company, so as we headed towards the airport and parked up we just seemed to cling to each other. We even created a scene as I had to leave her as she went through security check. We just could not let go of each other. I know people were looking at us but I just didn't want to leave her nor her me. Eventually she went through as we blew kisses to each other. She doesn't know this but I turned and just cried. I cried and thanked the Lord for giving me such an amazing person and that He had given me such a love for her. That same love is what I carry for her to this day in spite of everything you are about to read that has transpired over the next twenty years.

And We Lasted Ten Weeks Together

With Prisci back in the United States and myself working to complete commitments in England it was all systems go for me to get back over there to my new family by July of that year, 1994. I had to complete some immigration paperwork at my end and Prisci had to sponsor me in to the US. Then the immigration department of the US embassy in London would contact me for a full medical examination and to have my official interview with them to be accepted into the country. Well, that was the plan anyway.

I had to see my violin students through to their end of school year exams which they would take around June time. I kept in touch with Prisci by phone which was really costly to do. I would send her money for her phone bill and mine got really costly so I had to cut it back a little. It seemed a long wait for that paperwork to be processed and I kept getting delays from Prisci over it. It seemed like she was holding back but I could not figure out why so I tried just to be patient with her.

It was approaching July and still no paperwork so I arranged to fly over on the green waiver form like I had done in the past. The trip went well and I brought two large, or maybe three large cases with me. Prisci came and picked me up in her brothers' large pickup truck and promptly ran straight over my toes while I waited for her to pull up to me outside the airport! She jumped out all apologetically, laughing at the same time of course! She looked great and I could tell that she had made up herself for me which made me feel special. Well, you can probably guess that we did not go straight to socialize with the family after being away from each other for so long!

However, in spite of our very strong physical attraction towards each other, I had been noticing that my zeal and intimacy with the Lord had started to wane for some reason. I started to really ask and seek the Lord, but I could not hear Him. Time and time again I did this but nothing. What was going on? I could not understand and what's more I realized that I had lost the fear of the Lord in me. It was like my heart had hardened but I didn't know what I had done for this to have happened. I knew His Word, the Bible and checked myself over and over again but I could not get any understanding nor answers at all.

The kids were being a handful too. It seemed to me that I was getting tested to see if I was really committed to them all, including Prisci. The pressure was on as I moved into their duplex. I was struggling from the start. Jeremy, the older of the two sons was a very active child, and he was into everything. I mean everything. He also had a great giving heart though, very forgiving and loving, and that part of him I wanted to see grow more as it was something very special that many young people and many older ones just do not have to that degree. Bianca was testing me to see if I was worthy to parent the boys I think. She was so used to doing that job, so it was hard for her to let go. Unfortunately, I messed up there too and I got demanding that all the kids learnt how to have a man back in the house as the head. Prisci, started to pull her hair out as arguments started to ensue between us. She was really trying to get through to me and I just was not getting it. I was clueless when it came to making and developing relationships. I had never been taught how to, so how could I know?!

Things got worse and arguments increased and I could not understand why all this was happening to us. Jeremy tried to leave home on his bicycle and we had to go bring him back. Jacob just loved that he had a dad but he was also into sneaky mischief and Bianca at times tried to act like she was my superior. Prisci, already overly stressed, finally broke and police were called in on one occasion and, well in the end I just had to leave the house. I had been living there but ten weeks! Prisci kept going on about me marrying her just to get a green card and that was a ridiculous charge to make, I was there because I loved them all. I was just lost, over my head and very stressed out myself.

So there I was walking down the road with one suitcase in hand in Tulsa, Oklahoma, just stunned and my heart aching. I got to a public phone and called Drew, the best man at my wedding. He came and picked me up and took me in to his house a few miles away. They had purchased a house for him and Jamie to live in. He was ticked off at what had happened, but restrained himself overall from saying too much about it. I had started a newspaper route which somehow I managed to get without having a social security card valid to work and no US driving license either.

I was allowed in the United States to drive for up to one year under my English driving license as long as it was current which mine was. So when I went to stay at Drew's house he kindly gave me use of one of his vehicles to continue doing the route so at least I could make some money. After the route each day I used to go to a local MacDonald's and give them my overs, my excess papers. After doing this a few times the manager came up to me and said that I could order for free any breakfast each time I came in. That was kind of them.

Drew was into a fairly new venture of his that consisted of buying, fixing and selling houses for a profit. 'Flipping' houses was the term used for this. I started to help him by doing the fixing and he would pay me for my work. I was most grateful but knew that this was to be a temporary situation. I was still in great emotional turmoil with regards to what had just happened with my wife, family, and myself.

Days and weeks went by but nothing seemed to improve with Prisci. I got notice that she would pay for my air ticket back to the UK (with some of the money I had been earning in the UK that should have been forwarded to myself). How charming a thought that was! Doesn't she know that I love her?

    Drew referred me to another man who needed some help in construction. This man, Mr. Wes, did not have much in the way of finances so he offered to pay me either at a low cash rate or twice as much in pizza vouchers! I switched between the two and soon had about $80 plus in pizza vouchers! I did not even like pizza too much. I used some for food and kept the rest on me just in case the need came along.

    Drew mentioned something about a fitness place called 'Balleys' that he went to and he took me there as a guest. While there the Lord told me to join. I thought that to be a rather crazy idea as firstly, I had no stable income and it was an expensive set up. Secondly, I also found out that not only was it not cheap, but you had to sign up for at least a year at a time. Still, if the Lord tells you, you better do it so I did and somehow got approved on the credit check that they did.

    I was really hurting over what had happened at the house with Prisci and the children. I would find myself just wondering around at times just feeling so empty inside and full of heart ache. I knew that the Lord was with me through this time but I just continually struggled to be at peace. Once I was just walking and a man called to me and we got talking and he invited me into a group of believers and they had me lay my hands on them and pray so I did and the power of the Lord filled that room and greatly affected us all.

    On another day I was hurting so bad that when I went into a Wendy's place to eat, something unusual happened. I sat down and had my Bible with me which I placed on my table. The place was packed as lunch time had just started. I had a table right in the middle of everyone where I had sat down at and was about to eat a salad that I had put together from the food bar. I couldn't eat, I was hurting inside so much so I opened my Bible and started reading instead. I sensed the presence of the Lord around me but thought no more about it except when the waitress, the lady who came around to clean the dirty tables etc. came towards me a few minutes later, yet she stayed about ten feet away from me. She got my attention so I looked up. She looked scared. Also, the whole eating area was empty, I mean completely empty! It was the middle of lunch time, what happened? She nervously asked me,
"What are you reading?"
I could not raise much of a smile due to the pain in my heart but I answered,
"The Bible, from the book of John."
And with that she started to back away from me. It was the most unusual behavior. I asked her,
"Where did everyone go?"

"I, I, I don't know." She said with a shaky voice,
"This has not happened before."
I just ate and then left.
I had left a message to get to Prisci that I wanted to see her and that I would wait for her in the Oral Roberts Prayer Tower gardens at a certain time. I got there early and waited and prayed, and waited and prayed. The set time came and went with no sign of her. I waited and prayed some more and still nothing. After about an hour and a half I cried and left, feeling broken and rejected. It was then, as I was walking my way back to Drew's house some miles away that the devil just did his very best to encourage me to just throw myself off the bridge into the Arkansas River and end all that pain and misery. As you can tell, I didn't follow that 'advice'.

I went to the Balleys Gym one day as instructed by the Lord. They had this huge hot tub that ran the full length of the swimming pool! It was really great as you could even swim in it. After taking a quick swim in the neighboring swimming pool I went into the hot tub. Then, the Lord spoke to me, as I was swimming in this giant Jacuzzi,
"Go to the end and rest on the side."
Well, I did that and pulled myself up on the side and as I did so another man came up to me from out of the tub and sat himself right beside me. He was a kind looking man maybe in his late forties or so. He had a warm smile and introduced himself as Rick. I could see by his eyes that he was a believer in Christ and in the first few sentences we exchanged together confirmed that for both of us. I did not pick up any dishonorable intentions at all and when he asked me where I was staying I told him, and I said that it was time for me to leave there so that the young married couple could continue their lives together. He then offered me a room in his house that was near Lewis and 11th street. We later exchanged numbers and within a few days I moved in with 'Mr. Rick' as he came to be known.

Mr. Rick was a kind man and loved the Lord. He lived in this small corner house with three very large dogs, a garden full of all kinds of shrubs and plants including a banana tree! Oh, and yes, he had this whole collection of canaries that he bred and took care of.

His house needed to be cleaned and organized to say the least and he didn't seem to mind me doing some of that work so I was glad to be able to help him out a little. He lived like a typical single man whose house had started to need attention inside and out so I did a little here and a little there so as not to embarrass him.

I stayed there a few months and by now my ninety-day green card waver had well expired, so now I was in the country illegally. I had hoped that Prisci would have been willing to reconcile but it seemed not. Eventually I had to come to terms with going back to England so I started to save up for the flight, but that was not going too well. I also called the US immigration department anonymously to find out my legal status. I asked them if I voluntarily left soon to go back to the UK would I still be allowed back into the US again. The officer said that yes, as long as I left on my own accord that would be fine. Having sorted that out, I booked a flight in the December of 1994 to return, heartbroken over my marriage that had barely even started. A wonderful Christian family in England paid for my flight back. I didn't know what was going on in Prisci's heart, but I was so in love with her that it really hurt bad.

    Now one day, just a few days before my return flight to England, I was in Mr. Ricks house on my own and I had started to play my violin to the Lord when the Lord spoke to me,
"Play along with the cassette tape you were given."
I knew exactly which tape the Lord was referring to. He was referring to the one that the lady on the lawn at Benny Hinns church in Orlando Florida had given to me by violinist Maurice Xxxxx. I went and got it and played the music on Ricks machine. The Lord then said,
"Play along with it."
Well I tried a few times and did start to get into some of it, but it was going to take time. As I worked at doing this the Lord stopped me again saying,
"Get the big phone book and call Maurice Xxxxx."
I stopped playing and put my violin down. Now, I had already been told by someone that this Messianic Jewish man lived in Tulsa (a Messianic Jew is a Jew by genealogy who has accepted Jesus, Yeshua, as the messiah). I thought that to be quite a coincidence from back when I was given that tape in Florida. So, I went and picked up the large Tulsa phone book that was one of a few that were piled under the coffee table. I placed it on the coffee table top and as I did so it opened all in one motion. I looked down at the page and there it was right where I was looking to the top left side of the left page. I read 'Maurice and ??? (cannot recall her name) Xxxxx with the address and phone number. Wow! Could this be the right number and address? All I could do was call it, so I did and a lady answered the phone. I explained what had just happened to me starting with playing along with the tape and then asked the lady if this was the house for Maurice Xxxxx the violinist?
"It is" came the cheerful voice as she introduced herself as his wife.
I said,
"I think that I need to see Maurice if that was possible?"
"Sounds like you should." She replied as I confirmed the address with her. Then she continued,
"However, he is in Israel right now and doesn't get back until next Tuesday."

Now my flight back to the UK, if I recall correctly, was scheduled for that same week on the Thursday. So I asked her if I could see him on Wednesday and she agreed a time in the evening.

Wednesday came fast as I was preparing to leave. I drove to get to Maurice's house and was welcomed in by his lovely wife. They had three children I think and one was a fairly new born. I met Maurice and we sat and chatted for a few minutes. I told him all that had happened and I asked him if I might possibly have a copy of the sheet music to play along with his tape, and also did he have just the backing piano music at all? He said that he had both of these but he always believes that people value something when it costs them so he wanted to charge me whatever the Lord placed on my heart. Well, I had already changed what little US currency I had into English pounds sterling and all I had left was about $40 in pizza vouchers! So I explained all that and offered him the pizza vouchers. He accepted and he gave me the written sheet violin music and a backing cassette tape. I warmly thanked him.

I was about to depart when someone else came to the front door. He was a well-known and respected Christian book author. I cannot remember his name but I think his last name started with a 'Z', like Zimmerman. I was invited to join them both for a while then we all prayed together. I had told Maurice about my marriage situation and Maurice gave his two cents about it and said that the marriage was not from the Lord. I was gracious to him in that, as I knew it *was* from the Lord, and there was something in his voice that concerned me. I politely thanked both of them again and left. I sadly discovered later that I had discerned correctly but for reasons of privacy I do not want to mention anything in this book. I was to 'bump' into Maurice a few times over the next few years in Tulsa even though he had since moved to a different State.

So, on the Thursday of that week, Drew and Jamie saw me off back to England once I had said goodbye to Mr. Rick. In England I had arranged to stay with a wonderful Christian family in small village called Waverton, near the city of Chester where my children were still living. I was going to do some more work for the lady, Leanne, who was a metal corrosion consultant to the oil and gas industry with a home office where she operated out from. I had already been teaching her two boys the violin before I left the country and their dad, John, was a teacher and piano player, so we all could join in making music together. Both Leanne and John were good singers too. Anyway, as Leanne had given me some sales work to do while I was over in the US we had stayed in touch with each other, so they knew what was going on. It was these wonderful people that were kind enough to pay for my return flight as I was struggling to raise the funds. They picked me up from the airport in Manchester and took me to their home. I was so grateful for their kindness.

And so that is what happened. Off into the night sky I went, leaving my estranged wife and family behind. I was so unhappy but had to trust in the Lord; what choice did I have?

Back in the UK I readjusted back to English life again. Of course I had nothing but a few clothes and my violin to my name. I stayed a few months with John and Leanne but it started to become clear that I needed to move on. On top of everything I was still found myself full of lust and was not giving off pure vibes I don't think, even though my conduct around them was always good.

Being separated from Prisci and in this state, together with a lack of self-control even though I resisted much many times over, I just could not get this driving lustful force out of my heart, all I could do was stifle it, resist it, deny it but it was always there waiting to come up again. Cursed be our old selfish and lust ridden flesh! So, I fell into sin during this time and kept away from the church and could not find the presence of the Lord, not even to lead me to repentance. I kept asking the Lord to forgive me and all I would hear was,

"I do." But it never seemed to heal me inside.

I met this woman of similar age to myself on the street one day and somehow we connected in an immoral way and before I knew it I had her number and address and arranged to sneak around to her place to be together. I arranged this at almost midnight one day so as not to be noticed. She lived in a terraced house (like a continuous row of townhouses) in the old part of Chester down a few side streets.

Parking was hard as the road was narrow and other vehicles were parked up tightly together. I saw one open spot so I started to reverse into it which is what you do to parallel park closely together. I got my car in and, as I got out of the car, who's car had I just parked in front of, and who was coming out to that car that very moment and saw me? None other than my Christian musician friend Jim. The Lord was doing this to warn me not to continue. Jim looked shocked to see me, and I made some pathetic rushed and most guilty reply to him, some lie about seeing someone. He took it but I felt bad inside. Still though, even with that warning from the Lord I still went ahead with my sinfulness.

It was not long before we were rubbing on each other etc. etc. and we were just at the point of no return when I was about to commit sexual adultery when the Lord burst through to me and showed me this woman as a repulsive house fly buzzing underneath me. I was so shocked that I just flung myself off from her and came to my senses. She wondered what the h**l happened but I could not tell her. All I could do was to sit on a chair and look down and twiddle my wedding ring around on my wedding finger looking at the cross that is carved out of it. She came over and saw me and tried to curse that ring and I stopped her, asked for her forgiveness and left.

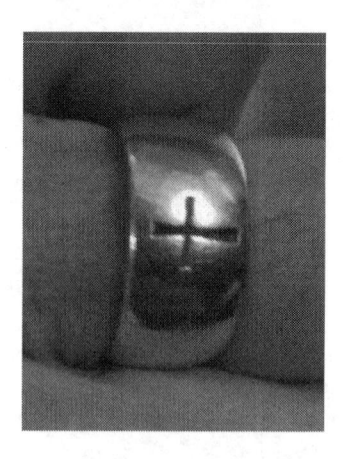

I got before the Lord and truly repented (The ring my wife had specially made for me with the cross carved out as you can see).

How could I be so unfaithful! How could I even contemplate such evil? It's not hard, my dear reader, when you have filled yourself with so much lust and perversion over the years. But you would rightly think that with such a profound experience in coming to the Lord, that I should be more than able to resist and conquer all such temptations. For years I never had the answer to that. And I have to even admit that I really think that my sin as a believer in my eyes was eventually greater as a 'saved' soul than before I was saved! How can that be? But I was to discover that the depths of darkness in a man's heart goes far deeper than most of us are willing to even admit and deeper than most of us are willing to go. For me, I was going to commit suicide anyway, so I had nothing to lose and everything to gain. I would continually over the next twenty years tell the Lord to do want He wanted with me, including test me, refine me and, as my wife would so eloquently put it later,
"Pound him to dust Lord!"
The Lord was to answer those prayers.

I had reconnected back with Keith Winson, that young prophet that turned back to the Lord after I picked him up drunk on the country lane, (we have gone back in time a little in this chapter so this obviously was before he died). He was doing well. Keith was a great barber and he offered to keep my hair cut for free and would not let me pay for it at all. His little terraced house was just off the main street in Saltney, Chester, which was just a few streets away from where my x-wife Karen and our two children Charlotte and Jemma were living. I was there one sunny afternoon during the spring of 1995 having my hair cut. Afterwards I left him and started walking back up to the main street (we do a lot of walking don't we! Well, I did not have a car still anyway!). Just as I turned into the main street there was a glass fronted business shop of some kind and the Lord caught me just as I walked by it. He said,

"Go in."
I was just passing the door so I put my hand on the handle and walked straight in. Inside the front was a simple open area and there was a counter that ran from one side to the other to separate out the front open area from the back section. I walked up to the counter as a young man from got up from one of the few open plan desks there. He was dressed in a suit and came up to me asking me if he could help me. I asked him,
"What kind of business is this?" as I had not even looked at any sign on the building before coming in.
"We are an employment agency and I am the manager." He stated and,
"Are you looking for a job?" He inquired and I said that I was whereupon he asked me,
"Do you want my job?"
What! Well, okay! I asked him more about it and got a number of the head office in another city which was an hour's or so drive away. I left the leaving manager and thanked him.

    After calling that number I set up an interview with a director of the company in the Chester office within a few days. As I went in for my interview the Lord told me what income to ask for and it was significantly higher than what the previous manager had told me that he was getting. I sat down with the director and he seemed fine about me starting and when he offered a starting income I just gave him my figure and left it with him to take it or leave it. He thought about it for a few moments and then agreed. I now had a job! Manager of an employment agency. Boy, was I in for some fun there, more than I had bargained for!

    The job was to manage existing work contracts and make sure that there were appropriate staff that got to the job sites on time so that everything worked well for the customer. Nearly all of the work was manual labor, the majority of that being jobs that most people really would prefer not to do. Jobs like working in a chicken factory, a beef slaughter house, and various food production facilities. I had about eighty places to keep filled when I started the job and by the time I left, just over a year later I had got to a maximum of over one hundred and seventy positions to manage. We also bussed in nearly all of the workers as few had, or could afford, their own transportation to the job site. Therefore, I had a small fleet of three minibuses and drivers to take care of too.

    I soon found out why the office was really basic in its set up. The entrance area had chairs set around its circumference except where the door was and the front counter area of course. The kind of people that came to work were, how should I say, a little rough around the edges. They were mainly low educated young men that came in acting tough and cursing etc. together with smoking as the norm. Most were from three of the roughest neighborhoods in the area, Blacon, parts of Saltney and Deeside. This job was going to be a challenge but I, by the grace of God, was confident and I needed something to get my mind off from my marriage situation. One of the first changes I made very clear was that there was to be no bad language and no smoking in the office.

I was allowed to have one secretary and currently did not have one, so I contacted the local government employment office and soon they were sending ladies over for me to interview. I ended up hiring this lady a little younger than myself who was capable of doing the job but was also not too pretty that it would cause a raucous with the workers when they would come in and wait for work or their minibus ride. She was also street wise to some degree in that she could hold her own with people if she was picked on and again, I thought that was a good quality to have in this environment. So I hired her and she stayed with me for most of the time I worked there.

I moved out of John and Leanne's house and moved into a small flat (apartment) literally a five minute walk up the street from the work office. I had met another Christian brother who had been having trouble with the person he had been sharing living accommodation with, so he decided to move out once he had found someone else to share with, which ended up being with me. I had found this place and he liked it, so I helped him move in.

The move for him though did not go smoothly with his previous roommate. I went up to his old place to help him move only to find them both almost in a fist fight outside on the front lawn. Tempers were raging mainly by his old roommate who had his fists clasped and was ready to slug it out for some reason. My new friend, Steven, was no match for this man (and nor was I really) but I quickly got out of my car, walked straight up to them, planting myself in between them both, and just stared into the other man's eyes. I just did it, I did not plan it out, it just happened. The man was still angry and red faced with fists about ready to fly and, cursing up a storm he was suddenly disarmed I think, wanting to know who I was and to get out of the way as he tried going to my side to reach my new friend. I just kept between them and did not say a word but continued to stare in his eyes. After a minute or so he backed off and, almost growling at me said,
"Are you one of those born again Christians? You are, aren't you."
I acknowledged that I was and he turned and left us!
So my new friend Steven and I moved into this small two bedroomed flat and that is where I resided while I worked at the employment agency.

I had the responsibility to open up the premises six days a week before 7am in the morning. There would often be people already waiting to get in at that time, some to wait for their ride into work and others in hope to get some work. As this kind of primarily manual labor type of work fluctuated with production demands. Sometimes I did not know how many people were required at a particular job site all of the time, therefore I had to maintain a reserve pool of people as it were, of last minute workers to try to fill in those gaps. That meant that one such willing person might be working in grain factory one day, then spend a few days on a food production line, then end up at Boeing extending the runway or something! It was a real juggling act for me.

Oh, and yes, more complications. As is I guess not uncommon between neighboring rough areas in a region, there was the aspect of gang territory and rivalry to contend with, all mixed at times with regular drug and drink abuse. There were fights, or potential fights for me to deal with and obvious drug use and hung-over people that I had to remove for the day, or ban for a few days. And these people were not shy in expressing themselves either!

In spite of all the challenges, there were many opportunities for me to be kind and helpful to workers in need and so the job was demanding yet also rewarding. My two minibus drivers, David and Martin were also a handful at times. Martin only had one working lung so he could not do manual work; therefore, I hired him as one of the drivers in order to give him an income. He was from Saltney, so all would go fairly well with the Saltney folk that he transported but not too well with a mixed group. One such man from a different neighborhood, an older man of all things, had it in for Martin and news came one day that this man had punched my driver in the face during work hours. That man did not turn in to work for a couple of days after that incident, so I went to call on him at his home. He managed to escape meeting me, so I left messages for him to come see me. He did come but had the gall to turn up and plonk his behind in a chair in my waiting area with all his buddies around him a few days later, expecting to go to work. That morning the front area was full and all were waiting to see what I was going to do. Even my secretary looked worried. I looked up and saw this older man, who was probably in his forties, a really rough looking character, joking around like he was all in control and no one better mess with him. With everyone watching, I stood up and went to the front counter, opened up the divider and walked into the front section right in the middle of the group and walked up to this man and told him, "Stand up."
He looked up at me and said,
"No."
"Stand up." I said again as I stared into his eyes.
He joked a little and got up. I was taller than him but it was not a fight I was looking for. All was quiet in the office. I turned my head to one side and said,
"Hit me here. This is where you hit my driver right? Hit me." As I pointed to my left jaw.
He was shocked and did not know what to do. Everyone was looking at him as I still repeated myself,
"Hit me right where you hit Martin."

I waited for a minute but he did nothing so I looked back at him and said, "What you did to him you did to me. You coward, get out of here and do not come back."

That man all but ran out of there totally embarrassed. I went back to my job. The Lord was still with me.

The only thing that I can recall that came against me throughout my position as manager was when one of the said gang leaders came and threw a house brick through one of the front windows when the office was closed. I found out who it was and did not prosecute but I did not allow him to work for me again.

I also invested in a blue minibus as the Lord grew the business for me. I purchased the bus from a Roman Catholic private school that had upgraded to a new one, so I was confident that it had been well taken care of. This bus I then rented to the employment company on a monthly basis which gave me a decent income on top of my salary.

So I continued working at the employment agency for just over a year when things started to not work out between myself and the directors. Something was going on that I could never really find out the reason for it happening. However, life was moving on and an amazing event took place, a miracle to me that I will cover in a couple of chapter's time. It took place just before I left the agency.

Ice Skating and the Gypsies Come to Christ!

Through a small church in a village called Buckley I got to know a man called Terry. He had for a long time been involved in the 'gypsy ministry', as it were and was very familiar with their ways. Terry had invited me to a gypsy camp that had established itself some time ago on open fields a short drive away. He was the person who had been kind enough to drive my car from Manchester airport when Prisci and I went on our honeymoon to Spain.

Within a few months it looked like these gypsy people had been there for years. Even though they could have set up on public or private property, these tough headed, tough hearted and just plain tough people could only be moved on with a court order and a usually a large band of police.

These gypsies were not the true Romany Gypsies that would migrate throughout Europe. The Romany Gypsies were very neat, tidy and clean folk that often brought a trade or skill with them from which to make a living. No, these other gypsies were ruthless, tough and were rather skilled at breaking the law! Once, I saw some of the children from such a site walk down one side of a high street (a main street that is) in a small town. In and out of the shops they quickly moved, passing people walking in the street and pick-pocketing some as they moved on. Voices and commotion would be heard all the way from where this little band of thieves had come. They were only between six to maybe ten years of age too! Once they had enough booty they would simply appear to vanish away before the police would turn up.

When I went visiting one of the gypsy camps with Terry I was warned not to take any valuables there at all. Even Terry's car was nothing special for this very reason I think! As we drove into the camp all eyes were on us. Actually not so much on us, but rather on Terry's car. You could see them looking at the tire tread depth to see if it was worth blocking up the car and taking the wheels, which probably would only take them less than a minute to do together! All we would have to do is be distracted just for that one minute and boom, four wheels would vanish away! Terry wanted to meet with someone so he wound down his window as a little swarm of muddy and rough looking children came around the car. Most of them were not looking at us though, rather looking into the car to see if there was anything worth having. Terry called to a man and asked where this person lived and the man pointed to this little caravan in front of us a short distance so we slowly bounced up and down on the uneven mud track to that home.

Terry did not want to move far from his car I could tell as he honked is car horn and got out. I followed him out and noticed that the children had not followed us. I looked down at the car wheels to make sure those bumps were not because our wheels had gone! We were good still. A woman came out with her children I guess. She was an old Romany as it happened and usually she would be on her own with her four children, but for some reason or other she was with all the other gypsies on this site. She was not happy about being there and said she was going to move away soon from the site. She must have been in her forties or maybe fifties. It is really hard to tell the age of a gypsy, they have such a hard, outdoor lifestyle that their complexions get very rugged early in their lives. It seems that the cultural norm of keeping oneself young and pretty as best as possible was skipped over with these folk! After a short talk, Terry and I left, and with everything fully intact!

About a month later or so Terry called me and said that this Romany family had left the site but he was not sure where she was in her little caravan. Word had it that she had moved into the Deeside area which was where I was now renting a room very close to the North Wales International Ice-skating Rink.

I had been taking my two young daughters that were from my past marriage to Karen to the ice skating rink for fun. They had enjoyed it but *I* had *really* enjoyed it! So much so, in fact, that I started taking group lessons and quickly passed through those to individually coached lessons.

My female teacher and I had a blast. Imagine this, one six-foot adult on the rink during private lesson ice time, together with about a dozen or so other students… all teenagers or under and all flying around me! After a few weeks I started to progress well and really enjoyed the balance, control and strength that was needed to be a figure skater. Shortly after that I was offered a job there as a part-time ice steward during the public sessions to make sure all on the ice behaved and also help take care if there were any accidents. A few weeks after that I became the only full time ice steward at the rink, after I had left the employment office job. Being full-time at the rink was great for me as it gave me open access to the ice at any time to practice my skills. Sometimes there were ice skating competitions, ice hockey practices or games. Occasionally there were curling competitions held there too which was always fun to watch.

The rink was resurfaced at least twice a day and I got to know most of the staff there. It was quite a skill to accurately resurface this rink as the surface was now naturally uneven. Some years past the ammonia based freezing system had punctured and caused water to seep deep into the ground and refreeze. Apparently the authorities had it inspected so as to totally redo the ice but it was going to cost far too much. The water that had leaked had frozen to a depth of some forty to fifty feet! This underground iceberg had fractured and upset the surface so now it was down to the skill of the man in the big ice machine to work the ice to compensate. He did a great job too! Often, as soon as he had finished I would be out there, just me practicing on the 'clean' ice.

Drinking gallons of 2% milk with high protein and consuming plenty of carbs together with working out in the gym kept me busy! Oh yes, and I had to do ballet classes too for stretching! Within my first year I was working on all my single jumps and multiple spins and, of course, if you know anything about figure skating, I was working on those insatiable circles that every skater has to do! I believe they still require you to pass the circles even in the Olympics!

I had not found out where that gypsy family was but for sure they were in Deeside as the children had been seen on the rampage down the high street at times. Looked like they picked up the bad habits of the regular gypsies.

So life carried on at the ice rink. I was really improving and once just by a sheer fluke, I got my recognition as an ice skater. I was the only one on the rink and, without my prior knowledge a couple of professional coach scouts were there talking to some of the local coaches. I had been working this routine and was in the process of it doing out there on the ice. As I executed some neat foot work sequence I then followed with a couple of small jumps and ending in a low to raised spin. I hit the spin (probably for the very first time out of a hundred attempts) perfectly, down I went on the front ball of my ice skate then I pulled up and in tightly as I whisked into an eighteen turn spin on the spot with zero travelling! I stopped and went to the side and the scouting coaches were asking about me! I laughed inside but it was nice to be called out in a good way! I never did do that spin as well ever again!

    A friend of mine, Jim was a fellow musician and he was also great with electrical audio gadgets. He found out that I had bought a violin from the flea market and had been spending hours and hours turning it into a golden sequined instrument. I wanted to play on the ice rink against my background music that would be played over the main speaker system in the rink. I was doing it for fun. I had learnt to skate a few dances, like the waltz on ice so I thought it fun to see if I could skate, dance and play all at the same time! Jim came and rigged me up with a cordless microphone for my violin and sure enough, there I was doing all three things. The local newspaper got hold of the story and I ended up on the front page! See:

Sequinned fiddler on the ice

A DEESIDE man with a golden touch on the violin has put his musical skills on ice to delight fellow skaters.

Mr Robert Ewens has been entertaining visitors to Deeside Ice Rink with his unusual talent – dancing on skates while playing his gold-sequinned electric violin.

Mr Ewens, 33, of Queensferry, has been playing the violin since he was 10, and studied at the Guildhall School of Music and Drama at the London Barbican.

He started skating six months ago for the first time ever and took to it "like a duck to water" thanks to his teacher, Hayley Pardo, from Pentre.

Skills

Mr Ewens said: "I'm doing it for a bit of fun and at the same time putting my violin and skating skills together."

His dazzling violin has not always been so bright but thousands of sequins have brought it to life.

"It was blue when I bought it, which was far too dull. I wanted something special and came across the gold sequins. It took me hours to stick them all on. There's more than 30 metres on there!"

One of the biggest difficulties is being able to incorporate the skating, especially the jumps, with the violin-playing.

Robert Ewens with his golden violin at the Deeside Ice Rink.
Picture: MIKE ROBERTS

One day a lady who also worked there came up to me for the first time. I had seen her there many times but we had never spoken. What she said just blew me away. She asked me,
"What is it that you have? I want it too?"
Now, some may wonder what on earth she was talking about but I knew straight away. You see, I had the Lord Jesus Christ and His Holy Spirit inside of me and it was Him that she was asking me about. Further questioning by myself verified this. She said that she had been watching me for some time and noticed that I was different from everyone else. I suggested that we just went outside in the sunshine and chat about it. We talked in the main car parking area. She was the daughter of the big boss! I

told her all about Jesus and the Kingdom of God. I didn't tell her about church, no, but the Kingdom of God, yes. She listened intently and after hearing me out she said that she wanted this too. So we prayed and she prayed and she repented and accepted Jesus Christ the Son of God as her personal Savior and Lord from that moment onwards for all of her days. She left with this warm smile on her glowing face. I felt so honored and humbled that the Lord would use me like that.

    News came that a single gypsy caravan had been seen down a dead end road off an old industrial site near the river Dee where it was tidal. I drove over there and found the family. They were surviving on stealing and, well, more stealing I guess. I was invited in and as we all crammed into the tiny living area the mother started to talk about religion and that she was all Roman Catholic with Mary mother of Jesus this, and Mary mother of Jesus that. This was before I had even opened my mouth to tell them about who Jesus really is. Finally I started to talk and she listened and she heard the simplicity of knowing Jesus and why He is the only way to God the Father. We overcame any obstacles that her religion had caused and she opened up her heart, and while crying accepted Jesus Christ as her Lord and Savior. Her eldest daughter did the same. The younger boys all looked scared (the first time I have ever seen gypsy boys scared!). I left with the mother thanking me and asking to come back (which I did, bringing them some food with me for them).

    Then, bad news came from Terry one day just after they had converted to Christ. The caravan had exploded up was the message so I got straight into my car and dashed over there. All the way there the Lord kept telling me that they were all okay. I arrived at their caravan, well what was left of it that is. The whole top and sides had been blown out. No one could have survived that blast. What had happened? I got hold of Terry, who was having a terrible time in a town some way north of Deeside. Apparently, word had got out that this family had become Christians and turned from being Roman Catholic. Some person had gone by and tossed through the window some kind of incendiary device that had also caused the propane tank in the caravan to explode. The family just happened to all be out together at the time.

    Terry was with the local authorities in this town up north trying to explain that you should not put gypsies up for the night, for not even one night in a hotel, even in a very basic hotel. Well, the authorities did not listen to Terry and on the first night in this hotel this one family caused over ten thousand pounds (about $15,000) of damage and had to be removed. It just freaks gypsies out to have to live in brick walls and have carpets and bathrooms etc. I guess they were just trying to rearrange things to make it more like home for themselves! Somehow a used caravan was found for them and they moved out into the countryside for a while before heading south to a town called Wrexham to be with friends.

Now to fit all these events in to my life timeline goes like this: After visiting Priscilla in the December of 1993, we got married on April 2nd 1994. We were then separated for almost two years and it was during this time while I was in the UK that all these things happened. During this period I was being tested by the Lord who was revealing and dealing with various issues in my heart that we all have to some lesser or greater extent.

Lust in my heart, that is sexual lust is a most common thing found in a man. So common that outside of being a born again Christian it is often considered 'normal' and if you do not display it at the expected times then you may be even considered odd. This is true for English culture anyway and I am sure it is the same in the US and other western countries at least. Sexual lust starts to be developed into a habit usually during adolescence and I was no exception to this. By the time I was sixteen I was so sexually driven that often all I would think about had something to do with sex. This was to become my norm as I progressed into adulthood. I thought nothing odd about it. Later, as a Christian I knew that it was wrong if directed outside my marriage but it was still there inside of me. Priscilla was a gorgeous Hispanic lady and I had the hots for her indeed. And, she being a hot blooded Hispanic lady that she is, was mind blowing for me when it came to passion, far more than I could have ever expected.

But, lust is lust and the truth is, is that it has no boundaries no matter how well you try and discipline yourself. You know where it should be contained to but sooner or later it will break through those self-imposed walls. This happened to me once we were separated after being married and I was stuck in the UK for that long time. It was not long for me to start wanting to have some kind of sexual activity. As much as I fought against it I never could fully overcome it.

It was while I was at the ice skating rink that I started to notice one particular girl who would skate around and always pass by me smiling at me or making it known that she was there. She was young but did I care? Nope, as I said lust has no boundaries. There was me at age thirty-three or so and she must have been just over eighteen! Shameful to say the least but again, when you are filled with lust nothing is rational. It did not take us long to get into conversation. She was eighteen, so she said, and she had her younger brother there with her, she had had a baby when she was under aged, and the baby was with her mother where she lived. We soon got into activities that we should not be doing and even when I visited her mother and found out that all this girl had said was true in her life (I needed to check that she was at least eighteen and of age), her mother approved of us!

One day at the rink her brother left early and she made up some story about needing a ride home. Of course, lusty me fell straight for that one and offered to do so once the public session was over that evening. I did, however I needed to go visit that gypsy family before they moved down to a town called Wrexham, so I told her that we would make that visit first. On finding the caravan in the middle of the countryside on a country lane, the children recognized me as I pulled up. The next thing I knew was that all three younger ones were inside the car with their hands everywhere! I ordered them out and had to get a little tough with them. The girl stayed in the car as I went inside the caravan to see the mother.

They were doing fine and were ready to get transported to join a few others in Wrexham. I was happy that she was joining some people that she knew rather than being out on her own. It was then, for some reason I checked my wallet in my pocket. It was gone! Those little rats, they pick-pocketed me! The mother was not a happy camper at this news and threatened to beat hard whoever took it if it was not returned with everything in it! Still, it took her a few minutes to get them to release it. I don't think they took anything else. They did tease me about the girl though.

After leaving the caravan we drove back northwards towards the girl's home. She asked me to pull over and then started getting all hot and physical with me. But, I could hear the voice of the Holy Spirit of God speaking scriptures of sexual purity to me. Then I kept looking down at my wedding ring and eventually the girl saw me looking at my ring and she got annoyed at me. I looked up at her and said that I could not do this. I am so glad that we did not go too far. I drove her home and that was the last encounter we ever had, thankfully. This is one of a few things in my life that I wish I had never, ever done but it did happen so it is here for all to read. I noticed that the more I would follow my lust the more I would stop being close to other believers in Christ and my appearances in church would diminish.

Oh Lord! Please deliver me from myself!

The Miracle Return to the United States of America

Just before I had left the employment agency and went to work at the ice skating rink full time the Lord told me to,
"Give your whole pay check to Keith Winson for he needs it."
Hmm, that was a good test for me. So, in obedience I did just that. After I gave my whole pay check to him I found out that he was raising funds to fly to South Africa to expand his influence as instructed by the Lord.

It was around this time that the Lord led me to the newly forming church in Mold that I have already talked about in the Paul Medford chapter. David (one of the drivers that I had at the employment agency) and I both attended that fellowship and we got to know the pastor, Pastor Idris, very well. I was working with the pastor, praying with him and the church was praying too for my marriage to work, but nothing had happened on that for months and months. I had gone through just about every emotion and every level of faith regarding my marriage. I had broken down and cried profoundly and just felt totally at a loss, worthless and such a failure, to being all joyful and happily trusting and knowing that the Lord would bring us all back together. Up and down and even sideways did that pendulum swing inside me until one day the Lord again spoke to me,
"Have you noticed something?"
"What?" I said to the Lord.
"No matter how you think or feel, it makes no difference to Me. I am going to do what I am going to do how and when I want to do it." The Lord said.
I was corrected. As if I could make the Lord bring something to pass according to *my* will, feelings and thoughts, like I could twist His arm so that He pleased me! As if I could tell my maker when and how it should all come to pass, or even if it will come to pass. He had, in that moment shown me the futility of my efforts over all these many months. I had given my life to Him and that was it. He owned me and my life. I needed just to accept and be at peace in Him, doing the best I could just one day at a time. Incredibly simple really! I was just complicating it because of my own wants and desires.

You see, dear reader, leading up to this correction by the Lord, I had thought it best to divorce Prisci as she was not going to come back to me I thought. I knew that the Lord brought us together but hard and hurting hearts can make us deaf to the Lord and it becomes easier to listen to the voice of man and do the wrong thing, making things even worse. So, that is what I was doing, following my own hurting heart and the advice of man. I had found a 'Christian' solicitor (attorney) who said that there was this 'Paulean Theory' based on what the apostle Paul wrote about believers and unbelievers separating and she said that if one party is acting like an unbeliever and was separating themselves then you were okay to file divorce papers. Really it was a lie and a manipulation of the Word of God, and I knew it in my spirit but I went along with it.

So, then the Lord did this correction and then He told me that I could not divorce my wife. I told my flat mate, Steven who, over all this time had never said anything on the subject at all. All he said was,
"I know," in a gentle and loving way.
I went to sleep that night, a Sunday night I believe and had a dream. There was Prisci and I sitting opposite each other in the living area in our flat talking to each other. It was so real and I knew we were meant to be together.

The very next morning I usually get to the business premises to unlock five minutes before 7am but on this day, for the first time ever, I found myself there way early and at 6:15am I was sitting at my desk doing nothing. One or two early birds arrived, workers looking for work and my secretary arrived early too. Then it happened...

My office phone rang and I automatically picked it up but just said, "Hello." rather than the usual business answer.
A little sweet and gently voice answered,
"It's me."
I started to cry as I got out of my mouth,
"Prisci!"
We could not say anything to each other at all at first, we just listened to each other breathing I think. This was a miracle! All the people in the office were looking at me starting to cry like a baby; their tough boss reduced to tears but no one ever said anything about it to me. I cannot remember what we then talked about but it didn't matter; she was there with me and I was there with her.

From then onwards we started to regularly communicate together. She said that it was the Lord who gave her a check inside to delay all the paperwork for the immigration requirements. I told the church and Pastor Idris and all were so delighted. Pastor offered to call her and he did, so we all conversed together to sort out a few issues. Pastor Idris was a good man and a genuine follower of the Lord. He was funny too, being a short rounded Welshman with that typical Welsh accent.

I had switched jobs, leaving the employment agency and was now a full time ice steward at the International ice skating rink in North Wales. Suddenly I had forgotten all my wrong ways and I was focused and on purpose to leave England and get to my new family. However, through talking with Pastor Idris, Prisci said that she wanted to come over to see me, so I arranged for her travel and shortly thereafter she was flying across the Atlantic Ocean to me. I was so overjoyed and yet a lot more sober about it from what I had gone through. Nothing seemed to matter than to take hold of my darling Prisci in my arms.

I waited at the exit point at Manchester airport for her flight to come in. I kept looking at the electronic notice board for the arrivals. There it was on the display board, 'On Time', and then 'Landed'. People started to come through the exit corridor a few minutes later. Where was she? I eagerly looked but did not see her. More people came but still no Prisci. I refused to accept that she was not on the plane. The number of people diminished to the last few trickling through. I just refused to stop searching. If only my eye sight could bend around that corner so I could see her. And there she was, my beautiful, my most precious, my darling, Prisci. I went to her and just held her and while doing so took a deep breath of her into me. Yes, the missing part of me is here.

"Prisci" was all I could say then,

"I love you" I whispered in her ear.

I took my wife back to Chester which was an hour or so drive in my car. Previously the Lord had done something rather special for us. Firstly, I was wondering where we should spend our first night together for I could not take her to my flat where Steven was as that would be awkward. Well, one day as I was driving up the main street in Saltney towards Chester, the Lord had me look at my speedometer and read the mileage. He said, "When the mileage gets to XXXXXX (Sorry I cannot remember the real number) turn in on your left and book a room."

Rather odd instructions I thought, but I did know that there were some bed and breakfast places up the street and a few guest houses too. So, as I drove I kept an eye on the mileage and sure enough I arrived at the Lord's number and there, right there, was an entrance to a guest house so I just turned in and parked. Getting out I saw that the house was well kept on the outside, a Victorian aged house by the looks of it. I went up and rang the doorbell. A man answered and invited me in once he knew that I was looking for a room soon. I told him that I wanted a special room for my wife was coming from the US. He replied after checking on the availability that the only room that he had available for that date was the honeymoon suite! Well, I guess that was what the Lord wanted us to have so I booked it.

Also, again before Prisci came over, I inquired as to whether Cherry Cottage was occupied or available. It had been rented to a relative of my other friend Jeff so a family was living there after I had left the cottage. Well, would you believe it, they had recently moved elsewhere and new people had not been found so the owner, God bless her, gave it to us for free as we used it for our first honeymoon! I was *so* made up and grateful.

So Prisci and I went straight to the guest house honeymoon suite and, to be honest I am not going to tell you much more about that other than clothes went all over the place as quickly as possible! ☺

From the guest house we went to Cherry Cottage for a few days. I also took Prisci to the Ice Skating rink where I had been working. The people in the café and the staff there thought she was fantastic and came afterwards and told me so. We also did something rather special in the church with Pastor Idris, we said our wedding vows to each other again.

Now, Prisci had come over for one specific purpose. To find out if I was really committed to her and the family and not just wanting a green card or something. I never did even think about that as a motive and to this day, getting a green card has never been an issue for me. I told her that I was fully committed to her and our family and I meant it and she believed me. Time flew by far too quickly and it was not long that I had to see her off back to the US. Prisci was now happy about proceeding with the immigration process and would go back and submit the paperwork.

This I believe all happened in 1995 so when our wedding anniversary came around in April 1996 I determined in my heart to make a surprise visit to her for that anniversary. I booked the flight and packed and was soon flying excitedly across the Atlantic once more to visit my baby, my Prisci. I flew the day before our wedding anniversary, on April 1st and soon landed at The New York airport where as usual I had to pass through passport control. I had my violin with me and my hand luggage. You pick up the checked-in cases once you pass through the passport control area and then take them to your connecting flight.

Now, a few months before flying I had had some concerns in the back of my mind. I was married to an American so I was told by the US Embassy in London to go to the non-immigration side of the Embassy to get a visa approved for me to travel as a visitor. After waiting in line for hours I went up to the window and explained the situation that I wanted to go as a visitor and my immigration paperwork was in process. This male officer said that he would not let me in as a visitor as I might stay there with my wife! I showed him from my passport that I had already been there as a married man and had returned, but all he said was that I needed to go next door to the immigration department and see if they will issue a temporary immigration visa pass to me. Upon which he then kindly stamped my passport:

Denied Access into the United States of America

Well jolly-dee! That's just great! I had no option I thought now but to go around the corner and ask the people at the immigration department if they would help. I didn't hold much hope in that as it was they who sent me to the non-immigration department in the first place! And sure enough I was correct. They told me that they could not issue me a temporary visa as not all of the paperwork was in yet. They did suggest that I might try going under the green waver card, that this might work for me. It was my last option it seemed and so that is what I did.

So there I am crossing the Atlantic and having landed in New York, I was now in line for passport control. No big issue I thought but all that hassle at the Embassy in London worried me in the back of my mind. As I went up to the officer and handed my passport all went well thankfully and minutes later I had passed through and was waiting for my luggage to turn up on the carousel. Then I heard it, a firm male voice…
"Mr. Ewens."
"Mr. Robert Ewens."
I froze and would not turn around. Then came the firm hand on my shoulder and as I turned around a rather large officer asked me to confirm that I was he and I did.
"Please come with me sir." He commanded.
He led me to rooms to the side of passport control that seemed to be a secure area (now where have I seen this picture before!). Inside I was asked to sit down and wait in this open area. I waited and waited, and waited! Being told nothing at all was a little frustrating so I decided to speed things up a little. I took out my violin and started playing to the other people waiting with me and any officers that cared to listen in! That worked and shortly I was asked to take myself and my stuff into a small room. Oh boy, in for another treat I was as this Hispanic lady officer came in on her own and proceeded to try and nail me with deliberate false entry into the US with the full intention of not leaving. She went on for over an hour and all she heard from me was the truth of my intentions. I must admit, I was beginning to wonder if she understood my simple replies or she just liked to repeat herself multiple times or something! So, eventually I got tired of her and told her that I wanted to see the head officer and was not going to carry on repeating myself to her and I then kept silent. Amazingly she just got up and did what I asked rather than take offense. A moment later and this large white senior looking officer came in and sat down. He explained who he was and that he was in charge of the immigration security. I explained my position and he acknowledged that I was telling the truth, and that I had been stopped because the immigration department had flagged my name as having been here in the US before and had overstayed my ninety-day limit. He informed me that they were arranging to have me flown back to Manchester on the next flight back.

Great! Whoopee, I get to see the sun set on the way and the sun rise on the way back! That's one expensive viewing!

Those officers that I had spoken to back when I left the US on my own accord lied to me, they just wanted me out of the country! The senior officer let me use the phone to call Prisci.

Now Prisci would be at work I thought so I dialed her work number. Someone else answered and then put me through to her.
"Hi, honey. It's me!" I said.
"Where are you?" She inquired as she could hear my voice very clearly.
"I am in New York and was on my way to see you for our anniversary but the immigration department has pulled me aside and said that because I overstayed last time and because we are married, that I cannot come into the country so they are sending me back on the next flight to England."
There was this silence at the other end and then,
"April fools right?" She inquired.
It was April the first! She thought I was kidding her!
"No, baby, this is for real. Really, maybe my luggage will get to you but I will not!"
She got it and was so shocked I guess and then she felt bad for me. She also thanked me for trying to get to see her too.

Well, after my call, two officers came to me to escort me through a maze of doors and corridors that eventually lead us to the outside and to a plane that was docked for loading passengers. I had insisted that they please check that I would have my luggage in the airplane so I could get it at the other end. They said that yes, that had all been taken care of (another lie). I had checked this with them three times in all. Up these little steps I went that lead to the entrance door of the airplane as I was then checked on to the plane by the hostess. For some reason I was not embarrassed but rather ticked off still at the whole sequence of events.

The flight was very empty thankfully and the staff on board were very kind to me. I even got to fully stretch my six foot plus self out along the chairs to make a bed to get some sleep. And, sure enough, I got to see that sun rise a few hours later as we came towards the UK! And did my luggage make it back with me? Nope, Prisci called me as I had put her name and number on the cases beside mine. She had received a call saying that my cases were in Tulsa! (Maybe I should have hid in one of them!). I got her to explain the situation and the airline company, American Airlines I think it was, had the cases flown back to London, from there they were couriered across England and into North Wales to me. What a long journey those cases had! The ordeal was over…finally. Moral of the story, don't go your own way even if it is done with the best of intentions, but rather, follow the Lord!

It was 1996 and finally I got a date from the US Embassy in London that I needed to go there for my official medical and interview to see if I would be approved to go or not. I was confident as the Lord had brought us back together. In fact, I was so confident in the Lord that when He told me to quit my job, book my flight, give away my car, leave my accommodation and pack, I did so without hesitation. I just wanted to be with my Prisci. Besides her short visit, it had almost been two years and for me that was two years too many!

Now the instructions that came with the interview date I read while on the way down to London. It clearly stated that I should on no condition think that I will be given passage into the United States of America and that I should not do any of the following:
-Do not leave your job
-Do not book a flight
-Do not make any changes to your living situation
-etc…
UNTIL after your interview with the immigration department.
Oooops!
Now, wouldn't that be a big booboo if I did not hear from the Lord this time! I had even changed my currency and had my flight booked for that same week!

Well, on arriving at the Embassy, I first noticed a long line for the non-immigration department. I remembered being there the previous year when I was denied entry into the country by an officer during the so-called interview that I did not even know was the interview! He had stamped my passport 'Denied Entry into the United State of America'. Now I was back to the other side, the immigration side and there was no line at all. I went up a flight of stairs and into a waiting area where a dozen or so other people were waiting. An officer called to me and I went up to his cubicle counter. He took my name and checked me off his list and told me to go wait with all the others.

It seemed that we were all there for the same reason and by the time everyone was there, we were a group of about twenty or so people. To pass the time we started chatting with each other. During this time an officer would call one of us up to check some details and when I was called, the officer went through all the documentation and had me complete a form with a whole list of questions about who I was, and who Prisci was etc. etc. There was one question however that I skipped. It was 'Have you ever been denied entry into the United States of America?'
Once I had finished I returned the form to the officer who then proceeded to tell me that he had reviewed all my documentation in preparation to my interview this afternoon and had found one vital document to be missing. This was the letter of financial sponsorship that Prisci was to have completed and mailed in to them. She had told me that she had done everything, so I told the man that. Still, he could not locate it and he said to

wait and see what the interviewing officer has to say about it. Things were not looking too good right now for me.

Before lunch time (we were to be given an hour lunch break before interviews started) we were all escorted out and down the street to a medical practice where blood testing and other tests were done on us all. The results seemed to be obtained almost immediately somehow. I knew this because one of our group was found to have HIV and he was denied entry on that basis and had to leave. As far as we all knew, the rest of us were all passing the examination. As a group most of us went and had a quick lunch so we were all getting to know a little more about each other, or at least those who did not mind talking about their reasons for emigrating. We all went back to the interview room where we sat down together and were called up one at a time to an open booth counter that we had to just stand in front of. Everyone could pretty much hear what was being said; nothing was really private there at all which surprised me.

At one time a couple was called up and they were denied entry because they did not have the letter of financial sponsorship. My heart sank so I opened up my Bible to read and comfort myself saying that I trusted the Lord. The man in front of me turned around to me and saw me reading it. Looking at me he said,
"You trying to get some divine intervention?"
"No," I replied, "Just trying to keep my peace."
No sooner had that brief interaction taken place when I heard my name being called up. Oh, Lord, here we go. Standing in front of this officer I watched him go through my application and all the relevant paper work. Then he looked up at me and said,
"There seems to be two things here not completed. First, the letter of financial support is missing. Do you know why?"
"No sir, I know my wife sent it so maybe it got lost somewhere or something." I replied a little nervously.
He looked at me and I at him. There was something about this officer that was strangely familiar but I could not put my finger on it. Then he then proceeded to ask me all about my wife and her job and I answered as best as I could. I tell you, you could hear a pin drop in that place. No one behind me seemed to be doing anything but listening intently. I felt all these eyes on me from behind. You see, most knew that I had got rid of everything and had my flight booked and it all depended on what happened today, right now.
The officer finished writing and then continued,
"The second thing is that you did not answer one of the questions. Have you ever been denied entry into the United States of America?"
I swallowed and thought better to always tell the truth so here goes. And just before my mouth opened to answer him I got it. This was the *same* officer that I had met in the non-immigration department a year prior, the

one who denied me entry and stamped my passport! So I boldly looked at him and said,

"Yes sir, and it was *you* who denied me!" He looked back at me with a straight face. Then it broke into a little grin, then a smile as he said,

"Yes, I recognized my own initials over the stamp mark."

The Lord told me to look down so I did and to keep very quiet so I did that too. After a long pause I heard pages ruffling and then 'Thud!' of a heavy stamp and he announced,

"I shouldn't be doing this but you have waited long enough Mr Ewens. You can go; you are approved."

I looked up at him and burst out with the biggest smile and almost jumped over the counter and kissed the man! Yes! Yes! YES! The officer handed me my passport together with some paperwork and as I turned around there were a bunch of mouths just wide open and big eyes looking at me! They were just as shocked as I was! Sitting down and trying to collect myself a little before I left, the man in front turned to me again and said,

"Well, I guess you got your divine intervention after all!"

He was sure right on that! Thank you Lord! You are so good to me.

   Arrangements all made and two days or so later I had said my goodbyes to everyone which included my two lovely daughters, aged about six and eight. That was the hardest thing in my life to do and to this day I do not know how I did it. I was really broken up as I gave them both, Charlotte and Jemma, a big hug and kisses. Driving off with tears streaming down my face so much I could hardly see where I was driving, the Lord burst through to me and told me to put praise and worship music on and praise Him. That was the last thing I wanted to do. I wanted to turn around and take them with me but I forced myself to sing and gradually my sad tears left and I was thanking the Lord that He would for sure take care of them. Nevertheless, that whole event was impossible for me without the Lord helping me, carrying me.

   So, yet again, there I was traversing the Atlantic Ocean for the umpteenth time! This time though I was fully legal and had a new life laid out before me, and the reception at the other end should at least be welcoming this time!

The Ugly Heart Returns with Vengeance

Back living with Prisci in Tulsa was to be a whole new experience. After being separated and how the Lord brought us back together, as well as confessions as to my immoral behavior in the UK, we somehow started to embark on this life in marriage together. It was hard to say the least. Prisci and the children had been renting a three bedroom duplex very close to one of the worst apartment blocks in Tulsa known for violence. Prisci's sister Kathy lived in the other duplex that joined ours for a while before she moved away. Prisci's parents were not at all happy with the location of where Prisci was at because of the neighborhood's reputation. I found out later that the annual murder rate in Tulsa was similar to that of the entire country of England! Guns were the norm here and that took a while to adjust to.

While I was in the UK Prisci called me to say that the duplex right next door to her parents was available to rent and should she move us there? She also mentioned in the conversation that her parents were for some reason concerned that I was going to split up her daughter from them so, wanting to show them that this was not the case, I had agreed to the move. This ended up not being a wise decision at all. I was all new to this and was struggling to adjust to the new lifestyle, the Hispanic culture as well as to getting to know my wife and her very diverse children.

I was for sure being tested by the children to see if I would endure and be worthy to be called "dad" or not. And, of course, I needed to understand Prisci with all that she had gone through already in her life. And, I needed to work and start to provide for my new family. I really wanted Prisci to be at home while her children were still growing up. She had missed most of this joy as her parents had pushed her to go to Oral Roberts University fulltime and then on top of this she had to work multiple jobs to support her family, so her mother took care of the children most of the time during the day. I could see that this grieved Prisci and I wanted to help solve that for her.

However, did I have the wisdom, insight and relationship skills to help make a smooth transition? I surely did not at all. I didn't even really know what the word relationship even meant! Seriously, the way I was brought up in England I had no life lessons on what relationships were all about. To me a marriage was to provide and have sex and have a good time as a family together as much as possible with good morals. In my first marriage I did not have the love of God inside me but now that was different, so I was starting all over again but had a weak foundation to grow from.

I stumbled my way through the first few weeks with my new family. Jeremy, my eldest son was about eight years old back then. Once again, I was getting stressed out and, because of my lack of relationship skills and my heart seeking the Lord for wisdom yet not finding Him, arguments ensued. Prisci was doing her best to get through to this stubborn Englishman who was still new in the Lord compared to her, but she was achieving little success with me. As for me, well, I was the Holy Spirit filled savior of the family! Oh, yes, (full of arrogant pride I was) I was there to fix this family and make us all godly together. And, by the way, just to let you all know, I am the new head of this household! Now, wouldn't you say that this kind of attitude was a clear recipe for disaster?!

I could drive Priscilla's Red Ford Fiesta or any other car around in the US using my British driving license for up to one year but it was good for me to get the US license too and Prisci was trying to get that through my self-righteous skull amongst other things. She did suggest that, once I had got my Social Security Card amended to show that I could now legally work in the US, I should start temping. As I thought that this was a good idea, I went ahead and did this. After registering with a few agencies and being tested on certain computer skills, I was offered a few jobs. I am not sure of the order of the jobs but I do remember working for a company called Decision One on 71st and Yale as an analyst for data in customer service. I also did some project and analysis work for Pitney Bowes in downtown Tulsa at a sub-location under Shell Oil. I then worked for another company working the customer service fraud detection department.

At one time I interviewed for a job in one of the three tall CityPlex towers that then belonged to the Oral Roberts University at 81st and Lewis. High up close to the top floors a company was renting space and doing a debt recovery service. I successfully had interviews and was offered a good salary plus commission but back at home with Prisci I was not at peace about it. Talking to her in the kitchen one day about the job, I said that I was tempted to take it, and then I realized what I had just said. I was tempted, and at the same time the Lord spoke to me saying that this company was built on corruption through to its core and not to take the job. I shared this with Prisci and we agreed for me not to take it. It was only a couple of years later that this became evident as the company collapsed and the owner was taken to court for various law infractions.

I got a job temping at the head office tower for the Bank of Oklahoma downtown Tulsa. At this job I was filling in for a lady who was on her maternity leave. The job was to simply log and cut the oil commission checks for individuals that had those small oil 'donkeys' on their land that were producing oil. It was an interesting job seeing how much some of those checks were for each month!

I started to get more interested in computer software programs during this time at the bank and started to automate some of the procedures rather than repetitively doing them over and over again. I had done this at one of the previous jobs working in the fraud customer services department using tools that they had provided, in order to increase speed and efficiency. At that job we were monitored as to how many widgets we could do in a certain time frame. I got so good at using these computerized short cuts, macros as they are called, that I was soon noted and was kept on when others were being dismissed. Back at the Bank of Oklahoma, I investigated the Microsoft product Excel and found out that it could do a huge number of things so I got permission from my immediate boss, another Priscilla to work on this. It was not long that I was able to deploy some automation to other people too and her boss, the department director, Mr. Terry, agreed to create a fulltime position for me as an efficiency programmer. I was having fun learning and helping others in their work.

Now, this Mr. Terry was a good man. He cared for people and he knew his job. Unfortunately, some months after he created this position for me, he had to leave the bank. He really had done nothing wrong but he stood up to certain work ethic principles and would not compromise, so he was basically dismissed. He took no action against the decision as far as I am aware. My wife, Prisci on the other hand felt that I should stay in touch with Mr. Terry so I got his cell phone number and very occasionally called him and prayed for him.

One day the Lord impressed on Prisci that I should call Mr. Terry so I did. He had a new job working for a company called First Data Corporation. He was some kind of manager there and was liking his job and the company. I thanked him for helping me at the Bank of Oklahoma and I said I would like to keep in touch which he was pleased to do. Then, only a couple of weeks or so later he called me. He asked if I would like a new job. There were two computer programming jobs that were to be combined into one position and would I like to do it? Without any hesitation I said yes. I also found out that he had been promoted to general manager of the whole facility. That's not a bad promotion in just a few weeks! The Lord is good to those who stay faithful to Him and this was a wonderful example of that.

So, within a few weeks there I was, working at First Data Corporation learning a new computer language or two, or three actually, and getting my head down working hard. I had been given a substantially improved remuneration compared to what I was getting at the bank. It was at this job that I started to settle down and establish my skills and talents in business. I really enjoyed the thought of making other people's jobs less tedious and boring. I would come up with all kinds of ideas, especially when programming for the call centers which was a large portion of where I worked. For example, I found a way to merge two seemingly incompatible computer interfaces while retaining the personal name and location, etc., of the operator working at any particular workstation. From this I could also monitor errors that they would sometimes make on their computer so I would create these little funny pop-up comments to show in the error message that would then appear on their screen. Oh well, it was a little bit of fun amongst a programmer's dull life!

Unfortunately though, your heart tends to follow you wherever you go, including from one job to another and my heart was far from pure. It was not long before I was looking at pornography at work and fantasizing about it. Now lust is a driving force and tends not to stand still when there are opportunities to do more and that's what I did. Internet pornography became live chat videos and then phone calls for phone sex. My world started to spiral downwards into darkness. The times of walking close with the Lord had long vanished and my fear of God completely gone. I even remember once at home going out into the front lawn and crying out to the Lord as to why is this happening to me. Why do I not fear Him anymore? No answer came. I was struggling to even hear the voice of the Lord my God at all.

A Double Life Style and the Hypocrisy of it

Life was getting harder. Prisci was picking up that something was not right. We would often fight then make up and, looking back on it there was not much real peace in our home. Over the next few years we bounced (mainly due to my decision making) from one church to another as my double life carried on. My heart was divided and really, I could not even see my own heart. I was becoming more and more self-righteous in the church, as if I had the right to judge others and say the will of God. As I played the violin it enabled me to play in various church praise and worship teams but this became an even greater burden in our married life as now people could see me and weak females became attracted to me. I, in my hypocritical pompous English way would deny that it had anything to do with me. I was innocent!

    Now, the Lord did use me and honored me especially when I repented of my sin no matter how many times I continued in my sin. God also brought individuals across my path directly or indirectly to challenge me to confess, but I was just too stubborn back then to do so. I just could not understand why my heart was so hard.

    It was not long before Prisci found out that I was up to no good. While working at First Data Corporation I had started to cross dress in secret again and even got to the point of researching and paying an online herbal doctor to guide me to feminize my body. All this was wrapped up with a sexual drive and I got to the point of thinking and believing that "well, if I want to be female then I must be interested in men." Like I have said before, lust never likes to stay still and will demand more and more of you and this was the direction that I and my stubborn heart was heading, causing havoc in my marriage and family too. Prisci, being a fighter and an Hispanic too, did all that she knew to do through those years to try to get through to me (thank you, my love. I love you so much forever).

The Never Ending Downward Spiral

My job at First Data Corporation improved. I was given my own private office and a pay increase. This 'new' business improvement methodology came into the corporate realm called Six Sigma, and First Data had decided that it was a good idea for the whole company to implement this process improvement system. Now, the Tulsa division was just a small part of the corporate company which spanned across many states in the US and abroad. Its business primarily was to service third party credit card transactions. The head offices were in Omaha, Nebraska and the corporation had over thirty thousand employees worldwide at that time.

One morning I met Mr. Terry, the general manager, as we both were walking into the entrance of the building from the parking lot. After a little polite chit chat on how work was going he mentioned this new company wide initiative called Six Sigma and asked me if I would like to be the representative for him to do this thing.
"Yes, I'll do it." Came straight out my mouth again.
I had absolutely no idea what Six Sigma was at that time and by the sounds of it, neither did Mr. Terry! Soon it became clear that it was some kind of process improvement methodology that had been improved upon from other similar methods. I was to be a specially trained person who was free to work with all people and departments to bring about change and improvements that would streamline the overall operations and result in a higher quality of work and less waste, a type of internal business consultant. It was hitting big in the corporate world as an excellent way to improve profitability which meant more money to the shareholders. This is why any stock market trading company that implemented it usually had the benefit of seeing their stock values go up. This, of course, happened to First Data.

I was sent to Omaha on various training courses that basically covered two main areas. One was project management and the other statistical analysis. The training was grueling at times but I was thoroughly enjoying the nature of the job and the status it gave. I was now in management status, had a company credit card, and shared a personal assistant who would book in my flights and accommodation etc. I was starting to be the new Tulsa Six Sigma specialist with a title of Six Sigma Black Belt once I qualified. Training took about six months and was a great growing experience for me. I got to facilitate all kinds of meetings and also to train others in the Six Sigma way. The methodology I found to be excellent and I really took to it.

Unfortunately, I discovered that what they warned us about in training was to happen a few times when I was back in Tulsa. They warned that in order for this process to work well, we would need to break down any 'silo' mentality in the organization. You know, those people that like to just control their domain and woe to anyone who dares to intrude on their territory! This is one reason why I reported directly to the general manager and I had his blessing to work in and through all departments to do my job. The good news was that I am a polite person and tend to get on with almost anyone, but I still had those stubborn bulldogs to deal with.

    To become certified as a Six Sigma Black Belt I had not only to pass all of the rigorous training modules but then I had to show that I could run a process improvement initiative from start to finish. Then, to get certified I had to take my skills and go back to Tulsa and either create new income or create savings (or a combination thereof) of $1,000,000 a year! Some, actually, many of the other training Black Belts that passed through the training successfully (only I think about 20% made it through) worked in much larger divisions than I did. This meant that they only had to complete one or two projects in order to attain that dollar goal. But little me here in the isolated Oil Division had to work my butt off for two years to finally get there. Good came out of it though as I got thoroughly grounded in the whole process keeping my boss Mr. Terry in the loop at all times. This was a wise thing to do as at one point the direction from the corporate head of Six Sigma changed, as it was finding itself under pressure to produce dollar results more quickly. Six Sigma Black Belts found themselves just diving headlong into areas that had not had the proper preparation that Six Sigma demands. I saw this and explained to Mr. Terry that I was not prepared to follow this way as it was self-defeating to all that we were taught just for the sake of putting some dollars on the books. He agreed with me and let me continue to train others, map all processes and complete the ground work first, before embarking on process improvement projects. It worked, after a few more months I had teams in Tulsa trained, I knew exactly where and what to measure to collect accurate relevant data in order to start improving things. Projects just started being rattled off and I had completed some fifteen projects by the end of year two. I got my certification in 2002. Here it is:

Once again though, if you give a person the ability to do wrong that is in their hearts, and you give them the money and time to do so, then you have all the ingredients to fall into bad stuff. And that was me again. Now, my sin (calling it in Christian terms for something that is morally wrong, that I should not be doing as it is destructive to all and not pleasing to God) had progressed to meeting other men for encounters. After all, I was a female right and that is what females do, go with men. I watched male pornography and spiraled further down that slippery slope of darkness. Somehow though through all the shameful things I did, I never actually had sexual intercourse with anyone male or female but did do sexually immoral stuff. There was a grace of God on me in spite of my wickedness to keep me from catching anything. Sorry to be so crude but that's just how it was back then.

It really is appropriate here to throw in a scripture from the Bible from the New Testament, the beginning of the book of Roman's that warns against such immoral behavior:

Rom 1:16-2:11

16 For I am not ashamed of the gospel of Christ, for it is the power of God to salvation for everyone who believes, for the Jew first and also for the Greek. **17** For in it the righteousness of God is revealed from faith to faith; as it is written, *"The just shall live by faith."*

18 For the wrath of God is revealed from heaven against all ungodliness and unrighteousness of men, who suppress the truth in unrighteousness, **19** because what may be known of God is manifest in them, for God has shown *it* to them. **20** For since the creation of the world His invisible *attributes* are clearly seen, being understood by the things that are made, *even* His eternal power and Godhead, so that they are without excuse, **21** because, although they knew God, they did not glorify *Him* as God, nor were thankful, but became futile in their thoughts, and their foolish hearts were darkened. **22** Professing to be wise, they became fools, **23** and changed the glory of the incorruptible God into an image made like corruptible man — and birds and four-footed animals and creeping things.

24 Therefore God also gave them up to uncleanness, in the lusts of their hearts, to dishonor their bodies among themselves, **25** who exchanged the truth of God for the lie, and worshiped and served the creature rather than the Creator, who is blessed forever. Amen.

26 For this reason God gave them up to vile passions. For even their women exchanged the natural use for what is against nature. **27** Likewise also the men, leaving the natural use of the woman, burned in their lust for one another, men with men committing what is shameful, and receiving in themselves the penalty of their error which was due.

28 And even as they did not like to retain God in *their* knowledge, God gave them over to a debased mind, to do those things which are not fitting; **29** being filled with all unrighteousness, sexual immorality, wickedness, covetousness, maliciousness; full of envy, murder, strife, deceit, evil-mindedness; *they are* whisperers, **30** backbiters, haters of God, violent, proud, boasters, inventors of evil things, disobedient to parents, **31** undiscerning, untrustworthy, unloving, unforgiving, unmerciful; **32** who, knowing the righteous judgment of God, that those who practice such things are deserving of death, not only do the same but also approve of those who practice them. **2** Therefore you are inexcusable, O man, whoever you are who judge, for in whatever you judge another you condemn

yourself; for you who judge practice the same things. **2** But we know that the judgment of God is according to truth against those who practice such things. **3** And do you think this, O man, you who judge those practicing such things, and doing the same, that you will escape the judgment of God? **4** Or do you despise the riches of His goodness, forbearance, and longsuffering, not knowing that the goodness of God leads you to repentance? **5** But in accordance with your hardness and your impenitent heart you are treasuring up for yourself wrath in the day of wrath and revelation of the righteous judgment of God, **6** who *"will render to each one according to his deeds"*: **7** eternal life to those who by patient continuance in doing good seek for glory, honor, and immortality; **8** but to those who are self-seeking and do not obey the truth, but obey unrighteousness — indignation and wrath, **9** tribulation and anguish, on every soul of man who does evil, of the Jew first and also of the Greek; **10** but glory, honor, and peace to everyone who works what is good, to the Jew first and also to the Greek. **11** For there is no partiality with God.
NKJV

Strong words indeed that should be soberly absorbed by us all. This perfectly describes the path that I was on. A good name for it is the spiral of degradation and I was starting to hit the lower regions of it.

Now, in the corporate world as a certified Six Sigma Black Belt I was called upon to travel to other parts of the corporation. Denver, Omaha, New Mexico, and Delaware were the main locations I travelled to. And, on many of these times my wicked dark heart was ready to act out. Eventually I switched bosses from Terry in Tulsa to a lady in Omaha at the head office. I found out later that Mr. Terry had arranged this as he was going to have to cut back staffing in Tulsa which would have included myself, so he went out of his way to get me switched to a more secure position. What a great man he was to me.

It was amazing to me though how, while even in the midst of all my entangled and perverse sin, the Lord still made appearances to let me know He was with me. He even still used me at times. Like the first trip I went to see my new boss in Omaha. I had heard that she was highly trained to oversee Six Sigma and had a special initiative lined up for me.

Walking into the main First Data head office where the corporate CEO resided, I went up to the security reception desk to get directions,

"Through that glass door and straight ahead", I was told as the security man pointed it out for me.

Thanking him I walked tall and upright knowing that I needed to give a good first impression of myself and walked…

… straight into the glass panel to the right of the door whacking my nose on the glass! For some stupid reason just before I was going to place my hand on the door handle of the glass door I noticed that to the right was a gap so why bother going through the door when I could simply walk around it! How stupid can you get! Well, I guess they kept their glass so very clean as to not even notice it is there. My new boss's secretary saw all of this as she came running to help me as I held my nose. How embarrassing! Well, it humbled me and that was good, otherwise I would not have been used of God for what happened next. My nose, thankfully did not bleed and I was okay; only my pride took a tumble.

After waiting just for a few minutes my new boss, an attractive middle aged lady who held herself well came out to greet me and invite me into her office. She did not want to know about my work achievements at all. She said that she had spoken to Mr. Terry and found out all that she needed to on that score and was fully satisfied with my work results. No, she wanted to know about me and no sooner did she say this that I sensed the Holy Spirit's presence as I talked about Jesus Christ and all that He had done so far in my life. Within ten minutes she was sobbing and, and I had no idea what to do! This was my new boss for heaven's sake! I waited patiently as she finally calmed down and she hugged me and thanked me. Getting her face in order she escorted me out.

She became a very good boss to me even though I rarely got to see her over the next couple of years. The special initiative she had for me? I was to train in mergers and acquisitions then I was to go over to Delaware State to be a part of a small team of selected Black Belts where we were to map out and find synergies between what First Data did and what this other company did that we were to merge with soon. This was the start of many long stays away from home travelling often twice a month from Tulsa to Wilmington, Delaware for a week or so visit at a time. Eventually I was given a directorship position as the corporation had decided to shut down its entire Six Sigma organization.

Sometimes when I could either afford to, or had managed to save enough air miles up, I would take Prisci with me. We had some good times together and sometimes even when I went on my own all went well. But there were also those trips where I just could not wait to dress up and find a gay bar or just go out if I had the courage to do so. I never went with anyone at all and had no desire to either, but I got more and more risky and just did not find the answer as to why I wanted to be this way. It was like being on drugs I guess, to get the next high. I learnt to stash clothing and stuff in Wilmington that I could access at any time I was over there.

[Interruption: Present day as I am typing and remembering all this: It is May 3rd 2014 and I just want to let you, the reader, know that I am really hating writing all this down. My heart is really sad and I am disgusted at myself with my biggest regret being how I impacted my wife Prisci. This is really hard for me, I have to keep stopping and take a break. I am sad. I think I will go shopping at Walmart.]

    This secretive second life went on in Wilmington for over a year I guess but God was not ready to let me fall completely. Whether I liked it or not His hand was on me and He had His purpose for allowing me to fall many times but I was not to see this until my time in the 'wilderness' to be refined was to be completed. I had once asked the Lord,
"How long, Lord?"
And He said that as it was with Paul (the Apostle) so will it be with me. It is believed that Paul spent twenty years from the time he was made to leave Jerusalem and until he started his ministry to the gentiles. Twenty years was the figure I got, I had about thirteen more years to go from this point in time. This all started on the day I got married to Prisci, April 2nd 1994. All I remember throughout this period was flitting between lust and sin and repenting and crying out to the Lord for His help. Sometimes it was just a heart cry,
"Where *are* you Lord?"
I knew He was there and I knew that He was in control even if I could not see it. I knew that I belonged to Him and He was working things out for His glory and for His purpose. All I had to be was willing and He who knows everything about me, that in my heart I was His, no matter where I was or what I was doing.
    Regarding the desire to be more female and to present myself that way I would say that if there is one thing that would get me really upset and angry today is a Christian that would say something like this to me as to why I was not overcoming this behavior;
"You get yourself delivered but pick it up again because you want to." Or,
"You are just refusing to give up this desire."
Why does this upset me so much? Simply because none of these people have any idea as to how I have pleaded with the Lord to deliver me from this. They have no idea as to the intensity that I have fallen down at the cross of my Lord and Savior. They have absolutely no idea what it is to be this way and the degree that you have to deny the core of who you are.
    So, why was the Lord not answering my prayers? Actually He *was* but that is all yet to be revealed. And, you never can see what the Lord is doing in your own life while you are going through it as He demands that we walk by faith and not by sight. If we got the understanding on His plan

as we went through it, how many of us would start to 'help' Him along? Answer: All of us would as we love to be in control of our own lives, or at least think we are. The trouble with this is that our perspective and level of understanding is far too shallow compared to God's, and the Lord wants to have and will get the glory, He will not share it with any of us at all. Sorry, that is just the way that it is. And that goes for me too!

So here I am dragging my beautiful wife and family through all the impact of my sin as I still try to be a good dad and provider. Finally, the Lord set me up for a fall in Wilmington. The directorship position that I was given was not the right position for me. I was on fire to do Six Sigma but now I had a bunch of project managers under me that I had no clue really as to what they did! I was a round peg trying to fit into a square hole. My boss became aware and, I think that people were getting concerned about me as my sin was starting to show in the work place to some degree in my behavior. As previously mentioned, I was given this directorship position as the corporation had decided to end all the Six Sigma operations so we were either given a directorship position or got laid off so I chose to take the job. My boss felt responsible to take care of me, so rather than technically fire me as things were not working out, she had me laid off with full pay and benefits for six months.

At the same time the Lord was dealing with me and confronting me once again about lust and my pride. I got my notice of being laid off as of December 31st 2005. I had to collect the 'good' stuff, that is basic luggage consisting of our clothes and toiletries etc. that my wife and I had kept in Wilmington for when we both travelled and stayed there together. All my 'bad' clothing etc. I had, once again, dumped in a local dumpster vowing for the umpteenth time never to do that again. I was becoming more convicted of my sinful, lustful life.

As Prisci and I were about to leave from Tulsa to Wilmington, she was inspired by the Lord to take a set of teaching tapes on prayer and fasting with us to listen to. This last trip was to be unusual in that I had rented a vehicle and we were going to drive there and back. It was the only way that we could get all our stuff home without paying high luggage charges to an airline company. All the way there I was generally quiet and Prisci just kept playing the tape series. We were both hardly alive really. She was so worn out battling and being impacted by my sin. I was more than tired of not overcoming like a real Christian is supposed to and I hated, absolutely hated myself for hurting the love of my life (I still have not fully forgiven myself not only for then but for right now too). I hate hurting people.

When we finally arrived after taking two days to get there, we unpacked in the hotel room. I needed to go for a walk outside as I could feel that I had to confess my sin yet again to my wife. I went out and found

a well-used trail into the woods. All I could feel was like I was dying, like death. Then, to my surprise the walk confirmed this too. First there was an animal carcass rotting on the ground with flies all over it. I passed by it and looked up and saw that some of the trees were also dead. Continuing on I came to a river that was shallow but crystal clear. Fishing! I thought but then looked and read a sign,
"Do not eat the fish. This river is polluted."
Death seemed to be everywhere to me. I returned back to the hotel room knowing that I was to come clean with my wife. For once, she was not all hot tempered and fired up but quiet and gentle with me. She softly asked me,
"Is there something you need to tell me?" I broke down and confessed. She said that she wanted to be flown straight home. I freaked out (my wife said I was demonized in my behavior). Then, through all this the Lord reminded Prisci of a website that she had found a year prior to all of this. It was a place for men caught up in sexual sin to go to get free if they really wanted to be free. A place of last resort.

    Now, prior to my confessing all my sin to Prisci I had for some unknown reason to myself, re-routed the journey home to drive further south than the way we came to Wilmington. I had routed it to pass through the top half of Kentucky. This ministry that Prisci was looking at on the web was located in that very part of Kentucky. Not only that, but we were to almost to drive right past the location! Prisci said to me that if I would go to this place, then she would not divorce me. I sat down in front of the computer screen and read a little about this 'Pure Life Ministries' for men, a live-in program for men. It was for a minimum of six months! 'Coincidently' that was exactly how long my severance pay was going to be for. I agreed and I called them and we arranged to visit the place in two days' time. I cancelled one project meeting that I was to take as I was in no right state of mind to attend.

    So off we went, leaving Wilmington for the last time and headed towards this men's retreat program at Pure Life Ministries, Kentucky.

Our Cry for Help Not Fulfilled: The Powerless Church

You see, we had attended so many churches here in Tulsa with my wife dragging me it seemed at times to get help from the leadership, from counselors and whatever programs the church had to offer that might get me better but none worked. Some helped in the short term I guess, but I was still a mess. We went to counseling, private and through the church. We prayed and fasted which did make a difference. We did 'Healing of the Heart', 'Restoring the Foundations' and 'Breaking generational Curses' classes amongst many others. I had hands laid on me and I remember those who would not want to touch me being there too, praying at a distance like I was some evil entity, so be careful not to defile oneself by getting too close to me. I confessed my sin and repented of my sin. I...I was worn out and so was Prisci. We got to a place where we were also done with church, the powerless church. We did more to blame ourselves I guess than just dumping all the blame with the church but really, they intended to do good but the power of the Lord was not there for us.

Well back to the Kentucky trip. By the next day I was driving to a hotel not too far from the Pure Life Ministries offices in Dry Ridge. We actually went straight to the offices instead of going to the hotel. I was given an application to take away and complete and return the next day and they would set up a meeting with the person in charge, a pastor to interview me to see if I qualified for the program or not. They only took serious applicants that had tried all else and still had not overcome their sin. That sounded like me I thought.

Completing the application at the hotel was a little long winded as they wanted to know all that I had been up to, for how long and where and how did I come to Jesus etc. etc. I decided to fax in my application as they had provided a fax number. The next morning I got a call from Pastor Jeff who went through my application and asked me some questions. He then invited me into the program immediately. He arranged for Prisci and I to tour the retreat site that day which was a little drive away in the countryside located on just over forty acres of land.

The campus or retreat, whatever you want to call it, was amongst the rolling hills of Kentucky and you have to travel for about ten miles off the main highway along this winding road that seemed to go on and on and on. Finally we took a right turn and then shortly afterwards right again into a small parking area surrounded by a few whitewashed buildings. We had arrived and I was nervous. I had no idea what I was getting myself into but so far these people seemed Godly to me. A large black man who went by the name of Mr. Ken gave us the tour and then we were invited to stay for the evening meal.

The program could hold about fifty men at any one time but they were expanding to hold more as the demand was growing for this unique ministry. If you did not have the money to pay for the entire cost of the program ministry and board, then you worked. You would go to work through an employment agency, at a designated place through one of their approved locations together with other people from the program. Mr. Ken gave me the 'house rule' book. Yes, a book it may well have been. There were tons of rules! You could bring only one case and a personal bag. No radio, no books other than your Bible, no music unless approved by staff, no smoking allowed at all... and on arrival, your bags were to be inspected as you unpack them! No touching of any other men in the program allowed at all, chores must be done well and on time…gee the list went on and on.

The visitation experience got worse, at the evening meal Prisci and I were invited to eat at the staff table. Staff got two napkins but all other people only got one. Staff got the nice glasses but the men just got the plastic beakers or something like that. Before eating a person would pray and we all ate. But, oh dear, oh dearie me, many of these men in the program were just weird. They stared too much or just acted I don't know, odd. I thought, I am going to join this bunch of crack heads and weirdo's?! Oh well, I had made the commitment.

Prisci and I decided that it would be better for me to start early in January 2006 so I think my start date was set for January 2nd 2006. I had to get us both home and do some preparations if I was to be away for so long. First Data had given me one last project to finish in Amarillo, Texas in December which is what I did as my date for being laid off was set at the end of December. Prisci kept me occupied at home building her a bedroom unit down in the garage for her. Others in the family also knew what was going on. Generally in a Hispanic family everyone quickly gets to know what is happening anyway. All that was left was for me to go.

Starting to Break – A Retreat in Kentucky

The days leading up to the departure were hard for me to bear as I still had no idea what kind of Christian experience I was now heading towards. I had read many testimonies from people that had been set free from their sexual sin and other things too, so that was encouraging. You could just get up and leave if you wanted to. You were not forced to stay. However, I resolved in my heart before the Lord that I was going to stay there until *they* said I was okay to leave. So, six months minimum it was to be.

I had booked a long trip on the Greyhound bus that would depart from Tulsa and arrive the next day in Cincinnati where someone from Pure Life was going to pick me up, take me to the retreat and check me in. Prisci and I went to say goodbye to our daughter, Bianca, at her home. She came out and came over to me as I did not want to get out of the car. She gave me this huge hug that she has never done before and said,
"It's going to be all right, dad." Made me cry.
At the bus terminal a good lady friend, Archana from my First Data days was there together with my family. I hugged everyone and boarded the bus with Prisci and I miming,
"I love you", over and over again to each other.
And so the bus pulled away and yet another unknown adventure was about to start in my life.

The journey was hard and the bus was packed with young soldiers off to boot camp on the East coast somewhere. They seemed quite happy just to crash out and fall asleep anywhere and on anyone including myself for most of the way! We had to change busses in mid journey which meant getting our luggage and checking it back into the next bus. I was all but glad to get off at the end of that ride.

A pleasant man, younger than myself, met me from Pure Life. Robert was his name and he said he was an intern there. He had gone through the program as indeed had all the staff. I was glad to have someone to chat with so I started rabbiting off about what the Lord had done in my life and how he led me here. But I quickly began to notice his look towards me. It said something like "You are so full of yourself. You need to be quiet." I got quiet.

Big Mr. Ken met me and took me to the first 'holding pen' as it were. Called the Lazarus room for obvious reasons if you know your Bible (Lazarus was raised from the dead by Jesus). I had to share a bunk bed with a room full of other men, total occupancy about twenty. Some I found out had just arrived a day or two before, others had been there for some weeks and other new arrivals were expected. I had to open up my suitcase and unpack its contents while being watched by a staff member. I only had one half of a locker and one drawer to keep all my stuff in. I was expected to make my bed every day and to use the laundry room to do my clothes washing. I was to use the buildings own kitchen and eating/studying area and was to clean up after myself. I was allowed one bag of food in the freezer and half of one shelf in the refrigerator and I was to put my name on anything that was just for me. Rules, rules, rules, it went on all day long. How you were supposed to follow them all without fault I had no idea. It seemed however that some other people there were deliberately breaking some of the rules. Staff would sometimes call someone out on the carpet, as the saying goes. Right out in front of everyone too. This seemed more like a military base in disguise to me than a Christian retreat! I got ready to do my best to help out and follow the rules.

I had to pay my keep a month in advance and then another month up front to Pure Life to help me settle in and get work. It was all very strange for the first two or three weeks but I soon adapted to the routine. I was given a job in a factory somewhere. I cannot recall all the places I worked at in those six months, but I do remember a warehouse that did garden equipment and ornaments, a place that distributed the Fram oil and air car filters, and Leslie's Pool Supplies where I worked for most of the time during my stay.

Now the Lord kept placing me with another man who was a little older than myself. His name was Amos and we just kept being put together, whether as prayer partners, on the same job site, even on the same job line or next to each other. He arrived close to when I had, so we were pretty much on the same page in the program. God used Amos to help me and visa versa (we have stayed in touch ever since).

Our schedules were pretty busy and we only really had Saturdays off, that is if we were not asked to work overtime at the workplace. Hourly rates were low but we all worked hard, as it is written, as unto the Lord. For $8.25 an hour with others getting even less at other locations, you could not do much with that once you had bought food and paid your keep.

We had chapel on the campus three times a week with accountability sessions and reading of the founders book 'Sexual Idolatry' by Steve Gallagher. That was then followed by discussions.

What I really did like about the whole ministry was that it was Biblically based. The ministry also recognized that unless the person met directly with the Lord then not much was going to happen in that person's life, so they set up the whole environment to deny any cravings of self, they greatly reduced the possibility that someone could continue in their sin, and did all that they could to fill you with the Word of God and encourage you to spend more and more time seeking the Lord. A lot of the services and even personal ministry was Holy Spirit led and each person was treated with respect as a child of God, yet were also not given any room to act anyway ungodly. They called it being merciful to challenge someone who was not acting honorably towards the Lord, which it was. I would be most interested indeed for the staff to accurately discern my life once you get to the end of my life story, (Actually I did contact them a few times and was quite pleasantly surprised at the counselor's reply).

I was allowed one ten minute weekly call to home unless there was an emergency and I loved to just hear Prisci's voice on the other end of the line. As we were not allowed cell phones at all, we had to take turns to use the pay phone that was located in the main dining area of each building. Prisci, I missed her. She had started a job with our eldest son at Cartridge World back in Tulsa and seemed to be enjoying being there. Prisci was doing well to pay off the credit card balances from the salary she was getting and the full salary I was still getting from my previous employer. I also did what I could with the little income I had working in Kentucky. Providing I was frugal I could save and send her money as well. At one time I managed to save a thousand dollars and sent it home. I wanted to do my part. By the time I was on this retreat Prisci and I had been married for some twelve years.

Looking back, I am amazed that I seriously did not contemplate suicide at times. I never seemed able to get my life together. Maybe understandable if I did not have the truth about life but *I did* have that, I had Jesus, I met Him. He touched me! He changed me so why am I now worse than I was before I even got saved!! I did not understand.

Almost without exception there will be at least one time during your stay at Pure Life Ministries that God will break through into your self-made life and when it happens you will know. You can see the fear coming on a person as they are truly convicted of their sinful ways and you can see that their pride has been more than just challenged, it has been dismantled to some extent. As men are humbled by the Lord through their own willingness, He starts to break through. As the person gets closer to the Lord's holiness he gets to see his own ugliness. It is a fearful and awesome experience that produces all kinds of responses. I have seen full grown men that have been in the ministry for years bail out. People can come up with the craziest of reasons why, all of a sudden, they have to leave the program. In just a total of almost seven months that I was there businesses all of a sudden needed attention at home, someone got sick, or they needed to deal with attorney matters, and the all too common "This program is not working for me." were just a few 'reasons' given at that critical time. Other people were just sneaky and left in the middle of the night. The staff are usually very discerning though and would often manage to help the person change their mind and stay to complete the program and their walk with the Lord.

My first major encounter with the Lord happened I think around week six. We had learnt to cry out to God to reveal the condition of our hearts and I had been doing this privately before the Lord for a few weeks. I had started to struggle again with lust after my counselor one counseling session took it on to challenge me by saying,
"Okay, Robert, this has gone on long enough. You, this nice Englishman..."
And as he continued with me just staring at him, he picked up his little wooden cross that was on his desk and flashed it before my eyes and said something in the name of Jesus Christ. I felt my heart jump back inside of me.

The very next day I was so full of lust and anger at everyone and everything. I went to work as usual with the van load of people I would usually go with. We left at 4:30am and I was feeling so angry but kept quiet, bottling it all up inside. At the job site I just started lusting after whosoever I wanted to. It was horrible seeing myself do this. Eventually I told my friend Amos and a couple of others. Back at the ranch (as we called the retreat) I spoke to a couple of other ministers that were in the program as I went looking for my counselor, brother Brad, to tell him what was going on. My friends and other ministers agreed with me that I needed deliverance. Clearly I was possessed! I had a demon of lust! Finally, I found my counselor taking a walk outside one of the buildings. Telling him what was going on I said that either I was possessed or I am the devil. He just smiled at me and said,
"Well, I don't know much about deliverance but I will pray for you."
You don't know much about deliverance! What are you doing here then! I thought to myself. He gently touched me and asked the Lord to reveal

Himself to me. I walked off thanking him but thinking that was all a waste of time. Wisdom was to prove me wrong and him right though.

I was now staying in the second building having progressed out of the Lazarus room where I first started out. So after my counselor prayed for me I went to the second building still not happy at all. As I walked through the study/dining area there were a few men quietly studying. One looked up and saw me. He was concerned for me and asked me if I was okay. I said no and he offered for us to go outside to pray. I really needed to do this but with this one goof? He was the one that would deliberately break all the rules and act so immature and *he* wanted to pray with me?! I said no as politely as I could muster and then the Lord arrested me on the spot and I froze. I turned back to him and begged him to please pray with me.

We went just outside the front door and sat down on this old wooden bench seat. As we were not allowed to touch we each sat at either end and prayed. I cannot remember what he was praying at all, as straight away I just broke down and sobbed. I felt so, so ugly and dirty inside. It was as if the Lord was finally answering my cries to reveal my heart to me. Again, it was as if the Lord Himself backed just enough away from me to show me myself without Him. I have never been so scared in my whole life, dear reader. I was truly in dread and I was horrified as to the wickedness of my heart. There was not one, no not one thing in my heart that was good or clean. I was awe struck about my condition and great fear seized me at that time. I have no idea how long we were there for as it seemed like an eternity but I guess at some point I went up to my room and, exhausted, went to bed.

The next day was no easier and people could clearly see that I was going through something. Happy, positive Rob was sober, quiet and in deep remorse. For that whole week I felt so dirty inside of me. I feared going to chapel on Tuesday and Thursday. I felt that if I went in I would defile the place with my ugliness so I begged the Lord not to make me go. God was merciful to me and, for some reason or other that never had happened before nor afterwards while I was there, both the Tuesday and Thursday sessions were cancelled.

The next chapel service was to take place and I remember walking up the steps, fearing to go inside. How could I, it was a holy sanctuary and I was so filthy? As others quietly entered, I delayed a little and waited outside. Then the Lord told me to walk in. Weeping a little as I did so, the Lord showed me in an open vision this sheet descending from heaven. The sheet was blood red and it was of the blood of the lamb, the blood of Jesus Christ. It covered me and everyone there and the voice of the Lord spoke again,
"Now, you are clean."

I sat down at the front most available seat as we were trained to do so that there would be no gaps in the rows, and bowed my head and cried quietly, grateful for Jesus' blood. The Lord had humbled me and also answered my prayer and had separated Himself from me enough for me to see myself without Him, like He had placed a mirror in front of me with Himself behind the mirror. To this very day, that encounter with the Lord greatly affects and humbles me.

Life at 'the ranch' went on with its usual schedule of disciplines, but I was changed inside. It was like a huge chunk of me that was previously in control of my sordid life had taken such a blow that it could not ever come alive again, for I had seen myself as I really am.

On Saturdays we could go do our grocery shopping in Walmart but we had to be at least a group of two people and we had to stay within ten feet of each other to hold each other accountable against doing anything ungodly. We had learnt to avoid eye contact with magazines, and other people that might be attractive in the wrong way to us. For me now though, all that was gone. What I mean is the lust factor had gone. I just saw people, human's with souls walking around. For the first time that I could remember, I had peace about myself and about being with people. This has continued to this very day too, and I thank God for His work in me. It truly is our merciful God who changes us from the inside out, and when it is *He* who has done the work in us, then it is done indeed.

A few weeks later Prisci came on an arranged visit. I was given permission as they do for married couples, to stay at a hotel for the night. It was a strange experience as for over four months I had been so careful not to let my fleshly desires be misused that when it came to even undressing before my wife I felt like I was doing it for the very first time and I was shy. She noticed and made a sweet little comment to me. The time together did not go too well though, as I was still in the middle of what the Lord was doing in my heart. I think she understood that; I hope she did. I did and do love her very much.

I soon progressed to the third and final dormitory area which is reserved for those approaching graduation. This was a smaller section and we had smaller rooms with maybe just two bunk beds. It made it easier to talk and build relationships. By now I had been at the retreat for over four months and I recalled my very first day visiting with Prisci and how I saw the men there as weird. Now I got to see that I was no different from them when I came in! I was just as odd and weird, but I just could not see it.

Towards the end of my stay at Pure Life Ministries I had this amazing experience of the cross of Jesus and His resurrection. I had been allowed to bring my violin and there were certain times when I could go to this room under the chapel to practice and worship the Lord. The Lord had placed on my heart to play the piece Via Dolorosa and I had managed to get hold of some backing music to it. The piece means something like 'The Way of Suffering' and depicts Jesus as He goes to the cross.

There were actually two rooms beneath the chapel. One large room with long tables and chairs set up for people to study at and a small boiler room which was but ten feet square. I had used both to play in and used the boiler room, which was accessed through the main room, if there were other people in the larger room so as to disturb them as little as possible. On this one particular day, however, there was no one there at all, but the Lord told me to use the boiler room. I switched the light on and, after warming up playing a few things the Lord had me play the Via Dolorosa. As I played I could see Jesus being beaten and bleeding as He carried the beam for the cross and as the Roman soldiers called at Him and whipped him to keep going. Jesus was on His way to the cross for all of mankind, to make the ultimate sacrifice and to make a way for us to go to our heavenly Father. Just after I had finished the piece and put my violin down, the lights went out on me. I guess the electrics had blown or something. I went silent. It was pitch black in that room. There was zero light from anywhere. I felt like I was with Jesus in his tomb, behind the rock in the cave. I fell into a deep sleep.

I have no real idea just how long I slept for but when I woke up the room was still in darkness. I fumbled my way to the door and then opened the outer door to let some light in. Packing up my violin I went to my room to put it away. I then went for a walk along 'the ridge' as it was called. It is an area of wild grasses over the top of the brow of this hill before it dips down to a cross that has been built there (see photo above). Many people spend time before the Lord at this cross and I had done so a few times too. Unusually, there was no one there but rather than sitting on the make shift bench I went and sat down near a fir tree for shade as it was a hot sunny day. I stretched myself out and before I knew it, I was asleep again. I awoke some time later and for some reason, as I lay on the grass, I turned around and there it was. A big black snake over six feet in length about three feet away from me staring straight at me. I jumped up and must have scared it as it quickly vanished into the undergrowth. I had no idea what kind it was or whether it was dangerous or not (I found out later that it was not harmful to people; it's called a rat snake locally).

Startled, I heard the Lord say to look at the cross again so I did and He then directed me to walk past it and continue down the steep hill saying to me,
"Go through and beyond the cross."
As I descended into the undergrowth I could see the analogy of the Lord going down to Hades and the graves as the scriptures describe.

Shortly after this, a few days I think, the Lord said He was going to complete my journey with Him at Pure Life. Nothing happened at first but then one evening, on the third day since my 'tomb' experience, I was quietly studying in the main house living area together with others doing the same, and Jesus just appeared in front of me. I stared and was not sure what to do. I looked at the other people but no one else was paying attention to Him. I guessed that they could not see Him. He did not come up to me nor talk to me but just gestured to me with His hand to follow Him. He turned and went through the kitchen so I got up and followed. I looked around at the other people but still no one saw. I followed Jesus through the mud room I think it was called. He did not need to open the door to the outside, He just went through it! I opened it and went out. It was night time and there was Jesus standing on the tarmac looking directly at me. I stopped and stared as Jesus raised His hands up to the sky, and He just floated up and vanished from my sight. I had no idea what to say but found myself saying out aloud,
"No, don't go, I need You."
He said,
"Follow Me" from the heavens.
I raised my hands at the place where He departed from the ground but the vision was over. The next thing I knew Pastor Jeff with his wife flashed his car headlights at me as I was standing right in his way. Feeling a little foolish just standing in the parking area with my hands held high, I smiled and moved out of the way.

I was released by the Pure Life Ministry staff to graduate after six months and two weeks from when I had arrived. God had done a work in me and really a lot more happened over those six months, but this book is not the place to go into it in detail. Sufficient to say that this is a genuine ministry and I have a high respect for all those involved.

Upon arriving back home though while around the dining room table with Prisci and her sister Kathy it became clear to my wife that the Lord had indeed done a work in me but yet it still was not over.

Who *Am* I? The Answer Profoundly Revealed

"Who am I?" Is a great question. It is not, "What am I?" nor, "What do I do?" But who am I is a question of being. It deserves a chapter all on its own but really the answer is short and sweet, so this is going to be the shortest of all chapters.

Who *Am* I? Is the question.

The Answer:

I am a spirit being that has a soul (mind, emotions, and will are all tied into the soul) and I live in this earthly body, i.e. my spirit lives in this body and it is my spirit man, my inner person, who is the real me.

I was not ever really in touch with my spirit at all most of my life and it was only when I accepted Jesus Christ, God's Son as my personal Lord and Savior that my spirit man came alive and I could see and recognize it. It was like God's Spirit came into me and woke up my spirit.

I am a spirit.

I have a mind, emotions and a will to choose… a soul,

And I reside in a body.

A Whole New Understanding of What This Life is About

Now I know what the Lord meant when He said to me,
"For two years I will reveal Myself to you and on the third year I will deal with you."
If you remember, the Lord spoke this to me shortly after I got saved. I was flying so high in the Spirit of God that I cared not to pay attention to the latter part of His words. Wow, I surely got to find out though! Years upon years the Lord has been exposing and refining my heart. The Word of the Lord was accurate and true. I got saved around early April time in 1992 and it was two years from then when Prisci and I got married, the start of

the Lord dealing with me. And ever since then the Lord has been 'dealing with me' just as He said He would.

So where does this chapter title come in here? I had gained a new understanding of what life was about and more specifically what life in Christ Jesus is about through being at Pure Life Ministries. Being religious is not and was not it at all. Even just being spiritual was not it either. Nor was being successful in some way or other even in ministry. Nor was it just about getting saved and born again in Christ though that is essential in order to enter into the Kingdom of God from our fallen state. I discovered that life has everything to do with the heart of man being changed to conform to God's heart so that He can rebuild His Kingdom. God is, if we are willing, refining and purifying our hearts to prove us faithful and worthy of His Kingdom, His Kingdom that He made a way for us to go to through the cross. That's why the Apostle Peter and James said that we should not be surprised at the firey trials we go through in this life and even to rejoice in them. This life is a temporary place, a passing through and is a testing and proving ground for eternity as spirit beings which we are.

It is so, so easy to focus our minds on the daily earthly activities that we get involved in. Doing this, doing that; do, do, do, and more doing, that it is not hard to get carried away and lose focus on the eternal truth. Everything in this world is subject to change and is continually changing whether we like it or not. Nothing really stays the same. We don't, that's for sure!

So the whole meaning of life is very different for me now. My desire is for others to be free from the bonds that chain our souls to earthly things through coveting, lust, pride, materialism, etc. etc. I want people to see that first and foremost we are spirit beings that are temporarily housed in our physical bodies and we have a way to live this life such that not only do we have peace with ourselves in spirit, soul and body, but more that we have a purpose while temporarily here on earth to find and live in God's Kingdom by following the journey that Jesus Christ Himself set before us. This is not achieved through religion, it is a very personal journey within oneself. Christ just showed us the way that's all. Neither anyone nor even He can make us take that journey, we have to want to go there ourselves. This is my endeavor and by the grace of God He will use me in some way to make a difference in lives of other people for His purpose. It is an awesome road to travel, most humbling, yet most rewarding. Please read on.

Living Through the Pain of What I Did to Others

This is the worst part of my life to face. I hate hurting others yet have found myself doing this at times. The closer you are to someone, the more likely it is that you will hurt them or be hurt by them in some way at some time. It seems to be a human dynamic that we just cannot avoid. I have heard of one or two marriage relationships that have claimed that they have never argued and always only did good to each other. Unfortunately I know (actually knew as they are dead now) two such couples that claimed this utopia. The trouble was, they hardly even communicated with each other beyond the basics of polite conversation! I even wonder if they really did get to know each other even if they were married for over thirty years!

So my biggest regrets are related to those closest to me. First and foremost is my beautiful wife, Priscilla, or Prisci, as I have always called her. It is 2014 and she and I have been married for twenty years. I have never loved anyone else on this planet like I still love her. I feel totally at peace with her presence in my life. She has done her utmost to be my help mate through these twenty years. She has had her own issues to face and I have always seen her, if not at first, but sooner rather than later, admit when she has said or done something wrong. Her heart I see and it wants to do well. Her level of mercy towards others is far greater than mine. She has gone through a lot in her life and I never wanted to add to it, but looking back over the past twenty years I have done just that. The internal battle to be at peace within myself has taken its toll on our marriage. Until I can walk in the fullness of what the Lord has for me spirit, soul, and body, I will not be able to be a real blessing, I feel, to her or indeed to anyone.

My children have seen their mother and I go through mainly my issues over the years and have made their own judgments. I wish I had been more of a dad to them. I did enjoy our trips out camping to the lakes, cycling down the tracks in Tulsa, and going to the movies together amongst other activities. I even enjoyed (most of the time!) home-schooling them! They are all very special to me. I hate to think of any negative impact my life has had on them.

Bianca the eldest now, married with three children has always been a little strong headed but I find her very lovable and she has a genuine passion to help others in need. She loves me I am sure but I know that I have affected her, or at least her thoughts and feelings about me over the years.

Jeremy and I are very similar in many ways which I think is one reason that we clashed a little. My heart has always been for his best in everything I have done for him. I hope that he sees that. He has a heart of gold and still has the ability to forgive where others struggle to do so. I love that young man.

Jacob, who bonded with me from the start has matured well and is married to a wonderful young lady, Christy. Jacob is strong where others are not and in a crisis he will be a strong rock for people and he can do it not only to his own detriment but he has the ability to help two opposing sides at the same time to some degree. I know that my actions have really devastated him at times but I think that he has gained some real understanding of things that happen in life and rather than judging, he has learnt to love and accept things that he does not understand himself.

Then there are the other relatives that have seen what we have gone through in our married lives. Oh, how I wish I was just 'normal' whatever that is supposed to mean. But I know I am not, I have always known this. I don't want to be different, but I am and there doesn't seem to be anything I can do about it other than accept myself as I am; the Lord knows that I have tried over the years to change, to conform.

Looking farther back in time to my first marriage to Karen before I became a follower of Christ I often wonder what my life did that was good for her and our two children Charlotte and Jemma. Both girls still live in the UK, but neither now seem to want to be in touch with me, and Karen, last I knew was still bitter towards me and thinks I'm a cross-dressing nut case. My older brother also thinks I am weird.

Lastly, there are all those peripheral folk that you automatically impact with what is going on in your life. The impact can be directly because you knew them or indirectly if they get to hear about you.

All I can say about all the bad things and bad influences is for those people to please find it in your hearts to forgive me and know that I did not, and do not, desire in my heart to do anyone wrong.

I feel that this chapter should be much longer, but either I am not wanting to dwell here too long or there is no more to say on the subject.

Final Steps of Recovery into God's Righteousness?

Some twenty years as a Spirit filled, Word of God believing Christian married to a wonderfully compassionate, believing wife, years of ministry to others at times, but mainly being on the receiving end within the church, must surely end in a wonderful marriage and testimony to the Lord! I mean, in almost twenty years we have gone through a lot together, so it is about time that the rough waves of the sea calmed down and we can just relax and enjoy each other, our family, and the blessings of a God that wants us to be prosperous in all things. We have done our fair share, more than our fair share, of tests and trials in this life. Sure sounds good, and looking back we did have short seasons of peace and easier living. Prisci though would often say that she was just waiting for the next bombshell to come along, whether it be through me or some other circumstance. As usual, we did not have to wait long.

I came out of Pure Life Ministries in July 2006. I had tried to get back into work as a certified Six Sigma Black Belt business consultant. I got close to a couple of jobs but the door just would close on me without me doing anything to cause it. Eventually Prisci said that we could not just survive on credit cards and she was right of course. I had to get work so I started by getting a job working the late night shift at the local Walmart Neighborhood store stacking the shelves. Now *there* is a drop in the old hourly rate from $48 per hour in the corporate life to $8.25 an hour stacking shelves! But I was grateful to the Lord.

Prisci then suggested that I take up painting curb numbers. Painting curb numbers? I had never heard of that! She explained that people would go around handing out flyers in a neighborhood and then would go around painting curb numbers for payment. I started to look into this on the internet and found out that it was a plausible business to work. Looking further into it and applying some of the skills that I had learnt as a Six Sigma Black Belt, it was not long that I had a little red pull along cart with me as I walked down the street, full of brushes, brass number stencils, cleaning tools, primer paint, finish colors, reflective coating, a sealant and all the needed cleaning stuff.

The plan was to develop a way to efficiently paint a good quality curb number that would last and that could be done in one visit within a short space of time. After a bit of practicing I got that part of the plan working well. Next was to create a good flyer that people would be attracted to read and even call me to book in their painting. I was going to cover about three to four hundred homes in a neighborhood where many needed their numbers to be painted for the first time or they needed to be redone.

We started and it sure kept us fit delivering all those flyers! Our grandchildren and daughter even helped us out a few times. We could do the set number of flyers in half a day so that was good. The flyers were in color, printing them three to a page on our home computer and printer to save money.

It was not long when my phone started to ring and customers were booked in for the Saturday scheduled painting day the following weekend. The flyer asked people to call in or they could simply mark on the flyer what they wanted to have done and tape it to their front door so that I could follow their instructions.

Saturday morning would roll along and off I and my little red wagon would start on our journey around the streets. It was fun, as long as the weather was good! I soon got efficient at not only doing the numbers but also calling on neighbors just to check if they wanted their numbers done. By the end of the day I had made a good sum of money for a day's work, usually between $350 and up to around $600. From this humble start was to grow a full handyman, remodeling and landscaping business.

Some years before I got laid off in my corporate job, which was before I went to the retreat in Kentucky, Prisci and I had purchased a house off 31st Street and Memorial Ave in Tulsa. It was a corner house on a fifth of an acre and it had been previously purchased by Drew, the best man at my wedding. He was into 'flipping' houses if you recall and had been working on this house for a while when I started looking for one. He showed me the property and it was a good size with good potential. It had previously been a rental house and, as usual with many rental dwellings, had not been well maintained. Also, the lower wall of the house had totally collapsed which was why Drew bought it at a cheap price. He had workers to rebuild the wall, add nine concreted steel peers around the lower side and back of the house, and had done some work inside too. He sold it to us also at a discounted rate making very little off the sale but wanting to help me out and get on to his next project.

So we bought this house in September 1999 and I borrowed and additional $20,000 against the value of the house to spend on home improvements that Prisci wanted to have done. New kitchen cabinetry was definitely needed and when we were about to move in we discovered that the suspended kitchen floor was rotten including under the old units. Drew had his workers come back in to replace the floor but the cabinets started to fall apart so we knew that we were going to have to make this a priority! Our kitchen was out of bounds for weeks as Prisci, bless her heart, had to cook in a bedroom or dining room. I even remember her once straining spaghetti in our shower! With the floors repaired finally, we found a great Christian missionary who built beautiful solid oak cabinets and he and his friend did an excellent job for us. We finished the cabinets ourselves. To put a little reality on this story, here is our house before we had done much work on it:

We lived in this house for a total of about ten years and it was while living here that many trials and tests took place. We also did a ton of remodeling work. Take a look:

As you can see, it no longer looked like a basic plain rental house. All that you see, is what we did.

Rather than paying for a contractor to do all the work I decided to take the work on myself, so much of the $20,000 was spent on tools and raw materials. My wife kept me pretty busy!

Like I hinted to earlier though, while living here came the biggest tests and trials both for myself and in our marriage, as described a little in the previous few chapters. This was also the house that both of our boys left from to start their own lives. Jeremy was to be set up in an apartment on his own as he did not want to follow house rules that Prisci and I thought were of good virtue. Jacob eventually left in an upset and we did not see him I think for almost two years as he got his life together as an independent young man.

In reference to the title of this chapter, the answer was no, this was not the final step into righteousness at all. More events were to unravel over the next few years…

A Prayer and Lives are Saved

It was coming up to Christmas time in 2004 and I really wanted to make a difference doing something that year (yes, I am going back in time here to before I went on that men's live-in retreat). I thought about having my family go to the St John's Mission here in Tulsa to help serve meals to the homeless, or something like that. Days went by and Christmas Day was approaching and I had done nothing to get this prayer answered. We did not follow religious traditions of Christmas anymore as much of its true meaning about Christ is covered up or not even mentioned these days. We did not do the tree or decorations, so that is why I thought to do something for others.

    Well, I guess I messed up that year as I had been so busy working on my house remodeling jobs that I did not organize anything special. I had been working a lot in my garage cutting up two by six planks of raw pine into smooth ¾ inch routed planks for a new wood floor that I was working on upstairs. I had been working hard on creating these custom planks for some weeks and much of the upstairs was completed (see the previous house pics again). Well, I was now working in the boys' bedrooms where I was cutting five inch wide planks. It was a Sunday evening I believe and I just had this one pile to go through so I got up to go down and work on them. For the first time ever, my wife Prisci said that I should take a break and rest. I said no, that I just wanted to finish this last pile of planks, so down into the garage I went.

    I had already cut the two by six planks to the right length and ripped them through the table saw. Before passing them through the planer I had to rout along both long edges so that the pieces would connect together when they are laid. My small but efficient router table was already set up with the router and half inch bit already set into place from the previous time I used it. I was ready to start so putting on my safety goggles I switched on the machine and heard in my head the voice of a man from church talk to me! His name was Kevin and he was an experienced carpenter. I heard him say,

"You know that you do not have the guard on that machine."

He was referring to the router table guard which is a clear plastic cover that goes over the actual router bit as a protection from accidents. It is lightly hinged so that when you pass the piece of wood towards the high speed router bit that is sticking up from underneath the table where the router tool is mounted, the guard rises up to allow the wood to pass through. I had tried to use this but for some reason that I cannot even recall right now, it kept getting in the way for me so I had removed it. I had to be careful of course whether the guard was on or not as routers can do some serious damage!

I started to work and the pile was getting low. I only had maybe a dozen pieces left to do. Then I heard the Lord say to me,
"Take a break."
But I did not. I only had a few left to do! Then, I thought, I will take a break. So, as I was passing another piece of knotted pine through it happened…

The nature of knotted pine makes it hard to have a constant speed when you pass it through the router. Wide soft grain in the wood will cut easier with less resistance so it cuts faster. A knotted portion will go much slower. I was passing this piece through when, for some stupid reason I looked up and across to see how many pieces I had left to do. At that same time (you know what is coming right) I must have hit a really soft place in the wood and the wood just shot through the high speed bit. The wood shot through… and so did my right hand. It all took but a second and flesh was shot around the room as you heard a short grinding sound, all in the blink of an eye. I felt this huge dull pain in my thumb which I quickly raised up to my face. Half of it was missing. Not only had my thumb gone over the half inch router bit, it had also gone down the hole around where the bit comes up from underneath. All I had left was a stubble to the joint and portions of loose flesh flopping around the side. What amazed me was what I cried out,
"Jesus, please forgive me!"
I turned the machine off and ran upstairs sticking my thumb in my mouth as I went. Upstairs my older son Jeremy and his mom, Prisci were watching television. Prisci had her back to me so when I declared that I needed to go straight to the hospital she blew it off, knowing that I was always doing something to myself! I mean, the last time was when I was working down in the garage cutting wood on the table saw. I was just completing a cut on a three foot length, taking off not even an inch strip and somehow it got itself hooked to the blade teeth which shot it at high speed back towards me, hitting me perfectly between my legs if you know what I mean! It drew blood too! Anyway, Jeremy looked over at me as I took my thumb out of my mouth and he gasped saying,
"Yeah, mom, dad needs to go right now!"
So we rushed off to the St John's emergency downtown Tulsa. I got checked in by the intake nurse who nearly fainted when she saw how bad it was. I was soon taken through to a cubicle where the on duty doctor came and looked at it. Then he numbed it by injecting something in and around my thumb. Finally that throbbing pain lifted. The doctor started to fold out the flesh and pointed out to me that the tool had ground down my bone of the top half of my thumb to just above the joint. He took one of his metal tools and showed me the top of the bone and tapped it showing that it was the bone. He said that all he could do was try as best as possible to stitch some of the flesh back together and bind it up and page the hand specialist

to take a look at it. It would need to be operated on within a certain number of hours as it was classified as an open wound. He also said that I had lost the top of my thumb and that the surgeon would probably just put a flap of skin over it leaving me with half a thumb basically. He left to page the specialist to come in to look at it before he bandaged me up.

I was not happy, and I was not satisfied with the suggested end result. I had to have my full thumb in order to correctly hold my violin bow. I mean, it is essential, no option. I closed my eyes and prayed a short prayer to the Lord saying that none of His bones were broken and so can it be also with mine, so shall it be with mine please.

The specialist turned up and we found out the he was someone very special who had come to Tulsa from the top hand surgical establishment up in New York, I think. He was Jewish and had an excellent reputation. He took a look at my thumb, frowned this way then that way and said no more after a close investigation and booked me in for surgery at 6am the next morning but I had to get there even earlier for pre-op. We left the hospital and went home. It did not look like I was going to be able to fulfill my prayer to the Lord after all.

Prisci and I got up early and she drove me in my gold 2000 Ford Ranger pickup to the hospital. After doing some paper work, I was sent to the pre-op where basic heart pressure and other things were looked at. After about an hour I was called into surgery. They had given me the option for either a local or general anesthetic and I had gone for the local. I wanted to see the operation! I was put in a wheel chair and taken down various corridors and finally into the operating theatre. Boy, was it cold in there! They explained that it was like that to keep the possibility of infections to a minimum. I remember one of the nurses asking if I would like to listen to music from the radio. I said that I would so she asked what kind and I replied Christian worship please. She didn't seem to like that very much and made some kind of comment as she put it on for me.

They hooked me up to various machines and started to add the anesthetic saying to me that they were going to put me under a general for this surgery. I was in no state to argue with them. The Jewish surgeon came in and said that he had been up all night and had not slept at all thinking about my thumb. Great, I thought, now I have some sleepyhead going to work on me! He then said that he thought he could save my thumb. Then, just as I was going out cold, he said that *all* my bone was there, none of the bone was missing! My lights went out.

The next thing I knew was that I was in the recovery room feeling a little sick. My thumb, actually my whole hand and forearm was in a solid cast. My thumb and fingers had no definition, I just had one solid round cast over the whole hand. I was to stay in the recovery for I think two hours before they released me to go home. They said that I was scheduled to return in three weeks just before Christmas Day, but to let them know immediately if there were any problems at all. I would not be able to move any of my fingers or thumb until after the cast was removed and please not to even try to attempt to move my thumb away from my finger as it was buried in it. Buried in it! They explained that the surgeon was skilled enough to lift a flap of my index finger and bury the top half of my thumb under it. Then, in three weeks the surgeon would disconnect my thumb from my finger, and the flesh from the finger would be alive on my thumb and he would graft a new piece of flesh to the finger from my arm. I was still in a daze but understood.

    Prisci drove me home and life went on as best as possible with me and my one active hand. Fortunately, I am now left handed when it comes to writing although I eat right handed, and I am more right footed. The three weeks seemed to go by fast and it didn't seem longer than yesterday that I had just come out of surgery and here was Prisci once again taking me back to have my thumb and finger parted.

    It was another early operation so the traffic was light as we travelled into St. John's hospital before the rush hour hit. After checking in I went through the same process that I had gone through three weeks prior and soon I was out under the general anesthetic having the same surgeon finish his work of art on my hand. I still had absolutely no idea how all my bone came to be there as the intake doctor clearly showed me the top of my ground down bone.

    Once again I awoke in the recovery room where I was to wait for two hours for the anesthetic to wear off. However, they got rather busy in there and the nurses had me discharged early as I had someone to take me home. So, still rather sleepy and feeling groggy we left the hospital, with Prisci, of course, driving us home.

    The way home was via Riverside Drive south out of Tulsa that runs right along the Arkansas River. So, as Prisci drove droopy me southwards with the river on our right side, I was looking forward to fully recovering from my stupid disobedience down in the garage. I was so, so grateful to the Lord for making my thumb at least complete for me to be able to play the violin again but I still had not seen my poor right hand now since that day! Even now it was back to being fully cast as the grafts had to be given time to heal up.

    It was rush hour and traffic was moving well but lots of it which is usual. Then, all of a sudden we heard this car screeching sound and, looking to our left we saw a gray car next to us moving in the same direction as we were, head straight into the oncoming traffic. It all happened too quickly to say anything as the car amazingly did not hit any other vehicle as they swerved out of the way and horns went blasting. I think Prisci slowed down automatically a little which was a good thing as that gray car took a sharp right, straight in front of us before heading back out into the oncoming traffic. All I saw was this black woman who seemed

to be slumped over her steering wheel. More cars swerved out of her way and then she must have put her foot on the gas pedal for some reason because she accelerated and again took a sharp right heading for the front of our truck. Prisci did a great job as she did an emergency stop, exclaiming at the same time,
"She's going in."
I knew what she meant. There is a short grass verge by the side of the road that goes up to a public track that people use to take walks, go jogging or cycling down by the river. On the other side of the track is a sudden decline down to the water's edge. Now, where this was happening was just a short way north of the 21st Street bridge and here, unfortunately for this accident, the water is backed up so it is not just a foot or two deep like the rest of the river in this area, but many feet deep. This car did exactly what my wife exclaimed. It accelerated up over the track (thankfully not hitting anyone) and took off and landed in the river. I could not see the car land due to the drop down to the river. All I remember doing was praying to the Lord for but a moment then, as Prisci came to a complete stop she said that I jumped out, threw off my jacket, wallet and cell phone and ran down to the water's edge. I do not remember to this day doing that but I do remember swimming to the sinking car that was now some thirty feet I guess away from the water's edge. The water was freezing but I guess my adrenaline level must have raised up so much I did not care. Holding my right casted hand up out of the water I soon quit that and swam with both hands to the car. The woman inside was hysterical. She was shouting,
"My baby, my baby!"
At the same time I noticed two other people running up from the bridge and dive in to join me. I seemed to do a few things all at once. I looked towards the bank but only saw people gathering and looking on. I saw that the two men were about maybe thirty seconds away from reaching the car. I noticed that the car was clearly sinking and had but two minutes before it went under, and I needed to check how deep the water was. Maybe it was only a few feet deep there. I shouted to the woman to wind down her window to get out as I held on to the locked car door handle on the passenger side that I was on and plunged myself down, pointing my toes down to touch the bottom. All six feet of me plus my arm length went under but I found no bottom. I came up and again did my best to get through to the woman to get out through her window. People were shouting to break the glass but I am glad that I did not follow that as the water on my side had reached the glass and would have flooded the car and sunk it faster. I made my way around the front of the car just as one of the other men, a younger man probably in his twenties arrived. I don't know what happened to the third man. I said to help the woman out through her window and somehow we both got her out. She was not a petite black lady,

so she was quite a handful for skinny one handed me. I told the young man to get the child in the back as I dealt with the woman. That's when she decided to shout at me,
"I can't swim!"
She was starting to panic. All I could do was to grab hold of her with my good hand, my left hand. I pulled her strongly to my face so that we were face to face eyeballing each other and I said in a loud and very firm voice,
"Today, you swim!"
With her close to me with me holding on to her clothing near her neck and shoulder, I swam as best as I could dragging her to the shoreline. A man waded in to help her out. He had a bandaged arm too! I went back out to the car to see that the young man had successfully rescued the child and was holding him above the water as he passed the boy to me. In turn I went back and passed him to the same man in the bandage.

    Prisci took the little boy into the truck, stripped from his cold wet clothes and we had a blanket there which she used to warm him up as well as putting the cab heater on full. I jumped into the passenger side and some people came and told us that the ambulance was on its way. Prisci was concerned that the mother was okay too and we found out that she was. She had drunk a little of the river water but that's all. She got reassured that her little boy, who looked about two years old, was fine.

    A few minutes later the emergency services all arrived but there were only two ambulances. One of the paramedics came up to us in our truck and asked to take the child. I was to go in the second ambulance together with the young man. I found out that he was in the US air force and was on the bridge when it all happened, proposing to his fiancé! Now for some reason the ambulance only had one of those hot air inflatable body suit things that raises your body temperature back up. And guess who got it? The young fit and healthy air force man! I got a blanket. Not that I was complaining at all but I just noticed it at the time. So, back we went to the same hospital that I had just left. Prisci followed on behind.

    Back into the emergency ward I go and I am thinking that I am getting far too familiar with this place! Straight into a private room and now it is my turn to use one of those blow up heat bag things. They took my vital signs and said I was hypothermic. I felt fine, but okay. They brought me some food to eat which I devoured. I was so hungry! Then various law enforcement and emergency people started to parade through being nice and thanking me for what I had just done. What was funny though was what the ambulance men said to me,
"Wow, we found the only person in the whole of Tulsa with zero body fat to jump into the freezing river!"
We all laughed.
The medical staff at the hospital informed my hand surgeon that I was back in there again and what had happened. They did not know if with my hand

getting all wet, it would cause problems and did he need to come and take a look at it. Apparently not, and he said that I was so fully pumped with antibiotics that it was a very small chance of anything bad happening. He was right, my thumb healed up nicely.

What an ordeal. I really did not think much more about it, as I was once again released to go home. However the media obviously thought otherwise and we were filmed at our home by channel two and six, I think, and the Tulsa World newspaper did a feature on it.

It did not stop there, the next thing we heard after a week or two was an invitation to visit the state Capitol in Oklahoma City to meet the Governor, Governor Brad Henry. The AP, Associated Press, did a release and I started getting all kinds of congratulations coming in. I still thought it was no big thing. I was there, I could help and God helped me do so. Thank you Lord I say, and let's move on. Anyway, I was to go to the State Capitol to receive a 'Hero of Oklahoma" award together with the two other men that had helped.

And just to show this, here is one of the official pictures with me testifying to God's goodness with the Governor to my side:

Here we all are together with the lady, her child and Governor Henry. The Governor also awarded the three of us a date of January 28th to be dedicated to us for what we did in the State of Oklahoma:

STATE OF OKLAHOMA

EXECUTIVE DEPARTMENT

Proclamation

Whereas, three extraordinary Oklahomans -- Joshua Johnson, Robert Ewens and Jerome Wade -- witnessed a car careen off a bridge and into the dark, icy waters of the Arkansas River on December 23, 2004; and

Whereas, Johnson, Ewens and Wade acted swiftly and decisively, as all three rushed to the scene; and

Whereas, the three men dove into the water and rescued the driver, Detura Bills, and her two-year-old son, Brandon; and

Whereas, these three remarkable men displayed the traits of true heroism, having acted bravely and without hesitation to do everything within their power to save the lives of others; and

Whereas, their example is a source of inspiration for all Oklahomans and all Americans;

Now, Therefore, I, Brad Henry, Governor of the State of Oklahoma, do hereby proclaim January 28, 2005, as

"Joshua Johnson, Robert Ewens and Jerome Wade Day"

in the State of Oklahoma.

In Witness Whereof, I have hereunto set my hand and caused the Great Seal of the State of Oklahoma to be affixed.

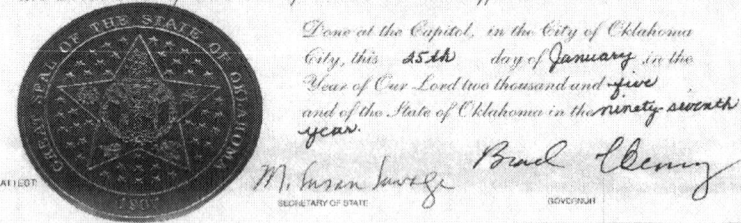

Done at the Capitol, in the City of Oklahoma City, this 25th day of January in the Year of Our Lord two thousand and five and of the State of Oklahoma in the ninety-seventh year.

SECRETARY OF STATE

GOVERNOR

My prayer then got answered on December 23rd 2004. Well what a life I am leading you may say. Will it ever stop? Nope, I don't think so…read on reader…

242

The House gets Destroyed!

Then came the big disaster. The winter of 2007 was particularly severe in Oklahoma. We had a massive ice storm that lasted for a few weeks. It was so severe that the weight of the ice was toppling trees and causing huge power outages everywhere across the State. We were to be without any electricity for over three weeks (for some reason we were one of the last zones to be restored). All you could hear would be cracking sounds then "BOOM!" as another portion or whole tree fell to the ground. It was eerie to look outside especially when it was dark. It looked like some scene out of a late night horror movie but during the day, especially as the sun rose and set it all looked so beautiful. Beautiful, yes, dangerous to be out in? Absolutely!

After that great ice storm which sure kept me busy cutting up and hauling branches for my customers, we had yet another phenomena, hail storms that caused extensive roof damage across Tulsa and surrounding towns. We were no exception either as in April our roof took a small beating, and we started to have water leaks in the living room. I contacted our insurance agent and they eventually sent a disaster insurance person over to us from Arkansas even though we were not in any of the official disaster areas. The lady representative came and cut us a check explaining that our policy would only basically cover for the materials and part of the labor due to much general wear and tear on the shingles. We also had two layers on the roof which meant that we had to totally strip off the entire roof and replace it with a single new layer of shingles. She said that she knew that it was very hard to get a roofer at present so I could do the work myself as I was a remodeler and did roof work at times.

However, the weather remained unsettled for the next couple of months and I could not secure a delivery of the required roofing materials. Finally in mid-June 2008 I arranged delivery for the materials. I had waited for the weather to be more settled and by mid-June the hot weather was starting. I chose a weekend when we were to have clear skies and no clouds as I had to strip off all those shingles and tar paper. My two sons kindly came over to help too.

By the end of this sunny weekend, actually by Sunday morning we had all those shingles stripped off and dumped in the rented dumpster that was parked on our driveway. All we had to wait for was the new materials to arrive first thing Monday morning, scheduled for 7am.

I had been checking the weather leading up to the weekend and all was good. However, on Sunday, all of a sudden for some reason unknown to myself, the forecasters seemed to change their minds and said that there was a 20% chance of thunderstorms. Then the percentage went up to 40% and then higher. So by the time it was dark my wife and her sister were in agreement that I should put up a covering on the exposed roof. Now, this roof did not have the regular eight by four ply or OSB sheets that most houses have these days. No, this 1963 built house had one by six planks laid horizontally with half inch gaps between them. I got the 0.6 mil roofing clear sheets and new tarps from the local hardware store and was up there that evening in the dark nailing them all down as a precaution. And so we all went to sleep…

      At 2:30am I was awakened by the sound of water. Water that was close by. Water that was… in my hallway! I got up and put on the light and water was pouring, literally pouring into the hallway out of the attic fan vent cover. I ran outside and, opening the front door the rain just hit me. We were in the middle of a huge thunderstorm and it was pouring down. I ran down the steps to look back up at the tarps and sheeting, and saw that strong winds were ripping them of like they had never been nailed down at all. I ran back inside to see more water coming in through different places in the ceiling. I cried out to the Lord to stop this and,
"Why Lord why!"
Prisci was up and Kathy got up as did Jacob. I got Prisci and Kathy out to go to a relatives as quickly as I could as sheet rock started to fall down off the ceilings. All my nine years of remodeling was being destroyed in one night! Jacob stayed with me to help but there was not much we could do. I called my insurance company and got through on the emergency call line where a person reassured me that he would add it to the existing claim and get the adjuster around as soon as possible. It was work in progress on an existing claim he was telling me as a big piece of ceiling sheetrock fell down right on top of me. He said that I needed to get out and go somewhere and keep any receipts so that we could be reimbursed later. I took his advice and Jacob and I left as still more and more rain entered the house.

      Early in the morning I went back to assess the damage. It had been a freak storm with gusting winds and rains that deposited almost three inches in all, most of which I think was in my house! The house was a disaster. I could only find a few pictures, here, take a look:

Well, I removed any remaining plastic and tarp sheeting off from the roof to let the hot sun dry as much as possible. Then I went to the local hardware store and purchased more tarps and sheeting as well as more wooden batons and long nails. I called the delivery people to delay sending me the new roof materials until I was ready for them. Walking inside the house it became clear to see that water had got into every room and had poured down stairs through the venting system and down the stair well too. I was trampling through eight to ten inches of a mixture of soaking sheetrock, attic insulation and all kinds of household items. Well, I thought, this has happened so I better do what I can. I bought snow shovels and soon my family came and joined me in this big cleanup to get everything that was wet out as soon as possible as I knew that mold could be a real issue if I did not clear out all this moisture quickly.

    After chasing up the insurance company a few times as I had not heard from the adjustor at all, they finally called and arranged to come out that day. On arrival there were two men, one was the adjustor and the other one apparently was too but he was also in construction. Once they looked at everything the construction man said that it would take him a crew of half a dozen men six months or so to rebuild the house like I had custom made it. It was obviously going to cost a lot of money. They left without making any commitment which bothered me saying that I had to do the phone call interview first. Well, that phone interview came when a young man who sounded new to the business (and later admitted to me that he had just started with this insurance company) called me and recorded what I said had happened and how the rain came in due to strong winds ripping of the appropriate sheeting that I used. He then placed me on hold for a few minutes and came back on the phone saying that he had just spoken to his manager and,

"We are sorry but you are not covered on this insurance policy as you did not have a roof on your house."
WHAT!!!
I was flabbergasted! I was speechless. First I was told that I was covered when I called at the time of the incident and to keep receipts for reimbursement including staying at a hotel etc. and now I am not covered at all?! I argued my point but the poor and rather embarrassed insurance associate did not know what to say so he placed me on hold again and then once more came back saying the same thing to me. I asked to speak to his supervisor and, after much insisting, I got him on the phone. He would only say the same thing too, even though it was people from this same insurance company that told me that I could go ahead and do this work myself and that it had been filed as an existing claim that had already been approved and paid out (the original roof repair claim). I found out shortly afterwards that they separated out the two claims, I guess so that point could not be made an argument against them.

    I was not going to be defeated like that. I really felt that this was an injustice. So, after speaking to a few of my wonderful neighbors who helped in any way they could, I called the local television channels, channel two and channel six. I also called the Tulsa World, our local newspaper to see if they were interested in the story. Soon, both television stations and the Tulsa World were there to film and take pictures as well as interviews. The story made the front page of the newspaper the following day and that same day appeared on the television evening news.

I also got hold of the Oklahoma Insurance Ombudsman in Oklahoma City and made an official complaint. I had to wait a few weeks until I heard back from them as they had to get a written report from the

Insurance Company and then do a review before they could make any comment. In the mean time we had to find somewhere to live and Bianca, our daughter, and her husband David, kindly put us up for a few weeks until we had worked out what we were going to do. We had no savings in reserve so I had to work out how we could fund to buy something else, with the understanding that I still had a full mortgage payment to make on the house that we could no longer live in, or to rent something somewhere.

Prisci and I toiled over renting an apartment or house to buying something. Unfortunately, due to our financial situation, there really was no way to get a mortgage, or should I say a second mortgage. Then Prisci came up with a marvelous idea. Let's buy a mobile home she announced and immediately I witnessed that was the way to go. Prisci had lived in mobile homes and she knew all the pros and cons of having one. What was good now is that the quality of construction had greatly improved since Prisci had her home many years ago. But how on earth we would finance one? I had to leave that in the Lord's hand.

We started shopping for mobile homes. We looked at new and good-condition used homes. We found out that the top elite homes were manufactured by Palm Harbor and they had a sales show room and homes here in Tulsa. The next best seemed to be Oak Creek Homes who also had a local sales office in Tulsa. We looked at other new homes too, but it was these top two manufacturers that caught our attention so we spent time looking at various sizes and layouts. Prices were not as cheap for a mobile home of good quality as you may think. Spending $70,000 just for the home would not have been hard to do. Financing such a sum would have been though! So, flitting between the two top manufacturers we got a break. The sales lady at Oak Creek told us of a dozen or so new homes that had been built in the factory in Texas that the company were selling off cheap. If I recall correctly, she said that they usually sold for $44,000 and were being sold off for $36,000. We could still have some choice in colors of walls, countertops and have extras such a storm windows, extra insulation and a larger water tank etc. We liked that idea and, on seeing the floor plan we seriously considered it. First, however we left there and went back to Palm Harbor. We had been praying for the Lord's favor in this matter and wanted to see if Palm Harbor had any specials. We saw the same sales lady there that we had seen before, and we were really open with her about what Oak Creek was offering. She looked at all the details and she knew of their reputation and construction. She surprised both Prisci and myself with her reply which went something like this:
"This is an excellent deal. I would love to sell you a home but you won't get a better deal than this. I would take it."
That was our confirmation. If the competitor can say that then we knew we were being favored and we were most grateful for her honesty and help.

So we went back to Oak Creek and started the process to purchase the new home. I went through their financing company that they usually used and found out that I would have to raise $9,000 as a deposit. That was going to be a challenge in of itself. You see, purchasing a mobile home is not like getting a mortgage. No, a mobile home, as it is technically mobile, is categorized more as a trailer, a vehicle so it is like applying for a car loan rather than a mortgage for a house.

While I was doing the financial juggling, Prisci was enjoying herself choosing all the colors and extras that she wanted for her new home. I had no idea where to get the $9,000 from but eventually came up with it from a mixture of our own income, an unsecured bank loan with our always very helpful credit union, and a bank overdraft.

The next thing that we had to work out was where were we going to put it? So, our next many evenings and weekends were spent driving to numerous mobile home parks in and around Tulsa. Mobile home parks can quickly change in a few years from a well-organized community to a chaotic shambles of trash, unrepaired vehicles and poorly maintained properties that more resembles a junk yard than a nice place to live. The key to a good park is to have a sound management structure and admittance procedures in place where the basic ground rules are followed. We looked at those very small parks that maybe only had a couple of dozen homes on them to the larger five hundred plus sites. Location was important to us too. We did not want to be too far out of Tulsa, nor in a place where all you could hear was the continual roar of traffic and be subject to breathing in carbon monoxide as part of our gaseous diet! Lastly, we also wanted to be at least reasonably close to our grandchildren who were on the West side of the city.

The ideal place turned up for us, Cherry Hill Mobile Home Park located just on the West side near to where the I-44 crosses the Arkansas River. The park was hidden below a cliff line; it had quite a few mature trees for shade which we liked the idea of, and most of the lots were well kept. There was a club house, offices, showers if needed, a laundromat and a swimming pool. Maximum capacity was probably just over the five hundred mark at a guess, so enough generated income to have a few full time employees to keep the park and its population in order. Once we had met with the current management, we were happy to move in there. We also got a rental discount as we were going to move a brand new home in. I could see that Prisci was happy and I determined in my heart to make this work for her and give her a really nice home.

With all the financing somehow approved and in place, the home was delivered and set up at the beginning of October 2008, less than four months from the date of our house disaster. Prisci already had plans to paint most of the inside walls and she soon had me being a busy bee doing that. Then we moved items from the house that were still salvageable and got those organized. In some ways, we were really just both glad that we had a place to live. But God blessed us more than we realized as this new home, location and neighbors really became home to us as we got to know more of the folk around us.

I don't know how, but Prisci always manages to create this list of projects for me to do! It's a new home, surely there cannot be many things you want to have done to it?! I was wrong, as usual! Actually, I really love doing stuff for my wife so there I soon was building raised flower beds, herb gardens, grape vines, window boxes, window shutters, patio tables, new baseboards and trim, etc.

One of the first projects that she said that we needed to do was add rocks to under the home and around the sides to make it more clean and easier to get underneath. Also, a three foot rock edge around the home really helps preserve the vinyl skirting. Add a long deck stained to match the home with numerous tikki lamps all over the place and Prisci was enjoying her home more and more. Now, I say her home, not our home, as I kept telling her that this was her home and I was doing these projects for her. She corrected me on many occasions saying that I was doing them for us not just for her. You know, sometimes I may not know why I say something at that particular time, but I was to find out later that I was the one being accurate. Although it did take a few years to get the bigger projects done, here are a few pictures of her home that were taken in 2013:

Only a year or so after we moved in, we had been away for a day or two somewhere, and on the return found that the small quarter inch water pipe that feeds the refrigerator had somehow developed a hole. Water had been coming out from behind the appliance, under the linoleum flooring that the home came with throughout, and the floor was sagging in the kitchen, hallway, and dining areas:

Yes, this is me in the picture doing the repair work!

I filed an insurance claim and we were very well taken care of to repair the home. So much so, in fact that as I was going to do the repairs myself, we

252

had enough funds left over for me to lay Allure flooring in the bathrooms, kitchen and utility rooms, as well as new laminate flooring in the rest of the home! The additional floor projects were completed over a year or so period. The house was looking good. Well, I thought so anyway.

The Old House and the US Coastguard Finds Me

It was during this period of time, from late 2008 through to probably 2012 that I worked on rebuilding our storm damaged home. However, although the damage happened in June 2008 other than emptying out the house and getting it dry and free from any mold, I did not work on it much at all until late 2009. This was because we did not have any money to really work on it, and also because we were in the process of suing the insurance company and we wanted to know the outcome first. Our attorney was very good at what he did and he strongly advised that we hold out as long as it takes as the insurance company would do all they could to delay the legal process. He was right, they did exactly that and it took almost a year just to get a mediation date even set.

Having come from England and having been in the lower court system through one of my jobs, I was quite shocked to find what 'due process' looked like at mediation. The chosen mediator happened to be someone that our attorney went through law school with. He had advanced to being a state high court judge until he retired to do such jobs like this mediation. Definitely a wise and well-seasoned person who knew his profession well, so it was well worth listening to him.

On the day of the mediation hearing Prisci and I turned up about ten minutes or so early. As we walked in another well-dressed man also came in and I picked up that he was representing the insurance company. Up at the reception he said that he had just flown in from California. So, he's the big-wig guy they have brought in I thought. He turned and looked at us and I smiled at him saying something like,
"Looks like you had a long flight in."
And smiling,
"Welcome to Tulsa."
He was not my enemy, he had come to do his job. Must be a hard one to do sometimes.

The local office that was hosting the mediation was not apparently supposed to allow the two parties to see or talk directly which is probably why the man looked at me rather awkwardly. He was quickly ushered through out of our sight. Then they came to get us and placed us in a conference room where our attorney was waiting for us to arrive. Once we had settled in the host office sent in the mediator and, like I have said, our attorney and he knew each other so after introductions they did a little past chat talk together. He looked like one of those old judges too! White balding hair, skin starting to wrinkle, yet he held himself well and there was a sense of overall peace in himself that he knew exactly what he was doing. The mediator gets paid handsomely to go over both parties arguments and then to use his knowledge and wisdom to help settle the issue here in mediation rather than going forward to court hearings. He made it clear what his role was and that we did not have to agree to anything that may be offered if we did not want to do so.

Finally, we were informed that the other party was ready to proceed. They were all in some other room down the corridor. The mediator was to literally walk between the two parties to try and resolve the case satisfactorily to all. First he left us and spent maybe almost half an hour in the other room before returning. Then he came back in to us and sat down to offer his advice. The main thing he said was that if we decided to take this case to court, we were almost certain not to get awarded the bad faith portion of our claim. Now this was the largest portion that our attorney was claiming on our behalf.

As our attorney was not able to find even one case through the history of the court circuits of a similar case that was won by the individuals suing an insurance company, then we really only had the opinion of the jury to decide and that would be very risky. This was even more so in our case as the insurance company also felt strongly that we had broken the contract by not having a complete roof prior to the incident occurring, irrespective of any work in progress. Taking that as being so, then about two thirds of our claim was gone already. Leave what is left and take away our attorney fees and mediation fees and if they negotiate down the rest by 50% of what is left we will not be getting much at all. I pondered this as the mediator added one final nail to the full claim approach as he told us that if we did decide to go to court then there was always the possibility that we may lose the case or it be thrown out of court. We may even be required to pay the court costs and the insurance companies expenses!

Okay, so no bad faith portion is an option now. So what next, I was about to ask, when our mediator said that we needed to give him an amount to offer to settle. Now, if we did settle here today then that was it. We would have no more recourse against this company and we would be sworn not to disclose who they are (notice I have not mentioned any names of the parties involved other than ourselves). Our attorney said that we should start with the full amount anyway. So off trots our mediator to the other room. Five minutes later he is back with a counter offer. Let me give you some rough idea of what ratios of dollars we are talking about here. Let's say our initial offer was $350,000. And guess what the return offer was?

"$2,500," The mediator told us on his return.
You're kidding me! I slumped back onto my chair with a look of amazement. I just stared at my attorney who did not seem too bothered. So, I shut up as he gave another figure which was everything less the bad faith portion that he did include in the first amount. So now we are already down to just over $130,000. Off trots the mediator again only to return five more minutes later with,
"$23,000."
This does not look good to me. That won't even cover my attorney fees! Our attorney changes tactics and has already found out that this top man that came in from California has another appointment in the early afternoon. So, we do a stalling tactic and have coffee and chat and do nothing as the noon time starts to approach. I still could not believe that this was the process by which such issues are settled. Full grown men playing some silly game of who can get the most cookies out of the cookie jar or keep them in there. I asked the mediator and my attorney about this and they said that yes, this was how it is done but worse than that, they said that it is this same process for medical malpractice and even death claims! I said that people must be devastated going through this and our attorney sighed and said yes, that would happen at times. Well, I guess it's all about money.

Prisci at times I think wanted to take it to court but I kept getting a check in my spirit not to do so but I said nothing for certain. As minutes went by and noon was approaching our attorney went and offered a very slightly lower sum than before. Then goes our $250 per hour lovely mediator trotting back down the corridor to the other party. Back comes a slightly increased sum but more than we reduced and I think our attorney thinks that they want to get this over with. He offers a smaller amount again and again a larger increase comes back. I said to our attorney,
"Do they know what amount they are willing to go to?"
He said that they do, so I said,
"Then why are we playing this silly game and why don't we get straight to the point?"
He shrugged his shoulders and continued the process. The mediator came back with a final offer. It was a reasonable sum and something I could work with, just but Prisci did not seem too happy. I made the decision to accept rather than risking everything at court. I said yes to their offer, providing they paid half the mediation fees. They agreed and papers were drawn up and monies arrange to be wired into our attorney's account on our behalf. Our attorney also was then kind enough to reduce his fees significantly which we both appreciated him for doing that for us.

A few weeks later we had the remaining funds from which to pay off some debts that we had incurred through this ordeal and money to spend on materials for me to remodel the house a second time! We had also fallen way behind with our house mortgage payments by agreement with the bank but we needed to catch back up as we had over $8,000 in arrears. In the meantime, we had this new home that Prisci wanted me to work on and I had to also work my self-employed handyman and remodeling job to earn some money somewhere in the middle of all this.

Without a doubt, it was the grace of God that gave us the strength and patience to work through all of this. Here is one crazy thing though, if I had listened more and been less stubborn we may have avoided the whole house disaster. The very night of the storm we had invited our daughter, her husband and children to dinner. Kathy, Prisci's sister, was there as well as she had been living with us. Our two boys, Jeremy and Jacob, I think were there also so we had a good size gathering and people started to comment on the 'what if' situation. That is, what if it rains before the materials arrived? We had just been working taking the shingles off so most of the roof was exposed though it was not to be until later the next day when I covered up the entire roof when the weather forecast changed. What if indeed I think as I look back to that meal time. What if I had not been so sure and prideful that nothing was going to happen and what if I had listened instead and waited longer to remove the shingles? Well, for certain, I really did mess up on that decision even though I did what I was supposed to do to protect our home before the storm came.

So battling on, we kept on going. Gradually I get the new ceilings up in the old house and added the insulation. One project after another gets completed. One day while I was working on the house I get a phone call, "Mr. Ewens?"
"Yes." I replied with an uncertain voice as the questioning male voice seemed to carry some authority with it.
"This is the attorney for the United States Coast Guard for the Mississippi catchment area."
"Sir," he continued, "Do not be alarmed, I have been trying to track you down for over a year now."
"You have?" I said and "Why?"
"You have been awarded the silver lifesaving medal from the United States Coast Guard following a thorough investigation as to the events that led to you together with two other men saving two lives out of the Arkansas River."
I perked up now that I knew I was not in trouble for something! Well some good news for a change. Apparently, the next in line to the admiral had made a house call some months ago in an attempt to contact me. Now they wanted to setup a time to present me with this award. They said that I could invite the media etc. but I was not really interested in publicity so I did not do so. They arranged a date at the local Port of Catoosa training school. Prisci and I went to receive the award and then we were taken on a tour of the whole port. It was most interesting; the Port of Catoosa I was

told is the world's largest most inland port and it plays an important role for the economy here.

Why Can't I Overcome and Get the Victory!?

Life just seemed to be one trial after another and all the way through these years Prisci was hoping that we could just settle down and enjoy our marriage and life together. I wanted that too but inside I still was not fully at peace. I still had not really found my first love, the Lord Jesus Christ like when I first got saved and the Lord just kept on reassuring me that He was here with me and just be patient. I did not have the fear of the Lord either and it continually worried me but the Lord would not reply to me on this. I just did not understand what was going on and why I, or should I say we, kept on going through these repetitive cycles of events that would be destructive to our relationship. I loved Prisci yet found myself being led astray going down this female deal road. I knew better, yet it would not seem to stop even when applying all the Christian tools.

In the end the conclusion, the only conclusion to this female desire to dress and be like one and all the perversions that seem to always go along with it, was that I was just refusing deep in my heart, and in my soul to let go of it. Or, you could conclude that I did truly repent all the times that I did and the Lord did truly set me free but I went straight back and picked it up again. Like the scripture says, like a dog returning to its vomit.

Was this me? Really, am I just so won over with this that all my future holds is my doom and destruction for me and misery for my wife, that is if she stays with me? It was now 2012, eighteen years of marriage and I felt we were still in the same place on this issue as on day one. Looking back I am still amazed that I didn't consider suicide and that Prisci stayed with me. But God was there with both of us and I knew it.

        Was my conclusion right above? It was not only my conclusion but that of others too, including my wife. Where had the redeeming power of the cross gone? Why did it not *totally* deliver me but at best just offer a short season only to reappear even stronger and more defined? I did notice that it seemed to be less and less sexual over the years but it was all sin to me however you evaluate it. It is my flesh, my wicked heart and I am deceived. Plain and simple.

Selling our Old Home

By 2012 our house had been on the market for two years with no offers at all. Realtors seemed a little puzzled and started to come up with reasons as to why it was not selling. Prisci and I really knew why. It was not time for it to do so yet. Also the Lord kept pointing out to me that the lower main supportive wall on the north side of the house was bowing out. This was the wall that had originally collapsed before we purchased the house. It had concrete and steel peers in it so it did not make sense to me why it was pushing out again and maybe in danger one day of all collapsing again. My conscience was pricked and I realized that I needed to fix this before the house would sell.

        The challenge was, where was I supposed to get the money from to pay for that kind of work? The job was beyond my skills and equipment. Thankfully, my wonderful Credit Union that I had been with for many years now were happy to loan me most of it. I decided first to get a structural inspection done and I looked back in my old house purchase information and found the person who did the inspection on this house prior to us buying it. I called his office and arranged to meet him one day at our empty and still not selling house.

        The structural inspector was a really pleasant man who had been in this profession for years. He remembered the house and he went around and saw the lower wall bowing out and inside a widening gap from the concrete blocks in the garage to the concrete slab floor. He inspected the peers and came back to me and said that the peers had held well and were not the problem. He said that he believed that whoever rebuilt the concrete block wall either did not put enough steel rebar in, put it in incorrectly, or there was none there at all. The wall should be tied in to the foundation but seemed not to be. The slab in the garage should be, and was, free floating so that was good. Remedy? Support the garage ceiling, knock down the entire block wall and rebuild it correctly. Push the upper wall back into place and drop it on the newly constructed one. Sounded like a big job to me. He recommended a company so I called them straight away and was given a really good price for all the work involved. Still just over $8,000 was no small sum.

Although it was summer 2012 I was not in any rush to get the job done as long as the house did not fall down beforehand! I had had enough of disasters. It was I think March 2013 when they came and did the work. Mainly Mexican workers but not all and a good job they did too. They even took out and poured almost half of the garage slab. I had arranged to do all the cosmetic work like replacing sheet rock, mudding, taping and painting etc. so by the end of April the house was in good selling order. Here are some pics of the work. I wonder if you can see why the wall was moving in the first place:

You see those hollow concrete blocks in the top right picture that were laid sideways for some (stupid) reason? Well, guess what, there is no way rebar goes through that. They did not even use rebar there at all! Unfortunately, it was my best man's business that had done all the work and he has long gone out of the country so there was to be no recourse on what he had done here. Anyway, the company I hired did a really great job and put it all back together, even managing to push the whole wall back into place before lowering it onto the new block wall.

The only bad thing about the wall deal was that the very next day after the workers left the house, the house was 'broken' into and the gas range that I had put there to help sell the house was stolen. Kind of odd situation really as the people got in through the back downstairs window which had not been locked (the workers used the window to take out some of the rubble (see bottom picture above) when excavating. And the thieves had all the right tools to correctly disconnect and switch off the gas pipe. The front door had been forced in but it looked like the stove was taken out through the back patio. I got the impression that the front door was kicked in as an afterthought to make it look like the point of entry, but, hey, what do I know. Another insurance claim.

I knew that the house would sell exactly when the Lord wanted it to do so. Prisci and I both knew this. It was one of the pieces of puzzle that was going to fall into place exactly when it needed to for all that was coming next in our lives. The house was to finally sell in the summer of 2013 whereupon I paid off our debts as the Lord had instructed, but not before even more things were to happen…

Chapter Five – My Destiny in Life. Sanctified and Commissioned unto God for this Very Purpose.

I am Nearly Fifty: A Terrible Shock

I just cannot believe it. This is ridiculous, this cannot be for real, no, no, NO, NO, NO! Surely, after all my wife and I have gone through the desires of my flesh are crucified with Christ, and I will no longer be swayed to and fro by the tempter. Surely, as and when the devil tries to tempt my wicked heart when I am weak to seduce me away, I have wizened up by now to see it for what it is and simply cast the occasional wrong thought down, so I can get on with being a good Christian man and husband. Surely my precious wife and I can settle down to a peaceful marriage as trust is rebuilt?

The business was being blessed by the Lord. ERS (Ewens Restoration Services, LLC) had been more profitable each year ever since it started in 2006. My nephew Triston had been my main helper and we worked well together. However, a year prior I had encouraged him to get a full time job and he got one working for the small construction company that my son Jacob was also working for at that time. Although money was not in abundant excess, Prisci and I still managed to help others in need around us, pay our bills, and live.

Well, the peaceful marriage part did start to happen and I can recall Priscilla even coming to me and saying things like,
"I was actually thinking nice thoughts about you today" and "I actually like you today."
We would pray over our meal in the evening, then be together to talk a little, watch a movie or sometimes read, and very occasionally read the Bible together. Surely, this was the beginning of something good that we both were searching for, a time of peace and restoration. But it was not to be…
..and who was at fault, yet again…me.

Thoughts to cross dress and be feminine started to come and even though I confessed to close friends and let my wife know that I was having thoughts, they persisted and got stronger. Like a pig with a nose ring, like a dog returning to its vomit, I, yet again, finally gave in after weeks of repenting to the Lord and casting down trillions of thoughts. I was not blind nor ignorant so I knew exactly in which direction it was heading. First, one skirt, then a dress, a bra … a mirror to dress in front of, get sexually aroused and I am hooked, yet while all the time speaking to God to deliver me from this vice! Speaking and declaring God's Word as I sinned before Him. Nothing happened.

It came to a head when I confessed after Prisci discerned, and we fought and we separated for about three weeks. I went to stay at the old house we are selling, living downstairs in the 4th bedroom. I was devastated. So was Prisci, and she was lead to go on a forty day fast. I was broken, both in disbelief and hope. I just could not believe that we were going through it all over again. I reviewed all the counseling, the studying, the confessions, the prayers, the efforts by all and the pain suffered. Those three weeks were agonizing for me and my wife. After twenty-one days of fasting, Prisci called me to come home and talk. I did and we reunited. I returned all my man clothes that had been delivered to my house back to our mobile home across Tulsa. For me the saving grace came while praying and listening to God and I heard Him say,
"You have not yet resisted sin to the point of shedding blood."
My head dropped and I agreed with the Lord. Even self-indulging sexual sin is just that, sin (missing the mark, not a perfect thing to do).

    We had also been attending a small Messianic church fellowship that met downtown. The pastors were there for us, though we had reservations about them on some fundamental Christian principles. The pastor's wife at one time said to me that I needed to cleave to my wife. This was a golden nugget for me that I held on to, so when my wife and I got together again, I lived by this and would let her know that if I was struggling, that I would let her know that I needed to cleave to her. Oddly, she did not seem able to really hear me, I felt. Her hurts were too deep and it would take weeks for her to even start to relax just a little bit. I hated myself for the pain I caused. Deep regrets indeed to my wife and family, and in the face of my God. What a wretch I had become, such an evil selfish heart.
..it was not the end…

    Summer 2013: Within a year the thoughts and desire came back even stronger. After confessing this to my wife again I separated out of the house and went back to the empty house that we still had not sold. I went with the purpose to expose my heart to God and do all my heart's desire and throw myself at the Lord. The battle was on between the desires of my flesh and evil heart, the devil, and the Lord my God through Jesus Christ. The acting out, denying, and confessing even to other brothers and so, so much praying and wrestling with God went on and on for about four months.

    While living in that empty house to do all that my heart desired, I really wrestled with God over my life. At one time I got fully dressed ready to go out and just stood in front of the mirror and argued with God for ages to look at me as I pleaded, and pleaded with Him to set me free from this behavior. I remember arguing with God, almost shouting to Him,

"Look at me! I'm a *man*. Why do I want to be like this?!!"
Finally, I saw the Lord's face… Smiling back at me! Saying,
"I look way beyond your flesh."
What's that supposed to mean! I got mad at Him but I knew it was useless, I have already given my life to His purpose and glory, not mine. I went out. It's really interesting to note that as a man, that is dressed and acting as a man these past 20 years, it has been hard for me to flow in the testimony of Jesus Christ. Even if I really wanted to, I could not. It was like I was bound and I would often pray to the Lord to loosen my tongue to share His truth of the Gospel and to testify of His goodness. It never happened. However, now, for some crazy reason, I was going out dressed as a girl and my tongue won't stop telling of Jesus! Now how ridiculous is that! Even when I did my best to look as a woman I never 'passed'. I am over 6ft tall, have a huge Adams apple and a large hooked male nose! Look; see:

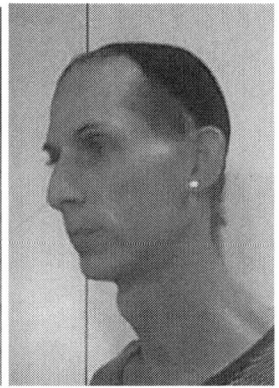

And I just found two old pics of myself that were taken back then:

Just a couple of days after I believed that I had done all that was in my heart to do regarding dressing and being a woman (which strangely ended in wearing pierced ear rings as the final touch at that time), the Lord led my wife and I to connect back to Pure Life Ministries. Prisci had kept away from me for quite a few weeks but her online research with other believers (mainly) had recommended that she should stay in touch with me and edify me as a man, and a man of God. Otherwise it was said, she could lose me as I would never turn back.

Pure Life Ministries had a 'Purity Weekend' coming up in St. Louis which we both went to. It was for the men so my wife was given a private area outside of the sanctuary where she could watch the service on a television screen. I knew the message that was to be given which was fine, I had come to repent if the Lord would accept me where I was at. I was still struggling to let go completely. At the altar call I stepped forward and as I got down on my knees before the Lord I saw a white cross come down to meet me. Light shone from out of it as I repented of my actions, my wicked heart, and all that was evil in me. During the time that we separated I never acted nor desired any sinful sexual activities with anyone else.

On the way driving home from the Purity weekend I wrestled with coming home to Prisci which would mean stopping all cross-dressing activities and turn away from it all. I finally got to that point in my heart where I could choose to do so and so I took a deep breath and I said that to Prisci. She double and tripled checked my decision with me. So that is what I did.

Prisci came with me to the old house to pack up all the ladies stuff I had acquired. She was brave to do this. I remember whining when it came to packing the rich blue performance (violin) dress that I had worked on and never got to perform in.

Once all was packed we (my wife and children) agreed to have a burning party at my son's house in Claremore as he was storing those packed boxes there. So, come the day we went and had a burning party and all was burnt. Everyone saw my actions as sinful…and so did I.. my wicked heart and my flesh acting out in an area that I was clearly weak in as I had given myself over to it so many times in my life. This, I was certain was the accurate, the correct understanding of my life. Life is about self-control, self-discipline of all things in the Lord and we do it as best as we can and the Lord helps us when we fall or fail. However, this desire over the years towards being female and all the sinful activities that go along with it is marriage destroying (as Prisci would continually tell me). It HAD to end. I was so, so, so tired of 'pulling the rug' out from underneath my wife and then have to look into her eyes and see the pain that I had caused. Enough was enough. I vowed to Prisci that if it ever, ever came back, I would leave the house as I was not going to play that destructive record again. I also looked my younger son, Jacob, straight in the eye and vowed that I would never do it again.

Once again after all that turmoil peace gradually started to return to our lives. I had absolutely no desires at all to repeat any of that behavior in my life, not even passing thoughts and was determined not to do so. Surely God had finally broken this off of me.

I am Fifty: The Prophesized Start of Ministry

Looking back a little to June 25th 2012, my fiftieth birthday: This was the year, at this age, that the Lord had told me some six years or so prior that my ministry would start (I say 'my' ministry but I automatically assumed that meant mine and Prisci's as she is my wife, my covenant partner). Fifty came, and fifty went. The only really significant things about that year was we finally found a relatively new church in Owasso that was being founded on the fivefold ministry and there was an apostle there laying the foundation. However, when we first went there the Lord spoke clearly to me as we walked through the doors for the first time, something that I kept to myself as I had no idea at that time why He said it to me. He said, "This body is not for you; it is for your wife."

The other significant thing that seemed to happen was that Prisci started more into being pre-menopausal. Prisci has always tried to do her utmost to meet my needs and edify me as a man and I think, considering all that I had put her through to date, she was truly an amazing lady not to have dumped my sorry as... you know, a long time ago. Going through this stage of her life I really did my best to understand, so was careful not to push her to come together too often. There were many times she just was naturally just not interested so I would back off. As this continued I actually started to get disappointed at myself and even started to pray for my sexual desire to abate. It was like I was done with sex. I also started to realize that my approach to sex seemed a little different than maybe what is normal for men overall. For me, it was more important to make sure my wife was satisfied than for me to sow my oats, so to speak like a typical testosterone filled man would act like. Therefore, as her natural desire dropped, so did mine. Sex, more accurately sexual lust, had caused so much pain in our lives. Looking back on it, I really believe God answered my prayer as my sexual drive and desires declined. I had no other sexual desires other than to be with my wife. I had gladly kept myself for her for many years now, even through all the previously mentioned activities. It got to the point where I no longer wanted sex at all. It was a gradual process that I really didn't fully notice until much later.

So, did the 'ministry' start? Nope. I had thought that now I was, really, really once and for all free from this female acting out stuff that God would start to use us to minister to others in this bondage, especially to husbands and wives. We would be a testimony of how the Lord can and will set you free from this sin. And somehow, by God's grace and mercy He would use us in some way to set others free too. I mean, that's how it works, right? You overcome and through your testimony others get set free. That's the Christian and charismatic way of the Kingdom of God. Right? I can imagine it all now; Prisci and I travelling to various churches and groups giving our testimonies, I will play the violin and the presence of God will manifest, Prisci will share her love and compassion and use the God blessed gift of wisdom she has and God will do the rest. Hallelujah, praise the Lord! Right?

Wrong again!

This Insanity Has to Stop!

Stop the insanity! Enough is enough. Twenty hard years of playing the same record doing all we could from what we knew to do to have a normal life and Prisci and I were more than tired. Tired of ending up at the same place. I was tired of always being the 'sinner', the guilty party that family looked at as the bad one. If only this desire would finally disappear but it had not done so for whatever reason one wants to attach to that.

Christianity blames the individual as having a hard heart, selfish heart, deceived mind, demon oppressed soul, weakness of the flesh to overcome, lack of Biblical or spiritual knowledge, lack of surrendering to the Cross of Christ, etc. etc. I had gone through them all and ended right back at square one. Self-rebuke and denial were the other tools I used. No, it was time once and for all to face myself before God and stop this insanity. Doing the same kind of thing over and over again and expecting a different result is crazy. It was time for a big change…

I am Fifty-One! Did I Miss God?

I was confused; I know the voice of God yet nothing seemed to happen. If the Lord said that ministry would start at fifty then what happened? I sort the Lord privately on this matter once I had turned fifty-one. It was late June 2013 and the Lord was silent on the subject. I was confused. It was like for almost twenty years now I had been collecting all these pieces of a puzzle, actually a really big pile, and none of the pieces would come together.

July came and went and so did August. After three years of waiting we got a buyer on the house. A young Christian couple with two lovely children and they loved all the work that we had done to it. For sure, we had spent a lot of time and money on it over the years. The purchase went through and I obeyed the Lord to clear our debts as much as possible which we did. I got the sense that the pieces of the puzzle were about to all fall into place.

Somewhere around late September something started to happen inside me. On the outside I was usual active Rob busy providing and working and doing life with my wife. Inside I felt separated from the world. Finally, I heard the voice of the Lord answer me.
"You did."
"I did?" I replied, "I did what?"
"You did start your ministry at fifty."
I got still before the Lord for understanding. The Lord showed me that He had separated my heart's desire from all perverse sexual desire and activity. That what remained in my heart was pure and would not count against me. I got great inner peace.

But then the most unexpected thing started to happen…and in a different way this time that had never happened like this before…

I saw the desire in my heart to be more female than male. It was still there now even stronger and clearer but this time untainted with sexual desires or perverse thoughts of any kind. I was struck dumb before my God. I was speechless.

It took me some time to get before the Lord on this and during those weeks the desire to act female and dress that way grew and grew. I confessed to some close brothers but it continued. This time fear and dread was absent, shame and guilt gone. But I knew I had to tell Prisci and when I did during a phone call I cried that I had failed to overcome and that I believed that I would never would overcome. For weeks I had not acted out at all. In fact I had strongly denied myself to act in any way at all. I had given my word to Prisci and I had looked at my younger son, Jacob straight in the eye after the last session and burning party, and given him my word that I would never act out again. I was determined to keep my word to him and to Prisci, but crying to Prisci on that phone call I realized that I was unable to overcome this in my life. For twenty years as a believer and about the same length of time previous to that I had faced this issue in my life and beaten myself up over and over and over again about it. I knew what I had to do. I had given Prisci my word that I would not put her through this again.

I told Prisci that I had to leave and packed my stuff and moved into my shop office about a mile away.

I arranged I think in November 2013, or somewhere about then to have lunch with my son Jacob. I told him what was going on with my life. I knew Prisci was convinced that I was doing wrong before God and all the rest of the family would either think I am sick, or crazy, or that I am just choosing to follow the desires of my flesh and that I am following the devil and not Christ. Jacob however, said something that totally touched my heart. I explained how all those desires were back even stronger and how I had refused to act out at all because I had given him my word that I would not do so. My heart was grieving and my soul lifeless and sad. It was like how you would be if all of your immediate family had been suddenly killed in a bad accident and you had just been informed. It is an indescribable pain in your heart.

I asked Jacob please to release me from my word to him as I was unable to overcome. Years of prayer, pleading, casting down trillions of thoughts, fastings, men's retreats etc. etc. and I was unable to achieve freedom even in Christ. I knew that the cross of Christ and who He is was not the problem; it was me.

As we sat down together at a Chinese restaurant in Owasso north of Tulsa, Jacob told me in all love that he had seen all these years of my struggles, that I had been a good dad, and good provider, and that he loved me for who I am and that I would always be his dad whatever happened. He released me from my binding word to him and suggested to me to basically to go for it, to live according to the real desires of my heart and discover who I am. He was not saying that he agreed with what I was going to do or that he understood it, but he loved me enough to know that this was very real for me and that he loved me enough to accept me as I am. I was deeply touched. Jacob had once come to me the previous year when I was at the house just to tell me that he loved me no matter what happened. I love that boy. I know all my children love me from where they are and according to what they believe.

I went back and sought the Lord again while in my shop office. I thought about what the Lord had said according to the purity of my heart that He said I had. I asked the Lord concerning this desire. He smiled again at me and told me that this was how He had made me to be to bring Him glory…

WHAT!?

I was silent in disbelief, checking over and over again that this was His voice, and it was and I knew it. He gave me Psalm 32:1-2 amongst many others:

Ps 32:1-2
  Blessed *is he whose* transgression *is* forgiven,
  Whose sin *is* covered.
  2 Blessed *is* the man to whom the Lord does not impute iniquity,
  And in whose spirit *there is* no deceit.
NKJV

Then He started to present before my eyes all those pieces of puzzle that I had been holding onto with no insight as to how they were to fit together. Right before my eyes He started to put the pieces into place on events that had already happened. Even events that I thought had nothing to do with this or His will, but He showed me His hand at work. He held on to some pieces and did not place them down. One piece was my desire to be more female. He held it and looked at me and I stared at the piece and at Him. Before I could say anything He said again,
"This is how I have made you."
But before He placed the piece down He said,
"I am sending you to them as one of them," referring to other people that face the same issues and that have been judged and even kicked out of churches, and to the lost the hurting and those who get depressed and suicidal.
I argued with the Lord, "But Lord you are God. You could remove this from me for you can do anything."
And the Lord replied in all love and wisdom,

"If I had then you would have never have gone to them. You would have gone to church on Sundays, and stayed at home with your wife, living in the prosperity and good health that I have given you, and these lives would have been untouched by Me." I sobered up and admitted that He was perfectly right.

The Lord continued,

"I am sending you to them as one of them. I command you to walk upright before Me and honor Me with your body."

After taking that in I said,

"I can do that Lord," knowing that the Lord had already delivered me from all perverseness over these twenty years to leave this desire pure.

Then the Lord broke me completely by saying,

"Then I grant you the desires or your heart," as He placed the TRANSGENDER, my identity piece of the puzzle down.

I lost it totally, lost it right there. I wept and wept and could not stop for some time. I just could not believe that this was happening to me. Joy, peace, elation all combined together to give thanks to my Lord my God as He released me inside from all the self-inflicted denying and condemning of who I am right from my childhood. My memories just 'popped' down a long series of events, each releasing who I am. All that repression coming straight to the surface and was being released out of me. All the condemnation and guilt was being released out of me. I was coming alive again. The Lord was setting me free!

    I found myself raising my hands up to the Lord and thanking Him and praising His name over and over again while I cried. The Lord had set me free to be me. Me, you understand, ME. I can be ME Just *ME!*

    I have never looked back. I have no regrets on this and see the mighty hand of the Lord in my life. It is the Lord who placed that piece of puzzle down for me and it made the puzzle whole even though it is not fully complete as my life is not over yet.

This is a true statement:

    At Last! Freedom from the Bonds of Sexual Immorality.

    The Lord had orchestrated the whole events of my life. Now, I could see that the deception of sexual drive and lusts and desires was what had been holding me back from seeing and accepting myself as I am, and it was the Lord, yes the Lord Jesus the Christ, the anointed One, our Messiah Yeshua, who has done it all. Not the hand of man, and least of all mine but the hand of God who has done this work. My Christian theology the Lord showed me was in error regarding His call on my life. I was not to be 'set free' from this desire and way of life. He told that He was sending me into dark and dangerous places (remember, as He had had prophesized over me in past years on three continents by anointed people of God) and that these places were not as I had thought, dangerous like going to gangs, communist countries or the like, but rather to the lost and rejected people, the transgender, transsexual, gay, lesbian and bi-sexual. He said that He was sending me as one of them (that is transgender) and that I was to submerge myself into that whole lifestyle while obeying those two commandments; to walk upright before Him and secondly to honor Him with my body. He will do all the rest.

Then He gave me two years to literally 'make myself as pretty as I can be and that He would be with me on this'. Wow!

WOW! WHAT AN AWESOME GOD WE SERVE!

Next, see how quickly the Lord moves in a life when you are submitted in all joy to Him. But first we need to understand who and what I am other than a child of God. The word Transgender I had heard of before of course, but I had always denied myself even the possibility that I was such a person. As I had labelled being transgender as a form of sexual sin, I had never bothered to look deeper into it. It was time for me to do a lot of research. First we will look and define the word and then go into the whole subject in more detail.

Thank you Lord. I had found my first love again and could once again love the Lord my God with ALL my heart, soul and strength.

Transgender: Definition

Here are some definitions of the word transgender as found on the internet (any bold text is my emphasis):

Oxford Dictionary:

1) "tranz'jender"
   adjective

   adjective: transgender; adjective: transgendered

   Denoting or relating to a person whose self-identity does not conform unambiguously to conventional notions of male or female gender.

Wikipedia:

2) Transgender is the state of one's gender identity (self-identification as woman, man, neither or both) or gender expression not matching one's assigned sex (identification by others as male, female or intersex based on physical/genetic sex).[1] **Transgender is independent of sexual orientation; transgender people may identify as heterosexual, homosexual, bisexual, pansexual, polysexual, or asexual; some may consider conventional sexual orientation labels inadequate or inapplicable to them**. The precise definition for transgender is changing but nevertheless includes:

- "Of, relating to, or designating a person whose identity does not conform unambiguously **(clearly)** to conventional notions of male or female gender roles, but combines or moves between these."[2]
- "People who were assigned a sex, usually at birth and based on their genitals, but who feel that this is a false or incomplete description of themselves."[3]
- "Non-identification with, or non-presentation as, the sex (and assumed gender) one was assigned at birth."[4]

A transgender individual may have characteristics that are normally associated with a particular gender, identify elsewhere on the traditional gender continuum, or exist outside of it as other, agender, genderqueer, or third gender. Transgender people may also identify as bigender or along several places on either the traditional transgender continuum or the more encompassing continuums that have been developed in response to recent, significantly more detailed studies.[5] Furthermore, many transgender people experience a period of identity development that includes better understanding one's self-image, self-reflection, and self-expression. More specifically, the degree to which individuals feel genuine, authentic, and comfortable within their external appearance and accept their genuine identity is referred to as transgender congruence.[6]

National Center for Transgender Equality:
TRANSGENDER TERMINLOGY
Updated January 2014

Transgender: A term for people whose gender identity, expression or behavior is different from those typically associated with their assigned sex at birth. Transgender is a broad term and is good for non-transgender people to use. "Trans" is shorthand for "transgender." (Note: Transgender is correctly used as an adjective, not a noun, thus "transgender people" is appropriate but "transgenders" is often viewed as disrespectful.)

Transgender Man: A term for a transgender person who currently identifies as a man (see also "FTM").

Transgender Woman: A term for a transgender person who currently identifies as a woman (see also "MTF").

Gender Identity: An individual's internal sense of being male, female, or something else. Since gender identity is internal, one's gender identity is not necessarily visible to others.

Gender Expression: How a person represents or expresses one's gender identity to others, often through behavior, clothing, hairstyles, voice or body characteristics.

Transsexual: An older term for people whose gender identity is different from their assigned sex at birth who seeks to transition from male to female or female to male. Many do not prefer this term because it is thought to sound overly clinical.

...

Genderqueer: A term used by some individuals who identify as neither entirely male nor entirely female.

Gender Non-conforming: A term for individuals whose gender expression is different from societal expectations related to gender.

Bi-gender: One who has a significant gender identity that encompasses both genders, male and female. Some may feel that one side or the other is stronger, but both sides are there.

...

Sex Reassignment Surgery (SRS): Surgical procedures that change one's body to better reflect a person's gender identity. This may include many different procedures, including those sometimes also referred to as "top surgery" (breast augmentation or chest reconstruction) or "bottom surgery" (altering genitals). Contrary to popular belief, there is not one surgery; in fact there are many different surgeries. These surgeries are medically necessary for some people, however not all people want, need, or can have surgery as part of their transition. "Sex change" is considered a derogatory term by many.

...

Transition: The time when a person begins living as the gender with which they identify rather than the gender they were assigned at birth, which often includes changing one's first name and dressing and grooming differently. Transitioning may or may not also include medical and legal aspects, including taking hormones, having surgery, or changing identity documents (e.g. driver's license, Social Security record) to reflect one's gender identity. Medical and legal steps are often difficult for people to afford.

Intersex: A term used for people who are born with a reproductive or sexual anatomy and/or chromosome pattern that does not seem to fit typical definitions of male or female. Intersex conditions are also known as differences of sex development (DSD).

...

National Center for Transgender Equality ▪ 1325 Massachusetts Avenue NW, Suite 700, Washington, DC 20005 (202) 903-0112 ▪ ncte@transequality.org ▪ www.TransEquality.org

Definition of Transgender according to the current medical profession:

References are made to the DSM manual. This stands for the **Diagnostic and Statistical Manual of Mental Disorders.**

Prior to May 2013 the medical field had transgender listed as an illness, a mental illness of some kind. From 2000 onwards this classification held, being written in the DSM-4 publication. The term used was Gender Identity Disorder, or GID. **In the DSM-5 they became more accurate and classified it as a Gender Identity Dysphoria.** More of a genuine medical mental (brain) condition that could be found to have physical or genetic source. Here is a section from Wikipedia on the subject:

http://www.ask.com/wiki/Gender_dysphoria?qsrc=3044

Gender dysphoria

From Wikipedia (View original Wikipedia Article) Last modified on 5/272014.

From Wikipedia, the free encyclopedia

Jump to: navigation, search

Gender identity disorder (GID) or gender dysphoria is the formal diagnosis used by psychologists and physicians to describe people who experience significant dysphoria (discontent) with the sex they were assigned at birth and/or the gender roles associated with that sex. **Evidence suggests that people who identify with a gender different than the one they were assigned at birth may do so not just due to psychological or behavioral causes, but also biological ones related to their genetics, the makeup of their brains, or prenatal exposure to hormones.**[1]

Estimates of the prevalence of gender identity disorder range from a lower bound of 1:2000 (or about 0.05%) in the Netherlands and Belgium[2] to 0.5% in Massachusetts[3] to 1.2% in New Zealand.[4] Research indicates people who transition in adulthood are up to three times more likely to be male assigned at birth, but that among people transitioning in childhood the sex ratio is close to 1:1 ....

Gender identity disorder is classified as a medical disorder by the ICD-10 CM[6] **and DSM-5 (called** *gender dysphoria*).[7] Many transgender people and researchers support declassification of GID because they say the diagnosis pathologizes gender variance, reinforces the binary model of gender,[8] and can result in stigmatization of transgender individuals.[7] The official classification of gender dysphoria as a disorder in the DSM-5 may help resolve some of these issues because gender dysphoria only pathologizes the discontent experienced as a result of gender identity issues.

The current medical approach to treatment for people diagnosed with gender identity disorder is to support them in physically modifying their bodies so that they better match their gender identities, an approach that conceptualizes them as having a medical problem that is corrected through various forms of medical intervention.

The old DSM-4 showed the condition as a mental disorder:

http://www.ask.com/wiki/DSM-V_codes?o=2801&qsrc=999&ad=doubleDown&an=apn&ap=ask.com

DSM-IV Codes are the classification found in the **Diagnostic and Statistical Manual of Mental Disorders, 4th Edition, Text Revision**, ... The DSM-IV codes are thus used by mental health professionals to describe the features of a given mental disorder and indicate how the disorder can be distinguished from other similar problems.

Whereas the DSM-5 became more accurate:

The *Diagnostic and Statistical Manual of Mental Disorders*, **Fifth Edition**, abbreviated as **DSM-5**, is the 2013 update to the American Psychiatric Association's (APA) classification and diagnostic tool. ... **The DSM-5 was published on May 18, 2013, superseding the DSM-IV-TR, which was published in 2000**... Notable changes include ...; **a revised treatment and naming of** *gender identity disorder* **to** *gender dysphoria*, ...

Gender dysphoria
Further information: Gender dysphoria
DSM-IV gender identity disorder is similar to, but not the same as, gender dysphoria in DSM-5. Separate criteria for children, adolescents and adults that are appropriate for varying developmental states are added.
Subtypes of gender identity disorder based on sexual orientation were deleted.
Among other wording changes, criterion A and criterion B (cross-gender identification, and aversion toward one's gender) were combined. Along with these changes comes the creation of a separate gender dysphoria in children as well as one for adults and adolescents. **The grouping has been moved out of the sexual disorders category and into its own.** The name change was made in part due to stigmatization of the term "disorder" and the relatively common use of "gender dysphoria" in the GID literature and among specialists in the area. The creation of a specific diagnosis for children reflects the lesser ability of children to have insight into what they are experiencing and ability to express it in the event that they have insight.

Actually, dear reader, there is a ton of information out there in Wikipedia on the whole subject if you wish to dig deeper. Sufficient here I think is just to mention the above points and not get too bogged down.

So, where do I stand in all of this? Here is where the Lord has me; I was born, as far as I am aware with fully working male body parts, that is my sexual organs. However, my physical brain is not so masculine at all. I have always had female behavior attributes but hid most of them during my life. Is my chromosome makeup XXY rather than XY or some other combination? I know not. I am rather convinced that if my brain was compared to a typical male and female brain physically one would find that it is created far more female than male (see articles and videos referenced in appendix 1).

In the past I would have fallen into the cross-dressing category, the transvestite category, gender-queer (a term I do not like as it sounds demeaning to me!), and gender non-conforming. Once the sexual aspect was removed by God once I was fifty, it has become clear that I am a transgender MTF, male to female, two-spirited as the Native Americans call it. However I am not a full transsexual, a person who is going to change their sex organs through surgery as best as they can have it done. I do not believe that God made a mistake when I was created and born. I am fully convinced that my heart (spirit) and mind (soul) clearly identify more as female than male but my sexuality is male. It seems to me that I have spent a life time trying to rebuff these truths, to deny and to change this but now I have accepted this in myself. For me, my heart and soul dictates who I really am with regards to gender and gender expression.

I can also be categorized as being bi-gender because there are still some male attributes about me but the female attributes are far stronger. If someone asked me what percentage I considered myself to be in each court as it were, I would say that I am about 10-15% male and 85-90% female in my heart and soul.

Like I said, sexually I am definitely heterosexual according to my physical sex organs, I am only interested and attracted to females and, as a married person born as a man, I am only interested in one woman, my darling wife Prisci, period. So medically, I am a typical person that has Gender Dysphoria. Wikipedia describes the word dysphoria as:

http://en.wikipedia.org/wiki/Dysphoria

Dysphoria

From Wikipedia, the free encyclopedia

Jump to: navigation, search

Not to be confused with Diaphoresis.

Dysphoria (from Greek: δύσφορος (dysphoros), from δυσ-, difficult, and φέρειν, to bear) is a state of feeling unwell or unhappy; a feeling of emotional and mental discomfort as a symptom of discontentment, restlessness, dissatisfaction, malaise, depression, anxiety or indifference.

Basically, the body indicates one gender yet the wiring of the brain indicates the opposite gender to some greater or lesser extent resulting in a mismatch. If you cannot do brain surgery to correct it, then have the body line up with the brain. Simple! Problem resolved.

The Desire of My Heart: I am Transgender

It is mid December 2013 and here I am seeing God's plan laid out before me. I knew that I was going to get so, so much bad reaction to this, especially from those close to me, but the Lord said the He would not leave me nor forsake me as I move forward. I joined the transgender support group at the Equality center in Tulsa. I started to meet others and listened to their life stories and I did a ton of research on the internet on the whole subject. I went to see a psychologist who knows about such issues to confirm my life (not that I really needed to, as a true transgender person knows who he or she is if they have done any amount of soul searching in their lives). She confirmed what I already knew about myself, that is, I am a transgender male to female, or X3 as they sometimes call it.

    I went to see a Christian doctor who specializes with transgender people, an endocrinologist. He was in agreement, too, as to my condition and put me on a dose of the estrogen hormone as soon as we had results from a blood test that I did that same day. I was to return in one month to do another test and progress from there. During that time he had to be more committed to being full time at the hospital. He had to drop all his transgender and other private clients so I was referred to another similar doctor who ran all kinds of tests including an EKG. That doctor, once he heard my story, increased my dosage and added a testosterone blocker and some estrogen/progesterone cream to apply topically.

A month later I feel that my life is finally coming together. I love my wife, Prisci very, very much but I cannot be someone I am not, I have to be who I am, and so far and maybe forever she rejects this as being my true self. I desperately want us to be together but I cannot force myself upon her. She has to love and want me as I am, or reject me. We are still separated as of March 2014.

The Lord placed a mature Christian brother, Jackie, actually the correct term we use is 'sister' as she is also transgender, in my path. We are both praying for other transgender folk we know, for them to turn to the Lord. We do not want to hear of anyone around us committing suicide or doing harm to themselves. I am sharing an apartment with this good trans-sister in the Lord and we honor and respect each other.

People are amazed just at how quickly it is all coming together for me in the transgender community. It is the hand of the Lord I know. I am not doing any pushing at all, just obeying the Lord one day at a time. He does the rest. As of March 2014 I am out and about now as Robbie Dee Ewens some 90% of the time and it is increasing.

The Lord Jehovah is good. Although some of the things He has asked me to do have been hard, I am doing them. For example, while driving to the lake (the lake near Tahlequah, Oklahoma, called Lake Tenkiller where I try to go each weekend if possible) where we have a live-in cabin boat docked at the Burnt Cabin marina, the Lord would point out one particular church of the many I would pass by. He kept telling me that He wanted me to go there, to attend the services as Robbie, as who I am. This went on for a few trips until, as I was passing by again one day, He told me to attend that Sunday morning so I took note of the service time on the board. He also said that He wanted me to dress up as best as I could with what I had with me. I was to get ready early, go to this country restaurant down the road called Big Red, have breakfast and go off to church from there.

I knew that this really was not a good idea. Hey, we are in the Bible belt as they call it. And conservative Christianity is the mainstream theology, very right wing I guess you can call it. Yes, the same judgmental side that *I* was on more and more these past years! (Gee what a hypocrite I have turned out to be!).

So, I did my best to not let my mind get too carried away with what was going to happen. Sunday early morning came and I strip washed in my little cabin boat and got dressed in this really pretty black velvet full length dress. I had good accessories, good two inch heels and did my face up as best as I could. Off I went in my little Ford Ranger pickup to the restaurant. Now, the Lord had already had me go to this place a couple of times previously and He graciously had this wonderful lady waitress called miss Bonnie who was also a believer in Christ there to serve me.

I remember the first time I went in through the doors to that country restaurant. It was fairly busy and as I walked in locals were chit-chatting away to each other then, once I entered... silence fell and all eyes were on me. That was a tough one. I did not know whether I should stand and wait or try and find a seat and hide myself in a corner. I stood as tall as I could, smiled and said good morning to those gaping mouths and cat eyes staring at me. Gradually they turned and started mumbling to each other on their respective tables as a waitress (Miss Bonnie) came to me and was really nice and found me a seat. Over the first two visits she found out more about my walk, my faith and 'new' life. One of the biggest misunderstandings about transgender folk is that the male-to-females (mtf) are homosexuals. That is usually the very first thing that men especially think when they see you, or when first in conversation. That sexual orientation and behavior of some deviation from what God *originally* intended is always present. Got good news, the two are very separate. Being transgender is about your identity not your sexual desires at all. Proof, you can put a hundred transgender people together and you can always separate them out into different groups relating to sexual behavior. Traditional Biblical sexual behavior is there too. I am one and my roommate another and I know there are many others out there too. True also though is that many, many are caught up in fornication, lust driven homosexuality and all kinds of other activities, but then so are many of the everyday population too! The bad stigma and media surrounding what society makes transgender people out to be on the whole, often promotes transgender folk to these pathways, with the church being one of the guiltiest parties of all as they are in the better position to do something about it!

Many older transgender people, I have found have abstained from sexual activities completely. You should hear some of the evil stories from some transgender girls of how the church has judged them and kicked them out unless they change their ways. I am going to digress a little before I continue my story of going to the church.

Let's look at the conservative charismatic church of today. The one that I have been a part of for so many years (well, was. I repented with regards to judging others). Many good biblical standards. A genuine desire to seek the Lord. Lots of props and programs to seemingly meet the needs of every family and most life situations. And such a choice of where you, or more hopefully, where the Lord will guide you to go. For example, there's the right thinking church, the do good deeds it's-all-about service to others church, the, you must have faith church, of course the famous prosperity teaching church, the we are all about missions church, etc. etc. Got the idea? The list goes on and on. Is there something wrong about these focuses? According to the Word of God, no then yes. No, because all these emphasis' are sound biblical teachings and principles. Yes, Because the Lord says that a false balance is an abomination to Him. Here is a question to help you think on that; when did you last hear about being in the fear of the Lord and sharing in Christ's sufferings, finding out what that means and participating in it? I could go on a lot more here but suffice it for me to say that many church bodies today have teachings from the pulpit that tickle the ears of the listener. Sure a few challenging sermons here and there that themselves may challenge, even convict but let's not take it further and continue on that vein for too long please (listener may have to either change or leave and then what would the church money collection look like after a few months of that?!), but please let's go back quickly to something more... "positive". Sorry, but the truth is, is that the church is in a state of apostasy, having a form of godliness but denying its power. Enoch prophesized that this would be the current state of the church and of course he was right as he walked with God.

So going back to my story you can see that it is not surprising that I had reservations about going to this conservative country Baptist church. Anyway, after leaving my wonderful waitress, Miss Bonnie and telling her where I was going, I departed to the church.

All the times that I have passed the church before, this Baptist church, the somewhat large parking lot had been virtually empty and I assumed that this was one of those big premises that a few used so most of the pews would be empty. WRONG! The parking lot was already packed when I got there. I did not know then that most came earlier to do bible classes before the service. After checking with the Lord again, I drove into the parking lot. I had to park on the far side, some distance from the front entrance. Well, out I got and I walked, all 6' 3" of me including heels towards the double glass entrance doors.

I could see four men at the doors. I guessed that they would be greeters but as I got closer three of them seemed to back off and vanish, leaving one older man there who kindly opened the door to me and welcomed me. Now, I had already determined that I did not just want to come, only to be asked to leave and that it would be better for me just to turn around a leave right there and then. So I asked this kind man if I would be accepted or would I be judged and asked to leave in which case it would be better for me not to enter in the first place. He said quite clearly that I was fine to come in. So I did. I went into the main auditorium and sat on a pew near the back so as to not draw too much attention to myself.

It was a traditional service with a pretty much set format. It was a little like going back in time compared to all the more modern charismatic churches I have been to over past years. Still, they preached the gospel and had real individual testimonies. They had what they call a 'welcome' or 'fellowship' song time where the musicians played and sang while

everyone else went around shaking hands with each other. This would be interesting. It would be the first major display of where these folk were at in their hearts regarding myself. This is what I observed both on the first and following visits (yes, I made it through the first day!). Most older ladies with their husbands would come up to me and genuinely shake my hand, always with the wife coming to me first though. Older aged men who seemed to be on their own were sometimes okay with me. Middle aged wives on the whole were cool with coming to me with genuine love in their eyes, some it seemed you could almost pick up that they understood where I was at. Men with few exceptions kept away, especially if they were testosterone filled and carried themselves to display their image of 'what a man should really look and be like'. I even saw some men straightening up their posture and strut their manliness before me! Also the younger girls, the teenagers and those in their early twenties just about all kept well away from me and some would look at me with 'dagger' eyes as if to say,
"Just who and what do you think you are…freak!" (just my interpretation, I could be wrong).
Then you get the few, some older ladies and in particular one family with two older daughters, that extended themselves to talk and chat with me and I saw no judgment in them at all. This family, and may the Lord bless them richly, even three visits later took me out with a few other friends from the church for lunch after the service and did not even bat an eyelid to anyone else's reactions concerning me. I had found Jesus there in amongst these people.

After that first visit I received an email from the pastor wanting to chat with me. Here we start I thought looking up to the Lord as if to say,
"You know where this is going to end up so why did you send me there in the first place."
A few days later the pastor called and we chatted for some time. Once he realized and chose to believe me that sexual immoral behavior was not a part of who I am, he indicated that it was okay for me to continue to attend providing my motive was good. I assured him that it was and that I was looking for a group of genuine believers that I could make some friends with and worship together with as myself, a safe place (ho, ho, ho). You know, the church is supposed to be a sanctuary and that word means that it is supposed to be a safe place for anyone and everyone, a place of refuge.

I was invited after the first service to attend one of the bible study groups the following week and I did so with a good group of believers with a husband and wife (deacons) team running the small group of about fifteen people. I was invited to join that particular group by a mature lady in the church who played the piano. She seemed to focus in on this one fifty year old plus group and I heard the Lord confirm it. So that was the one I went to the following week. What was interesting was that on my

first visit to the group, just as I was walking in to the church, the Lord spoke to me and told me to pay particular attention to the very first few words that were to be spoken to the group as it was directly for me. I went in, was made welcome although a few of them seemed a little uncomfortable (mainly men). And the very first words to the group were spoken by the deacon wife,
"The Lord wants you to embrace the new identity that He has given you." You can't really add to that! Of course, she was referring to our 'new' identity in Christ Jesus but for me, because of the Word of the Lord beforehand, to me it had a double meaning.

    By the third visit I was starting to get to know my bible group folk a little and they were more open to asking questions. They were all genuine even though a couple of the middle aged men were struggling a little it seemed in understanding who I am. I had copied some information about being transgender just to try and help the group understand, giving the full version to the deacons and later that morning to the pastor and a single sheet was made available in the group for anyone who wanted one. I was just trying to help them and make it easier for them to ask questions if they wanted to.

    Okay, so now let me tell you how I handled going to the bathroom in this conservative Baptist church. The answer upfront, not very well! You see, I was at a point back then when I was still finding my way in society as to how to do things as a transgender person. So there I was at church and it was windy outside and I needed to freshen up a little and brush my hair. I asked someone the directions to the restrooms and, following their directions found the two doors labelled 'Mens' and 'Ladies'. I looked at one and then the other door. If I went in to the ladies would I be breaking the law and causing trouble for myself? If I went in to the men's, how would the men react? I was in a little bit of a dilemma. I had heard from other transgender ladies that we should use the ladies' bathrooms, but I just could not stop thinking that I might be breaking the law or something (truth is, transgender ladies do use the ladies bathrooms in Oklahoma even though in public places it legally is referred to as an act of civil disobedience). So, into the men's I went.

    It was just a few minutes before the service was to start so there were a bunch of men in there. Oooo, you should have seen their faces as I walked in. Men at the urinals started to hide their stuff and went all red faced while others mumbled something to each other and yet others got out asap! I smiled and went up to the mirror and proceeded to brush my hair as the restroom door opened up and in walks an elder of the church but upon seeing me at the mirror exclaimed,
"Oh, Sorry!" and quickly proceeded to turn, leave and close the door. He thought he had gone into the ladies!

I had clearly chosen the wrong restroom to go in! The following week I used the ladies but while in there I got a few strange looks but no comments, that is until the pastor called me that following week. The women were not happy either so exactly where do I go? I ended up compromising and using the pastor's private bathroom.

But then it just had to happen, didn't it. The predictable. Another call from the pastor which sounded like it came after some kind of leadership meeting together with some complaints from members of the congregation. This call had a different tone to it. Sure the pastor was his usual polite self, but he was concerned about the information I gave out (about being transgender given to the group deacons), and the impact on his church (he didn't say that directly but that's what it amounted to). Use of bathrooms as just mentioned and concerns about myself and their church doctrine regarding gender were also an issue with him.

Isn't it so odd how the church says that the most important part of us, that is who we really are, is our spirit man, our inner self, as it were, and the next most important part is our soul, that it must be saved, and that our bodies are last where we are to honor the Lord with our body. Yet, when it comes to our identity beyond hopefully belonging to Christ, we all of a sudden reverse that order. It is our flesh now that determines who we are. So now, if your inner man relates to being female and your soul confirms this also with thoughts, desires and actions etc. but physiologically you are male, then we have to change the physical brain, soul and spirit of that person to conform to the flesh!

Just as ridiculous is the lie that God only makes males or females, that you are one or the other in sexuality and gender identity. Wake up people! (please excuse for exuberance on this but come on now, get real please) God makes or at least *permits*, even physically, a whole spectrum of sexuality and gender variations. God has never said otherwise, it is man who has amassed this conclusion from the scriptures and in doing so has ostracized and demonized other souls that God loves, the kind Jesus also came to save. You may want to refer to the famous first two, Adam and Eve, but that was in paradise, where man had not fallen. We don't live there now! We are a whole mixture and there is more than enough evidence out there to show this. Does this change God's ideal for a man and woman? No it does not, but the effects of the fall show in all our lives in many different ways.

We seem to think that after Jesus came all things are restored back to the pre-Adamic sinless state! Is it my fault that I and many others are what we label transgender? Is it the persons fault that they are in anyway imperfect and not like Adam or Eve? We have forgotten mercy and live more in judgment when we expect someone to be anything more than who they are, expect them to change, or blame them if they do not change.

If, as in the blind man born that way from birth, he was not considered blind because of either his or his parents sin, then how can we not apply the same to transgender people, or anyone else that is not perfect to that matter which includes us all! Jesus clearly stated that neither party sinned and went on to heal that man:

John 9:1-7
> Now as *Jesus* passed by, He saw a man who was blind from birth. 2 And His disciples asked Him, saying, "Rabbi, who sinned, this man or his parents, that he was born blind?"
> 3 Jesus answered, "Neither this man nor his parents sinned, but that the works of God should be revealed in him. 4 I must work the works of Him who sent Me while it is day; *the* night is coming when no one can work. 5 As long as I am in the world, I am the light of the world."
> 6 When He had said these things, He spat on the ground and made clay with the saliva; and He anointed the eyes of the blind man with the clay. 7 And He said to him, "Go, wash in the pool of Siloam" (which is translated, Sent). So he went and washed, and came back seeing.
> NKJV

Jesus may yet come and heal me too, to make me like Adam (or Eve?), the question is that if He does, will He change my brain, heart, mind, my soul, or will He change my body to match these? Anyway, I am getting on my soap box a little too early in the book here but no wonder why my twenty years doing all those things asked of me and my wife got us absolutely nowhere in the end on the subject of gender identity, in spite of doing my utmost to change.

    I even personally know of two people that physically have a physical sex mixture (Intersexed) and I have heard their hurtful church related experiences. Read this true story (I will come back to the pastors second 'chat' with me after this)…

    A close Christian brother, Art, has known me for probably seven years or so. We first met at a non-denominational church and gradually we got to know each other. We do similar remodeling and repair work. He is part of a Christian organization that help train youth and he just works to raise enough beyond donations to keep afloat, as it were. An honest man of God married to a good lady too. Over the years we have shared some of our struggles together and he was aware of my situation. His belief was, and still is, is that it is the devil tempting me to act out wrongly, to come and steal, kill and destroy the Christ in me and anything godly. So, anything I do that is contrary to what he believes the Bible teaches about is a deception and a lie in his eyes. During these past few months he has been like a tick on my back to try and get me fixed to fit his and the majority of the conservative churches view on this (and what was mine too once). I give him credit, he really has been trying real hard with me. Sadly, his doctrine has blinded him. He too says that God does not make mistakes and you are as according to what is between your legs when you are born.

I told Art that I went to visit for the first time a transgender young lady in her twenties, let's call her Rachel. At the age of thirteen her parents consented for her to start female hormone therapy because Rachel from early childhood was insisting that she was a girl and wanted to be one. However, Rachel was physically born as Richard (fake name) and looked like a typical boy with all boy parts intact. The parents were Christian believers and because of their child's behavior consented to the hormone therapy when she was thirteen (anymore details surrounding that I do not know. For example, I am sure they went to see a behavioral therapist or a psychologist). One day, after they were all in their church wherever it was that they attended, a lady who I guess must have known about all that was going on, went up to this young Rachel and told her that,
"*He* was an abomination to God."
Well, I am sure you can imagine the impact that had on her as a young teenager. I asked my friend Art, even though the lady at the church was wrong to come out like that, what she said, was she right in the eyes of God and scripture? His reply seemed a good one. The following has been copied from the text messages we sent each other but should be fully understandable. Some spelling corrections have been made but the content remains true. He said that,

"He is not an abomination but what he is doing is an abomination to God. By changing our bodies in this way is saying that God made a mistake, and he doesn't make mistakes. God loves all people but he loves them too much to leave them the way they r. He will take off one layer at a time if we allow Him to and we will be transformed into who He designed us to be."

This is a typical response from someone in ignorance on the whole reality of gender yet thinks he can answer anything in righteousness based on his current understanding and use of scriptures. I then went ahead and mentioned that this person then got a girlfriend and, although Rachel did not tell this to me, I asked my friend Art that if they married would that be acceptable in God's eyes, after all, according to you he is a male anyway and that's that. Art would not give me a straight yes or no answer but said that:

"God will not c him in a healthy marriage because he already violated God's principals, he went against God's will by changing his body. Rob u know better than that! Two wrongs don't make a right."

Art went on to text the following:

"How many times do (did) you go to counseling for this issue? U cannot change ur DNA no matter what you do." (Gee I think that that is our point exactly right there! DNA includes the makeup of your brain and how your soul works does it not!)

Anyway, back to Art. I then told Art that I then was told by Rachel that at the age of sixteen she went to hospital for some further examinations for some reason that I do not know. And guess what they found? He, this Richard as my friend Art refers to her, who should not be messing with HIS body, actually was more female than male! The hospital found a womb and uterus and SHE was producing active eggs too. In fact her male parts were sterile. For some reason the uterus never got to connect as the male organ developed on the outside. I challenged Art with this truth and had to resend the text a few times… he never answered me. Later he said that I was trying to trick him and have an excuse to change myself. When we finally met face to face (I was as Robbie which totally shocked him), he kept at a distance from me with a miserable facial expression all the time. He still said I was trying to trick him.

"No," I said, "I don't need someone else's life story to justify my life actions. The whole point of this true story was to show you just how judgmental we have become and how we start to play God in other peoples' lives. Yet, we also know (I hope) that we are powerless outside of Christ to change another person so why are we judging and not leaving God to change a person if they need to be changed at all?" I pointed out that Rachel's mind knew exactly who she was even before any sexual physical evidence was discovered. Art still could not hear me and he had no sorrow over the fact that I pointed out that he has passed judgment on thousands and hundreds of thousands of genuine transgender people (I am of the understanding that there is estimated some 900,000 plus transgender people in the US alone). The conservative Christian mindset. I call it what it is, what I was and want to be totally free from… being a religious, spiritual Pharisee.

Reader, please do not misunderstand me. I love the Lord my God with all my heart, soul, strength, and mind and I love the real body of Christ, the Kingdom of God. I hate the false doctrines of man. I have been just as guilty judging others and am sure will be found guilty in the future too somewhere, but the Kingdom of God demands us to repent from such ways to allow His Spirit, His grace, and His mercy to flood in. I am seeking His Kingdom to manifest here on earth. With the exception of a few individuals, some small groups and a few other rare occasions, I have yet to find the Kingdom of God in any manmade, doctrine controlled, organized church body. I guess I can get off my soap box again now. Time to get back to that "chat" with the Baptist church pastor...

As I mentioned, the pastors tone was different this time. He made his agenda obvious when he started to question one item on the sheet of paper that I had given him regarding 'Do's' and 'Don'ts when understanding and communicating with a transgender person. The item he focused on referenced that it was a good idea to ask the transgender person what gender pronouns they would like to have used when spoken to. The pastor referenced some doctrine that they adhere to (called 'Family Values') that states that a person is either male or female according to their physical makeup sexually. He did not want to listen to, and never directly addressed those of us who have some or both parts naturally and did not acknowledge the development of the brain in the area of gender either. I could tell he was on his own pedestal and I could see what was going to come next: "Maybe, as you (meaning me) said that you did not want to cause an upset, might consider 'toning things down a little' as some people in the congregation are finding it hard with you there to accept you. Maybe you (here it comes) could look more androgynous (!!!)."

I said I would first pray about that (I was already getting angry inside and did not want my emotions to dictate my response to that crazy 'suggestion'. He wanted me to start jumping through hoops. No longer being allowed to be just me, I now had to start to change to conform at least on the outside. I did ask him (could not fully contain myself), "So a little less on the makeup? Don't wear a dress? No jewelry? Smaller boobs? I mean pastor, what are you saying here?" Sounded like he got a little embarrassed.

We ended the call. And after a few hours this is what I emailed him:

(2/14/2014) Dear Pastor XXX,

Having let my emotions subside a little I feel that I can now reply to some of the topics we discussed in our telephone conversation today.

Our most sacred and usually most protected part that makes up a person is their true heart, their inner man as scripture sometimes refers to it. When I first came into Baptist church, being led by the Holy Spirit to do so, it was not easy. Actually it was really, really hard as I knew what I was going to be in for to some degree. What made it, and still makes it hard is that I went in fully exposing my heart, my inner man to either be accepted or rejected. It would have been far, far easier to have dressed in men's clothes and acting as a man as I have learnt to do over many years. At least that way I would have readily been accepted and none of all this would have arisen. I could have just continued to hide inside myself and conform. And that would have been the lie continuing in my life yet again. When I act as a man it is exactly that, an act, my heart is not there at all and my mind is only there because I have learnt to discipline and train it but it's not who I am sir.

      Now, you ask me, due to the doctrine of your body (your church body) regarding such gender issues, to conform to some degree so as to be less confronting (my word), more approachable etc etc. I little bit less of this, more of that, wear less or none of that... Please understand that my outward appearance is an expression of my heart that you are playing with here. Just as a man does not get up in the morning and think, okay today I need to act and present myself as a man so I will wear these clothes and act this way...no it is automatic for him to do that because that is who he is in his heart, his inner man. It would be alien for him to get up and put on a dress, makeup and act feminine to any extent because this not who he is inside. Now, as you know I have spent over 20 (years) before I got saved and 20 since getting saved doing all I can change my inside to conform to my flesh. In the process God has delivered me from all kinds of sin that one can image that this can lead to. Yet, in all His marvelous works in me, He has allowed this to remain. The prophet Jeremiah that you referred to is correct regarding the wickedness of the human heart. The new covenant also talks about us purifying our hearts and to walk with a pure heart. Psalm 32:1-2 was given to me by the Lord as I fought against taking this road. I know that the Lord has called me into ministry in this manner. I see His hand every way I turn, confirming, providing and leading. None of which is contrary to His Word, but often contrary to man's theological interpretations (i.e. doctrines of man). We have so easily pushed away His Holy Spirit and grieved Him so that He cannot perform due to our man made doctrines and have become more like spiritual Pharisees to some greater or lesser extent. Sorry, I am getting on my own soap box here, but do you hear my heart and passion for the real presence of the Lord to change us...from the inside out. When man creates a doctrine that looks good to him and applies it, all we can do is try changing ourselves from the outside in, even if we call it the other way around. Jesus our Lord, on the other hand always knew how to address the heart of man and did it with piercing accuracy. Pastor, if I start to 'tone things down' regarding my presentation of gender then I am on the path (yet again) to conformity to who I am not, contrary to your 'family values' theology that says (I believe something to this effect) that one should conform to the physical gender one is born with. That means that the flesh of a person is to take priority over the persons soul and heart.

Yes, first and foremost we are to be truly saved as the very foundation of our being when the Spirit of God shines in our hearts to conform us to His image. Then we go forth and live it out hopefully not in any deceitfulness but out of the integrity of our hearts. My heart is grieved at your request however gentle you put it across to me. I see where it is headed and I cannot be myself. Yes, I can discipline myself to even be fully as a man in mannerisms and dress code, I can be there like that this Sunday but you won't get the real me. There will be no life in me. Is that what you want from me because that is the direction that request takes me.

I think it better I leave and let you have your church back to normal and you can put it down to a learning experience and go back to how you all were before I came on the scene.

All praise to many of your wonderful congregation that stepped out and made me welcome and some who extended themselves further and did not judge me at all but are willing to ask and learn and act in love. And to a few who took me out for lunch last week and did not bat an eyelid because I was the way I am but accepted me.

I am sad to make this choice but I understand you need to follow your rules and need to well, I am not sure really why you even went there on that subject other than certain people making comments and you coming up with this moderation suggestion as some sort of compromise and conformity to your teachings? I don't know, I am guessing but I am glad that you are being open with me, I really respect you for that. I do not want to disrupt your church.

May the peace of God in our hearts guide us.
God bless you Pastor XXXX XXX.
Robbie Ewens

And with that, one month later...I have heard nothing from him or anyone else at the church concerning my attendance. I pray for them. I have to admit, though, that I really wanted to include something like the following in the email (I actually thought I did include it until I went back and re-read it all):

"As you and your leadership are asking me to change my presentation and to look more androgynous, then surely that if I submit and conform to this change in my identity presentation to look more masculine, then to avoid you yourselves from being hypocrites, should you also not be just as willing to do the same? In which case, I will dress more masculine and maybe all the men in the church including yourself could compromise in the same manner, so maybe if you all wore skirts we would all look the same!"

Okay, I know, it was probably better that I did not include text like this but do you get to see my point here? We are such hypocrites in the church at times. Another quick example, a more masculine dressed and acting female 'Tom boy' is perfectly acceptable in most churches but an effeminately looking and acting man is most certainly not accepted, even if he is honoring the Lord in his conduct.

'True' and 'False' Transgender People

I have to be really careful using a title like this, as I do not want to cause any unnecessary offense or misunderstanding, and I do not want to invalidate any credibility of the contents of this book. Having said that, I do need to make a clear distinction between what I term a 'true' transgender person and a 'false' transgender person. For the transgender person reading this all, I ask please for some grace to hear me try and explain what I mean, and why I am making this distinction at all. Firstly, you need to know that I am looking at people from a spiritual perspective that takes into account the whole of a person, which is their spirit, soul and physical body, in other words holistically. I am not just looking at the physical makeup of a person, nor just the workings of their mind, and not even only the condition of their heart or spirit. And I am not evaluating, and neither does it matter as to what part of the transgender umbrella a person falls into. Lastly, I am not trying to redefine any current medical or psychological terms or definitions. But rather I am addressing and embracing all of these collectively. Keeping all this in mind, hopefully you will get to understand what I am about to explain.

Why am I making a distinction between a 'true' and a 'false' transgender person? I am doing so because we will find people that discover that they were not transgender as they thought they were and therefore revert back. Unfortunately, the Christian church as well as sometimes the individual may make a legalistic doctrine out of their personal freedom from being transgender, and declare that therefore ALL 'transgenderism' is wrong and everyone in it can be delivered from it. There are some (what percentage I have no idea) people who are motivated by temporary desires that drive that person to do what they are doing. These desires which I will go into shortly put a person's soul into bondage and truly that person has no peace in his or her heart at all but are driven on. For these people deliverance is for sure possible, maybe even desired even by themselves for they are not free but rather tormented inside. So, we will later hear of some of these delivered people and I rejoice that they were freed from their torment. Therefore, I am making the distinction up front between these people and those who are transgender who are at real peace and know in their hearts that this is right for them, where this is a true saying in their lives,

"I am presenting myself this way because this is an expression of who I really am inside."

'False' Transgender people:

So the 'false' transgender person is therefore the person who basically got led into this as a lifestyle by some means. The number of pathways that can be taken are infinite but to name one possible way as an example, we could look at the road I took. I dreamed of being a girl, did some fun dressing up a few times, then it all got sexualized and driven from adolescence into adulthood. Driven by lust I kept it as secret as possible because of fear, shame and guilt. And, if it was not for the hand of God in my life, I would be a driven, tormented transgender person to this day with no real inner peace. I could have found myself at the end of all my deliverances as not being transgender. That is why my testimony that you have already read shocked me to the core that I found out that I was a 'true' transgender person. That was not something I concocted. I was wanting that NOT to be the truth for me. And this is why it can be hard to distinguish between the two groups because it is not the path you take that determines if you are transgender or not, it is the identity deep in your heart when you are at peace. Remove all the driving forces, the invisible 'chains', as it were, and what you are left with inside is the real you. Once achieved if you find that you are not a transgender person then may you be wonderfully happy and rejoice that your real inner self matches your original physiology and you no longer have to go through what true transgender people have to endure.

The 'false' transgender people are those who in Christian terms are being driven by their flesh, which the Bible describes as the 'lust of the eyes, the lust of the flesh, and the pride of life':

1 John 2:15-17
Do not love the world or the things in the world. If anyone loves the world, the love of the Father is not in him. [16] For all that *is* in the world — the lust of the flesh, the lust of the eyes, and the pride of life — is not of the Father but is of the world. [17] And the world is passing away, and the lust of it; but he who does the will of God abides forever.
NKJV.

For non-believing people I would describe this as something like your own pride that is important to you for some reason. You want to be right about something, you want to look good, you want to be noticed, impress people, be important and successful and be accepted. Or you can go to the other extreme and belittle yourself as you think yourself worthless. Or you are driven through sexual desires and fantasies that seem to rage inside of you either at times or continually and you find yourself being driven like you are in this car and you thought your hands were on the steering wheel controlling your life, but you really are out of control. You seek to be like other images out in life to conform yourself to, hoping that you will feel better, and if only you could do this or that, or have this or that, then you would be happier. These are examples of things that you could do to just keep going and try to be happy.

Sooner or later though either a realization comes that what you are doing is wrong, that it never changes you inside, or that it is all temporary happiness at best. You try successfully or unsuccessfully to get out of your mess. Or, sadly, many in this situation seem to either react by getting mad at people, at God and at themselves, and may go into depression of some form. Some will even consider suicide as an option.

Now, here is the catch where someone may think that I am saying that if a person is being driven, as I call it, or prideful etc. then they are not a 'true' transgender person. Someone reading this could really misunderstand what I am saying, so please understand the following. I am going to re-emphasize my point here. It is fully possible and I know from my own testimony, that a person who is so driven and bound is indeed a 'true' transgender person, in fact I place odds that the majority of these people are indeed 'true' transgender but they are so bound and driven, probably mostly by pride and lust, that they cannot see through all that. They are tormented and driven by the need to see the real person that they are. If they do become free from their chains as I was and they get to see themselves as they really are then they would see one of two things and come to a realization of the truth for them in their hearts. They would either see that the desire to be and act transgender in anyway was just a driving false lifestyle and now that they are free from those driving forces they are at peace in their hearts and minds just to be themselves and that happens to line up perfectly with the physical gender of their body like it does with 98% or so of the general population. Or, they are free and see that they are truly transgender and now have a deep inner peace in both their heart and mind that they are so. No longer being driven they start to embrace their identity in peace.

'True' Transgender people:

The 'true' transgender is therefore that person as mentioned in the previous couple of sentences. They have a deep inner peace and a clear mind as to who they are with regards to their gender. Hopefully, they are not being driven, especially by lust and sexual lust being the most common, but they can rest in what is true for them.

What a 'true' transgender person does once they know who they are, really determines just how bumpy the road that they travel on is going to be. Isolation, personal trial and error, self-administering hormones, having poor mentors, listening to wrong information etc. can all lead to much heart ache as that person tries to find his or her way. Also, sadly most church bodies are either clueless or judgmental on such issues so they usually provide little or no help and, worst of all, can take the true transgender person down into self-condemnation and into bondage (like I did to myself). The worst thing that can happen to a true transgender person is that they get themselves all tangled up in behaviors and activities that they should not be doing and they lose their inner peace and end up acting like the 'false' transgender person that I described in the 'False' definition section above, who is a true transgender caught in bondage and is driven.

I am going to add something here simply because I know it is the truth and you can take it or leave it dear reader. I now know, without a shadow of doubt that I was the 'true' transgender that was bound and driven for years. I got free not because of me. I got free over a period of twenty years by the power of God working in and through me to purify my heart from all kinds of lusts and wrong desires (things that I should not be doing or desiring to do) and in turn renewed my mind to that which is pure and good. I turned to Jesus Christ, not as a point of religion or as some kind of crutch but as a cry for help; time and time again I did this and He never let me down. Did I ever feel and think that He did let me down? Heck yes, twenty years is a long time to be set free! But the end story, the end truth is that He did it and now I am truly free from bondage. My heart has peace and great joy, my mind no longer tormented so I have no lustful thoughts or covetous thoughts to have to continually deal with. And now my body is lining up with my heart desire and my soul can rejoice, and even now it is the hand of God working in me.

As we progress into the following chapters you will see me once again make reference to 'true' and 'false' transgender people with some additional comments used. Please, please, please reader do not think for one moment the when I use the word 'false' that I am using that in a negative way at all. What it really means is that you belong to the 98% plus of the population of those who have harmony with their body, soul and spirit that they were born with. Praise the Lord for you! Go in peace.

Changes to My Body

Physically there are changes already too. I have been doing both laser and electrolysis hair removal concentrating mainly on my face and neck. Nearly all the dark hairs are gone that the laser works on. The white and grey hairs have to be worked on individually by the electrolysis needle. Ouch! It hurts even when using some numbing cream. It's a slow process as you have to kill the root and to do that the timing has to be right, in that the root has to be at a certain stage of growth, where the root is in a bulb shape for either the electrolysis or laser to work permanently. I have found a wonderful, very experienced, and licensed lady in Tulsa, Vicki Sue of Advanced Electrology Clinic, who is excellent and you pay as you go. Even better, we are trading out with me doing handylady work for her to help pay for the treatment. I could be at this for at least a year or more.

Although I have always had soft gentle skin it is certainly even softer now and my body hair does not seem to be growing back as fast on my arms. I am eating more! I weighed 142lb when I was last weighed and I hope that will increase more as I am hoping to get to about 150lb (hopefully in the right places!).

My body odor has completely changed. No longer do I get that nasty salty, musky smell from my arm pits. Now it is just some sweeter smell that to me is just great. Getting a little bit more personal, odor 'down below' has dramatically changed too. I smell like a girl there now without a doubt!

Getting more personal, due to the hormones, I no longer get involuntary excitement in my male private parts and of this I am most happy. Going through a year where my wife really was not interested 95% of the time at absolutely no fault of her own I must strongly add, helped me get free from this sexual drive that has plagued my life for so many years. Being free from this is a wonderful joy. On this subject one may ask, "So where does that leave you Robbie, with regards to your own sexuality and desires?"

A good and fair question. The answer is that I keep myself for my wife and for my wife alone and I have no problem doing this even before taking hormones as the Lord has set me free from the bonds of lust of the flesh (wrongful desires) and when the Lord does it, it is done indeed. I am neither fully male nor fully female now. I was born fully male as far as I know with exception to my brain, my soul and heart (my inner spirit man) which are definitely far more female than male. So, with regards to my identity I see myself as a nothing, neither a man fully nor female fully and with that said I have no desires for anyone or anything else. But just to make it clear, being a transgender male to female (mtf), for me, has in no way changed my sexual orientation. I am attracted to females and only one specific female who is my wife, Prisci. I have dedicated my body unto God with all joy and peace.

From a Christian point of view you could almost classify me as a modern day Eunuch (but not really so) in some way. Eunuchs, back in biblical days, were either chosen before puberty, or freely chose to have their testicles removed (castrated) so they could serve in the kings court. Yet others it is stated were even born that way. Interestingly, the effect of castration is not only infertility but testosterone production is greatly reduced that would otherwise make the person have all those male features. Now the estrogen hormone in them will be able to kick in its effect more. If done before puberty then that 'male' will look and act often very feminine. Post puberty castration is less dramatic but feminization still occurs to some varying degree. Jesus Himself referred to the Eunuchs of His day in a positive light. That's the best way I can explain myself. It seems that the cost to be myself, as unto the Lord carries the price of giving up my sexual desires other than to my wife and this I have done and count it all joy.

It will take a good couple of years for my body to benefit from the hormones I am on. Breast development has already started. As a man I had laughable nipples. I mean, they were tiny, tiny, tiny! More like two pimples really. One month on full hormones has transformed them to over 500% in size and they now stick right out, are very sensitive and tissue behind them is forming. I am believing for up to 'B' cup size which would be perfect for my body, but it is unusual for a transgender chest to develop that much, especially for me as I have very little surface body fat on me. I may have to end up having small breast implants in a year or two. We'll see.

Another good question would be,
"So how far are you going to take this? What other changes to your body are you going to make?"
And the answer is already in my heart and mind. Firstly, I *myself* do not want to become a woman for that is impossible and is not desirable for me either. I am a transgender lady, no more and no less. I am not fully a transsexual lady, but I desire to present myself as a transgender lady and not as a woman. To me this means that I desire to change a few of my features that are clearly masculine but not carry on refining my appearance into some female model. Even though there are amazing transformations available in the specialized field of FFS, Female Feminization Surgery that can totally restructure not only your soft tissue but also your whole bone structure to look female, this is not the desire of my heart.

So I will be looking to do some basic work on things like my nose, eyes, lips, oh, and remove my Adams apple of course! Then, probably a full face and neck lift to finish just because of my age. As previously mentioned, maybe small breast implants depending on how much they grow over the next couple of years through hormone therapy.

I regularly go to see my endocrinologist after having a blood test done. Hormones are powerful messengers in the body and it is wise to have them regularly monitored. Pictures just of my first few months show how much change they can bring about in a body (pictures follow after the next chapter).

Finally, a good question would be,
"Why are you making changes to yourself? Is it not just for vanity and selfishness?"
And my answer is yes and no. To answer the first part of the question, I am making some changes to my appearance so that my heart, soul and brain are at peace with who I am with regards to my presentation. Up till now I never had anything to compare my whole life to outside of what was expected of me, both in looks and behavior, and I thought I was doing just great in life. Sure, even as a man I did not like my Adams Apple nor my large hooked nose, or my hairy arms and legs, but as a Christian believer just did my best to accept those things thinking no more of it other than that is just the way it is. It was only after the Lord got hold of me and told me how He had made me and why, that those buried desires came bubbling to the surface and I could, for the first time, see myself before God as I am. And this time, I realized that my dislike of certain features was only because they were male features and my brain is more female than male so they were alien to me. However, having said all this, changing anything outside of myself does not change my heart nor anything inside really but rather becomes an expression of who I am.

To remove my Adams Apple and hooked nose and clean up a few other features in my appearance can be said to be vain and even selfish to some extent, but it is more for identity reasons that I am motivated to go through a second adolescence and suffer the pain and rehab of surgery. I am following the Lord's instruction that He has given me two years to make myself as pretty as I can according to the knowledge of who I am in Christ Jesus, and as the transgender lady that I am. And in all this I am still not sinning, nor disobeying the Lord, but I am walking upright before Him and honoring Him with my body. Finally, I have to quote a very wise man, Solomon who concluded life this way:

Eccl 12:6-14
 6 *Remember your Creator* before the silver cord is loosed,*
 Or the golden bowl is broken,
 Or the pitcher shattered at the fountain,
 Or the wheel broken at the well.
 7 Then the dust will return to the earth as it was,

And the spirit will return to God who gave it.
8 "Vanity of vanities," says the Preacher,
"All *is* vanity."

9 And moreover, because the Preacher was wise, he still taught the people knowledge; yes, he pondered and sought out *and* set in order many proverbs. **10** The Preacher sought to find acceptable words; and *what was* written *was* upright — words of truth. **11** The words of the wise are like goads, and the words of scholars* are like well-driven nails, given by one Shepherd.

12 And further, my son, be admonished by these. Of making many books *there is* no end, and much study *is* wearisome to the flesh.

13 Let us hear the conclusion of the whole matter:
Fear God and keep His commandments,
For this is man's all.

14 For God will bring every work into judgment,
Including every secret thing,
Whether good or evil.

NKJV

Changes in My Behavior

I love to dance, but there was always one problem, I was terrible at it! As a musician you would think that it would be natural for me but I was so self-conscious and stiff in my body that I really struggled to dance at all, especially in public. Yet, in my mind I was free and could see myself moving my body all over the place and just, just being free. So as the years went by this dynamic never changed. My beautiful wife loved to dance but we rarely did together, often commenting that I did not have a Rock and roll bone in my body! She was right too. At weddings I would force myself to dance, spending sometimes weeks prior to an event telling myself that I was going to do it and making myself dance when I got there. Fear, embarrassment were all too present every time. I thought that this was my lot in life regarding dancing.

Now on to the subject of socializing, how was I at that? I sucked at that too in reality. I would rely on my polite British accent and mannerisms to see me through any social event but it would not be long until I would isolate myself somewhere out of the way. Even in the middle of a group of people I would drift off into some isolated world of my own, missing most of what people were saying. If I had a specific role to play, like I was presenting a business opportunity or something then I was fine. I would don my business hat on and act it all out and most of the time people loved it. But my heart, it was hidden away deep inside of me. It would not come out, I could not let it come out and I was so self-deceived that I had lost touch as to why I was not able to do so.

Cooking, I like to cook and clean and even in my marriage I enjoyed doing so for Prisci as an act of love for her. It was never a chore to me but rather a small opportunity to 'be myself' in a small way. I had learnt over the years to work hard and as efficiently as I could, to be good at business and I was recognized for this. Indeed, these are good values but again, I used this behavior to mask true desires in my heart. Doing this for many years it all became 'normal' for me to be this way. People, family expected me to act this way, sometimes even wondering when I would start to slow down a little! Do, do, do! Lots of doing, little living and no real inner peace as I had closed off my heart deep down.

Compassion for others. This I lacked and it was obvious to me. I even would make a joke out of it at times but really I was very concerned that I had no real deep compassion for the lost, the hurting and the broken. I was a good person and did good deeds... sometimes. But, I never had heart compassion to get on my knees and pray for others with all my heart. I cared about people but that seemed to be as far as it would ever go. My wife, Prisci, on the other had was so amazingly compassionate which seemed to highlight my lack in that area. She would find someone that could not afford their rent payment and check with me then go pay it in secret for them. Or, she would go help cut someone's lawn that was struggling, or babysit some children when the mother needed to be working but could not afford child care. Many acts of love and compassion came out from her and I would just look at her in amazement. Where was my compassion?

One other thing I found hard to do was laugh, that is laugh a wholesome heart felt laugh. Usually I would just laugh along when others would think it odd if I didn't. I can count on two hands the number of times my wife and I both would laugh uncontrollably. At those times it was wonderful but they were too few and far between over a twenty year period.

Quote, "Lusting after other women" was a common behavior over the past twenty years or so but there was a unique reason for this that I was just not willing to face back then. I would somehow 'draw' certain females to me. They were all different, older, younger, tall, small, even overweight or skinny, or provocative or not. My wife (as women can do) soon could scan a crowd and know which females would be 'victims' of my 'lust' as it was described. It was horrible for her and what made it worse was that it all too often happened in church! Now I can look back with clarity and see what it was that I was drawn to. In each of these individuals there was at least one feature, either visual or behavioral, that my heart was grieving to be like. I had so deeply buried myself that I did not even allow myself to go there for fear of exposing myself as I am. I was never interested in the individual ladies at all; it was just something about them! God bless my wife for staying with me through all of this.

And lastly, shopping. I was the typical male shopper. Know what you want, plan how to navigate around the store as quickly as possible, and find the shortest line at the checkout and get out. Oh, but my darling wife would take her time and so often she would feel like she was dragging this lump of dead bones (me) around with her. Sometimes she would get ticked off and send me to either get something or I would go looking at the fishing gear or something. I was bad. When we walked through the clothing department at Walmart for example, I was never interested in the men clothes. They were just a necessity that I had to wear. However, I cannot ever remember not glancing over to the women's clothes and it was great when Prisci would wander in amongst them with me 'reluctantly' following. I did manage to discipline myself to look for stuff that I thought would look nice on her and this was genuine but my heart was elsewhere and my wife knew it too.

So did all the above change? It has and it still is. Like I am waking up from a deep sleep. Working backwards on the above list, I love to go shopping now. Really, I can spend a whole day in stores looking at outfits, jewelry, even groceries. Guilt free I am discovering my own dress style and colors. It amazes me the number of people that come along to help me at times.

The 'lusting' at other women has gone, period. Do I still look at them? Heck yes! But for a totally different reason now. I love to see how other ladies are presenting themselves so I can learn from it too. I often get into conversations now asking them where they got that dress from or what perfume are they wearing. The great thing of course is that I am totally non-threatening to them so we have good conversations.

As you will see from some of my pictures shortly, I can at last really smile and laugh openly. I have caught myself laughing so much and smiling so much that I never realized that my mouth could be so big! I laugh at myself and to the Lord my God, forever grateful for His mercy towards me.

The first sign of compassion outside of my marriage to Prisci came on the return journey from the purity weekend in St. Louis when I broke down in front of my wife over the lost and neglected souls that I had met in the gay bars etc. My depth of compassion for them even shocked me. Overall, this increase in compassion is still continuing in me.

I love to cook. I am not at all brilliant at it. My wife is much better than I, but I really do enjoy it more now than ever. Before, it was just a little area of escape to being me, now it is me so my level of enjoyment and satisfaction has increased.

I dance! I dance all the time to the Lord. The natural way I dance is just like a woman so no wonder why I had stifled it up over the past years! I love to swing my hips and move my hands and sway this way and that. Still a little self-conscious in front of others but I know that this will dissipate in time.

Finally to socializing. I am having a great time. Now that I am free, I just love to talk and mix with all kinds of people. Male and females alike, I am free to openly communicate now. Sure wish my wife would accept me now, we would be having a blast together. Really, if she could just look beyond my appearance and accept me for who I am, and not be bothered by anyone else's opinions or judgments, we would be able to have a really fantastic time together. However, I cannot allow myself to think like that as I am also a realist and I know that it is between her and the Lord, whether that ever becomes a reality for us both or not. The clock is ticking and I am hoping, I am praying that this miracle will happen before we get too old!

Pictures Before and During My Transition

So here are some pictures of me from my past to give you an idea of my appearance before any transition. Sorry that they are only in black and white but you can always go to my Facebook pages and see plenty there! (all pages are public viewing, find me under Robbie Dee Ewens) I will attempt to put them in date order from earliest to the most recent:

England 1981. Celebrating my parents 25th and my grandparents from my dad's side, 50th wedding anniversaries. From Left to right: My mum, me, my grandmother, granddad, my brother Roger, Rogers first wife, and my dad. Right is old photo when I played in the LSSO back in the 1980's.

Hero of Oklahoma award at the State Capitol with Governor Henry, 2006

Wedding day to Friscr. April 2nd 1994

Victory Christian Church Missions training 1997?

Certified Six Sigma Black Belt in business 2002

At a Pure Life Ministries conference banquet 2010

Handyman Rob giving a presentation 2010

Rob and Prisci off to Boston visiting late 2011

Jan 25th 2013: Rob and Prisci for a celebration dinner that we are hopefully finally 'free' to be a happy man and wife together?

Here are the more recent pictures since the start of my transition from mid-December 2013 to October 2014 (the pictures are as best as possible in date sequence from oldest to most recent):

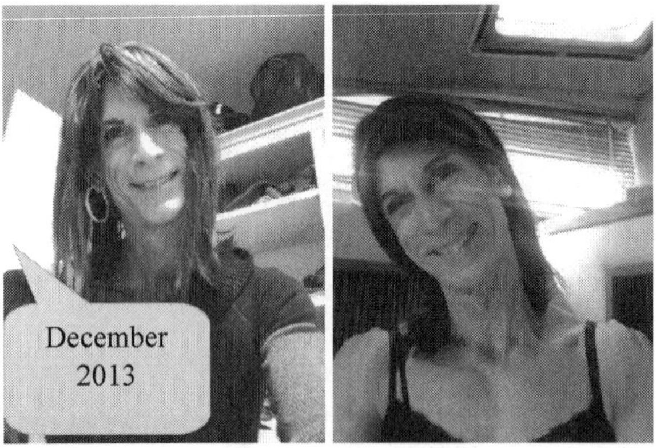
December
2013

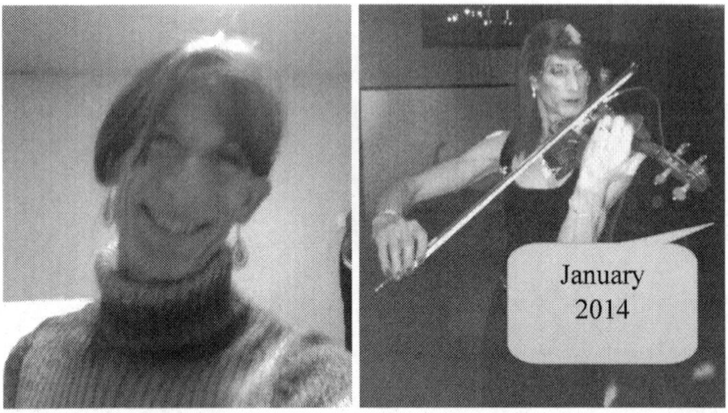
January
2014

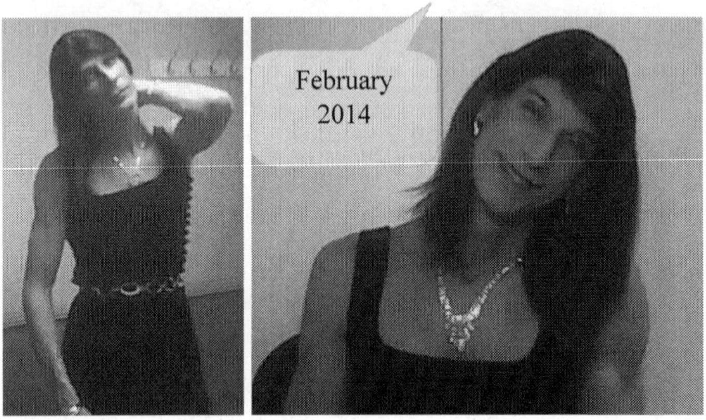
February
2014

March/April 2014

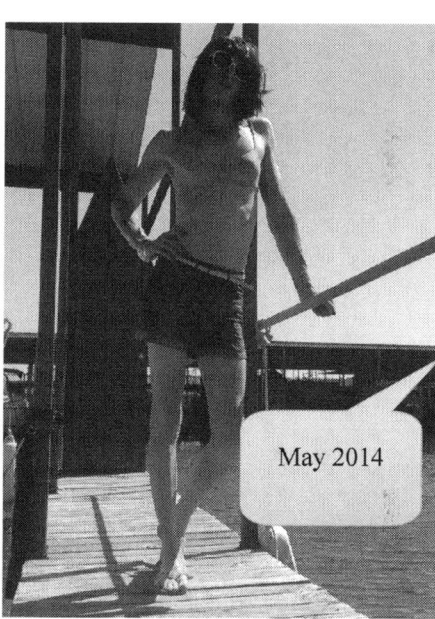

May 2014

June 2014

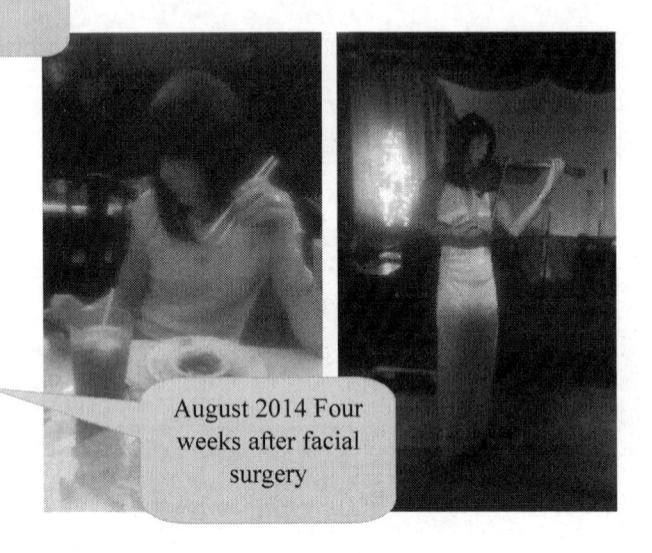

August 2014 Four weeks after facial surgery

October 2014

Persecution against Being Transgender

It had to happen sooner or later. People are not very good at adapting to change, especially when it puts them outside their comfort level. Even more so if it is going to put some kind of demand on them. Look what happened at the Baptist church in a previous chapter!

I had been participating in a business referral club for over five years I believe when my transitioning started back in late December 2013. As my transitioning seemed to progress at warp speed it was not long before I was about 85% of the time expressing myself as Robbie, Miss. Robbie if you please. But the truth was, I was afraid of the reactions from this unofficially recognized 'Christian' business referral club that I belonged to. I loved the people in the club, many of whom I have known for many years by now. The club was just over twenty people strong and new people would be invited to come along and, if suitable, would join if they wanted to. Some stayed for a season and left, others stayed and became solid members. The key for such a club to work well is to build healthy relationships with each other, even beyond just basic business acquaintance level. This I had done over the years. It was like a kind of family to me.

The format of the weekly early Thursday morning meetings was well structured. Each meeting started at 7:30am and would finish promptly at 8:30am. Various people would volunteer to hold different positions within the club for six months at a time. I took the administration position once but for some reason the Lord would not have me volunteer for more and even when I tried to a couple of times nothing came of it.

Each member would represent their own business and no two similar businesses were allowed to be in the same club. This was done to avoid any conflicts and the rule worked well for everyone I think. I was the handyman, the lawn and garden, and remodeling man. Each year the gross dollar amount of referrals increased with the club. The first year about $7,000 and by the final year 2013 I think it amounted to about $98,000 which was exceptionally high for my little, primarily one man band set up. That last figure represented about 70% of my business for that year and it was because of this large percentage that I had feared what might happen. There were some in the group that I knew would judge me and have a hard time to accept the tall skinny Englishman, as a transgender handylady.

However, the more I was transitioning, the guiltier I felt about hiding this from them. I have always operated out of the integrity of my heart, so I decided it best to speak to the directors of this club, who also happened to be the founders of the whole business. I had known them for many years, even prior to joining. They seemed to take it very well, especially the wife. It was at this point that I started to realize the level of ignorance, the total lack of knowledge people have regarding us transgender folk. I started to see a pattern of how people take what I tell them and they try to fit it into some current box of understanding that they have. I could literally be telling someone a truth about me and if it did not fit into their belief system then they could not process it accurately, but if they manipulated what I said a little then they could fit to a different understanding that they had and were okay with me! This seems to be far more common a phenomenon with the men than the women. Women look at things less in boxes and more broadly through relationships. We transgender ladies seem to do both!

Well the directors seemed to understand and, like me, were not sure how this could fit in with the group. I had already seen a few of the other long term members privately too. All but two seemed to have no issue with it. Their main concern was that I was continuing to do the same work which of course the answer was yes, and their overall comment was, "Well you are the same person, you just will look different!"
Exactly my very point but I knew not everyone would see it that way.

Seeing a few of the other club members resulted in typical mixture of responses. One would accept me and more so when they discovered that sexual orientation and behavior was a separate issue from identity. Another couple that were more medically trained were very compassionate and would pray and support but then were not sure how they could help and I respected their genuine hearts. I also got a sense that after our meeting they had some reservations; they just didn't feel comfortable discussing them with me. Yet another person was totally in ignorance but when they heard my story, accepted me and had no issues passing business to me at all. The same went for another good friend in the club.

One person that I also highly respected ran an electrical company that I had done work for quite a few times. A fellow Christian and as I had done work at his home also, I had got to know his wife and children to some degree. A really great family indeed, not perfect but real and continually doing their best to do life altogether as a family. I have to tell this story in detail as it is even funny in places.

I had arranged to do some work on a particular day at their home and arranged it so that I would finish late in the afternoon knowing that the husband would not get back till then. I texted both of them asking if I could speak to them about a major change in my life. They were fine about it and were kind enough to invite me for dinner at the same time. Now, so far I had always presented myself as a man as I wanted to tell them first, so they never had any idea what I was going to tell them.

Of course come dinner time the whole family was there, including their three wonderful girls so I could not really talk to them at that time. However, previous text messages with his wife who was upfront and wanted to check that I was not going to come out and say that I was gay, gave me an indication that she was in tune with the Spirit of God. I assured her that I was not gay at all, so she was fine about me coming.

After eating, the children went off to play, so at the dining room table the three of us sat and talked. The wife looked more composed than her husband. Looking back I can see why. The Lord had already informed her that I was transgender of some kind. The husband, on the other hand, had no clue so as I started I explained that I really needed to give some background before I come out with it as to do so only leads people to judge according to what they know and often what people think they know is full of error. So they patiently listened as I got to the point of calling it for what it was. Once I saw the husband look really angry and he came out and asked if I was having or had an affair with …(I'm not going to say who he said). He calmed down when I assured him that I was not, did not, and not with anyone else either. I also stated that this did not involve any sexual immoral behavior as we understand it as Christian believers and I have happily kept and keep myself for my wife alone and no one and nothing else.

"So, what is it then?" he asks with a little bit of frustration as his wife almost had a smile on her face by now!
"Okay," I said,
"It is probably best if I show you first."
Now, my cell phone was behind me and so I had to get up from the table and turn around and get it in order to show them a couple of pictures of me, Robbie Ewens, but as I was about to stand, by habit, I guess, I rolled up my sleeves. Boy, you should have seen his face turn red with anger, but he contained himself well. I turned, got my phone and opened up a picture of myself and showed it to him saying something like,
"What do you think of her?"
I cannot remember his comment but he did not recognize me. On showing the picture to his wife she smiled and said,
"It's you isn't it?"
She knew; and on that revelation and on seeing my picture again, he fell back into his chair just totally blown away. His anger departed as he told me that when I started rolling up my sleeves, he thought I was going to show needle marks and that I was a drug addict! He was relieved but also amazed at the news. Once it started to sink in he seemed cool with me and still is. She is great with me too. Great people and I think they understand that this is not some immoral sin but an identity conflict between my spirit and soul with my body that I am resolving by the grace of God and for His glory.

So all seemed to be going well with most of my key friends still on board with me, hopefully, as I transitioned. Still not sure whether to, and exactly how to bring it out in the open with the whole referral club I continued to plan to see a few other members about my changes. And that is where I blew it. I had arranged for the first time to take my tax return that I was in the middle of preparing, to the accountant at the club to review. I use good old Turbo Tax software and have used that method for years now. I was concerned as the software came up with about $7,000 plus in taxes due. I had way over-earned in 2013 to avoid paying any taxes but had not put any money aside nor paid any quarterly payments throughout that year. Also this was only my second year from switching from an LLC to a LLC S-Corp status and the latter is much more complicated. I knew I had forgotten how to match up a business return to my personal return so I was hoping that this well respected accountant could help me.

The trouble was, I had booked to see him late Wednesday afternoon. Now, at that time I was living on my own in my shop office with no shower facilities, so I had joined the local YMCA (more stories about that later!) so that I could shower and change there. I did so on this particular Wednesday but was running late so I had tried to call the accountant to reschedule or, for some stupid reason to see if he was okay for me to turn up as Robbie. I was going to be dressed as Robbie (I hate that saying, as it sound like it is someone else but me. It is not. It is the real me) as I had a transgender support group that I was going to straight from there. Really, looking back on it, I had set myself up to fail here. I had intended to see the accountant and tell him about my changes, but it all went wrong. I only finally got him to answer his phone after I had showered and was fully changed and sitting in my truck in the YMCA parking lot only ten minutes away! So, I took the plunge and told him that I was looking very different in appearance so was he okay still with me coming to see him. He was not quite sure what I meant and said, "You are dressed as a clown or something?" laughingly.
So I explained to him how I was and I let him take in the news and asked him again if he was okay with that or we could reschedule. He said he would soon find out when I turned up and to come. I should not have gone. He was not okay with it.

He was a mature man, a very, very nice man to know. He was once a church pastor and through all I knew of him, I really thought (in reality I wrongly assumed) he would be one person who would be able to not judge me and understand. How wrong could I be as I walked into his office at about 6pm that Wednesday! I saw that look of more than surprise on his face. He was shocked and could not hide it. After only a brief talk to him about myself he wanted to move straight on to reviewing my past taxes and current situation. He was very helpful to me yet also very uncomfortable. At the end I thanked him and explained that there was only a few people in the referral club that knew including the directors. I asked him please to keep this in confidence until I had seen more people and sorted something out with the directors. He said he would. And off to my transgender support group I went.

The following morning at 7:30am was the usual Thursday weekly meeting and I was fully intending to go, but the Lord put a check on me not to. I obeyed the Lord. I had been troubled over the recent couple of weeks as I was feeling like I was not being honest with everyone at the club and I was starting to feel guilty that I was deceiving them somewhat, scared to take the plunge and bring it out into the open. Early that morning the Lord woke me up over my concerns and had me text both directors at about 4am(!) explaining where I was at and that I was not going to attend today but wanted to get together with them both, as Robbie at their office to plan bringing this to everyone. I heard nothing back from either of them.

The success of me continuing in the club really boiled down to what the founders and directors were willing to do. If they didn't want any discrimination to take place and were willing to stick up for what is just and right then all would be well. Even though there would be a few that would still find it hard to accept and might even leave the group if they were so strongly opinionated, I would be able to stay and transition and continue supporting the group. If they both really judged me too and did not want me in the group, in spite of their apparent acceptance, then they would find a way to remove me.

The next thing I got was an email stating that my membership had been terminated and that all the current leadership was in agreement to terminate me. And, that the reason was due to excessive missed meetings as they do have a policy that you can only miss a maximum of three meetings in a revolving ninety day period. I called and spoke to one of the directors and he was most belligerent that I was over my limit and rules are rules and why should I be an exception. I pointed out my loyal five years of service and that this had never, ever happened before and that he knew perfectly well why I was having some attendance issues. I had missed five sessions in ninety days and he said that I had received three computer generated emails warning me of this that came from the same source as my final termination email. I challenged that as I had not received one such email (I even checked all my spam folders and still no sign of them and why should they not be in my usual In Box like the final termination email was received?). Not only that but the previous week that I had missed I had set up a substitute person from another group to cover for me. Apparently he didn't turn up but I was never informed of this. So, the director said that okay well four sessions had been missed and that is still one over. Arguing some more, he said that he would speak to his wife and they would get back to me.

Then one of my friends who was there at the meeting texted me saying that he was sorry I was no longer in the club! I called him straight back and discovered that it had not been announced, but since he had the job to keep the roster he noticed (already!) that my name was omitted from the list which had never happened before. He went and asked one of the directors who replied that I was not going to be in the group anymore! They had already made up their minds. But as, you will see next, they did not have the honesty to say the real reason why (my opinion but you judge according to the facts).

I found out that they had had a leadership meeting to discuss a few of us that had been missing too many weeks. Of them I seemed to be (as far as I was told) the only person terminated in this way at that time. We have never treated our members like this in all the years I have been there. These people all know that I operated out of integrity and we, as a group have shown compassion and understanding when other people have had life situations that have suddenly come up, sometimes for many weeks.

I heard nothing back from either director the following day, nor over the weekend so on Monday I texted them as I was still waiting a reply. I finally got a text back from one of them saying that their decision was final and good luck to me!

Now, let's look at this a little closer and ask the question, was I really terminated because I missed one too many meetings in a ninety-day period? If they were so concerned about my attendance and they are the leaders who know the facts about every person's records, why did neither of them call or text me that same morning before the meeting saying that they were concerned that I had reached my attendance limit and if I did not attend or have a sub they would terminate me? Why did they take the roster to the meeting without my name on it? Why did they, at that same meeting, tell one person that I was no longer going to be in the group? Why were they even considering taking such action if they knew that I was a key and loyal member to the group? I was the second largest financial contributor in gross referral dollars! And they had the ability to contact me to come if the number of meetings missed was such a strict issue as it ended up being with me. Or, was this really a convenient cover up for what really was a case of discrimination? You judge, dear reader.

Later I also found out that the accountant was part of the leadership team and that morning, just after the meeting had closed and people were milling around, that he had somewhat blurted out that he had had no sleep that night because of my meeting with him yesterday and that he was all shook up about it. I even got a call from one of the directors about this and she offered to do damage control. But it was really too late. There was at least one other person who heard him who did not know about it. Thankfully he was a good friend and I arranged to see him face to face to talk about it and, although he did not understand it, he was gracious to me.

I was out because of one too many missed days... hmmm really? Like I said, you judge. The bad news is that my referrals and business have been greatly affected which in turn greatly affected my earnings and therefore the money that I could give to Prisci. Was this because I was transgender? Was it because the directors backed out from doing what was right and just? So, basically I got rejected.

[Addendum: It is January 2015 and I have some great news to report. After all this happened a couple of months or so later I found one of the directors Facebook page and invited her to be a friend. She accepted and we passed a few brief comments together. Time went by and at the end of the year I decided to offer myself to play Christmas carols voluntarily at their annual Christmas party. She replied that they were not having one this year but a referral party instead. Then, mid-January I get a text from her inviting me to participate in a new start up referral group that would basically be non-discriminatory. I thought and sought the Lord on this and decided to say yes but I wanted to meet with them both first face to face to clear up past issues and my hurts.

We met at their office and both were very accepting of my presentation. We sat and talked for about two hours. Dear reader, please here this, they both humbled themselves and openly repented for what they did. It was genuine and touched my heart so much that tears were coming. They admitted why they did what they did and did not try to justify themselves more.

Before we even met together they had started to announce that they were forming this new group that was going to be non-judgmental and was going to have all people based solely on their work and integrity as good honest business people (rather thought that that is what being a Christian is about!). So I have agreed to join this new group and to start over. I hope others get to discover the truth about myself.

What changed? The directors said that they had been secretly following me on Facebook and they had then gone and done some research to find out more about being transgender. They knew in their hearts that they had done me wrong and have made amends. No matter what happens next, they are totally forgiven and I look forward to helping everyone once again. God bless them.]

In July of this year (2014) a close friend decided to invite me to the church that he had been faithfully attending some ten miles or so away in a small town called Sperry, Oklahoma. My friend, Jackie, is a wonderful Christian person in his mid-fifties and he had kindly given me a place to stay shortly after my wife and I had split up.

Jackie was a short, gentle and usually quiet man and would attend this small church in Sperry on a regular basis. The pastor of old knew him well and Jackie had a small group of friends there. It was home for Jackie. A new pastor took over a short while ago and Jackie seemed to me to be a little discontented with his ways, like he was more interested in telling his congregation what to do but did not seem to be doing those things himself. Jackie was always very polite but also not shy in pointing things out that he believed were just not right.

Well, the new pastor had been encouraging his congregation to bring in new people. Jackie was quick to respond and invited me a few times to come to a Sunday evening service. I knew that I was likely to cause a stir. These country churches are usually filled with judgmental doctrines of man and it does not take much to get them all upset. Finally, warning Jackie that this visit was going to be most interesting, I agreed to go.

I had met the pastor and some of his congregation some months prior when I was invited to go to the movies with them all, so it was not like they had no idea what to expect. Jackie had even sent the pastor text messages checking with him that it was okay for me to go. The pastor was, on a few occasions, supposed to have called or contacted me since that first movie outing, but he had not once done so. However, when Jackie had said that I was going to visit this coming Sunday evening, he did let Jackie know that he wanted to speak to me there. I was fine with that and could predict what was going to be said.

So off Jackie and I go to his church in Sperry. On arriving early I was soon in the pastor's office as he invited me in and closed the door. He was just finishing off his evening message on the computer but soon we were head long into the church doctrine of appropriate dress and presentation and gender is dictated by the organs you have between your legs... We bounced back and forth and got nowhere really so I just backed off letting him say and believe what he did. He explained that he had only closed the door to his office because I was a man in ladies' clothes. So, I got up and opened wide the door and sat back down again as we talked a little more. The service was about to start and I went and joined Jackie on the back pews together with his friend Linda.

The service was average. Some good singing and a good message. As usual with Sunday evening services not many people were in attendance, maybe thirty in all of a church that could probably seat three hundred or so. After the service I got up and waited out in the lobby area as Jackie went to use the bathroom. As the regular congregants exited past me I noticed a rather high number of judgmental stares and coldness by the older people. I just smiled and was polite as I could be. Jackie came out and home we went. End of story…No!

Jackie went to church as usual the next few weeks and I think that it was on the second morning service, after the service had finished he was speaking to another lady friend there when a man, possibly her husband, came up to him. Jackie had been talking with the pastor about my visit and the pastor had been telling Jackie that I was an ungodly influence on him.

The pastor said that I was corrupting him as being like I am is clearly ungodly and for me to live in his apartment was not good at all. So, at this particular Sunday morning service this elder asked Jackie a few things and then, before Jackie knew what was going on, all the elders (not the pastor) were around Jackie asking him into the pastor's office and with all of them in there Jackie felt overwhelmed like he was being cornered, even threatened. He was told that,

"This is over." And with that the next thing he knew they asked him out into the parking lot and was told never to come back to the church again.

It didn't stop there, the church called the local police on him too, to not to trespass! Jackie was all shaken up as he drove to the police station to find out what he had done wrong! The sheriff was out so he had to leave his details and go home.

Once Jackie was home, I found out from him all that had happened. I had been attending my usual church, Canvas church, and a group of us had gone out to lunch afterwards to fellowship together. I found Jackie all shaking and obviously upset at being so badly and wrongly treated by the very people that are supposed to show love and understanding! And what did Jackie do wrong in all of this? He invited me to attend that Sunday evening.

Now there is a real hypocritical twist to all of this story. Hypocritical on the church leadership that is, as Jackie, I believe, had informed the previous pastor about himself, or maybe I should say about herself. You see, Jackie is also transgender but always had presented herself as male and didn't change that so as not to upset the church. Trouble was though as Jackie's hormones and ways are becoming more and more female, sooner or later someone would pick up that something was going on. Jackie was always being careful on not causing any offense to anyone and here she was getting kicked out her church! Go figure that! Well I guess it's appearance that counts.

Overcoming the Fear of Man

I had separated from my wife that I love so much around mid-December 2013. I did not want to force her to see me go through transition as she was, not surprisingly, a more conservative Christian as the term is used, and not at all in agreement with me. All I knew was that I had put her through repetitive cycles of pain each time this strong desire for me to express myself this way would resurface throughout our whole twenty years of marriage. But now I was out of the home, living on the floor in my shop office (that was before I started sharing with Jackie).

It was a time, once again, to get before the Lord my God as I continued as best as I could to still work the handy-lady business. Once the Lord had given me the revelation as to His call on my life and how He had chosen for me to do it, it was for me then to obey Him one day at a time on how this was to work itself out. I had no real idea, especially as I thought the Lord was going to 'set me free' from 'transgenderism' and not tell me that He made me this way to be used of Him. He had reminded me that He was only answering my prayers to be used by Him in any way that He saw fit. And this He did, and at the same time granted me the desire of my heart to express myself as I am! Awesome God.

It seemed to only take me a couple of weeks before I had a starting wardrobe and makeup etc. I was only dressing partially as female more in an unnoticeable way while out in public. I wondered why this was so. I mean, if I am transgender and God has now given me peace in my heart about it, why was I nervous, scared, to go out in public and express myself as I am? The answer was the fear of man. Fear of man's reactions to me was in my heart and it had to be overcome. I am supposed to only fear the Lord, not man.

The Lord kept on gently telling me to dress up and go here then go there. Looking back I can see His wisdom on where and when He sent me. At first it was just out to the arts bar downtown Tulsa. This was a place frequented by straight, gay, lesbian, cross-dressers and all kinds of people. What I liked about the premises was that it was a non-smoking facility and the music was never too loud so you could still make conversation. I had also been there in the past, especially two years previously, during my attempt to battle it out with God and act out my 'wicked heart's desire' once and for all and get this out of my system. *Right!* That didn't work did it!

The people there remembered me and were, not surprisingly, very accepting. Straight away the Lord sent me over to this rather tall and sturdy-built transgender lady that was with a group of other people. We connected and that was to be the start of my getting to know people of all kinds. Her name was Krystol and she was, I found out, not transgender in the way that most people understand in that she is transitioning from male to female in some way, but rather more with what we understand as a cross-dresser. She identifies and has peace within herself as a person who is more female than most men to the extent that she does this and that is as far as she needs to go to express herself.

As I was not happy about living out of my shop office, a place where I should not be I felt, I would do my best as often as possible to get to the old cabin boat in Tahlequah. It was an hour and twenty minute drive south east of Tulsa on Lake Tenkiller. I would leave if possible on the Friday evening, though sometimes it would be night time before I left and would go as Robbie, dressed as I see myself. Then I would stay there the whole weekend and often leave to go back to Tulsa early Monday morning.

I was so, so grateful to the Lord as I still am and would sing, rejoice and praise His Holy name while traveling as well as every morning. Talk about the goodness of God, shout the goodness of the Lord! Never before had I experienced such freedom and liberty to just be me before Him. As a man I found it hard to really get into conversations with other people to any depth at all. I always had to distance myself a little, or worst still, I would use my knowledge and experiences with the Lord as a cover up to who I was inside that I had been in denial about all these years. Now I was truly free, I could hear the voice of the Lord once again just as when I first got saved!

While staying in my little cabin cruiser boat I spent my time praying, singing and dancing to the Lord. I was free in my body to dance before the Lord! I was like a new creation and kept shouting "Yes! Yes! Yes! Lord!" as I danced around (I am sure my dancing on the security cameras was most entertaining for them!).

The boat is moored at the very end of the very last dock at a private marina in Lake Tenkiller and while in dock the boat is connected to the main electric supply. I could blast praise and worship music to my heart's content. As it was winter time and often cold there, many boats had been removed and winterized but some remained and you would have the owners come down occasionally to check their vessels out. I did not need to winterize my 1987 Sea Ray 250 Sundancer (an appropriate name for my dancing to the Lord!), it was fitted with a thermostat controlled engine heater to prevent the water in the engine from freezing. It had an in-board, out-board engine and the outboard section was too far under the water to get frozen in Oklahoma. I also had a fan and oil heater in the cabin and usually left the settings on low to prevent any water pipes from freezing. Here is the old boat:

So, gradually I would meet one or two other boat owners, usually just the men. Their overall reactions to me surprised me. One or two did a double take look at me but no one mocked nor backed off but were most gracious to me. I soon got chatting (again, something that in the past I had to force myself to do with people) and they were most accepting of me as I am. I would briefly explain who I was and what transgender meant and for many it seemed an education for them. I have seen many of these people since and we are really cool with each other as if my appearance is not any different from anyone else. I wish I had people take some pictures so that you could get a visual fully of me back then but here are a couple that I managed to find:

They are not very endearing at all I know, but that is where I was then. I was just starting out. Nevertheless, even looking clearly like just a man in women's clothes I was starting to get out there before people. I did not want to make people accept me. I knew all too well what is in a man's heart, so I fully expected all kinds of reactions from all kinds of people. Besides, looking back over my whole life I can see lots of things I did and said to others so why should I be so surprised at others towards myself as I got out in public? Knowing this though really does not help you much to get used to it and overcome it. You have to get out there with peace in your heart knowing that what and who you are is right for you. You will not be successful if your real heart motive is to get acceptance from others to validate who you are and how you are presenting yourself. You have to know who you are inside first.

So then the Lord had me take my laundry for a service wash downtown Tahlequah. That turned a few more heads in my direction, but one day when I did it the lady serving me opened up and we had a great chat. She ended up passing my name and number to a student's university transgender group that met regularly in the local university. She thought I could help them. I have been going to that Laundromat regularly and they are all great with me.

While my laundry was being done the Lord had me either go to the Walmart superstore to shop and/or to the McDonalds to eat and work on my laptop (free Wi-Fi there). I got reactions at both locations. Many peopled just stared at me then would turn and laugh with each other. Some, especially if I looked at them, would look away. A few were amazingly really nice to me. I mean, really nice and I noticed the grace of God here that no matter where He would send me, He always had that one person or group to encourage me. The Lord had me repeat this same routine, the Laundromat, store and McDonalds over and over again. It got easier and as it did so the Lord had me go shopping to other places and it was not uncommon for me to strike up conversations and start educating people about what transgender is. Actually, more importantly it seemed, I would tell them what transgender is *not*.

Younger people, that are in their twenties and under down to about adolescent age tend to sexualize what they see and, together with many men that were, well I guess you could say prideful and judgmental, they would judge me as being homosexual. That misconception would become a common element in conversations and often I would see the people's eyes look with great surprise when I separated out sexual orientation and behavior with gender identity. I got into many a good conversation, often with other Christian believing people over this truth too.

I was starting to overcome the fear of man, overcoming the thoughts in my own head of what others think of me and allowing that to dictate or color what I do or not do. It is something that we all need to overcome in life, transgender or not. As a Christian, we should know this, but rarely get the victory as we do not do what we need to do in order to overcome.

So here was God teaching and guiding me through it all with His continual grace ever before me. You see, at the start of the transition you are not only unsure of yourself in public through fear, but you are really obvious in public. Put the two together and you come across as a total spectacle. Look at me, just over six feet tall and even higher if I wear heels! As previously mentioned, I have some very masculine facial features, a large hooked nose that is clearly a man's and a big Adams apple that protrudes out from my long neck and these features you just cannot hide unless one has an operation!

Back in Tulsa one day I had another one of those challenging situations in my early days out. I needed to go to the Walgreens store to pick up my first prescribed meds for hormone therapy, so this was back in January 2014. I was fully dressed and intended to go through the pharmacy drive-in at my nearest store. I pulled up to the window, where I received an odd look from the lady serving, as she asked if she could help me. Checking into her computer she said that I was at the wrong Walgreens and I had to go to the one further up the street towards downtown. Great, someone messed up. Oh well, off I went to that Walgreens.

It was about five in the afternoon so the roads were busy… and so was this Walgreens store. And… I could not see a drive through there. It looked like an older store so I thought that maybe it didn't have one. It was packed and it took me a minute to even find a parking spot. I just sat in my truck knowing that if I wanted my meds, I would have to go into the store as I am. Taking a big breath after a little prayer as well as a,
"You done it to me again Lord," comment thrown in, I got out, stood tall, walked across the dark parking lot and went inside.

The place was very busy and the pharmacy just had to be on the far side of the store. As I walked towards it, I could feel people's eyes on me and I became very sensitive to those quiet comments that people would make to each other. Oh, and then there are those irritating little sniggers and chuckles you hear once you are just out of their line of vision. And, to make things worse, there was this long line of people for the pharmacy! Gee! Now I just had to stand behind and wait my turn. Again people looked around at me, again came the private little whispers, and again they would turn around trying to look at something else but always made sure they took a second look at me. Now, of the dozen or so people in front of me, only a few in reality did this. Most just kept themselves to themselves. It to me just seemed like it was everyone.

Then, as my turn got closer, the two servers saw me. One was a sweet short young lady and the other a big, macho muscle young man that probably thought he was God's gift to woman. He kept making little glances at me and just could not help himself from gaining a permanent smirk on his face. I just had to stand there and take it. What else could I do that was honorable before God, create a scene? So I stood in line wondering which server I would get.

    Thankfully, I got the young lady and she was very pleasant to me and just gave me the biggest smile one could hope for. And, she called me "ma'am" which brought a smile to my face. My meds were not quite ready so she went to the back and got them expedited for me so that I did not have to wait much longer. After serving another customer, she gave me my meds, and as I paid for them she did a most wonderful thing that I really wish I had a recording of. I guess that there was something about this young ladies personality or what I do not know, but she gave me my change back and said out aloud, in a loud voice while beaming a huge smile at me and looking at me straight in the eyes,
"Thank you, MA'AM! Have a wonderful day!" and the way she announced it cut straight through other people's judgments. It was like a knife cutting the atmosphere in two. The other assistant just stopped what he was doing, immediately took the smirk off his face as he looked at his colleague. All the other people seemed to go quiet. It was like a moment suspended in time, and I knew right then that I was going to be okay. Smiling back at her I said thank you, turned and left in peace thanking God for His mercy.

    I am a realist as well, so I did not walk in denial that I passed for female. In fact, the Lord's command to me is not to be a female nor to always pass as one. No, He told me that I was a transgender lady and that He has given me two years to make myself as pretty as I can be at this stage in my life as a transgender lady. After that, my work would start and that this is the calling for the rest of my time here on earth.

    I started to notice a shift taking place in how people reacted around me. The more I got peace at just being myself and less conscious of other people the less people laughed and made comments, and more people seemed fine with communicating with me rather than avoiding me. This was accelerated once the hormones started to take effect. It was not long after that when I was always out just being me with the only exceptions being homes I went to that had young children until the parents said it was okay, I did not want to put them in an awkward situation.

    Now the owners of the boat marina at Lake Tenkiller, near Tahlequah Oklahoma, are a family that live on the grounds. They are a really nice family and my wife and I had met the wife, Mrs. Karen and her two sons Jered and Richard who I guess were in their twenties. They were a Christian family and the husband was often away working I think she said on a farm that they owned so I never yet got to meet him face to face. Well, over the winter period I assumed that word got around from the few boat owners that I saw, as well as from the maintenance men, that there was this person down there dressed as a woman. But I never got to see the owners during this time and I wanted to in order just to be courteous and explain myself and let them know that I was not some freaky person looking to cause trouble on their marina.

    Weeks went by and then, finally as I was driving my truck up the hill from the marina I met with their truck coming down and they were waiting to let me pass so that they could turn into their long driveway up to their home. I was fully dressed and about to go for breakfast at the local red neck restaurant under the Lord's instructions. I stopped, smiled and waved them to turn in front of me. Now their big truck had tinted windows and I was wearing sunglasses so I had no idea who was in the truck. They paused then turned, then stopped, then backed up, then stopped for a second in front of me as if to contemplate talking to me, and then finally drove off!

    I few more weeks went by and I really felt that I needed to speak to the owners. By this time the Lord had me attend that country Baptist church on Sunday mornings. Finally, I was driving down the hill one bright and sunny Saturday afternoon and there was Mrs. Karen and her son Jered talking to a cabin resident by the side of the road. I drove past waving and smiling to her as they looked to see who it was and, recognizing my gold Ford Ranger with a white hood and business magnet signs, I was sure they knew it was me. As I passed them she did that 'who *are* you?' look with a second pause before she politely waved back. I had to stop, so I pulled up and reversed back up the road a short way, almost to where they were standing. The other residents went back to their home and I got out and walked towards them in my long black skirt, orange knitted top and hair, makeup etc.

    Walking right up to her I said hello in my softer toned voice (not that I planned that, but it just came out that way) she smiled inquiringly. Jered was standing a little back behind her looking on. I said to her,
"I have been meaning to see you to explain what was going on," upon which she said,
"I have been meaning to call Robert to ask him."
Err! I looked sweetly at her smiling and I said "Miss Karen, I am Robert."
"No, I have him on my list to give him a call." She didn't get it. I could hardly believe my ears so again I said,
"Miss Karen, I *am* Robert." As I deepened my voice. She took a step back and stared at me in surprise,
"Oh! I thought that maybe you were his sister and that he had sold the boat to you or something." She said with the deer in the headlight look on her face!
She finally got it. Gee, thought I was going to have to take my wig off to show her! Now, I think Jered knew, but had not let on. He just kept quiet throughout all of this discourse. So I got to explain about being transgender and that my wife and I sadly were separated. She had never even heard of the word transgender so it took a little bit of explaining. I mentioned that I

had been going to a local Baptist church and I knew that they went to church too but then she went and asked me which one. It was the same church that she went to where I had been visiting by that time for a few weeks causing no little stir with my presence. She declared,
"Oh, so that lady is you!"
She had seen me there but never had come up to me. I thought that I saw her too once, but was not sure, so I did not go to her either. Well I guess I left her with plenty to think on. Mrs. Karen has been very gracious and caring towards me. It is a great atmosphere at Burnt Cabin Marina for sure. I feel honored to be here.

Please let me make this clear, there were many, many times that I really did not want to go out and about but I trusted the Lord that He knew best, so I would go against my thoughts and feelings and just do it, often triple checking that it was Him telling me to go. Overcoming fear is not pleasant but necessary.

I am sure that I will be able to recall many other times too, but it is sufficient here to know the process that the Lord put me through. Not once did He leave me stranded. He always was merciful enough to make things end well yet testing and refining me at the same time.

As I became more and more comfortable going out I was told by someone (I cannot remember who) that there was a transgender support group downtown Tulsa that met every Wednesday evening. I actually had known about this even before my wife and I split up last year but was going to church still on Wednesdays so dismissed it and was still resisting myself back then anyway, wondering why I was drawn to it.

I went along during the daytime to the location after calling them. The Tulsa Equality Center on 4th Street is where the building is located. It was a little scary in some ways as this would be another step to me facing myself and transitioning, this time with others. I have my faith in Christ Jesus but what would these people be like? Also, it is the GLBT center, that is gay, lesbian, bi-sexual and transgender. Now, the first three refer to sexual orientation and behavior, the latter is not. Transgender is about personal identity. As a Christian I was very clear on the Word of God regarding my own sexual activities relating to lust driven activities in my own heart, so I was not sure about turning up and wondered what I would find.

When I first went in I was pleased in that people there, the staff that I saw, were respectable people and seemed to want to help. When I mentioned transgender they passed me over to this wonderful lady, Mary Jones. She was very helpful indeed. She told me about the group, took my details and gave me a contact person to call. The next Wednesday there I was all dressed up walking into the building again to my first meeting.

The meeting was upstairs in a large enough room to hold forty or so people. About twenty chairs were laid out in a circle and it reminded me of those AA meetings you see in movies. I wondered if I had to say my name and confess I'm a transgender like "My name is Robbie and I'm an alcoholic." I laughed at myself.

Sitting down with all the others, I strangely felt quite at home. What a bunch of misfits they were… and me too! The meeting was informal and people were given a turn to say what is going on in their transitioning lives. Over the following weeks I got to know them more and more. People from all walks of life, some high performers, others struggling to keep a roof over their heads. One thing we all had in common was not so much that we were all transgender but that we had compassion for each other. It was a safe place for people to share their hearts. I still go there to this day and try helping others there as much as possible, often wishing I could do more for them than I do myself. I was clearly changing. My focus was going off from me to others, which I knew was a good thing.

After just about two months the fear of man had pretty much gone and I started to be more comfortable going out and being out 20%, soon went to 50%, then 95%. Fewer people bothered me, fewer jokes and chuckles did I hear, and the more open to me people became. Why, because all of a sudden they had all changed? No, I had changed and the Lord had done His work in me. It was not a matter of self-confidence nor increasing my self-esteem. It was the Lord working in me to overcome a fear, the fear of man that should not be in me. I should fear the Lord my God and Him only. It is a beautiful example of the Lord who changes us from the inside out compared to our own attempts to change ourselves from the outside in. Am I perfected in this? No, but I am a long way from where I was.

YMCA Experience

One such story of how the Lord worked in my life to overcome the fear of man took place at the Tulsa Thornton YMCA over a three month period. If you can recall, I had joined the YMCA only because I could go there for a shower and change after working because when I first left Prisci I was crashing out at my shop office for that time and had no other way to keep clean.

I could use the family room at the 'Y' to shower, where I could lock the door and get some privacy. So I joined at a reduced cost as my income was low. At that time I was only confident enough to be not too obvious that I was transgender in my appearance. I felt like a fake though, like I was hiding my real self to people.

Staff would always smile and welcome me as I went in as I scanned my access card. All went well for a couple of weeks then one day I went in and found out that the family rooms were out of commission so I would have to use the men's changing area. Not too bad I thought but I needed to shave my legs and it would look odd for men to see me all pretty much hairless anyway. I also knew that gay men went there to look for potential partners etc. and I had no interest in that whatsoever. I also only had female under garments including tights (hose) to put on afterwards as a preparation to fully getting dressed when I got back to the shop. Nevertheless I needed to shower from working outside so into the men's locker room I went.

I decided to put on my men's swimming shorts that I just happened to have stuffed down in my bag and, after quickly undressing and wrapping my large white towel over my shoulders I went, bag and all into the six man open cubicle shower area. There was no one there, great! I went into the furthest corner and started to shower. Then I got confident to start shaving my legs so off to task I went. Just in the middle of doing this though in come a bunch of men to shower. Now I am feeling a little awkward here folks. I heard two men taking a quick look at me and one commenting,

"Maybe he wants to be more like a woman."

Well, he was right! But as I had not overcome what others think and say, so it affected me inside, but I made myself quietly finish what I was doing and, after they had left out I went to get dry and change. I changed as best as I could while sitting down on one of the plastic garden chairs that are spread out throughout the locker room. I was in one cubby area that has lockers on three sides to enclose you in. I dried and powdered myself and, got noticed by this older man who had his locker in where I was. He picked up what I was doing but pretended not to notice. He talked and extended his hand to introduce himself to me. I was very cautious but shook his hand and as we did he gripped it in a funny manner, I think to tell me that he was gay, which clearly he was I believe. I just looked at him, my eyes piercing his in such a way to say 'don't even try going there Mr'. He got the message loud and clear and left me alone yet still being polite. I dressed and left.

It started to get really inconvenient to drive all the way from my job site to the YMCA, shower, change and then have to go back to my shop office, undress and dress again in my desired clothing in order to go out. The Lord was prompting me during all this time to be myself out in the open more. In fact He was relentless and I even questioned why He kept sending me out so much. Still, I obeyed and I finally got to the point after a few more weeks to go to the 'Y' straight from work and have my complete change of clothing to go out in with me all neatly folded inside my ever expanding bag. Now, this would be interesting for sure I thought.

The staff were getting used to seeing me and indeed, there were a few there that I knew from past years attending the facility. Working there was also the granddaughter of the neighbor that lives literally just across from Prisci's mobile home. In fact, she had lived with her grandmother for many months and Prisci and I had got to know her too. Maybe I would not be there when she was to be in attendance I thought.

Wanting to do things in a decent way I thought it best that I should tell the staff about me as it was going to be pretty obvious taking those hundred steps from the family changing room to the outside of the building going right past the reception desk to do so. So, on my first day to do this I went up to the counter as I went in and asked to speak to the manager on duty and a very sweet lady came to me. I told her,
"I thought it would be best if I explained myself to you all and make sure you were okay with me."
She looked at me inquiringly, with a smile yet wondering what I was going to say of course. I took a deep breath,
"I am transgender and I use the family room for privacy to shower and change. I will be going in like this but coming out very different. Is that okay?"
She looked a little surprised then answered,
"Yes, that is fine just please try not to spend too long in those rooms as families use them too." She smiled and I smiled back.

So in I went looking more as a man, and out I came, over six feet tall, plus in a skirt, blouse and makeup etc. Lifting my head up and feeling that all eyes were on me (which of course was not the case although in reality many did take a look I am sure), I casually walked out, smiling to the staff as I left and thanked them. I had made it once and I knew that the word would get around about me so hopefully it would get easier. Also, the granddaughter was not there which was a relief to some extent. On thinking about that it was probably good for her to meet me maybe. I don't know.

The next visits to the 'Y' went well and I even started to just sit out by a table and do my nails there, ignoring the men that would walk by looking at me as they came down from the work out area upstairs. This is who I am and I am not ashamed of being me.

On another visit there, only one of the family rooms was working so I was going as fast as I could to get ready and get out of there as there was this sweet sounding lady who must have knocked on the door three times to get in with her young children. Finally I said that I would be out soon and was going as fast as I could, She was very polite and thanked me. Then I heard her tell the children that they would just wait outside for me to finish. I had to tell her I thought, so I did through the closed door mention that I was transgender, so please do not get too shocked when I come out! She seemed fine about that and said that that was okay with her.

A few minutes later out I came in this black and orange two piece outfit with makeup to match. It was one of my favorite looks. The lady beamed at me exclaiming,
"You look really great!" and she meant it too. What a blessing.

Then, on a Wednesday it happened. I had to shower and change and I was running late to get to the evening transgender support group that I was faithfully attending. I went into the 'Y' as usual, being well greeted with smiles by the usual friendly staff. Into the family room area where there are three such rooms, and… and they are all not working with all the doors propped open and a sign there. Oh great! That's just great. I went back up to the reception desk and asked one of the staff about it and apparently there had been a flood and the water had to be turned off. She apologized and saw the worried look on my face. I said that I was transgender and used those rooms for privacy. She smiled and said that they knew I was, and sorry, but there is nothing that they could do about it. She really felt bad for me I could tell but all that was available was the men's locker room and showers.
"Oh, well. This is definitely going to be interesting." I declared to her as I turned and headed to those locker rooms!
There was an average number of people milling around but I just went and undressed, showered and tried to think of how on earth I was going to get dressed around all these men. I made a plan to use the men's toilet cubicle to do that and not use makeup as I could do that in my truck. I would then wrap myself up in my large man's coat and just walk straight out which would, of course, mean that I would need to transverse the entire locker area in full view of everyone there. I left in an open locker my work clothes and just took my bag full of my change of clothes. I quickly wet shaved first and then went into the cubicle all as planned. Once dressed I went to put on my coat and… and darn it! I had left my coat back in the locker! Well I sure screwed that up, didn't I! Well, now I had no choice, I would just have to go out there as I am and so I did. After getting my gear from the locker, I just carried it all with me and proceeded out not walking fast, just at a steady pace smiling and keeping tall. All eyes were for sure on me and one last person to pass, and I was out though the door but not before he made some stupid sissy like comment. I didn't fully hear what he said and I was on the verge of turning to confront him when the Lord clearly said,
"NO." So I restrained myself.
I had made it. More experiences were to follow as the family rooms had a burst again and another time they were out for a few weeks for repairs. This all happened in my first months of being myself and as the Lord was dealing with me. I had not seen Karla, my wife's neighbor's granddaughter at all, but one day I did. On this occasion when I went there I was dressed not in man drag as I call it, but already presenting myself as I am, Robbie. I

went in as usual just to shower and change and afterwards met with Karla for the first time at the reception desk. She was awesome. Obviously she had heard about me but she was so accepting with me it touched my heart. We chatted for a bit about it all and she just said that she keeps things to herself and was fine with me. I got to see her a few more times after that.

I now had finally got to the point of being at peace going there and did not fear others looks, judgments or comments. I had broken through together with everything else that the Lord was having me do.

By sheer 'coincidence' I was later at my regular Village Inn on Harvard and 27th Street working on this book and having a cheap meal, that I never noticed Karla and her grandmother there having dinner together. After they finished eating they made a point to come up to me. I was surprised yet happy that they came over. Neither were judgmental towards me, just loving. We chatted only for a little while then hugged. I asked how Prisci was and the grandmother said that she was okay. Oh, how I was missing her a lot.

My training period seemed to be over. I was now free from the fear of man and could just be me in public. Now I am me all of the time and it is early June 2014. Hormones are working great, and all the expected body changes are taking place. Most of all I am very well pleased how fast my breasts are developing as I am almost an 'A' cup which is pretty good going from having absolutely nothing five months ago. Emotions feel balanced and are certainly more present than before. Big mood swings are totally absent so it seems that I am on the perfect mixture and dose of the hormones. My mind is so, so happy and I have no conflicts between my heart and mind and both rejoice at the changes to my body. I am getting more and more normal in being a transgender lady.

Taking care of my skin, getting better at makeup and gradually increasing my wardrobe through trips to the thrift, Ross, and Half Off Named Brand clothing stores are all normal to me. Really, it is completely normal now for me and I am not trying to get there, it is just working out that way. If I was really a 100% man doing this then I would never get to this place and certainly not in five months! I wonder what the Lord has for me next as my life moves on. If only Prisci was here to help me, that would make the whole experience totally amazing. I wonder what she is thinking right now? I miss her so.

The next few chapters are going to deal with Christianity and the church with regards to transgender people. The information is gained from my direct experiences and those of other people that I have talked to. I also will delve a lot into the scriptures, especially those that are often used to address being transgender.

The Church: Religion Verses the Kingdom of God and Transgender People

This chapter is an introduction on how I toiled and wrestled between the truth of who I am, biblical scriptures, understanding them, and the standard beliefs and judgments that come out of all that. I am not going to try to use scriptures to match 'my reality' as a transgender person so that I can convince myself or others that what I am doing is right before the Lord in order to continue. That would not be hard to do though, but just as easily the reverse is also true. You can take certain scriptures and use them to indicate that being transgender is a sin. So who will be right? To answer this I am going to look at the common scriptures that are referenced as I have lived on both sides of the fence so to speak. In fact, I judged and condemned being transgender as a sexual deviation, as immoral behavior and therefore sin, for much longer than I have gained peace with the Lord and with scripture to be who I am. I will also briefly revisit the terms 'true' and 'false' transgender definitions from a more scriptural point of view.

    To do this right I will first have to address the difference between religion and the Kingdom of God. Religion is man's best attempt to interpret the scriptures and apply them to our lives. Man comes up with a whole host of interpretations on a wide variety of life issues, many times in some kind of conflict with each other which is why you can go to one Christian church and be accepted then to another and be rejected. For example, one congregation believes that all sickness is of the devil and not to succumb to it so stand in faith to be healed! While another church down the street may say that God uses sickness to refine us and bring us closer to Him. Yet another church says that it is just an accepted result of the fall of Adam in the Garden of Eden so we can believe to get well but turn to modern medicine to get your healing. And another says that the fall caused sickness and that Jesus could heal you but it is not your fault if He doesn't, just praise the Lord if He does! And so it all goes on. That is the church of man's doctrine, religion. And with each particular vein of theology they back up their points of view with real life examples, testimonies and certain scriptures.

    Man in religion always attempts to help change us to be more like Jesus by applying principles and disciplines that can change a person from the outside in. At best this is temporary, as the heart has not been convicted and the person is now in bondage through applying 'boundaries' and rules to 'help' them overcome something in their lives. It all looks well and fine and godly but there is one critical presence missing. The presence and power of the Holy Spirit who is supposed to Himself lead us into all truth and liberty. If a person is in sin of any kind then it is the job of God's Spirit inside of us, His Holy Spirit to convict and take our heart to a place of heart felt repentance. Then once our heart has been changed the same Holy Spirit works inside of us and we no longer desire to do those things that we were doing to sin. This is true change, from the *inside out* and *this* is the Kingdom of God.

So here we go into Christianity land where we will eventually dissect the Scriptures and take a fresh look at them in light of being transgender. But first...

A Hearts Cry

Oh dear, Oh dear what a poor state the body of Christ is when it comes to people being different! Unfortunately, this brief section cries out of how manmade religious doctrinal beliefs will put man into bondage and self-condemnation. Oh, how we have taken some aspects, some 'principles' from the Word of God and made it a blanket rule thinking we are doing God a service. Oh, how we have lost our way and forgotten the amount of His great mercy given to us, to only judge others in and outside the body in a self-righteous, unrighteous way! Oh, how people and leadership allow themselves to be influenced to please man and take a way that seems right but is not. And how we have so easily become modern day Pharisees!

I could cry out I am sure on this matter for hours. Instead I am going to break it down some more, strictly in terms of transgender people and I will use real life examples.

My Argument

Before I start on this endeavor I feel I need to surmise my conclusions here first and declare my purpose. As you read on it will become clearer that the current charismatic right (that is those that believe that the Word of God, the Bible should be obeyed as literally as possible) church view of any form of transgenderism is a sin, period. No room for any maneuvering from this to the left or the right. What their argument then comes from is the stance that being transgender is sin and sin needs to be acknowledged by a believer and repented of so that the person may overcome their sin and walk in the victory Christ has given them. This was the theology that I too believed and followed for all these years. And they are quite clear that the problem is in the person's head, in their deceived mind and also in their heart which has these wicked desires, not a problem of the physical body that needs to be changed. I argue however, that for the majority it is not like this at all, and the pat answers from these Christian churches regarding transgender people are floored. There are what I term real transgender people in the world where the error as it were, is not in the mind and wickedness of the heart at all but in the body. The only people ever created that had perfect bodies (which includes the brain, the mind!) are Adam and Eve before they sinned, and Jesus Christ Himself. Medical science has just caught up and recognized that not only is the transgender condition real but that it relates to actual physical changes in the makeup of the brain. Transsexual brains have been found to match the design and size of the opposite gender. No wonder they, and we are communicating, and functioning differently! The church needs to catch up big time (see end of appendix 1 for articles).

    I make a distinction upfront regarding sin and the transgender which I must re-clarify right here. Non-believers in Christ Jesus are, according to scripture under the Prince of this world, Satan, the deceiver. Believers in Jesus Christ who are doing their best to follow Him, filled with the Holy Spirit are able, by the grace of God to be free from sin of every kind. A non-believer does not have God's Holy Spirit inside of them so they do not have anything beyond themselves to draw upon. A believer therefore is able to see sin for what it is and can repent and allow God, the Spirit of God to work in them to put to death the sinful desires of the heart which in turn will change the way the person thinks and behaves. Now an unbeliever may be so determined for some reason to overcome something and manage to totally stop the behavior, but their heart has not changed and will seek another avenue to express itself. In other words, the condition of the heart has not changed even though the outward behavior might do so.

    It is so, so common to have the issue of transgender be so entangled with the idea of sexual perversion or deviance as scriptures tell of throughout the Bible, that most people automatically assume that all transgender people are in lustful sexual immorality of some kind or other. Nothing could be further from the truth and besides my own testimony I know many transgender folk who are morally good in that area of their lives both in desire and actions. I know some who will not do anything sexually until they absolutely know that they are approved of the Lord (which is more than I can say for some people claiming that they are followers of Christ).

    Now, what I term as a transgender person who is not a true transgender has nothing to do with what they are doing in their lives necessarily, although that may be an indication. This is a driven person with sexual drive usually being the driving force or some other driving force of misplaced need in their lives, or some combination thereof. It doesn't matter, that person has no real inner peace. This goes for a believer or a non-believer in Jesus Christ. A believer can be just as driven by all kinds of lust and pride as a non-believer can. A believer or not, either one can still be a true transgender person underneath all that junk.

I have read testimonies (what few I could find) on the web of people getting free from the 'feelings', 'desires', 'thoughts' and the 'temptations' of being transgender and the constant torment that goes with that lifestyle. Praise the Lord! I say, for in their conscience they knew that they were being driven and were in the wrong. By God's grace He had mercy on them and made him or her free from bondage. Now, dear reader, do these true testimonies therefore prove that *all* transgender is a sin and you just need to see it for what it is and repent and allow the Lord Jesus to set you free? No, they do not prove this at all. It does show that some are driven by their own desires and sin forms and grows and leads people into the darkness and then they often get caught up in further dark deeds of the flesh. But there are true transgender people out there of which I have met many here in Tulsa, Oklahoma that are not driven at all. In fact, they really have a great peace about who they are. Confusion comes (especially if it is a believer and is indoctrinated like the way I was) because you are not allowed to accept yourself the way that you are in heart and soul by the very church body that you are attached to!

No, no, no! Shouts the church. We have to change this wicked heart, renew your mind and jump into the Christian 'toolbox' and God will set you free. And, if He doesn't set you free then the problem is with you and not God as the Cross of Christ is more than sufficient to set you free. Enter self-condemnation. It is a vicious cycle that takes a true transgender person into bondage not out of it! I have lived this for twenty years in the church. Saying that what is in between my legs dictates my gender is ridiculous like you are forgetting that the brain is also part of your body! Now the only body organ that I know of that can communicate is the mind, and people, it is doing just that! Is anyone listening?

So something did not go right somewhere from conception forwards and the result was a person who, to some greater or lesser extent has a conflict (NOT a confusion) between their body design and expected behavior, and their own identity in their heart and soul with regards to their gender.

Generally speaking, the church has it wrong! When there is a real true transgender person who knows in their heart and soul who they are, they should be fully accepted in all ways. We need to stop destroying that persons soul and grieving their heart over and over again so that we can get them to conform to what we see their flesh to be, while doing so all in the name of Christ and the Kingdom of God!

We need to consider God's grace and mercy and look at it a different way, that the body is the part that is out of whack, out of sync here. Help the person change their body to line up with their soul and heart in the peace of Christ Jesus, and you will see a person blossom in Christ. If that person is wrapped up in all kinds of sinful activities, helping them gain peace of who they are just might, don't you think, also help them to be free of sin that they may no longer need, because they have peace in Jesus Christ of who they are! This surely is applicable to believers and non-believers alike. Gee, a few may even discover that they are not true transgender after all, but the majority I think you will find are. And if you cannot physically operate on the brain to force it to be wired and function differently, then change the body to line up instead!

That, dear reader, is my stance and I repeat myself, I am so certain of this in these true transgender cases that if we could, as the body of Christ even embrace those transgender people that are still heavily bound in sin, especially sexual sin, then maybe we will see the delivering power of God's hand at work. So far the church as a whole is just judgmental about gender identity (primarily because they are lacking in knowledge on the whole subject). They bring no life of Christ Jesus to the transgender person nor to themselves. All they see is sin and judge accordingly. For a believer they say that he or she has a hardened heart, a seared conscience, is deceived etc. etc. and if they persist must leave the church or make themselves conform from the outside in, at least for the appearance sake of not offending people. Rather than lead the transgender person away from sin, depression, suicidal thoughts etc., they are actually pushing them towards these things. I have heard horrible true stories, plain evil words spoken to transgender believers already and I have not spoken even to fifty people yet on this subject! People who have been called,
"You are an abomination to God in what you are doing to yourself," and the like.
Shame on the church I say if you do this. God sees the heart of the person and He knows what is motivating the heart into action. We still tend to judge a person by their outward actions based on our past traditions and beliefs that sadly are sometimes founded on ignorance.

When a person is born intersexed then all of a sudden it is okay to play God, and to alter the body to one sex or the other even just after birth. However, if a person is allowed to grow up intersexed, or somehow it was missed at birth and discovered later in life then this can also be considered sin if the person has presented themselves as one particular gender, and then switches. I am sure that a study of what happens in the case of babies being operated on will reveal that sometimes it works out fine for the chosen gender and at other times not so because the mind, the soul has a gender identity too and if the wrong choice was made at birth regarding that person's body then there is a conflict that would need to be resolved. I have not found one *true* transgender person yet who has not transitioned AND stayed totally complete, whole and at peace with themselves and God (if they know Him). I have found one or two that decided to deny that in themselves and have done so (just like I did) for whole periods of time, sometimes years but it is always there in the background waiting to come through.

Because of the current charismatic conservative Christian point of view, all the Christian related material that I am finding that relates to, or could be used to relate to being transgender, has that sin-related slant to it as a premise. When scriptures are presented after this, they show what the person needs to acknowledge, what they need do in light of those scriptures, and no one can argue if they say that they believe the Bible. Case sealed, for you cannot go against the Word of God if you say that you are a believer in Jesus Christ. And, the solution is to renew the deceived mind and purge the wicked desires of the heart to conform to the body and that this is the Will of God solution. Lord have mercy on all of us that falsely believe that way like I used to myself. We have missed God and become self-righteous, like the Pharisees.

So here is my statement that I declare as truth before God:

BEING TRANSGENDER IN OF ITSELF IS NOT A SIN.

A result of 'the fall' in this world as an explanation to the condition and also to explain why intersexed people are born with any and all other kinds of defects, is fully acceptable. Or, as a result of the fall there is a weakness of the flesh, a thorn in the side or whatever fits your theology. The end state is the same no matter how you label it:

IT IS THERE AND IT IS REAL FOR THAT PERSON.

The question that we should perhaps be asking is, what is the right thing to do before Almighty God to help such people that are in this situation? I declare the following:

I AM TAKING THE STANCE THAT A BELIEVER IN JESUS CHRIST CAN BE TRANSGENDER AND IT IS ACCEPTABLE BEFORE ALMIGHTY GOD OF OUR LORD JESUS CHRIST TO LINE UP THE BODY WITH THE SOUL AND SPIRIT (HEART) OF THE PERSON AND THAT THIS IS MORE ACCEPTABLE TO GOD THAN YEARS, IF NOT A LIFETIME OF BATTLING THE IDENTITY ISSUE IN THAT PERSONS MIND, AND THAT THIS PERSONS HEART AND MIND ARE SOUND, NOT DEFECTIVE ON THIS ISSUE!

What counts more than anything here is the heart motive that GOD sees in that person, not other people's judgments on what they say your heart motive is and how you should be. To go with the latter creates a church of man, not a church of God where the Holy Ghost is free to act in and on our lives. Rules that seem right to man when formed out of some agreed interpretation of the Scriptures puts people into bondage and stifles God's Spirit.

Definition of a True Transgender Person

Moving forward from the earlier chapter on 'True' and 'False' transgender definitions let us revisit that subject to make sure we are all on the same page. What I refer to when I say a true transgender person is a person who really has been born with a gender difference that the medical field calls GID, Gender Identity Dysphoria (as published in the DSM-V dated May 2013). The body and the mind are in conflict as the body shows that they are one sex and gender, and the other, the mind and soul says that they are to some lesser or greater extent the opposite gender. This has been found present in children from as early as two years of age. If you search the infamous YouTube website for transgender children documentaries, you will find some quite revealing stories (see also list of recommended documentaries in the Appendix 1).

Whether the true transgender person is entangled in other tormenting and driving lifestyles and behaviors (sin in Christian terminology) or not, they are still true. Once free from all those things that drive them, they can see who they really are and gain peace in their hearts and souls that they are transgender and can now hopefully pursue it with inner peace. Many though have not heard or accepted, or have believed but rejected the message of Jesus Christ because they have been so badly judged by believers and have kept away from anything to do with church that so many remain true transgender but still bound.

You see, a true transgender knows in their heart who they are. They do not need to change anything about themselves in order to become or validate that they are transgender through appearance or mannerisms. They change their appearance and act the way they do *because* that is who they are.

Now, this definition does not include what to do about it. That will be discussed in following chapters. Now compare my definition of a True transgender to a 'False' transgender.

Definition of a 'False' Transgender

As previously mentioned, the word 'False' is probably not a good choice of words as it indicates something bad. In reality though it means the opposite here. False is good! Because these are the people that believed for a whole multitude of different reasons that they were transgender. What makes this group different though is that they were drawn into that as a lifestyle by lust, pride, by force, trauma, or by something that motivates them, drives them on which results in no inner peace but rather torment. As they have no real inner peace they look for the next 'fix' to try and move things on. These people, if they come to the truth about themselves often can have huge regrets as to what they did to themselves in the name of transitioning. Driven people with no peace, some fall into depression and even commit suicide. Others see the truth for themselves and get free and change back if possible and there, they find their inner peace (no, this does not mean that any transgender person who experiences depression or attempts suicide is therefore a false transgender).

These 'false' transgender people belong to the rest of the 98% or so of the population where their soul and body always did line up in agreement with regards to their gender identity, they never had GID, Gender Identity Dysphoria. They were deceived into going down that pathway for one or many reasons. The proof is that when free from torment and driving forces (sometimes through accepting Jesus Christ and being born again) that gave them no peace, the need to be transgender vanishes. Good for them. I hope we can help more of these people discover their truth as well as help the true transgender people change.

Once again, let me make it absolutely clear that a true transgender person can also get caught up and be driven in all ways as a 'false' transgender person can, so you cannot distinguish which a person is until they become free and gain real peace in their hearts.

The few testimonies of people that you can find that have been set free from 'Transgenderism' after turning to Jesus Christ are perfect examples of a 'false' transgender person. You can read their testimonies of what it was like for them in that life before they got freed. They all talk of guilt, shame, trying to be someone else, tormented, driven and unhappy inside of themselves. These are all obvious red flags to show that they were surely not motivated by true inner peace. Once set free from sin, the clear picture of who they are came out and for them they discovered that they were not transgender at all.

A Legalistic Church Response to True and 'False' Transgender People

Now to preempt what I am expecting the right, more conservative or apostolic side of the church to say, is that my definitions are just a cop out to face the truth. And that the truth is that all transgenderism is simply lust of the flesh no matter which way you look at it. Really? You really believe that this is the response that Jesus Christ would give? You really think that changing and mutilating our bodies is perverse and ungodly? You should read your bible more closely and read on in this book too.

I have a feeling that these churches will retract back to, or refuse to leave from their traditional understanding that what you are sexually physically born with always, always determines that person's gender and say that God does not make mistakes; that you were born male *or* female. If this is so, how I pray to the Lord that they could know what it is to be who we are. I think that the nearest way to get through to such people is to force them to do the following, to be who they are not, and see if they can change their brain gender as they so demand that we need to do to ourselves in order to be 'healed' and 'free'. So, as an example for the men:

For the next year you are to dress, act, and fully identify with the opposite gender that you were born as. Yes, you men are to only dress and act in all kinds of women's clothes from the work to casual and full dress. You are to do all the makeup and beauty stuff that ladies do to take care of themselves. You are to do all the basic home jobs and meet and gather together to engage in ladies chat times and you are to love those times and be fulfilled. You are to act more feminine to be just like ladies automatically do overall. Your whole goal is to renew your mind so that you have total peace as to being who you now are, a lady. Then, after a year you can revert back to all the manly things you had and did before. And I am sorry, just to sit there reading this and imagining what it would be like is no substitute for doing it if you want to get an inkling to what goes on with us.

Now, what kind of reaction am I going to have giving out this challenge? Think I will hear of even one person who will do this? What will men feel like after six months trying to live as the opposite gender as much as possible. For sure, it would feel unreal and most stupid at the start. Very uncomfortable and embarrassing. Maybe by the end of six months though you may have got used to at least a few of the changes, maybe not. But one thing I can guarantee for any true man, when he gets all his stuff back and his correct manly role back he will be *SO* pleased. He will trash the girly clothes, put on this rightful man gear and shout, "Yes, *this* is me!" with a great sign of relief that that ordeal is over with. True? Yes.

So now you know what it is like for us transgender people a little. Forced to conform to a gender that is not you. Then, when we can be ourselves it is "Yes, *this* is me!"

All that I am doing by pointing out two very distinctive groups of people from a Christian biblical viewpoint is this; I am showing that to blindly NOT take a look more closely may make it easier to apply the standard traditional beliefs of male and female and avoid having to put some more effort into this, but if you claim to want to walk in the truth with knowledge and understanding is this not better to do than just turn a blind eye and be right according to your current belief system? Are you not rather judging based on your beliefs and your current understanding to the meaning of the Word of God? You know, God really does not mind if you probe and start looking more closely into His Word in order to correctly divide it. Just because you may have followed, and believed a certain doctrine most of your life does not make it true or right before God.

If I, for example were to visit the apostolic church that my wife attends in Owasso, Oklahoma, dressed and acting as I am, when I walk in will not people judge me. When they realize who I am will they not judge even more?! If I insist on attending every week as I am will they not get the leadership to try and change me or to remove me? Oh, the doctrines and judgments of man! Could they not wait to even prove themselves right, that God Almighty will come to me and deliver me out of my 'deception' etc? Will I be subjected to yet more counselling and prayers for me to help me change, or will I be called hard hearted and calloused and be judged and cast out? You see, the church is quick to apply what it thinks is the truth, when really they are so much more guilty of being judgmental and therefore in sin themselves, than we are by just being ourselves! Also, I thought churches are supposed to have a sanctuary? And I thought that a sanctuary was supposed to be a safe place, a safe place for all to come and worship the Lord our God? Looks like we in the church have a lot to learn still.

To push my point further look at this email I received from a man who calls himself an apostle of the Lord Jesus Christ. He runs that apostolic church in Owasso. As for me the fruit of an apostle needs to be there fully for me to declare that he is one, and I was never there really long enough to get to that point. Persons like the Arch Bishop in Nigeria and a few of his friends in Christ, as well as the apostles of my first church, the Restoration church in England were clearly apostles by calling. You sensed that authority born of Christ in them and the power of God working through them. This man definitely had something there but, like I said maybe it was too early for me to tell so he may well be a true apostle.

As you can read, I had apparently messed up in communications to him and had not contacted him through all the drama that was going on between Prisci and myself. The email was received just two weeks before Prisci went and filed divorce papers against me. It starts with my email to him on March 23rd 2014:

Dear Brother D,
It has been a long time since I have attended the fellowship for obvious reasons of being judged and not accepted etc etc. Surprisingly to me I have not heard a peak from any of you but I know that the Lord commands you what to do or not and that is good.

There is a section in a book that I am writing that the Lord has told me to send to you so I will say no more and send it to you. Please be aware that it is draft form so there are probably some grammar errors etc.

I do not consider this information as personal so please share it or not at your discretion.
The God of our Lord Jesus, Yeshua keep you and everyone there at peace and in His will.

Ms. Robbie Ewens

- The church: Religion verses the Kingdom of God and the Transgendered

Oh dear, Oh dear what a poor state the body of Christ is when it comes to people being different! Unfortunately, this chapter is going to tell a dismal account of how manmade religious doctrine will put man into bondage and self-condemnation. Oh, how we have taken some aspects, some 'principals' from the Word of God and made it a blanket rule thinking we are doing God a service. Oh, how we have lost our way and forgotten the amount of His great mercy given to us, to only judge others in the body in an unrighteous way! Oh, how people and leadership allow themselves to be influenced to please man and a way that seems right but is not.

I could cry out I am sure the heart of God on this matter for hours.

Instead I am going to break it down some more, strictly in terms of transgender people and I will use real life examples of just how ungodly the body has become.

Groups of people claiming that they are a…
(…I will stop here as you have read it all in a previous chapter.) Now for his rather predictable reply a day later:

Rob,

I wanted to let you know that I had received your email.
I'm certain I could refute your statements with other texts from the scriptures to substantiate the view Holy Spirit has given to me just as you has used certain texts in order to provide validity to what you feel is right. However, I will

not choose to do that. I will say that the last time we visited you told me you would contact me to let me what your choice was and if you were going to follow through with this false identity of purpose. Priscilla had also spoken with me and said that you were going to call and share your decision and that you were going to go elsewhere. I never heard from you. I'm sorry if you feel it was my responsibility to track you down. I preach the gospel of the kingdom and equip people to walk in true identity. I do not chase anyone regardless of their condition. After all of our conversations over what you knew was right in the scriptures and how you identified the sin you dealt with. I am sorry to hear how you have now chosen to use the same scriptures to support the life you wanted to live.

Contrary to what you may or may not think I do not hold the position that certain sins are worse than others. Sin is not an action. Sin is a condition. I do not believe any sin or situation is too big for Yahweh to redeem. I do believe however that we are the variables in the equation that needs to change not the rules or Yahweh's order.

D **XXXXXX**
Apostle

This email makes me cringe because it comes from the premise that being transgender is a sin from the outset. Do you see the use of the word 'feel' as if it is a matter of feelings to be a certain way. He uses his listening to the Holy Spirit against my feelings indicating that he is correct as God, the Holy Spirit is always right, especially over feelings. Then the use of the word 'false' which is a judgment word to try to tell you that you are wrong and if wrong then in sin. He also worded it in such a way to suggest that I had acknowledged that it was a false identity and I was going to contact him to let him know if I was going to go on that pathway or not. I never once said it was a false identity, that is his input there. Writing FALSE IDENTITY clearly shows where he is at regarding being transgender. Oh, if only he was one too,,,.how his tune would change. I wonder if he, as a believer would have been willing to battle against it in himself for twenty years like I did? Would he have been so sure that he would battle forever? Or would he finally realize like I have had to, that being transgender is not a false identity nor a sin?

Then the reference to me knowing what was right again shows that same judgment. And then to feel sorry that I am using the same scriptures to support the life I wanted to live! Sure, man I can think of no better way to be joyful in life than to be transgender! I mean it's man's life long desire for all physically born men right! Give me a break please.

To his final paragraph I agree that no one sin is worse than another. Like maybe judging is the same as lust, which is the same as getting sick, or not getting healed, or, not walking in faith or in the Spirit?! Sin is a condition I agree and I also totally agree that no sin or situation is too big for God. So, as predicted, the blame has to be passed on to me. I am the failing variable in the equation for God does not change, He is the Same Yesterday and today and forever. I am just so defective that over twenty years of the Lord dealing with me I just am to end up in this totally sinful, self-deceived lifestyle that I am just choosing so that I can feel right.

This email is just a perfect example of the total misuse of the Word of God that does nothing other than be right and brings not the person into freedom and liberty but into self-condemnation, guilt and shame if taken into the heart and submitted to in this manner, and I have already been there too many times to travel down that road again. Christ came to set people free not to put them into bondage. Man again is doing his very best to help, but it takes the light of God inside of us to convict us if something is sin or not, bringing godly sorrow to sin, not some interpretation of the agreed division of the Word of God. This, and all phone conversations with this man of God did not result in any such sorrow. What this wonderful man has no idea about is how many times over the past twenty years I have already been there on this and how the Lord did deliver me from lust of the eyes, of the flesh and pride of life (as the Bible refers to the main sources of temptation and sin) and left me with this, my identity in its purity. I tried to tell him this but his doctrine blinded him and he could not hear me I don't think.

So, on the same day I replied and never heard back from him again (not that I was expecting a reply):

Dear brother D (assuming you still classify me as a brother in the Lord that is),

I also want you to know that I received your response. Not that I was expecting one but I am glad you did for one reason at least. I want to apologize for not getting back to you way back at the end of November last year to tell you of my decision as you referred to in your reply. I was under so much stress at making the decision knowing full well the typical response I was going to get. So, please forgive me for not doing that.

With regards to the rest of your reply, I was sad of both its content and judgmental intent and how you don't seem to see that I have been and lived where you are coming from, but you have not and cannot see where I am, yet you judge me! However, I am not surprised as most believers that try to live the current charismatic understanding of the scriptures all respond that way. I just thought that you might be a little different but alas not so, very predictable. I could (and I must admit am tempted to) tear into your reply, especially those comments like "you have used certain texts in order to provide validity to what you feel is right" kind of comment because all you can see is, quote "I am sorry to hear how you have now chosen to use the same scriptures to support the life you wanted to live" saying that this is my will and not God's. And I know it is pointless to even point out to you your stance, because you have the truth and I am the deceived one, right. So I will not waste my words on that. How you can even make that last comment bemuses me when I clearly wrote (assuming you did read it all) "Being transgender is hard, really hard and no person in his or her right mind would even consciously choose to be this way. That is an insane idea. I assure you that every transgender person would have loved to be born with the body and a soul and spirit that all line up perfectly like probably yours does. " Still, I am going to stop here other than to say that at last I am free in Christ Jesus, my Lord, my Savior and in Him do I trust. Finally, I have great joy and peace in the Holy ghost as when I first got saved. I have my first love back.

God bless you, your wife and family and I thank you with all my heart for the love and actions you and the body are doing for my wonderful wife Prisci, who I love and keep myself for at all times.

Robbie Ewens
...Oh and just to help you be a little more judgmental about me...
My picture ☺

Okay, so I got sassy there at the end, I'm sorry but do you see what I am saying here? Let's move on to actually reviewing the scriptures.

Scriptures: Introduction

Groups of people claiming that they are a part of the body of Christ can be found everywhere here in Tulsa, Oklahoma, the buckle of the Bible belt as it is known. Over the past twenty years I have been in many such congregations, sometimes as a member of the praise and worship team, sometimes involved in other ministries, and sometimes just as a member of the congregation. Over these twenty years here in Tulsa I am truly grateful to all those that availed themselves and have been used by the Lord to help others. No doubt about it, there are many great deeds being done by most such bodies when it comes to reaching out to help others and for this I know the Lord is well pleased. However, I am going to look more at what really happens inside the body and here things are not often at all holy and pleasing to the Lord. To do this I am going to look at the scriptures then at other related Christian and non-Christian material. Then we can take a look to see if the churches are really acting correctly towards transgender people or not.

Looking at the Scriptures and Discussions

The Bible scriptures are very clear with regards to what we do with our sexual behavior although how we go about interpreting these scriptures can vary. Throughout various books of the Bible it most clearly states that it is all reserved between a man and a woman in marriage if we are to obey and please God. Now, I know that I could stir up a whole hornets nest on this next passage and I am fully prepared to go there on this topic. However, right here, now, and in this book, I am not going to do so. 'Gays', 'Lesbians', 'Bi-Sexuals', all have their biblical arguments or simply reject scriptures, or say that they mean something else etc. etc. I have studied many of the arguments but, like I said, I am going to skirt around this for now as I am focusing strictly on gender identity not sexual orientation and behaviors. I will say this though, if indeed being transgender is not a sin before God, how does God judge our sexuality? By our sex organs or to the extent our brains and souls are gendered? This is one reason that most churches just want to stick with the male and female strict categories as they just don't want to go there because you can go on to say, gee, what if medical science then proves that the part of a gay persons brain is physically created to be attracted to the same sex?! So then the argument relating to those all-so-clear scriptures in the old and new testament would need to be revisited and looked upon as LUSTFUL acts, driven by lust that makes it sin. Or, are we to say that they were created as an abomination to God?! Born of the devil, damned through no fault of their own?! I know, I know, I'm starting to stir the waters right here and I will no doubt have to address this whole issue one day, and I will as I gain more knowledge on the subject. This is one reason though, the lack of clarity here that there are transgender people that fear the Lord and have chosen to be celibate until God gives them peace regarding their sexuality.

With regards to sex though, it is interesting that it is done away with completely in the new Kingdom, that is after Christ returns and Revelation is all played out according to the scriptures. Can you imagine that! No sex at all. Maybe we will be so elated in the presence of almighty God that this sex issue that we seem to be so hooked on and driven by here on earth becomes a total nonevent. Read the scripture coming next to see where this is explained by Jesus Himself.

Matt 22:23-33

The same day the Sadducees, who say there is no resurrection, came to Him and asked Him, 24 saying: "Teacher, Moses said that if a man dies, having no children, his brother shall marry his wife and raise up offspring for his brother. 25 Now there were with us seven brothers. The first died after he had married, and having no offspring, left his wife to his brother. 26 Likewise the second also, and the third, even to the seventh. 27 Last of all the woman died also. 28 Therefore, in the resurrection, whose wife of the seven will she be? For they all had her."

29 Jesus answered and said to them, "You are mistaken, not knowing the Scriptures nor the power of God. 30 <u>For in the resurrection they neither marry nor are given in marriage</u>, but are like angels of God in heaven. 31 But concerning the resurrection of the dead, have you not read what was spoken to you by God, saying, 32 *'I am the God of Abraham, the God of Isaac, and the God of Jacob*? God is not the God of the dead, but of the living." 33 And when the multitudes heard *this*, they were astonished at His teaching.

NKJV (New King James version)

Jesus said that we will be like the angels in heaven and that there is no marrying at all nor any new marriages. Therefore, no sex at all is the only conclusion to make as the Lord is true to His word regarding any sexual activity outside of the marriage bed whether we like it or not. So, you see, sex really is not important in the new Kingdom, while here on earth it is one of those issues used to test and refine a person to see if they will seek to follow the Lord into His Kingdom.

Now, as we progress into the biblical scriptures, let us first start addressing how a body of believers may well be found to respond to a transgender woman (male to female) person that comes into the church. Use your imagination for a moment as I describe the scene. Here is your usual Baptist Church Sunday service about to start and, depending on the size of the congregation, you see familiar faces and are pretty much expecting a familiar format in general. The service will be maybe just over an hour in length and you usually have plans about what you are going to do for the rest of the day or not afterwards etc.

People are comfortable and have successfully managed to keep their own dark secrets away from other people lest they be exposed (come on now you know what I am talking about you 'nice' folk who read this and say "I am right with the Lord"). In fact, most like the church that they are in because they get to hear what they already agree with, conviction of the Holy Spirit is either absent or minimal and you don't have to come clean on anything unless you want to, and nearly everyone does not want to. Truth be told, the church has become more of a social fellowship that revolves around biblical principles and teachings, not the Holy Spirit.

And then it happens. Just before the service starts, in walks this freaky looking man all dressed in women's clothes. And what is the most common judgment that is made right here? A gay cross-dresser! Or possibly some may understand transgender and think that but ... must be gay, a homosexual. Others judge secretly in their hearts thinking, "we don't want *that* in here".

Then, if you have a heart, you think praise the Lord! He is in the right place for God to deliver him! I hope we all make him feel welcome. If you have some real compassion then you might even offer a prayer to the Lord for the poor man who is obviously caught in bondage. Your mind flits through what his traumatic past may have been like. Maybe he was brought up that way and in a family with no male figure, no dad present to stop him going under the influence too much of his mom and maybe all he has is sisters. Maybe those sisters made him dress as a girl and he never got over it. Poor man, or maybe he had some kind of other trauma that made him decide to be that way. Maybe the devil has deceived him away from a Godly calling and he needs to be set free to serve the Lord. Maybe…

What have you just done to that 'poor' man? Do you have any real understanding of what or who he or she is? Can you even begin to comprehend why this person is dressed that way and acts that way? Do you realize that because of your own beliefs you have already judged that person?

In the far left kind of churches, you accept him as is and leave it at that as far as possible maybe even thinking that it is fine and not a sin to be that way. The trouble is, is that these church bodies are often so far left that they have left the foundation of the Word of God and use some term like "we are to judge no one and it's all about love, love, love." All too often they have moved away from calling anything sin except maybe extremely bad behavior.

Back over to the far conservative and Apostolic right you get the stricter literal implementation of the Word of God.
"Though shalt not dress in clothing of the opposite sex. It is an abomination to the Lord!" They all say.
To be more accurate:

Deut 22:5

5 "A woman shall not wear anything that pertains to a man, nor shall a man put on a woman's garment, for all who do so *are* an abomination to the Lord your God.
NKJV

And they say,
"Have nothing to do with the effeminate man."

Or again, to be precise:

1 Cor 6:9-10

Or know ye not that the unrighteous shall not inherit the kingdom of God? Be not deceived: neither fornicators, nor idolaters, nor adulterers, nor effeminate, nor abusers of themselves with men, 10 nor thieves, nor covetous, nor drunkards, nor revilers, nor extortioners, shall inherit the kingdom of God.
ASV (American Standard Version)

The Youngs translation also has the same word 'effeminate' and it would seem that it could easily be applied to transgender people. All other translations that I checked have the word 'homosexuals" and looking at the meaning of that in the Greek is explained as 'as with a female' which clearly refers to the sexual act of a man acting the as it were in a female role. This has nothing to do with gender identity at all but sexual behavior. And if you look at the context of the scripture it is clear to see that this is the correct interpretation. The Word of God correctly divided.

It amazes me how particularly the more 'conservative' churches are, the more they are so blinded by their own doctrines. What right do we, for example, have to take a line of scripture literally and judge someone with it? For example, that one liner in Deuteronomy (Deut. 22:5). If you take it literally and make it a truth on its own then you judge according to it within the body. But, what about all the other verses in Deuteronomy? Like, if a man and a women commit adultery they shall both die!

Deut 22:22 "If a man is found lying with a woman married to a husband, then both of them shall die.
NKJV

If you take one verse literally then should you not also take all the others that way too? Or, do we pick and choose which ones are 'relevant' for today and apply those in a literal way and excuse the others? What was the correct context for this sentence to appear like it did back then? Was it (Deut. 22:5) meant to be applied to transgender people? Might it be more accurate to note that ungodly sacrifices were being conducted at those times and the male 'priests' would put on female clothing to perform the sacrifices. Or maybe we just choose to 'put things in modern day context" to justify our use of the law. And, regarding the Law, I think I heard something about that somewhere:

2 Cor 3:4-6 And we have such trust through Christ toward God. 5 Not that we are sufficient of ourselves to think of anything as being from ourselves, but our sufficiency is from God, 6 who also made us sufficient as ministers of the new covenant, not of the letter but of the Spirit; for the letter kills, but the Spirit gives life.
NKJV

The phrase 'the letter' refers to the letter of the law. How then can we claim that we are helping someone get free by having them 'fall in line to the letter of the law?' The Spirit of Truth, the Holy Spirit brings freedom and liberty yet we seem all too eager to apply the scripture and judge one another…of course….in 'love'. Hypocrites we all are for doing such evil to another! Once again man tries to apply his understanding of how things should be and look like, and tries to change a person from the outside in, using his application of the scriptures to confirm and justify that what they are doing is right, all the while the Holy Spirit cries out to let Him make any changes from the inside out! The first if obeyed is temporary, hear me, TEMPORARY. The latter, life changing and liberating. Also, if you really insist on applying this scripture literally and out of context then we still find that a true transgender person is not breaking the law as we identify as the opposite gender as who we are. Therefore, according to the letter of the law here, it would be sin for us to dress and act deceitfully as the gender we are not! For myself to dress and act all manly would be a sin as I now know that this is not who I am. Actually, if you research the scriptures accurately you will find that the garments being referred to relate to warrior garments for use in battle (you can find all this out on the internet), and this makes a lot more sense in time and context than applying it to transgender people of today.

True conviction of sin, *if* sin is present comes from the inner witness of the Holy Spirit upon our hearts that leads that person to Godly sorrow that leads to repentance and results in liberty and joy in the Lord, a time of refreshing in His presence! Man cannot, and will never be able to make this happen. If it is *not* sin and that person is not convicted of sin then that leaves the church in a place of passing judgment on that person if they think it is still sin. Being transgender is one of the many issues that seems to fall into this category. Because the Lord has not convicted the person of sin but the church has a doctrine that states it is sin, then that leaves the church to be religious and they do to that person what seems good in their own eyes to 'help' that person 'face their sin'. And, if the transgender person is still staying there at the church to submit themselves but no real change is happening, then the usual action by the church after a period of counseling is for that person to be dismissed from the body or they just leave if they will not conform at least outwardly. Or, even more sadly, the transgender person uses their own will to make themselves conform to the leadership and places themselves under self-condemnation and into bondage, all in the name of submission. I have experienced both and other transgender believers I have met tell the same story.
"Our understanding of the Word of God is that God made either a man or a woman." Is a very common line referenced to transgendered people.
On that basis, what gender you are is determined by what is, or is not between your legs. I know that I have already mentioned this in a different chapter but it really does need to be addressed again here from a Christian perspective.

People think that the flesh (body) overrides the soul (mind and its workings) and spirit (heart) of a person when it comes to ones gender. They also seem to forget that the mind, physically the brain, is also part of the physical body just as much as the sexual organs are. Because of this, transgender people, or those with some 'gender confusion' as the church sometimes refers to it (we are not confused at all. We are just gender different) need to renew their minds to fall in line with their flesh (body) and the churches interpretation of what you should be. You have to fall into the male or the female bucket. There are no other buckets available, sorry, that's just how it is says the church. And the buckets refer to gender identity and sexuality together.

Foolish people! Open your eyes and take a more careful look around you in your church and in the real world. You will see females that range from oozing femininity to, well mega 'Tom boy' mucho manliness in both looks, dress and behavior. Then men, you can find the soft, gentle and even effeminate and delicate person in body and soul, to the tough red neck tobacco chewing "I'm full of testosterone" man that thinks he is God's perfect example of what a man should be. A multitude of variations, a total spectrum.

Who is right here? And who is being deceived? Well, you might say that's really okay for these people to be that way as at least they are sticking to their natural body gender. Really, take a look to see how many women do dress in men's clothes and act manly. Is that conforming to their correct gender role? And where exactly do you draw the line to decide this? And where you drew the line ten, twenty, thirty years ago, is it in a different place now? If so why? Is not the Word of God the same, unchanging? A woman dressed in any kind of pants some years ago was not acceptable but now is okay? Openly you will see far less the other way around (that is men acting feminine) because society ridicules such behavior so it is done more in private or is suppressed but it is still there.

What you are saying in effect is that as long as they do not claim nor *do* anything to their bodies to change to, or towards the opposite gender then that is okay. But, the moment you get a more extreme case where the person's soul and mind and behavior line up more with the opposite gender, you cannot take it there, for now it has become a sin, an 'abomination to the Lord.' Jesus said that if a person even lusts in his heart towards a woman then he has already committed adultery. Do we then go and apply the law and stone them to death? Of course not. Does it only apply to lust by a man towards a woman? Or was He showing us a truth of the Kingdom of God that we are to apply to all issues of the heart? If the latter is true, then we are not as clean inside as we would like to think we are, right. In fact, would we not be guilty just as Jesus pointed out to the Pharisees of His day:

Matt 23:25-28

"Woe to you, scribes and Pharisees, hypocrites! For you cleanse the outside of the cup and dish, but inside they are full of extortion and self-indulgence. **26** Blind Pharisee, first cleanse the inside of the cup and dish, that the outside of them may be clean also.

27 "Woe to you, scribes and Pharisees, hypocrites! For you are like whitewashed tombs which indeed appear beautiful outwardly, but inside are full of dead *men's* bones and all uncleanness. **28** Even so you also outwardly appear righteous to men, but inside you are full of hypocrisy and lawlessness. NKJV

So now that transgender person has to do one of the following if they are a believer in Christ Jesus and desire to stay in the church body:

They can open up and become transparent as best they can and submit to the church leadership and eldership for correction. Oops sorry, guidance in accordance to the Word of God. Call it Biblical counselling. I know, I was a member of the IABC (International Association of Biblical Counselors) for a few years and fully believed in it too, for transgendered people! (again, I have repented). You can have times of 'victory' over your wrong thoughts and the desire to change to the opposite gender can abate for lengths of time. You can redirect any such 'fleshy' desires to Godly ones. YOU CAN CONFORM TO HOW WE SEE THE WORD OF GOD, says the church body, including maybe yourself too. And all the time the person is still really in bondage being placed even more in bondage by those who are doing their best to free him or her! And if you (like I did for many years) believe it too, then you also become your own worst enemy, placing yourself into chains.

Or the person can and sadly often is, hurt in their heart by what people say to them to the extent that they leave the church because they just cannot deny who they are inside. If they are brave souls, they may try a couple of other churches but soon get the message. We "welcome you as you are" ... for a while but we expect God to change you and, "if He doesn't then we will!" Okay, so I am being a little obnoxious, but come on, isn't it really like that? Those that you are submitting to start to place 'boundaries' around you for you to submit yourself to. Maybe you do follow counsel and make yourself fall in line, punishing yourself for having such thoughts and desires. Beating yourself up for years like I did, all in the name of Christ and my wicked, wicked heart that needs to be purified and my deceived mind that I have to renew so that I can get the victory and overcome! Piercing and grieving my heart over and over again. Religious fool I have been.

Or maybe you have gone through life for long enough to see the hypocrisy in the church so when the time came for you to 'come out' you prepared yourself as best as you could for their reactions, so you quietly left either just after or before news broke out. Let them carry on doing church the way they like to. You leave, sad yes as you still believe, just cannot be in fellowship. Again, this is what I did finally.

Or you leave for a few years, fully transition and then go back into the body in 'stealth' mode as it is called. No one but you and God knows and you have peace with God already on this issue in your life but cannot just be real and truthful to those around you knowing full well how they will react. I personally know of both male to female and female to male transgender people that are doing this right here in Tulsa. Some go to really well known churches too. Sad, but true. Oh, the doctrines and judgments of man.

Now, let us address again that statement "God only makes a man or a woman." This is the doctrine that many churches follow. Is it true? Does God indeed only make a man or a woman? Physically, absolutely not! And in the soul and spirit, absolutely not! But here is how the church gets around those of us who were not physically born either one or the other sex to some greater or lesser degree (i.e. the intersexed and we are only referring to sex organs here, excluding the brain).
"It was a genetic or growth error in the development of the baby in the womb somehow."
Okay, so the adults decide at birth what the baby will be and the surgeon goes to work and cuts out the unwanted parts and adds the new as needed with the technology we have available. See, we fixed it! The baby now fits into either the male or female bucket! Or, the phenomena goes undetected and the child grows up and at some time or other in their life it is discovered, leaving the child or adult in a situation to choose whether to have surgery to one gender or the other, or to stay as is. At this stage (actually sometimes from as early as a child can start talking) the person usually knows *in their soul, their mind as an outlet of their heart* what gender they are. As previously mentioned, a good study online of real life transgender children and adult documentaries will prove most revealing to those who do not know this.

And all this time where does the church take its stance? In different places. Some think it acceptable to play God like I mentioned above at birth and change the body and hope the soul agrees later in life. Or you can explain the condition as result of the effects of sin or the fall of Adam and still fix it to…well one or the other gender I guess, as long as it fits into the male or female bucket, after all, right, the flesh determines the gender identity of a person. Right? Third option for the church, look the other way, live in ignorance to the reality of the transgendered, after all (for the conservative and apostolic Christian believers) it's just a deception from the devil that your wicked heart and mind is buying into. Rather hard to apply that to the intersexed though don't you think?!

I personally know a few people that were born with mixed sexual parts, intersexed, each to different degrees. Some were obvious, others were not discovered until later in life. But, in just those few cases they all knew who they were with regards to their gender and I bet that there are far more detailed studies out there about this than my short observation. **The truth is, it is not your flesh that determines your gender! It's your heart and soul!** Now there's a revelation for you. Your flesh may confirm to you what gender you are but it does not command to your brain, your soul and spirit what you need to believe and accept you are. It is the heart and soul of a person that knows who he or she is. The church has it backwards and gets transgender folk all messed up to change the gender of their soul and spirit to conform to the body. It's as if we do not realize that the soul, that functions out from the brain is also part of the body. No? Yes! Here on earth, try having a soul without a brain from which to operate out of! The soul is a living part of a person's whole and out from it we control our body (or not!). Church! Quit beating up the transgender people and start listening to them please.

Here is a real oxymoronic situation. If a baby is born with mixed sex organs and the parents, often together with the doctors agree what sex the baby should be and the surgeon goes ahead and operates, then this is considered satisfactory by the church to do this. The parents decided. But if the person grows up as a believer in the church and decides to change him or herself due to some physical differences then they get judged and now are in sin! Seems rather hypocritical to mutilate a baby and say that is okay, but to change body parts around as transgender people do or at least desire to do is not. Not only that but a baby has no say in the matter, at least transgender people have understanding and a choice as to what to do to their bodies.

The brain is an organ too and is gender differentiated. In other words the female mind and brain is different from that of a man's (that's kind of a "durr" statement I know. See end of appendix 1 for articles). If a physically born man knows his brain is female is he just going to have to spend the rest of his days in torment having to stay bound in the male body, never having a sense of wholeness but always 'on the battle field casting those 'lies' down and correcting his 'wicked' heart? Having times of reprieve that the church uses to show that they can indeed be 'free' and have 'victory', only to find in reality that they are on the merry-go-round of acting out, guilt and repentance in confession, a sense of relief to it and even freedom for a season, only to play the record again, and again, and again? And this pleases the church?!?!?!

Is it really too hard to perceive that if a male can be born with some female parts that it is just as feasible that he could be born with a female brain rather than a male one? And then what do you do? Switch out brains? Do brain surgery somehow of which currently we do not have the knowledge to perform? No, of course not, you alter the body to fit the brain.

Time for us take a brief look into the scriptures and see if it is acceptable in the eyes of God to alter the body for some reason or other particularly with things that affect gender identity. Unfortunately, there is very little throughout the whole of scripture that directly relates to this subject. The nearest you will find are the scriptures already previously mentioned, the stories about the Eunuchs. The Eunuchs of which Jesus Christ made a righteous comment or two about regarding such people. And was it not an Ethiopian eunuch that got saved and baptized?

So what is a eunuch? In the old biblical days a eunuch was a man usually born a man (though Jesus said some are born that way that is as a eunuch), and this man either chooses to, or is made to be, castrated so that he cannot be tempted to have sex with those around him. He is then placed to work in the kings courts, thus keeping the king happy that his women are safe etc, etc (See Ester chapter 2). Having their testicles removed which, especially if done prior to puberty, results in a very effeminate man. This is because the body then has very little production of the testosterone hormone that is mainly produced by the testes (the Adrenal gland produces a small amount apparently). I understand that it is the presence of testosterone that kicks the body into developing male characteristics so without it and leaving the present female estrogen to do its work unhindered, the result is a more feminine looking and sounding person. That person will not develop an Adams apple, his voice will not break and deepen. He will not sweat like a man does and the typical manly odor will not be there. His skin will be soft and his muscle development less. He may even start to have a small sign of nipple and breast development. Even his way of thinking can be affected to be more relationally based rather than the typically male logical reasoning and 'boxing' that is characteristic of men. Emotionally he will be more sensitive too. In other words, he has become more feminine.

Did Jesus bring judgment upon these people? Did He separate out and judge against those that willingly had the operation from those that were born that way or were forced into it? No. He said nothing bad of them at all. In fact, He said the opposite, that they that choose to do it to themselves (gee, mutilating their own bodies! Effectually feminizing themselves!), that they do it for the Kingdom of Heaven's sake (see scripture below of Matthew 19:10-12).

Let us dig deeper and visit the Old Testament on this subject of eunuchs:

Lev 21:16-24 And the Lord spoke to Moses, saying, 17 "Speak to Aaron, saying: 'No man of your descendants in succeeding generations, who has any defect, may approach to offer the bread of his God. 18 For any man who has a defect shall not approach: a man blind or lame, who has a marred face or any limb too long, 19 a man who has a broken foot or broken hand, 20 or is a hunchback or a dwarf, or a man who has a defect in his eye, or eczema or scab, <u>or is a eunuch</u>. 21 No man of the descendants of Aaron the priest, who has a defect, shall come near to offer the offerings

made by fire to the Lord. He has a defect; he shall not come near to offer the bread of his God. 22 He may eat the bread of his God, both the most holy and the holy; 23 only he shall not go near the veil or approach the altar, because he has a defect, lest he profane My sanctuaries; for I the Lord sanctify them."'

    24 And Moses told it to Aaron and his sons, and to all the children of Israel.
NKJV

So you can read quite plainly here that in the Old Testament, according to law, a eunuch is classified as a defective person that cannot go to the alter of the Lord. Wow, hmmm church, are you treating transgender people that way by any chance? As it is written, the letter kills.

However, Isaiah wrote in the Holy Ghost:

Isa 56:3-5
  not let the son of the foreigner
  Who has joined himself to the Lord
  Speak, saying,
  "The Lord has utterly separated me from His people";
  Nor let the eunuch say,
  "Here I am, a dry tree."
  4 For thus says the Lord :
  "To the eunuchs who keep My Sabbaths,
  And choose what pleases Me,
  And hold fast My covenant,
  5 Even to them I will give in My house
  And within My walls a place and a name
  Better than that of sons and daughters;
  I will give them an everlasting name
  That shall not be cut off.
NKJV

    Did you read that! A eunuch who has mutilated his body, or had it mutilated and made it more female by cutting off the male producing part, can please God! And not only that, can be given a special place in the Lord better than those children who belong to Him! Now, of course the Lord is referring to those who keep themselves to please the Lord and that definitely includes being free from any sexual immorality. Motive of the heart is all important to the Lord so to become a eunuch for selfish reasons and not for the Kingdom of God would be a sin as I see it.

I am *not* saying here that transgender people are eunuchs at all. I *am* saying however, that it does show that for the right heart motive, altering one's body can be acceptable to the Lord.

Now to the New Testament and in the book of Acts chapter eight we see that it is perfectly acceptable for the Old Testament defiling and defective Eunuch to obtain mercy and forgiveness of sins and be baptized. Now isn't that a turnaround from the Old Testament! Here it is:

Acts 8:27-40

And behold, a man of Ethiopia, a eunuch of great authority under Candace the queen of the Ethiopians, who had charge of all her treasury, and had come to Jerusalem to worship, 28 was returning. And sitting in his chariot, he was reading Isaiah the prophet. 29 Then the Spirit said to Philip, "Go near and overtake this chariot."

30 So Philip ran to him, and heard him reading the prophet Isaiah, and said, "Do you understand what you are reading?"

31 And he said, "How can I, unless someone guides me?" And he asked Philip to come up and sit with him. 32 The place in the Scripture which he read was this:

"He was led as a sheep to the slaughter;
And as a lamb before its shearer is silent,
So He opened not His mouth.
33 In His humiliation His justice was taken away,
And who will declare His generation?
For His life is taken from the earth."

34 So the eunuch answered Philip and said, "I ask you, of whom does the prophet say this, of himself or of some other man?" 35 Then Philip opened his mouth, and beginning at this Scripture, preached Jesus to him. 36 Now as they went down the road, they came to some water. And the eunuch said, "See, here is water. What hinders me from being baptized?"

37 Then Philip said, "If you believe with all your heart, you may."

And he answered and said, "I believe that Jesus Christ is the Son of God."

38 So he commanded the chariot to stand still. And both Philip and the eunuch went down into the water, and he baptized him. 39 Now when they came up out of the water, the Spirit of the Lord caught Philip away, so that the eunuch saw him no more; and he went on his way rejoicing. 40 But Philip was found at Azotus. And passing through, he preached in all the cities till he came to Caesarea.

NKJV

And Jesus told of the eunuchs like this:

Matt 19:10-12-
   His disciples said to Him, "If such is the case of the man with *his* wife, it is better not to marry."
   11 But He said to them, "All cannot accept this saying, but only *those* to whom it has been given: **12** For there are eunuchs who were born thus from *their* mother's womb, and there are eunuchs who were made eunuchs by men, and there are eunuchs who have made themselves eunuchs for the kingdom of heaven's sake. He who is able to accept *it*, let him accept *it*."
NKJV

So if Jesus did not condemn such actions then should not we be given the same grace when our motive is right before God, to be whole and complete? I am a Christian believer. You have read my testimony here in this book. I keep my Lord's commandment for me to walk upright before Him and to keep my body pure before Him and I am doing so. And why, for the sake of the Kingdom of God, that by His great mercy He may use me for His glory in any way He sees fit. There are others like me too that also love the Lord. Church, why do you judge us? Please stop and accept the unique calling on our lives and maybe, just maybe the many other lost souls out there (especially the transgender people) that are bound in much sin might realize that they too can be who they are yet not live in sin. Is it not time to be used to free such people that their souls might be saved in the Day of the coming of our Lord, rather than passing judgment because you believe differently due to manmade doctrines based on subjective interpretations of the scriptures?

And so you have the eunuch, that man who in effect feminized himself, mutilated his body so that sexually he was no more. Neither male nor female but an 'inbetweenie', a 'HeShe', a 'Sissy Boy' or whatever the modern non-medical colloquialism is. An intersexed transgender person is sometimes forced into being who they are not, by choices made at birth but for many it is their (our) soul and spirit gender identity that would lead us to change our bodies to fall in line. Yes, we will mutilate, manipulate our bodies and present ourselves to line up with our real soul and heart identities. And you are going to judge us!?

Now I repeat myself, I am NOT trying to make the argument here that for someone like me to transition is the same as a eunuch castrating himself as the motive is different even if the end result could be seen as similar. No, I am not saying this at all. What *I am* saying is that Jesus and the Word of God does not condemn us doing things to our bodies but rather judges the 'why', our motive for doing so. God knows if what I am doing is out of pride or lust of some kind or any sinful desire, and He knows if my heart is true and pure on my motive. If it was a sin for me then He would not deceive me for all of these twenty years by convicting me of all the multitude of other sins I confessed to, and from which He corrected and delivered me from, and yet not do so of being gender different? Why would He not do the same with me being transgender? God is good, not evil, He is merciful not deceiving. He is the healer and He makes us whole the way HE wants to do it. We just have to be obedient and not judgmental about it. And please, for the sake of us all, please do not try the line,

"Well, on that issue, you didn't or wouldn't let go of it and God won't force you to do so."

If you want to see me get mad, which is a most rare sight I assure you, it would be over this type of ignorant comment. The Lord knows how many times and with what effort I have thrown myself into His arms, before His cross and repented and repented and submitted and cried out to Him. So, please do not even go there.

    Hey, I know, most Christians are in such ignorance (not meant as a derogatory comment) that they have no idea what being transgender really is. To others more judgmental, it would probably be far more accepting if I had castrated myself and said I was a eunuch! Then they could say something like,

"Well isn't that a little strange but, well, I guess it is in the Bible so it must be okay."

Gee, give us a break here, but tell me that that would not happen at least by a few.

    Look please do not think for one second that us transgender folk are just out to be rebellious and get some kick out of life for some perverse reason. Being transgender is hard, really hard and no person in his or her right mind would consciously choose to be this way. That is an insane idea. That is why so many of us have fought against it. All the transgender people that I have met including myself have spent countless hours, months and years soul searching and hoping that we are not the way we are. Life would sure be a big lot easier! I assure you that every transgender person would have loved to be born with the soul and spirit that all line up perfectly with their body. No, we have the short straw so to speak and we have to find and make a way to get through life, like this, the best we know how. We have to be courageous to go against tradition both in society and in the church. Please, please church stop judging us and gain some understanding here and walk in real love and mercy with compassion, then you can rejoice that you have truly helped a group of people in need of

God through our Lord Jesus Christ. Help those of us who know the Lord to continue to be free, yet now within the body of Christ where our gifts and talents may be put to good use as well as outside in the world. We are no less of a testimony of God's grace and mercy than you are, and should not be denied God called positions within the body.

It was an amazing revelation to me when God spoke to me and told me it was okay being the way I am and that He looks way beyond our flesh. So, I do not care if you want to label me a sinner, a fallen saint that could have been so much used of God, a person given over to his wicked heart and who will spiral down quickly, or a stubborn man who just wants his cake and eat it and does not want to let go of his sin. Or whatever fits your own personal belief system because it just takes us right back to judging. We have forgotten that Jesus said that Mercy is greater than (overcomes) judgment:

James 2:8-13
If you really fulfill the royal law according to the Scripture, "You shall love your neighbor as yourself," you do well; 9 but if you show partiality, you commit sin, and are convicted by the law as transgressors. 10 For whoever shall keep the whole law, and yet stumble in one point, he is guilty of all. 11 For He who said, "Do not commit adultery," also said, "Do not murder." Now if you do not commit adultery, but you do murder, you have become a transgressor of the law. 12 So speak and so do as those who will be judged by the law of liberty. 13 For judgment is without mercy to the one who has shown no mercy. Mercy triumphs over judgment.
NKJV

Isn't that what the cross of Christ is all about? Jesus took our judgment and gave us mercy.

Remember, I spent twenty years as a Christian doing all I could to 'Do the Word' from praying, denying myself, fasting, casting down trillions of 'wrong' thoughts and going on a live-in men's program for almost seven months in Kentucky, besides other things like the laying on of hands, confessions, repentance and accountability etc etc. My end conclusion is as Solomon's: All life is vanity and best to fear God and follow His commandments AND GUESS WHAT READER, BEING TRANSGENDER IS NOT A SIN! Now what you do with it can lead to sin, just as that is true for you 'normal' folk out there.

Transgender people have to face so much rejection on top of just the stress of transitioning in this world that depression and suicide is rampant. Apparently the US attempted suicide rate for transgender people as around 41% compared to the national general population figure of just over 1.6%. And what is the church on the whole doing about it? Adding to the rejection by judging us! Well done church, I wonder how God will judge your doctrinal beliefs over His Spirit? If you justify yourselves in this then just how do you think that you will escape God's judgment of you? Do *you* not fear the Lord?

To the retort of some close Christians that do not understand nor know that to be transgender is not a sin before God, I am finally free in my body. Christ set me free in my spirit when I got born again and my soul got really set free when sexual sin was no more and I could see myself for who I am in my soul and spirit without shame or guilt. Now my body is being set free as it conforms to my soul and spirit. Now I can shout hallelujah! Praise the Lord! Now, I sleep well and wake up each morning with a grateful heart and rejoicing in the God of my salvation for He has made the impossible possible to me. Peace and joy flood my soul and heart.

The sad thing is, is that there are close relatives and some friends that are still stuck in the bondage of judging that can only reply this way to me; "You are deceived." And "It is a false joy that you are experiencing and you are happy because you have given into your flesh and stopped fighting." Stopped fighting?! Absolutely! Praise the Lord! And rather than beating up my heart I can now guard it wisely and I can stop tormenting myself. Sadly though, those still stuck in judgment are waiting to hear the news that my season of 'enjoying my sin' is over and it all came crashing down around me.

Again, if you want to call this a weakness of my flesh well okay. But either way it is what it is, and I am who I am and God can use me like this and He will and He is! Watch the hand of the Lord at work all you who are waiting for the day of my fall! Grace and mercy are greater than judgment and if you do not know this then you are still stuck in doing works to be better, to conform yourself to your understanding of the scriptures while all the time the Lord is interested in your heart before Him to be free so He can use you and bless you. If this is you then I pray you wake up from your own deception that tries to keep us transgender folk from the fullness of Christ *as we are* without changing us. I pray you walk not in ignorance of who we really are but gain knowledge and understanding so that you may have truth and life and the real fear of God in you that is not based on your head knowledge of the Word of God but on direct intimacy with Him.

I love the real church. I have a passion for it. I miss not being accepted and being a part of the body (as of April 2014 I am now in a good fellowship). But I hate the lifeless man made doctrines that kill by the letter and stifle the Spirit. I pray that even the deepest false belief be exposed in your congregation for the Lord is already judging the churches and has found most caught wanting and falling short. Man's best intentions are not satisfactory to the Lord when we should know better.

If there is anyone out there that thinks or feels that I am in error of how I have interpreted the scriptures, or that maybe I have either 'conveniently' or by accident avoided certain other related scriptures then please contact me (my details are at the end of this book for communication). Or, if you believe that you have a real valid argument in the Lord against my original argument here that being transgender in of itself is not a sin before God, then again please contact me. If I am able to revise this book or create a new one specifically for correctly dividing the Word of God in relation to being transgender, then I will do so. I am not closed on this issue even though I am totally convinced in the Lord. I am a man, not God, and it is always possible that I have missed something so I am always willing to hear more.

If you know that what I am saying is the truth and your spirit (heart) bears witness, but you are either too stubborn or lazy to accept *and act* on this, but rather remain rigid and judgmental staying on your old beliefs, then know this; it is the Lord's hand that you will come against, not mine.

Looking at Other Material

So, in this section, before we continue my ever evolving life story, we are going to take a look at passages from material that other people have posted on the internet, or in print form of some kind. Due to the restrictive nature of current copyright laws, I can only extract portions to comment on (I am limited to a maximum of 300 words per article but there is a lot more I would love to have added to each one). However, you should get the idea of what I am saying with regards to the material presented without me having to wade through pages of their work. Hopefully, you can go online to look at the full articles if you so desire. Off we go…

Internet pages:

Here is a page off the website, a Christian website (http://www.exposethelie.org/article-database/christian-trans-gendered-it-is-not-who-you-are) from a wife whose husband came out as being transgender. I am going to point out and comment in [*script text* between brackets] as we proceed:

Christian? Trans-gendered? It is NOT who you are.

If you are a born again Christian, then you are not trans-gendered [*Really? That is your opinion that you are entitled to. Question is, is that really the truth or is it just something you believe to be the truth?*]

…

Just as light and darkness cannot be joined, the name 'Christ' cannot be joined to the name 'trans-gendered' [*Ooops, red flag! Making a big assumption right here that being transgendered is darkness and it is right here that you lose all creditability in your argument. No direct scriptural basis given that shows this, that proves this. And you will find from here onwards the use of scripture to tell believers what they should do to overcome this deception and if you are an obedient believer then you will have to follow all that the scriptures say…*]. The two are totally opposed to each other [*Opinion!*]. One is the Truth the other is a lie, from one the Spirit of Truth proceeds, from the other the spirit of error proceeds… [*Oh baloney! The two are not totally opposed to each other at all. You might as well say, "Just as light and darkness cannot be joined, the name 'Christ' cannot be joined to the name 'male' or 'female'. And if you think that my comment here is a lie then you have to be basing it on the truth that you hold to that man was created either and man or a woman only and it is the body parts, excluding the brain, that you have that determine your true gender and only that will Christ accept if you want to be joined with Him. So, hopefully you have read my walk in Christ in previous chapters and now you are going to tell me based on your theology and beliefs that I am no longer joined to Christ?!]*

These statements are not the same as saying that one who is a Christian cannot struggle with a trans-gender temptation [*is it a temptation? If it is sexually driven then I can clearly see this being the case and interpret it that way regarding the sexual aspect. But what of those of us who love the Lord and know the Word of God and know it is a soul and heart identity issue, and we live morally upright before our God (probably more so than many non-transgender Christians]*. Neither is it stating that Christians cannot choose to give themselves over to a trans-gender identity [*which is why I spent 20 some years as a believer fighting to overcome what I have discovered for myself is not something to be overcome but rather used for God's glory*]. Christians may choose, ... to give themselves over to another or allow another to take control. [*Here you can see how this theology tears at the very heart of us transgender people. Basically it is saying that accepting yourself as a transgender person is of the devil and you have chosen to follow the devil and not Jesus, not God, either in ignorance or by conscious choice. Odd though isn't it how the scriptures do not specifically call transgenderism a sin at all and the nearest we can find in scripture is Jesus Himself referring to men who castrate themselves for the Kingdom of Heaven!*]

...

Trans-genderism is a confusion of gender identity [*no, no, NO!*

it is not. It can sure end up that way and I am sure it does get confusing for lots of transgender people as they struggle with their identity but I can testify that the truth for me is not any confusion at all but gender difference. I am not confused at all thank you and neither are many, many other transgender people that I know].

...

Will your ruler be sin? Will your ruler be a 'trans-gender identity' or will your ruler be a 'righteousness in Jesus' identity'? [there you go again automatically calling being transgender a sin by comparing Jesus to transgender]

The Christian must make a fully determined decision, "I will not let trans-genderism rule in my life. [The beginnings of maybe years of trying to overcome, supposedly "fighting the good fight".] Trans-genderism will not be my defining identity. [And it isn't. Jesus Christ is. The word transgender is just that, a word, a label] My identity, whether it is my gender identity or my spiritual identity, is found in Jesus Christ alone." [Again, Yes my whole identity is found in Christ Jesus indeed. And my gender identity is as clear as yours. If you are born a natural man, then a man, if born a natural female, then female because your souls agree with your flesh so it is no issue. If you identify with Jesus Christ do you stop identifying yourself as a woman or a man? Does that vanish away? No, of course not. Same for us transgender folk. We are still in Christ and we identify with being transgender. What is the problem here really? Just who is being deceived here and who is placing people *into bondage?]*

...

The answer for the believer is to align their lives, their thought life and behaviour with the Word of Truth...

[Gee, please read my testimony on this for the past twenty years and what I have done to my wife and family because I failed to 'overcome'. And you want me to continue this for the rest of my life! That's plain evil and don't you think that the cries out to God over all these years were not sincere from where I was at, at the time and God is not merciful enough to 'deliver me'? No, let's just blame me that I refused to let it go. I wanted to be this way... that's sick thinking to fit your theology] This is the same Spirit who works doing a transforming and conforming work to the name of Christ. Yet it requires a daily diligence to align your life, your thoughts or actions, into obedience to the word of righteousness *[sounds great but, if you are a man try this for a year or two: change your thoughts and actions into that of the opposite gender and see how well you do! You may call that foolish as you are not that gender. Exactly my point! I can guarantee that this author is NOT transgender]*. "Having been set free from sin, you became slaves of righteousness. ... now having been set free from sin, and having become slaves of God, you have your fruit to holiness, and the end, everlasting life" (Roman's 6:18 and 22). Only the believer is free to choose who whom they present themselves, for Christ has set them free *[And I am free! Not that you could accept that]*.

END of web page.

May I gracefully suggest that it really is possible to use scriptures to make a good argument either way. The Spirit of Truth within each believer to lead that believer is far more powerful and acceptable to the Lord that our use of scripture to categorize and instruct that believer because it relies on fallible man to say what the scriptures mean and how they should be applied. If indeed, the person is deceived and belongs to Christ then we need to be really careful on how we judge. Modern day Pharisees we are when we judge like in this website article.

Here is another page from the same website:

God is not the author of gender confusion
Whether you consider gender confusion a mental illness, a physical ailment or a psychological condition, trans-genderism or gender identity disorder is a confusion of gender identity... *[NO, we are not confused at all. We have a gender difference. Our body and souls are not matching that's all. No confusion. One needs to change to be at peace and made whole in Christ, body, soul and spirit. And, it is NONE of the above mentioned conditions. It is a physical disorder, now, since May 2013 medically diagnosed as a physical difference between the brain gender and the body gender, Gender Identity Dysphoria.]*

...

Trans-genderism, trans-sexuality is a confusion of gender identity *[Keep repeating yourself but this is not true! And therefore your whole argument and use of scripture is invalid].*

[... more of the same about confusion...]

...no person can say "God made a mistake when he created me in this body" *[And why is God blamed here at all? How about a result of the fall, sin in the world or how else do you explain a person who is a true hermaphrodite? God did not say and nor do I say that God made a mistake. Or do you say that the devil made him/her that way?! I fully accept the natural body I was given but because my heart and soul is more female I have chosen to change my body to line up with how I am. Maybe you would be more accepting if I said that I will castrate myself for the Kingdom of Heaven as you can find that in scripture (eunuchs by choice)!].*

In regards to the inter-sexed condition, I realize this is a defining statement. God does not create imperfect forms. Deformity, inter-sexed genetalia, ill-formed bodily functions all occur because of the presence of sin in the world and the work of the enemy [*okay, so you believe this doctrine, as I mentioned above. The question is, however is it the flesh that needs to line up with the soul and heart (spirit) of the person or the other way around? And like the man born blind from birth that Jesus' disciples questioned Him about asking if the man was blind because of his or his parents sin right? Also, are you saying here that an inter-sexed person is the work of the devil? I think that I would recommend that you repent from this lie as soon as possible my friend. Interesting thought though, If Jesus came to me again and 'healed' me from my gender difference, would He give me a new heart and brain that was all male, or would He simply give me female body parts?*]. .. When this process of formation gets disturbed or disrupted or damaged It Is not because of God's error, but the work of the enemy. [*Author, do you realize that you have just judged thousands and hundreds of thousands of us transgender people as* being the work of the devil!? We were created by the devil, not by God. Wow, I really hope that you have repented from this statement for I do not want God to judge yourself in like manner. Sufficient to say to my dear readers of this book that if you are transgender, you are NOT a creation of the devil my friend. All those who, transgender or not, are fully accepted by God when we enter through the true door, through accepting Jesus Christ into our lives.] Yet God is also the one who can put right what has gone wrong... Nothing that ever happens is a surprise to God. [Author, you just totally blew it here. Here you expose your Pharisee mind set and beliefs. Firstly you clearly say that any deformity is because the devil, quote 'but the work of the enemy.' Have you ever thought that the sovereign God is God over all things, even the devil? Well, dear author, I guess that my confused, deformed mind and soul needs to change, or is it my deformed body that needs to change to match my soul? Hmm I think the latter is exactly what I am doing! With regards to a person born with inter-sexed deformity then, are you suggesting that they should remain that way or do you play God and decide what parts need to be surgically changed? Hypocrites! Judging according to the flesh and not the Spirit]

...

When medical science takes upon itself to heal, correct and fix physical abnormalities, ... to the pattern that God set in place in His original creation [Oooo, I have to jump on this. So, if we correct physical abnormalities, like sex organs and *lack of certain hormones, or too much hormones etc and align the physical body once more to the pattern of God (whole spirit, soul and body) where the body has been changed to align with the spirit and soul then there you have it, a transgender! Or, are you going to operate on the human brain and heart of that person to align it with the body?]*. Medical science has studied how the body should work they do so, so that they may restore the body back to its original properly functioning pattern. It is God who gave humanity the ability to use medical knowledge to aid the restoration to His pre-defined pattern. ... we use medicine to align that which is out of order so that it once again resembles that which God originally created. *[Yes, yes and yes! And this is why I am using medical science to correct my abnormality as you put it! You cannot use medical science to alter a person's soul gender identity, but you can change the body to the soul and there you have it, transgenderism!]*

...

In rare situations when a child is formed whose body has sexual ambiguity, because of the presence of sin in the world, it is for one purpose *"that the works of God should be revealed in him"* ... *[Still hooked up on the flesh identity and not the soul. Isn't it amazing that we are supposed to be so spiritually minded and not fleshly (carnally) minded yet we seem so quick to judge others according to the flesh and what they are doing with it! Also, I totally agree with the purpose statement of truth but you also need to include the soul, the mind gender identity besides the flesh. No solution offered here. What is the right thing to do before God? Mutilate the organs one way or another, brain surgery, or leave all things as they are?]*.

Enough of that, let's move on to another source.

Here is a different website that is also against being transgender (specifically in this article, being transsexual). This website is not Christian based it seems but rather uses psychology and the like:

(http://waltheyer.typepad.com/blog/2013/05/sex-change-transitioning-may-become-obsolete.html?cid=6a0133f43a41d9970b019102a67543970c):

05/27/2013
Sex Change Transitioning May Become Obsolete
...
Dear Walt, ... It demonstrates that the main factor in the brain that is responsible for brain growth and changes of the brain in those with GID:
1) Parallels the same brain neurochemistry and neurophysiology that is known to underpin various mental disorders in general [*And so your conclusion is...? We all have mental disorders? And if so, how are you going to fix us? How about a physical disorder?*]
2) Is directly the result of the way transsexuals are treated mainly in traumas and psychological abuse [*I seriously question this as a blanket truth*]

I can't pick and choose the objectivity of the facts [*Well isn't that great! You make two points and now state that you question their relevance!*]. I now need to present you the *objective findings* that neurochemistry and the neurophysiology of GID brains demonstrates that the brain is indeed changeable and that there is substantial evidence that ***GID brains are the result of psychological trauma*** [*Oh really, again maybe in some or many I do not know but I know people like myself that this is not true. Want to prove me wrong? I'll be a guinea pig for you!*] and that the changes are the changes seen in those with an array of psychiatric disorders. ...

This data support the hypothesis that the reduction found in serum BDNF levels in GID patients may be [*Theory! Which, of course is what hypothesis means*] related to the *psychological abuse that transsexuals are exposed during their life.*

Since BDNF is involved in neurophysiology and neurochemistry and is subject to change based on the environment, I am not confident that what seems to be a cross sexed brain structure actually is a cross sexed brain structure in any of the transsexual brain studies now or perhaps to come. It may be [*Theory*] that transsexualism is not ever a male/female brain issue and raises the possibility that *neuropsychiatric treatment will substitute and replace gender surgeries and hormonal treatments for all transsexuals.* [*It is a shame that these people are all stuck in the mind and its workings. Do they realize that humans have hearts, a spirit that drives what goes on in the mind?*] …Even if 10-20% of transsexuals may benefit from treatment with transitioning [*If! And only up to 20%. Not so much of a major truth discovery here then! I am sure it may work either temporarily or permanently for some, what do I know?*], the transitions and SRS may become outmoded in favor of neurological and neuropsychiatric treatments. [*I am starting to wonder exactly what this 'treatment' involves here*] *This study may be the one which starts the revolution to show that transitioning is idealistically an obsolete treatment.*

http://www.ncbi.nlm.nih.gov/pubmed/23702250
Walt went on to comment:
I wanted to post this study sent by the physician because it brings into question serious psychological issues that remain unresolved even after a gender transition is completed. [*And these 'serious psychological issues' are...?*] Neuropsychiatric treatments could make gender transitioning obsolete and could offer new treatment criteria. This gives me optimism that it may help reduce the needless surgeries and unnecessary suicides. [*Are you suggesting here that it is those who have 'needless' surgeries are the ones who commit*

suicide?! I sure would like to see the data on that assumption].

Walt Heyer, The Maverick Transgender *[You will find me communicating with Walt via email later].*
www.sexchangeregret.com

My overall response: So, a traumatic experience or two resulted in a person wanting to change their sexual identity? Well, I am sure that that is something that can and does happen, but I do not believe for one moment that that is the truth for all of us, including myself. Then the article goes on to say that it is the mind in error and we can "now look for neuropsychiatric treatments". What will be involved here? Drugs, electric shocks or psychiatric counselling aimed to change the way the persons brain works? Isn't this just more manipulation of a body part but this time on the brain rather than the sex organs? I want to add here, too, that if a person is still a lost soul and by that I mean the "God" connection (born again through Jesus Christ) is absent, then it is not hard to see why some people are transsexual, actually any form of transgenderism for wrong motives, and that if those motives were corrected, could result in that person no longer desiring to be that way ever again. Thus they would regret the things that they did and would desire to undo what they did. This falls neatly into my definition of a 'false' transgender person. However, this then cannot be used as a blanket truth for all transgender people and neither can it be used to prove that being transgender is of the devil and not of God. For a simple example, a person who for some reason in his life needs to get attention, then this would be a great way to do so. If this need was resolved, then they may discover that such a desire vanished because it really was not who they are. This is basic psychology. During my forty years before I accepted myself to be transgender, I went through all kinds of soul searching and counselling. I am at peace with being transgender. More than that, I am overwhelmed with the joy of the Lord that He would grant me the desires of my heart after all my begging Him to take this 'sin' from me. Maybe that is because I know I have Christ in me and He is my identity. I am a spirit and I have a soul that is connected to my body in which I live here on earth for a short season before I move out of here and get a new body that is not faulty in any way.

Okay, here we go travelling off to another Christian based website that also is sincere in helping people:

http://help4families.com/

A Matter of Survival (Part 1)
by Bob

...

I felt very much a freak of nature at one moment, a replicated form of my mother in the next. I wanted so much to emulate her... [*Clearly here he is not being who he is but rather trying to be someone else and as you read on, you can see that he really does not know who he is even though he is out there doing all this stuff. He is what I have defined as a 'false' transgender person.*]

... But the intrigue was quickly replaced by an overpowering sense of shame. [*His conscience convicting him of what he is doing is not right for him, hence the shame. I have no problem with this. It is the heart motive of why we do something that is what God judges and exposes and when the motive is some kind of self-seeking driving force of some kind rather than an internal peace with God through Jesus Christ, then you are going to have inner conviction, confusion and turmoil*]

I knew, too, that I had once again exposed myself to such an incredible risk of being caught. Why? ...

... my journal: I am intensely angry and confused! ... delight and disgust. Delight, knowing that I was at least for the moment accepted as the woman portrayed to the "unseeing" eye . . . but a freak, ... [*Proof of what I said above, he is clearly in sin as his conscience is convicting his heart that what he is doing is wrong. He is not being open and truthful, he is being covert and deceitful and is walking in fear.*]

I loathe all of this! How can I go on in this type of existence? Always longing for what I cannot have. Always in pain within. [*Again, this is clearly not right for this man. The opposite is when you have inner peace both with God and yourself and you are not being driven nor in sexual sin either by desire or action.]* ... And all the while suppressing the excruciating, instinctive knowledge that I am in the wrong.

...

Survival is what transvestism and transsexualism is about at its core. *[Sorry, yes and no here, Yes for those who are being driven, who have no peace like this man has already described about himself. No for the 'true' transgender person, for those of us who have great inner peace as to who we are and it is because of this we can ride the storms and overcome the challenges. And for the believer in Christ Jesus we have our Helper in our almost constant times of need, the Holy Spirit. The author will go on talking all about self: Self, me I and feelings etc. etc.]*

...

Because we have suffered a breakdown in our "psycho-social development," *[We have?!]* we have eroticized the other sex, ... *[Hey, hey, hey hold on there a minute. You are now introducing a whole new aspect into the equation that many of us transgender people understand and that you folk seem a little hard of hearing. GENDER IDENTITY IS SEPARATE FROM SEXUAL ORIENTATION AND BEHAVIOR. You can look at a hundred mtf (male to female) transgender ladies and you will find every range of sexual activity from celibacy to horrible perversions not even worth mentioning here. You can be transgender in the Lord and still honor Him. Read my testimony. The second point just thrown in here is that we are all trying to cure some kind of intense emotional pain! Well, I guess this man at least at this time was probably not a Christian believer by the way he is talking psychology terms. People, there is a cross that our Lord and Savior was crucified on and who made a way for us pathetic little us human souls to follow by His sacrifice. In Him is healing for our hearts, souls and bodies. This is where this man should have gone for healing. It is a typical psychological belief that emotional pain drives a person to do things that otherwise we would not do as a mechanism to avoid fully facing that pain. Who of us that have either not had such trauma or have faced any such pains and yet still are, or later become transgender?]*

… when a man refuses to accept himself, his eyes are directed to someone else, (typically his mother for the transsexual [*Woo, woo, woo! Slow down there Mr. psychologist. Are we really refusing to accept ourselves? It is insane to think that a man born a man, looks to his mommy and says that is me! Again, I am sure that there are cases out there in history where that has happened but no way can you lump everyone in that boat! Rather, by accepting ourselves, we gain real peace for all us 'true' transgender people!]*), finding himself stuck in some form or manifestation of the wrong kind of self-love [*At last it appears. I thought that this line was going to show itself far more than it has. Self-love all gone wrong as you should only be loving and accepting your body-given gender and not some false image that you are trying to lay over the top! I am surprised we haven't heard "low self-esteem" here as well*]. Failing to love himself aright, he will love himself amiss. This misplaced affection results in an inordinate, highly immoral, self-love of the woman of our own making that attempts to destroy our God-given sexual identity. …, I was delighted to at least catch a fleeting glimpse of mother in me. [*Gee, more psychology. Well let's look at that first comment, when a man refuses to accept himself. Again this may be true for some transgender people. In Christ Jesus, however, it is not about self at all. In fact, it may come as a surprise to know that we 'true' transgender folk would love with all our hearts to be one sex right from birth in spirit, soul and body. What a joy that would be! We would not have to go through all these trials that these people who judge us have no idea about. And as for this man, I am pleased he discovered his wrong heart motives and I guess later repented and got out of bondage. Praise the Lord! It is not like that for all of us though and it would be a grave error to claim even what we have read here as being true for all transgender people. Again, in this passage he is clearly trying to be who he is not, referring to seeing a glimpse of his mother in him. As Christians we look for God to conform us to the image of His Son Jesus Christ and it is that image we look to reflect through His work in us. This is only achieved by us continually choosing to do His will and not our own, and letting the Holy Spirit guide us and lead us into all truth so that He may use us in any way that He sees fit to for His glory. 'True' transgender people have to accept themselves as they are in order to gain peace.*]

Masculinity is something we have found most distasteful as transsexual males. [*Jumping straight on this one. True for you maybe Mr. Author. However, I do not look back at my childhood and all the way through to the present day at age fifty-one with any distaste at all regarding any masculinity. I am most grateful to God for all I am.*

...

We took instead the identity of mother, aunt, etc., in order to cope with the pain of a lost, forsaken, or rejected male identity. ... *[Oh what a lot of mush! I loved my male identity as I grew up, I had to hide away or change my more feminine natural behavior which was always there! I just learnt to hide it away as it did not conform to other boys' behavior and I would be teased so that was a good motive for me to stop. My point is this, I had no trauma or a poor man example. Who I am was inside of me all the time, just repressed. That is why it would boil up and various times in my life and because I had no wisdom of God and needed deliverance from sexual bondage, I could not see it for what it was back then.] Now tell me, Reader, if you were born a man and always thought and lived as a man and got saved in Christ, when you do die to self, did you stop being a man too? Did your gender identity just vanish? Of course it didn't and it doesn't. No different for us true transgender people. We were born to some lesser or greater extent with a conflict of brain gender identity from our physiology, so if we are born again into Christ, we still are that same way! Just saved souls now!]*

...

Now here is a wonderful testimony of a person being real and making choices regarding being transgender. As I cannot reproduce the full article I highly recommend that you read it all on the web. The website is

http://www.transchristians.org/archive/brooke-my-turning-around

Brooke started to transition, but then decided it was wrong. Since this essay was written, Brooke has returned to transitioning believing that transgender feelings cannot be healed.

I am 34 years old, struggling with gender feelings ... I am married with four children. I grew up on the farm in Pennsylvania and went to a Mennonite church.

...

Questions I have: Is TG God's will for my life? Would he put my wife and family through this? Is transforming a cure? Is being TG sinful? ... How can I be a father to my three boys? What will they turn out like? Could I handle losing my family? ...

...

... God would not want to break up families. He instituted marriage and family. What God joins together let not man take apart

...

... My prayer was, "God help me! Change me!"

...

... I was a good-looking young man with potential. I never saw this man before. This was the miracle I was looking for. I couldn't wait to get home to tell my wife.

...

I do not see being TG as sinful. But I do believe it is wrong for me to continue to live a TG lifestyle. I do still consider myself as being gender-gifted. Considering that I believe God has answered my prayers I will no longer be able to express myself as Brooke. I will miss being Brooke.
I see this as God pulling me from the clasp of the enemy. I believe Satan was trying to destroy my family, my life, my dreams, and my family's future ministry together. Satan was slowly getting me to accept his deception which was slowing changing my values.
But God Has won!!
May God bless you as you seek Him.
Love,
Brooke No More

[What a wonderful article, that if it was not for the added comment at the very top, would show that a man can, for very good reasons too, choose to stop on the transgender path. It takes a lot, a lot of effort and I can really relate to his story here. In fact, I could well

have been the author of this as I have experienced it all too, multiple times. It would even be inspiring me to try once more to stop, and indeed in my life right now (April 2014) my heart is aching a lot for my wife and I hate all that she is going through. I have been on the verge once again to quit this path not through any doubt or recognizing that I am in some kind of sin (I agree with this article that true transgender is not a sin) but to stop her and others from hurting. But I have been there before, quite a few times, and I get the same result as Brooke. My heart goes out to all people that are in a married situation with either a male or female transgender person. If we do choose to go back like this person did, and I have done so many times before, it will resurface because it is who we are, not something we just do. Even though I too walked down the same path of reasoning as Brooke did, you still find yourself right back at the start because that is who we are, as made by God. Far better to accept who we are and let God be strong in our weaknesses, than to spend a life time trying to conform ourselves to the image of who we are not, and thus causing revolving cycles of pain to others, and continually to ourselves for that is not love.]

Here is yet another angle to look at regarding a spouse's response that you really need to read the full article online. Sadly I think that this is uncommon but oh, if it was more to found to be this way. This wife is absolutely awesome to her man although she is only part way through the whole story. I went to the authors web page but it does not seem to have any updates at all so she may have not posted anymore after this one and I was unable to find a way to contact her:

http://minka.hubpages.com/hub/Living-With-Katie-my-Transgender-Husband

Living With Katie: my Transgender Husband
How Do I Cope With Being Married to My Transgender Husband??
... married 18 short years. Raising 3 children, working, living, ... I never imagined once that he was a woman trapped in a man's body. ... until he blurted it out six months ago. ... I simply shut my mouth and looked at him blankly .... He asked me if I was o.k. and I just nodded. Meanwhile thinking heavens above ... is it o.k.?? I love him of course it's o.k... But I was stunned ...
In my heart I knew from the very minute he told me that it was imperative that he step up and be true to himself and express himself and be just precisely who he needs to be.
...
prepared to just exist in his designated male body and put up with the self loathing and lack of bounce to appease his family, the masses, society, whoever. It was tough explaining to him that if he didn't step up and express himself and simply be the most fabulous him that he ever could be it would surely crush him and rot him from the inside out. He's my soul mate, my other half, my right arm for heavens sake. I wouldn't be able to breathe without him.... regardless of whether he's got a skirt or a shirt and tie on.
...
Sure I'm scared but not because of what people are going to think. I honestly couldn't give a flying rats what other people think about our life.

[Wow, this makes me cry just reading it. Oh my, what an amazing wife who loves her husband however he is and not only that, comes along side of him to help him without judging him. As to him, I can totally remember doing the same cycle of fighting against myself for the same reasons he did. I really wish that I could get an update from her on this and will continue to look out on the web for one. For my own life and wife, I know she loves me to this same extent, just has to overcome her fears and the legalistic judgments in order to see the truth before her. If she does, then I know she will see me and love me for who

I am. If not, then sadly she has lost me in preference to her beliefs and set values. I hope that her genuine love for me will rule in the end.]

Here is another good, yet short article from a transsexual in the UK. I found it on the Matt Sorger Ministries website:

http://www.mattsorger.com/miracles/article/i-was-transsexual-.then-jesus-came-into-my-life

Miracles & Testimonies
I was Transsexual .Then Jesus came into my life
Apr 5, 2012
Hi Matt, I crossdressed for almost 30 years, finally having surgery (2008) to become the woman i was told I could be [*Now there is the first red flag right here*]. After surgery and now having been baptized (2010) as Stephanie, God started showing me in dreams that I was caught up in an addiction that had plagued me for decades.
I believed i was a woman, had support from a leading hospital in London and my past was filled with parents and friends saying I should have been a girl [*Looks like he was talked into believing this is who he is, no self-conviction*]. Soon after I got baptized God started speaking to me, using my male name which i had not used for over seven years. ... and finally God spoke to me as clear as day, saying "Why are you ignoring me?" How could I go on being this "woman" when i was a man. However I had now had surgery, so how could I be a man again? I went to Hell and back, planned suicide, saw demons... I spent three days on my bedroom floor crying out to God, ... I now know God has a plan for my life. To somehow get my testimony out there and speak to trans people and anyone who will listen so that they can have the truth in their lives like I have...
... I am trying to become the man he created. Psalm 139 says it all to me. He knew me even before I was made and wonderfully made as well. I pray that by sharing this God will use me to speak to people showing them from my own experiences that there is life even after surgery as a man.
Steve Clarke, Aylesbury, Buckinghamshire......England

[*This is a good testimony of someone that seemed to automatically from a young age of being told that he should be a girl repetitively and by all things seems to have believed what he was hearing and continued on that pathway. So, it is really great news that he at least eventually discovers the truth for himself through God. However, he then makes the assumption then that his story proves that he has the truth about transgenderism for all transgender people. This is not so. Believers in Christ (using this group of transgender people as his story is about Jesus setting him free from being a transgender person) can and do have peace with God but this story shows signs of the driven aspect that I have referred to, categorizing him as a 'false' transgender person who could, and praise God, was set free. Great news for this man just hard on him as he found this out after all his surgeries.*]

See Appendix 1 for a list of good YouTube documentaries that will give you much insight into the reality of being transgender. Although I am listing just a few you can search YouTube for 'Transgender Documentaries' and find many good productions. There are also articles regarding the brain differences of transgender people.

Chapter Six – Moving Forward: The Future

Refined, Set Free and Sent Out. What Will it Look Like?

"Immerse yourself in this world," is my instruction from the Lord. And just a quick note to the true Christian disciples out there, immerse here does not mean follow the ways of this world, it means for me to still be separated out for the Lord's purpose yet be fully there in the culture, with the people.

It is March, 2014

Now, I have finally learnt (I hope) by now that the Word of the Lord, the spoken Word of God is always accurate and always does what it intends to do. I have also learnt (through countless falls) that exactly *what* the spoken word means is NEVER what I thought it meant with regards to the path to be taken for that word to be fulfilled. In fact, I can truthfully say that I have been 100% wrong on guessing exactly what the Word means and how it will play itself out. I have never got it right and so, over all these years I am leaving stuff like that in God's hands and instead just acknowledge Him one day at a time in all that I do. So I receive the Word and watch the Hand of God play out before my very eyes and the more I keep my grubby little hands off trying to control things, the easier it seems for me, for it to come to pass. As the psalmist said,
"Let go and let God."

"God is sending you into dark and dangerous places," was the spoken word by three different godly men, full of the Spirit on three different continents. For years I held on to this wondering what it would look like and all I could come up with was that I would go into places like Communist countries, to gangs, into Muslim radicle places etc. However, as usual, I was wrong. The dark and dangerous places that the Lord was always referring to are spiritually dark and dangerous, to the demons and evil spirits that people have hosted that has resulted in all kinds of perversion and uncleanness through pride and lust.

    My twenty years of marriage is just about to complete. Twenty years of preparation and I know not if my wife will follow me. At present all signs show that she will not and this is a price I may have to pay, although my heart cries out for her continually. I now know that it was for this purpose that all this work had to be done in me and I pray with all my heart that my darling wife, Prisci, will see this and break free from hurts and judgments, and that we still can, and are called to have an amazing life together. She may not. I have to put this in the Lord's hand. As much as I am so convicted of the Lord's direction, so she seems so determined that she is seeing right and I am the deceived one. Into Your hands Lord I once again I commit our marriage, the marriage where You in Your infinite wisdom had me change our vows to declare to each other that we would: "Stay together till death us do part through ALL situations and circumstances."

To my wife, Prisci I say,

"It is for this very ministry that we have travelled through so much, my dear wife, and in our lives before we even met. It is for His purpose and His Will that He has chosen us to be used to save the few that He has chosen. It is not about you nor me, it is for His glory and His Kingdom. All the refining and the prophesies lead to this place and God has chosen the method, not I. In my weaknesses will I boast that He may be strong in me. I have to fulfill the destiny that He has called me to and I will either be full of all joy with you at my side, my darling wife, or an emptiness in my heart will be there due to your absence."
"Oh Lord my God, keep us together I pray."

God is so awesome and wise and all powerful. One can only look back at the road travelled and see His mighty hand at work and all I can do is marvel in amazement. Yes, truly, He is an awesome God. And now, He has given me His close fellowship once more like He graced me with when I first turned to Him. Joy and thankfulness continually abound in my heart and His presence and voice are always so close to me to guide me and for me to trust Him. In spite of some of my situations, especially my marriage, He gives me peace and love way beyond my comprehension and worth. May the name of Jesus Christ, Yeshua be forever praised! Amen!

So what will it all look like? What does this future hold that is now to be revealed? Was it one huge deception and I never heard the Lord at all and I have moved into deep darkness and my soul is destine for hell and the grave? Some would believe and say so. I would have said so a few years ago if I met someone like me! How can I really know the truth to these questions? The Word of God, His glorious Word.

The fruit of the Spirit, the Holy Spirit of God is:

Gal 5:22-26
But the fruit of the Spirit is love, joy, peace, longsuffering, kindness, goodness, faithfulness, 23 gentleness, self-control. Against such there is no law. 24 And those *who are* Christ's have crucified the flesh with its passions and desires. 25 If we live in

the Spirit, let us also walk in the Spirit. **26** Let us not become conceited, provoking one another, envying one another.
NKJV

Eph 5:8-14
For you were once darkness, but now *you are* light in the Lord. Walk as children of light **9** (for the fruit of the Spirit *is* in all goodness, righteousness, and truth), **10** finding out what is acceptable to the Lord. **11** And have no fellowship with the unfruitful works of darkness, but rather expose *them*. **12** For it is shameful even to speak of those things which are done by them in secret. **13** But all things that are exposed are made manifest by the light, for whatever makes manifest is light. **1**
NKJV

So I judge myself against this truth and find that amazingly I seem to be experiencing all of these in my life. So next I take a look at how my life is impacting those that the Lord sends me to and I see some already turning and a few have already turned to God through Jesus Christ with real heart repentance taking place (stories to follow). Do I have real pain and suffering to those who judge and reject me? Yes I do, it grieves me deeply, but I am not walking around in some form of prideful self-righteousness or arrogance. I am a broken person who gets up every day rejoicing in the Lord and knowing that it is literally by His grace alone that I continue.

The Agony of a Pending Divorce

This is really too hard for me. My heart is all torn up. How can this be happening Lord, You are a covenant keeping God and I am crying out to You! I love my wife and she loves me Lord! How can I be doing this to her and say that I love her! How can we claim Your love and that it was and is You that brought and keeps us together when divorce is on the table? I'm all torn up inside. It makes me want to stop on this pathway and rather die inside for the rest of my life than to go through a divorce. I am not convinced Lord, that you want us to divorce but I have no answers. Do not keep silent on me Lord, we need You. You are our helper in this, our time of need. All You keep saying to me is five years. I do not think that I can hold out that long not having my love, by beautiful wife with me. How am I going to do this Lord? How is she? We are *one* Lord! This is too hard.

This is like an extended funeral that does not seem to end. A non-stop grieving. This heart ache is the same aching I experienced when I denied being who I was before I went to my son to ask him to release me from my promise to him, exactly the same. I know who I am, and the Lord has made this clear, but what a price to pay. What a terrible choice to have to be put through; have my wife but live not as me, not being fully who I am and continue on that destructive cycle that I have put her through for these twenty years, or be honest and live by the integrity of my heart serving the Lord but, by the looks of it, without my wife. I keep myself for her and no other and the Lord knows that this is true. I am truly in love with her but I cannot and will not continue to put her through the destructive pattern that we have gone through together for that would not be love now that I know why and who I am.

I feel like death. I just want to curl up in a corner and fall asleep and never wake up. This pain in my heart and mind is too much to bear. I miss my wife! I want her. I just cannot seem to let her go and I don't want to! Oh Lord help please. Help us! She won't change her mind about me. I am ruined. Even if she divorces me, her heart will not change, nor mine. We are bound together. Does she not see this? All that will happen is that she will get herself into some survival mode to protect herself. God made us one so why try tearing that apart? Maybe she thinks that by being transgender it is all my doing, like I had this free choice to be transgender or not. God knew, we didn't and I did less than a year ago. Through twenty years of marriage I did not know until last year. She has no idea what this is and she proves it by claiming she does and can relate. If that was true then she would understand but she does not. If she did then she would know what I know. She would fully understand that it has nothing in reality to do with sex and sexual desires and orientation, but I think she does not. She will never want me back nor want anything to do with me unless she can *see me* and I do not mean in the natural. No, by seeing I mean to see me, the real me, my inner man, my heart that is bursting with love for her. I love her perfections and all of her imperfections, it's what makes her unique. Both her body and behavior have changed since we first met and I have had challenges to overcome in order to accept her as she changes and some of those changes were not acceptable to me. I had to work through it and it took me years to overcome my own desires. By the grace of God though I have got there and now this, now this dear reader. How am I going to carry on now other than to extend the same grace and patience to her?

Divorce Mediation and Rejection

It is May 30th 2014 in the afternoon and I have just come out of divorce mediation, something that I believe should never have taken place and never needed to happen even if divorce was being taken by my wife against me.

I am feeling awful inside. My pain is over our marriage and to know what my darling wife must be going through. I understand why she is filing for divorce, and the only grounds is that I am transgender. I believe that she thinks that I have 'chosen this as a lifestyle' over being a man and her husband etc. She doesn't get that it is a genuine condition that is medically categorized and accepted pretty much worldwide. It is not a sickness nor a mind deception from the devil. As a conservative Christian lady that leans more towards the implementation of the Bible as it is currently being taught by the more conservative Christians, transgender is seen as something of the flesh due to wicked desires in the heart and a deceived mind. How do you get through to someone like that so that they can see that that very interpretation is the lie not the reality of being transgender? How do you get someone to see that a person's sexual desires and orientation is totally separate from one's gender? How do you get anyone to see that it is not a question of 'choosing a lifestyle' but rather being true to who you are, including who you are in Christ if you are a believer? Maybe she knows all of this but just does not want me anymore. She wants a man in the traditional sense, not a transgender person. I'm sorry that I am different, baby.

If I were not transgender then we would still be together. But it looks strongly now like she will not accept me this way and so I am just going to have to come to terms that this is the path she is choosing based on who I am, and her beliefs about who I am. She doesn't get that I am no longer in torment and bondage, but I am free, that the Lord has set me free. Not free from marriage, no, He hates divorce, but free in my soul and body. All the sin assigned to the transgender behavior before I knew that I was such, has gone and no longer has a hold on me nor I on it. I am in my rightful place now. The cost though looks like it is to be my marriage.

At mediation today I deliberately made sure that both parties were to be in separate rooms because I knew that she still had those beliefs about why I am the way I am being. She would be very emotional and I would be too, and we would not get down to the business side that the meeting should be about, as I am sure was explained to her. And, she has never seen me as I have mentioned.

I arrived at 8am and was led to a room by the assistant who was getting everything ready. I waited 45 minutes for my attorney (a wonderful transgender lady) and the mediator to arrive. I then heard the bell ring just before 9am and knew it was Prisci together will some moral support, probably my son Jacob and his wife Christy. My heart goes out to them being willing to be in the middle of all this. They, or at least Prisci, went into the other conference room. I think my son and daughter in law had to wait outside, I am not sure on this.

This is just heart breaking! This is all totally unnecessary. This should have been resolved not in the worldly court system but between believers. Where was her church if she was going to take this pathway? Maybe she is no longer going to church? Maybe the church didn't want to get involved for some reason. Maybe she did not tell them. Maybe they were giving her judgmental advice that supports her belief about being transgender and that in doing so she is being further made to be 'right' on her decisions? Maybe they have told her that it is okay for her to divorce me? Lots of questions, some of which I have lived in both quarters and have discovered the lies and the truths.

Could I have done more from where I was to reveal the truth about who I am? I believe I did my best to do so as I came into the knowledge of the truth but I am sure I could have approached it in a different way. I never was much good at choosing the best way to talk about issues I don't think. Does the Lord know about all this and is He in control? Is He permitting divorce when He is against it? Who here is hardening their heart? Am I? Am I hardening my heart to the Lord, which is what those that judge me would say? Is the fruit of my life as already mentioned in part fruit of a man in bondage, in sin, that has walked away from the Lord his God? Am I really being deceived? I ask myself these questions and all I get is total peace at who I am and I see the Lord's hand changing other peoples' lives around me. Oh, how I so wish my darling wife could see all this.

Heaven on earth for me would be for Prisci to see that I am a faithful person, to see that my sexuality is totally committed towards her alone, for her to accept me as I am, and that together we could help others that are bound in sin through the door that the Lord has opened here for us. Maybe I am pie in the sky dreaming but I am daring to believe this even though divorce is pending. I dare to believe in the vision God has for us and I dare to believe that in the end, Prisci and I will walk hand in hand into the ever bright pathway of our Lord.

But this was not to be, at least not at this mediation session. I had the mediator tell Prisci the truth about me honoring her and not being in sin and wanting and loving her and it all got rejected. She said that Prisci said she loves me but, as for who I am, she does not accept me. That is the one biggest rejections I think a person can receive in this life, from the very person you have fully exposed your life to and who has painstakingly stayed together with you, only to end up rejecting you. This hurts so deep I do not know if I will ever be able to fully recover from it.

Yet, there is a fire within my soul to get the truth out there to not only the public but to the church regarding transgender people. If the church would quit falsely judging and start to embrace us transgender folk, then just maybe the suicide rates would drop, more would get saved and the transgender might start to get free from the sinful lifestyles that many fall into for the sheer lack of love and support. The good news is, in my little experience here in Tulsa, that more Bible based churches are starting to recognize this and are beginning to understand the true nature of being transgender. This is a really good sign and it needs to increase.

Back to the mediation process. The mediator Ms. Monica, we will call her was a very focused, alert and experienced mediator. She was chosen by my attorney I believe, and I was told that she was not a judgmental person and that proved true. She was warm and understanding to both parties and I knew she would perform her role very well. After meeting with my attorney and going through some of the documentation that we had provided to all parties regarding our assets, expenses, and incomes, she first went to spend time with Prisci.

Now, of course, I had no idea what was being talked about, but I knew my wife was in great stress and really upset. I could feel her heart hurting so much I wanted to burst out of my room and go to her and hold her so tightly and never let her go. Why can't she just accept me for who I am? She loves me, I know, more than skin deep, more than soul deep. We love each other I know from our very hearts. We all change as life goes on. Okay, so I now look like a girl and act a little differently, so friggin what! It's still the same me! Just a free me at last once and for all. I live joyfully morally right, for the first time in our marriage, and *now* is the time to split?! Let go of the past and the pictures that we both thought it should look like between us. I had no idea this was going to be the end result at all, you, dear reader have read my whole story that has brought us to this point. None of this was pre-meditated on my part. I was just trusting the Lord by faith that He would see us through. Has the Lord let us down? Is the Lord into the dissolving, the breaking of a marriage? No, He is not, and He never will be. He doesn't even agree for divorce on the grounds of marital unfaithfulness, but He only permitted it due to the hardness of our hearts. Is this divorce due to my heart or hers, or both of our hearts being hardened? Or maybe neither. I have cried out to the Lord time and time and time again to reveal this and only get reassurance and peace in return. Please, dear reader, if you are a believer in Jesus Christ, please say a prayer that my wife and I reconcile together. I love my wife, I will not, and cannot ever not love her. I miss her so much it hurts. Does she not realize that by allowing myself to be me as I am now is a good thing? We are off the merry-go-round destructive cycle that we have lived for twenty years!

Why do our judgments that come out of our current beliefs cause harm and not good? I have seen and know this because I have been guilty of the very same, even with regards to transgender people! I condemned myself, as well as others, and did nothing to exude liberty and the freedom that Christ has given us and I failed to love as Christ loves, with agape, unconditional love.

Ms Monica then came back to us looking most concerned. I do not want to put in this book what was said, but clearly Prisci was, as I had detected, most upset. This mediator's job was not going to be an easy one and this was going to take some time. Sure enough, it did and we went right through to lunch time when the mediator had to end things. She had gone between both parties a few times and it became clear that we were not going to get a resolution today. The biggest obstacle was that my current drop in income and my ability to earn was significantly reduced, therefore the amount of alimony Prisci wanted just wasn't available. It is a different reality now I live in and I cannot go on my past income level. What was she not getting in the equation as to why I showed my real and also projected income as much lower than the past? Here are the answers to that question:

Firstly, I am a transgender lady and that means a few new realities in my life whether I like it or not. I am not as strong as I was before. I estimate that I have lost about 25-30% of my strength to date. I also have far less endurance. I used to be able to work hard for at least eight hours or more. Now, if I do six, I am doing well. And my speed of work has dropped too. These factors affect the income I can earn. I have to space jobs out more but still charge the same, whereas before I would overlap or run one bigger job and still do small jobs during the same time period. I just cannot do that anything like I used to be able to do.

Secondly, as you may recall that I referenced in a previous chapter, I was dismissed on a technicality from the business referral club that I had been faithful to for some years. I believe that I know the real reason why I was dismissed and it seems that I will not be invited back as a transgender person either, although I would love to be proved wrong. I was getting over 60% of my business from that club in 2013. Now, that has gone, but I am still getting one or two referrals sometimes from certain individuals from that club that I built relationships with and that do not wrongly judge me. Overall I think that I am taking a 75% or so loss now from that source of business, which amounts to somewhere around $40,000 gross or more a year. I have not found a substitute for that as yet. When I do, it will take me a few years for it to produce significantly. So, on this score I am starting over.

Thirdly, when Prisci took the business Dodge Ram pickup and trailer in April my ability to service my annual lawn care customers was taken away. Last year that figure amounted to about $14,000 of the gross income. This also cuts into my leaf removal and gardening income from those same customers amounting to an additional $6,000 or so annually.

Now, I have kept one customer only and I keep my equipment at her house so I can service her, so overall I have lost about $15,000 of gross income. All my other customers I had to contact and let them go as the growing season had just started. They have all made arrangements now with other lawn care businesses.

Fourthly, as pointed out to me by my attorney, I am now a woman in a man's world and that will have an effect on my business. I also add here that being a transgender lady also has its disadvantages because there are still others out there that are judgmental and may not want me to work on or in their home.

So, Prisci is making this big issue probably thinking that I am being deceitful and that I am earning a lot more, or could earn a lot more than I am currently doing. It's as if she thinks I can just continue as I was before being more of a woman, like a "That's tough" attitude and, "You chose this lifestyle but why should it affect me?" kind of approach. I could be wrong here but the communications from her attorney suggest this to me. There have been a whole bunch of accusations coming on paperwork, through emails and on conversations via her attorney since this all started.

So where is all this leading to with regard to a settlement? Well, we pretty much have agreed to the division of the assets. Prisci changed some of the values around but I was okay with that, and did not argue with her even though I believe she is out in reality by almost $20k in her favor, but I always made it clear to her that I wanted to make sure she had her home and that all in it was hers. I get the old boat. I am not greedy at all regarding material things. I had calculated her getting 60% and myself 40% of which basically my portion would be the business tools and equipment, so that I could continue working the best I could with all that I am going through. So the sticking issue is my ability to pay any alimony based upon the amount of any short or long term income projections as I am self-employed.

The ability for me to earn and why the changes have happened are directly attached to my being transgender as mentioned in the four points above. If this goes to court, then we will be dealing not just with dollars and cents but we will surely have to address the impact of a transgender woman in a man's world, with less strength and endurance, the loss of a major source of income that took years to develop, my wife's actions affecting the business, and how others will judge against me on account of who I am. These are all realities that directly impact my current earnings and my ability to earn in the future.

Now, I could quit the business and go get a fulltime job. Maybe I could get back into being a Six Sigma business consultant and earn $70,000 or more a year once I had retrained somehow (I would need to retrain to get up to the current standards and also because I have forgotten many of the details involved and things change after nine years). This could take me a year or two, so if I started off at a $50,000 job if I could get it, that's only just over $4,000 gross a month. Now deduct medical, taxes etc. and I will end up with less than I am making in my current business. I would need to start at an income of at least $70,000 in order to see a significant income to support myself and pay any alimony even to half what my wife was asking at mediation. I would end up working a full time job doing longer hours for same pay as the work I am doing right now!

Here is a question for both of us:

"Is our love for each other conditional or unconditional?"

If my wife, Lord forbid it, went seriously sick or had an accident would it be okay for me to divorce her because she has a lack of faith to be healed from either one? Or, because she does not look nor act right in my eyes anymore? Can I say that she knows that Jesus heals so, therefore, if it is not happening then it is her making a lifestyle choice to stay that way? I remember the movie, 'The Notebook'; would we be like that to each other or would we separate and self-survive, taking all that we feel we deserve from the other person?
    Finally, I want to express the following: I love my wife and she loves me and however this ends up that will not change. I know that she is doing her best with where she is at. We both are.

I love you Prisci; where *are* you my love?

People Start to Turn Back to God

Just to be able to accept other people and not be in judgment of them, even secretly in your heart, I believe, is a real gift of God. I also have found out that in my life I have had to painstakingly go through many tests, and trials, and sorrows in order to get to that place. Now, I can go into all the gay, lesbian, cross-dressers, transgender and whatever else is out there with love and acceptance in my heart toward all these people. My own self-righteousness has been shredded by the Lord and, because of who I am, I find no grounds for me to get all prideful and judgmental again. So I rejoice in my weakness as I am kept humble and have a constant reminder as to my past hypocrisies. Yet, in the midst of all this, my heart rejoices in the Lord and I am eternally grateful to Him for His work in my life. Out of this I cannot help but tell others about the goodness of the Lord. I continually share the truth of how it is my relationship, not religion, with God through Jesus Christ that gives me my foundation to be who I am.

So, you can imagine how I rejoice when I see someone's life being touched by the Lord. Other than the one woman at the ice skating rink back in the mid 1990's who came to the Lord while I was in the UK, I do not think that I was used to bring anyone into the Kingdom of God over that whole twenty year period! In the first two years of getting saved, during that period when the Lord was revealing Himself to me and sending me out on various trips, I was used to bring hundreds to the Lord in the presence and power of the Holy Spirit. Then it all stopped for these twenty years as the Lord refined me. And now, the Lord has done His work in me and I am back with Him again, more broken, but with Him. Already I can see three people that have returned or come to the Lord in a very real way and I have no idea as to how many others He is touching around me. All I know is that I love the Lord and I love people.

In the next few sections you will get to read about two of the people that have turned to the Lord. I am making no personal sole claim to their salvations as it is the Lord at work, not little me. Other believers have been involved too. However, I know that many more will come to know the true message of the Kingdom of God as the days, weeks, months, and years go by so I rejoice in this and am fully contented.

OYP

OYP is a private organization located here in Tulsa, Oklahoma. Inspired back in 2002 by a few key people and a small group of youths, they decided to establish a safe place for youth that were LGBTQ (lesbian, gay, bi-gender, transgender and gender queer). OYP stands for Openarms Youth Project and is geared towards supporting the GLBTQ youth throughout the Tulsa area. From this small group of people, through hard work and the support from a variety of private sponsors, OYP has not only survived but also grown significantly into a place that is safe for youth to attend on a regular basis.

The premises is a single story converted business building that has a performance and party room for a couple of hundred people or so, an open kitchen, dining, a comfortable couch group meeting area, and an area for used goods to be sold and a few offices. It's well planned out so that the youth have different places where they can 'hang out'.

There are strict ground rules as can be expected such as no smoking inside the building, no drinking of alcohol and no drugs etc. I am a volunteer there and we all comply with the standard reporting and confidentiality rules for the State of Oklahoma and it all seems to flow well. There are even training counselor's from the nearby university there to help work with the youth as the need arises. Including myself, there are several adult volunteer helpers who provide both practical and moral support to all.

    I remember my apartment-sharing friend Jackie mentioning this OYP place to me and Jackie was most insistent on me seeing the place. We went by there one Monday evening. It was closed at that time but as I peered through the window a young man inside saw us and came and opened the door and invited us in. Mr. Tom had been involved in the project for some years and did a great job of explaining all about the place as well as giving us a tour of the premises. He explained that the place was open to the youth on Thursday afternoons and evenings, and on Saturday evenings. The Saturdays were more of a social dance and drag performance night where over a hundred or so youth would regularly turn up. There would be a whole mixture of people, of different gender and sexual orientations. The Thursdays were reserved for a quieter time of sharing a meal altogether followed by a group meeting in the living area. Anything between a handful to over twenty youth turn up and it is a rewarding time for all as various subjects are discussed. The counselors would sometimes help facilitate the meeting together with one of the adult founders of the program. Alumni, that is those over 21 which is the maximum age to be a part of youth, would often turn up too.

    I remember the very first day I went along. It was the Thursday after I first met Tom. As I walked in, the atmosphere was, was great! No sense of people being judgmental at all. Excellent! I thought. Both adults and the youth can just be themselves here. Following visits, and to this day this atmosphere has remained this way. It is a healthy and safe place for all. I am there to help provide mentorship to whomever the Lord brings my way, especially to the transgender youth. There does not seem to be anyone there either who is strong in the Lord either, who can share the love of Christ to these wonderful young people. My heart goes out to them as they try to discover and navigate their lives. I pray for them all now and I hope that I can be of some value to them at some time. It is in its early days, but I am sure that the Lord is already at work there.

Accepted in a Bible Based Church

After expelling myself from the church in Owasso as I knew that they would be judging me and wanting me to do all the hoop jumping again to help 'free me from my sin', and after the experience with the Baptist church in Tahlequah, I was still hoping for a fellowship of true believers in

Christ Jesus that would recognize the work of the Lord in me and accept me for who I am without any overt or hidden agenda to change me.

Well, a young man, let's call him John that attended the same transgender support group that I was going on Wednesday evenings downtown at the OKEQ (Oklahoma Equality) Center had been touched by the Lord. John had been going to the group long before I turned up on the scene and he saw himself as a transgender lady (mtf). However, when he had started the hormone therapy he pretty much immediately reacted opposite to most of us. He found himself moving away from the desire to be female and his male gender just seemed to kick in. So he stopped the hormones and dropped the whole transgender path. I got to speak and share with him a little and a couple of us were praying for him. Then, a short while later he posted on the group private Facebook site that he was 'turning back to God'. This was awesome news! And he did turn back to the Lord too. He also has stayed in the group as a support to all of us. I think that is wonderful as he recognizes that he was not a 'true' transgender but a 'false' one and is staying around to help us true ones in any way he can. What a blessing.

I got talking to John a few times after his turning to the Lord Jesus. He mentioned in the conversations that he was part of a church in Tulsa that was very accepting. I quizzed him a few times about it. I was firstly concerned that it was a real church in that they taught and followed the Bible, that is the whole Bible. I was not interested in a group of people basically fellowshipping together under the umbrella of being a Christian church. We should be hearing and putting into practice the correctly divided Word of God through its preaching, teaching and by allowing the Holy Spirit to do His work in us while we all walk in truth and in love towards each other. Was this to be the place that the Lord wanted me?

I asked John to speak with the leadership to make sure it was okay for me to come. I was already getting tired of being judged and rejected. Not that I was getting a lot of rejection from individual believers, but I was in the middle of all the rejection from my wife and family so to add more was getting a little too much. I knew that the Lord loved and accepted me and that He was and is my rock, my foundation but I was also going through a second adolescence due to the hormones which compounded things.

So John checked with one of the pastors and all was said to be fine for me to come. Sunday came and of I went to this church which was renting some space called Agora which was a coffee house with facilities behind it for church services. I had been even more cautious with John on this as I had visited a 'church' group there some two years prior and found it to be way off track and they had lost their way (if ever they were there) and ended up somewhere far to the left and liberal. It was more like one of those all-inclusive group meetings of some kind and did not revolve around the truth of the gospel, the cross, and the power of God to transform us into the image of His Son. John, however assured me that this body was a different one and that as far as he knew the one that I was describing was no longer there.

All nicely dressed up and presentable I walked into the church and was noticed by this small group of mixed individuals but I sensed no harsh judging going on. John saw me and made me welcome and introduced me to a couple of people. Music was loud and upbeat and adults and children were chatting, dancing, running around prior to the start of the service. The service started informally and informal seemed to be a feature of this group of people. Appearance was not an important thing with them. That was a good thing I thought. Worship songs were all modern which was okay. More importantly I liked the words of the songs as they focused on our Lord Jesus and not on self.

After a few songs the pastor, also in an informal manner and dress started to address us all to pray and then he gave a short message which the content was good. This definitely was not the same church I visited a couple of years ago. What I got after I left this service after being encouraged to return, was that these people were not judgmental and they both believed in the Word of God, and that to walk in love and truth was the most powerful thing believers can do and that we need to make sure we are doing so with each other. This was healthy. I was happy to return again the following week.

However, the next few weeks got cancelled. The landlord and owners of the Agora premises seemed to be in conflict of some kind and the church was getting caught up in it all so they decided to look for other premises in Tulsa. It was not long before we got either texted or emailed with details that they were moving to 15th Street west of Harvard, only a few miles from where I was living. I was looking forward to attending more services and see if my first impressions and discernment were accurate or not.

I attended a couple of more services and I was pleased to see and witness the same healthy atmosphere with the people. The pastor's wife (who at the time I had no idea was the pastor's wife!) was most friendly and encouraging. I was invited to join them for lunch and so I did and got to share a little about my life, why I was transgender, and how the Lord has got me to this point in my life. I wanted, as I thought it was best, to share with the pastor and his other male leadership, but they were at the far end of the long table so that was not to be. I guess that I had also forgotten that I am more female than male, so it was actually more appropriate to speak with the ladies! Since then I have had a few female friend requests on Facebook and I am joyful that they have accepted me as female in gender. Wow, what a difference from that Baptist church in Tahlequah I went to!

I attend regularly this wonderful fellowship that is called 'Canvas' and am starting to get to know more people. And listen to this, dear reader, on the offering envelope where I filled in my details for their mailing list etc. they asked if I was interested in any area of ministry. I saw music worship and checked it off thinking no more about it after that. During the week I get this call from the music director asking me what I played and he invited me to join them on Sunday. I was a little cautious as I was not sure if I would fit in to their style of music but I agreed and felt honored to even be invited to join them. The band was still young with regards to flowing together but all seemed keen to minister in music. I went to the pre service rehearsal and after getting my violin hooked up to the soundboard system off we all played. It was different but I sense that the Lord wanted me there so I did my best to follow and fit in. It seemed to go well so I played in the service and now play every time I go to the service. I am enjoying this fellowship and it is starting to become family to me.

After my first service playing in the band I was so joyful that they saw me fit to minister in music rather than maybe judging me as not worthy as I was transgender, and therefore maybe in sin or something. This was a real demonstration of walking in love and not judging. I also think that they needed to hear, prior to all this that I was living my life morally upright before the Lord and was not in any deliberate sin, but rather a broken person who is all too grateful that the Lord would even see fit to use me in some way to the benefit of others. Following this first service where I played, I went to Starbucks, as instructed by the Lord..

Salvation at Starbucks!

So off to Starbucks I went as instructed by the Lord after the church service. I did go home first to grab some soup and crackers as well as my laptop. It is not unusual for me to be at this Starbucks that was located near 51st Street and Harvard. I had been there many times before and most of the staff knew me by now. As I walked in I got the,
"Hi Robbie, good to see you again," from one of the ladies working there. Customers would look at me making their own judgments about me. This is something that I have got used to and so it does not bother me. I know what is in a man's heart and the whole range of loving and not so loving things people can think. I am at peace with just being me and that is good enough for me in the Lord.

However, on this occasion there were no other customers there at all! I made some comment about where is everyone and I joked with the two ladies about it while ordering my hot tea. I set up my laptop and plugged it into the electrical power and sat down on one of the two comfortable lounge chairs. I was going to work on this book so once all my programs had finished launching and the internet had connected to the Starbucks Wi-Fi, I opened up this ever increasingly large Word document of this book.

A lady came in and ordered a drink of some kind. She then sat down on the other comfy seat next to mine. I am not sure who struck up conversation first but we started to chat and she brought up the subject of God and soon we were into a conversation about the Kingdom of God. She got her drink, stayed a little longer to chat then left.

Another lady came in and also ordered her drink and sat on the comfy seat next to me. I think she asked me what I was writing about or something and soon we were both talking about the things of God. She too got her drink and left wishing me well and I her the same.

A short while later a third lady came in. Now, during all this time there were no other customers there at all. This third lady must have been probably in her mid to late twenties. She was dressed in a three quarter length blue casual dress that was plain in design. She had numerous tattoos on her legs I noticed. She also walked a little Tom-boyish, if I may say that. As she walked in I looked up, saw her leg tattoos and just blurted out, "I like all your tattoos!"
She briefly turned around, smiling and said,
"Thank you." In a low toned butch kind of voice.
I thought no more about it and went back to this book, only to find her plonking herself down on this now famous second comfy chair! She asked me,
"What are you doing?"
And that was the start of a whole, long conversation on my life before Christ, my amazing conversion, and trials in the Lord and how I had to come to terms with being transgender in the Lord. Her name was Jessica and she seemed mesmerized by the story, but I was also sensing as I was talking that the Lord was in this meeting in a strong way. I was ending up my greatly abbreviated story when the Lord had me state my destiny, that being transgender and going to those that are like me was,
"…my destiny in serving God for the rest of my days."
Then straight away the Lord had me ask her,
"What is your destiny Jessica?"
She looked at me and then started to talk about how she had been kicked out of the church that she had attended for some years together with her mother. She had told her mother that she was a lesbian and her mother did not judge her for it. The church found out and Jessica was basically told to stop being that way, or she had to leave. She had no idea as to how to stop it as it seemed by her that it was a part of who she was I guess (I didn't know for sure as I was not there to tell her that she should or should not be that way. I was there to show her the way into the Kingdom of God

through repentance at the cross of Jesus Christ and let Him deal with any present sin in her life, not me). She then said that her mother was also confronted by the same church and that because she would not renounce her daughter's behavior, then she would also have to leave. This happened over two years ago and since then Jessica said that she has kept away from church and was not interested in the Christian religion.

Then, she said, one day she was in her back yard and she just fell down on her hands and knees, searching for an answer to that empty space inside of her so that it may be filled. She told me that the word, "Mona," came to her.

The 'Mo' she said came from Mother, and the 'na' was the Nature. She was going to worship Mother Nature. She got up and she said that she felt so filled and in a spiritual high. And this high she said to me continued for quite some time, many months at least. But she said it then waned and now she is back to being empty again. I explained to her that we can go through life with these temporary fillings from a whole variety of sources. There are plenty out there to choose from but only one is permanent. There is only one real God and that place that she is seeking to fill belongs to the one and only true God and the way to Him is through the door, through Jesus Christ. I said to her,

"It is like you can see the house of God but you are on the outside. You want to get in but have not found the door. You can go up to the house, walk around it and even peer into the windows but not get in. Jesus is the door Jessica and you have to go through the cross of Christ, repenting of all your sin, your wrongs, and fully submit your life to Christ like you have never done before. This is not religion, this is life, Jesus came to give us His life that He may come and live inside of you, personally."

As I continued I started to explain to her the complete difference between the Kingdom of God and what we usually find in a church and soon she was listening to me with real intensity and as she did so she started to cry.

Other customers by this time had come into Starbucks and I am sure a few at least were watching us. Jessica, weeping as I recounted that the true story of the cross and salvation was for us all in a real profound and permanent way. She told me that she wanted this so I spent three times making sure she fully understood what repentance was before we got before the Lord together as she repented there and then in Starbucks that Sunday afternoon. I could tell that her repentance was real and I saw the Spirit of the Lord come upon her as her countenance lit up afterwards. She had received Jesus and had gone through the door into the Kingdom of God and she left that place with the Spirit of Truth, the Holy Spirit inside of her for the first time in her life.

Art and the Horses

This is one story that I just have to include in this book. Remember my friend, my Christian friend Art that was having trouble hearing me and was out to try and fix me from being transgender? Well, we are back to him again, this time with horses too!

Art has never got off his belief that I am deceived, that I have quit the battle against my flesh and am not in the Kingdom of God but following the devil now. This is a perfect demonstration of how deceptive a belief can be in a person's life. As he is so convinced that he is right about me, that all that he sees, judges and does is filtered through this belief. I can talk and challenged him over and over again but unless he is even willing to look at really what being transgender is, and accurately matching it to the correctly divided word of God, the scriptures, then he will never see the error of his ways. Even though I mentioned on quite a few occasions that I have been where he is for many years and am now in a different place. I had to repent of my judgments to others and to myself, as well as drop and revisit this whole issue, but he still cannot seem to even appreciated that either.

Art had been mentioning to me and my wife Prisci for gee, probably a couple of years now, that there was this horse ministry in Arkansas where a gifted lady in the Lord uses horses to help people receive ministry. Neither Prisci nor I really took to the idea and life was doing okay back then. Still Art would often talk about it. Zooming forwards to this present time he mentioned it a few times to me and eventually I thought, well, who am I to refuse what the Lord might do. Maybe Art is right and as he sees me in sin even though I do not at all, God could still use this ministry to help in some way. I finally replied to Art via text messages saying that I would go. He then said that it would not be worth it unless I was willing to receive healing upon which I communicated 'healing for what Art?' So, he rephrased it to 'receive any ministry' which I guess to him meant the same thing and I was fine with that. If the Lord wanted to do something then I was all for it. I also determined in my heart, but without telling Art this, that if the Lord wanted to take away everything to do with me being transgender then that was okay with me as long as it was by His hand and was complete forever more. This is not the first time I have offered this up to the Lord, but it is good for me to do so. I did not tell Art because to his belief system that would indicate to him that I agreed that I was in sin which was not what I was saying at all.

Finally we got a ministry date set for Tuesday May 13th. I did not have much work going on so a midweek day was fine with me. Art picked me up and off we went for a hour and a half drive to see the horses and the lady. Art told me that the ministry was great and that he and his wife had done it. He started to talk to me about how it works but then backed off a little thinking that it would be best for me just to go do it. The journey there was most interesting. Originally I think he was hoping that I was going to go disguised as a man in man clothes etc. but I had made it perfectly clear that I was not going to do that. I felt that if I did that I was being deceptive and I wanted to be open and truthful.

On the journey there, of course it did not take long to be on the subject of being a transgender person. I was calm with him but had to get more firm at times as he was stubborn in not hearing me. It was like I could see his mind almost getting to a point of understanding, only then to ping back to unbelief in what I was saying. Then, when I started to mention about being on hormones he reacted with a distained look on his face and made some comment about it that I did not catch. I got a little ticked off at him as I thrust my developing breasts forward and said,
"What, do you think these are not real or something Art!? These are real."
Upon which he did something that shocked me. While driving he took his right hand off the steering wheel and gestured in front of him (not towards me) as if he was fondling my breast! I sat back and away from him staring straight at him exclaiming,
"You think this is some kind of a joke or something. Is that what you would do to a woman travelling in your car?"
He quickly replied,
"No, of course not, only to my wife."
Annoyed at him, I retorted,
"This is me you are with and I am serious about my life. Do you want to be slapped?!"
Art went red in the face and got quiet. We continued our journey not talking much more about the subject but rather put some worship music on and sang to the Lord. As we arrived to this farm-like place that had a mobile home on the plot surrounded with horse paddocks, we stopped and got out to meet the lady. She was a sweet short lady I think with native Indian blood in her. I had met her briefly at the church that Art attended, a Messianic church some distance from Tulsa that he went to on a regular basis on Friday evenings. She was very polite and did not seem to be bothered about how I presented myself. I assumed that Art had already told her about me and how I was going to turn up and that was all fine by me. I am not hiding anything.

She explained how the program worked. We were all going to go through each paddock over the forty acre site and look at all the horses. I was to look for the one horse that I found myself attached to, or the horse would find me. Also, she would watch how the other horses reacted around me. From this she could possibly help me in some way. I told her that I was not used to being around horses but that I was not scared to do this at all. She was fine with that. She also explained that all of these horses had their own story to tell, as it were. Some were rescued, some abused, others strays etc.

So off into the paddocks we were to go but before we even left I made eye to eye contact with this white, rather solidly built horse that had put its head through the fence some hundred feet away from me. Its eyes and whole manner I could identify with for some unknown reason. I told this to the lady. She said that we were still going to go in and see all the horses to see what else might happen. So off we went.

In the first paddock the horses were some distance away and we all walked towards them and then she and Art let me get closer. Nothing really happened there so we went on through a small stable area I guess where I met the white horse close up. I just could not stop myself from smiling and stroking her and got close up to her. Now you have to realize, I am not used to these big creatures at all so to be comfortable straight away to do this was exceptional to me. I wanted to take her home with me!

On we went and over the next half hour or so met with most of the other horses including one large white stallion. Although one or two horses followed us and myself at times, nothing significant seemed to happen. My whole attitude for this time of ministry was for me to receive whatever God wanted me to receive. I left it down to Him. All that He had told me to do was to relax and enjoy my time there and so that is what I did.

Back to near the house we ended up and after gathering a few chairs together the three of us sat together and prayed and then she started to explain all about that white horse that I connected with from right at the start. She said that this horse was often selected by people.
"Her name is Katie," then she called the horse by its Indian name I think, "Her name means 'Free spirited'." Got me interested now! She continued, "She is the mother of the big white stallion that you saw in the far paddock. And really she is the overall boss as she leads the stallion, who is the apparent leader of course being the stallion. She, being the mother, rules the stallion and therefore the whole herd. She is maybe over protective at times."
She didn't say much more than this by my recollection. All the time Art was to my side writing a few things down and then he quietly prayed and prayed for God to do something with me as she went into asking me about my life a little. I did so and told her about my walk with the Lord and coming to terms with being transgender. She probed a little then started off on this psychological route of me recalling my first time of feelings hurt about being myself. I saw that she was struggling to find where to go with me and I did not want to spend countless minutes or hours going down pathways that I have already visited many times in other ministries so I politely mentioned all this to her, still saying though that if it was the Lord telling her to take this route then I was fine to do so. I just wanted to let her

know that I had already done all that pain, forgiveness and generational ministry. She abandoned that idea and looked at me asking,
"Then why are you here?"
It was a fair question. My reply was,
"For two reasons. Firstly, Art has been nagging me for a long time, maybe well over a year to come here, even before I separated from my wife and started to transition. Secondly, I did not want to restrict whatever God wanted to do. If I did not come, how would I have ever found out what He might do?"
She was fine about my answer I guess, as we soon ended praying with her blessing my walk with the Lord and me blessing her ministry. Art was quiet.

    As we departed Art wanted to get a coffee, I guess to keep him awake on the return trip. We could only find a fast food Taco Bell so we went inside. I checked that he was going to be okay with me going in with him. He said he was, however I could tell that he was uncomfortable in his body actions but he was trying his best. Inside we got a little food but they had no coffee for him. A man came in with his pre-teen son who both saw me. Afterwards, outside Art asked me how I must have affected that boy and what was the father to say? I just looked at Art thinking "wake up Art. We are in the real world now, not in some ideal bubble." He just wasn't seeing it so I really did not say much.

    Driving back I saw Art shake his head a few times. Finally he said, "I really thought God was going to set you free today." And so I asked him,
"Did I do anything wrong there?" or something of that nature.
"No," he replied, "You were polite and made yourself available." Again, or something to that meaning as he continued,
"I really thought God would do something for you and set you free." So I turned to him, raising my voice a little and said,
"Art, you still are not getting it are you. There is nothing for the Lord to set me free from! He *has* set me free. I am free!" And for the first time, just for a few minutes, I saw his walls drop down only to be taken up again as he went back to his old rhetoric. I have to admit, I gave up and rested instead. I had told Art from the start of his trying to 'help' me that we were going to lose our friendship over this.

    We listened to some more music and when we got back to my place we said goodbye and I thanked him for all his time and efforts. So much had gone on between us that I forgot to give him gas money that I had promised him. Oh well, I could give it to him another time if there was ever to be one.

Translady Turns to Christ from Being Atheist

As previously referenced, I have been attending and supporting a weekly transgender support group that meets at the OKEQ, the Oklahoma Equality Center in Tulsa. It is a great place to meet other transgender people and to share our lives and support each other. There is no fixed agenda as such and we usually start off each meeting going over some basic confidentiality ground rules and then we take turns just to spend whatever time we each need to say how our week has gone. We then usually discover some particular topic related to being transgender and we share as a group our thoughts and hearts. The group is usually around twenty strong with a core group usually there each week and others that appear at varying degrees of frequency.

Now, because of confidentiality I am not going to reveal any identities at all and disguise further any comments relating to events. Below is a wonderful testimony of the Lord touching one person's heart that had been involved in 'religion' at one time and got burnt, as it were, and rejected, so she turned atheistic instead. Anytime I would share my own faith in Christ Jesus she would end up making some small but mocking, comment or gesture. This went on for many weeks although I took no offence to it. A short while later after some brief communications, she sent me this chat message after I had invited her to be my Facebook friend:

Dearest Robbie, Thank you so much for sending me this FB (Facebook) friend request. I looked over your most recent posts, and your transition is coming along great. Your posts about being a True Transgender Person was spot on!

I want to simply be accepted as me for me. It is the beginning of the life I have always dreamed of. To that end, I have been extremely selective about the folks that I friend on FB. At one time on my old page I had nearly X number of friends. Of which, nearly two thirds were trans-folk from across the globe. Their posts and stories lifted me up in transition. They helped me gain the confidence to grow, aspire and achieve the goal that I am nearly to. Please understand that I have no wish to stifle or in any way inhibit the content of your page. You write brilliantly. I'm just afraid that many of my newer friends on FB who have no clue about my past, might become suspicious about me adding so many beautiful and articulate trans women. To that end, I am not going to accept this request. This is just Facebook. Not life. You have been a wonderful friend and I look up to you spiritually. It was your steadfast beliefs that lead me to question whether or not my path of atheism was going nowhere. Which, as you are well aware, it was. I now count myself as a believer in Jesus

Christ. I hope knowing that, the sting of turning down your FB request will be quelled somewhat. You are most welcome to write me any time here on FB. Your Sister in Christ, xxxxxxx

Chat Conversation End

What an honor to be a part of someone genuinely turning to the Lord in a real way. Someone else in the group had been quietly praying for this person and another interacted a few times as she turned to the Lord. Thank you Lord for using us all.

It's good to know that we can make a difference even if you are not aware of it. Recently I received this text from another transgender person that attends the weekly support group:

Robbie! Hi! I just wanted to take a second to tell you that I really admire you, as a person, and that you're awesome. I always love hearing what you have to say.
You're just so real about things. You're typically my favorite person to hear from when I attend group. You're always interesting with whatever it is you have to say.
... I just think it's awesome that you're genuinely a caring, beautiful person, but you also let people know what's up and on your mind. I just like that you present to the world this very straightforward you-ness.

Isn't that a sweet thing for someone to say to you that you had no idea you were even influencing. I pray we all continue to support each other at the group in a real way. It has really helped me for sure. If you are transgender, or think you are, then I hope you do not isolate yourself away but join such a group. That way you will get the support and resources you need and maybe you can help someone else too.

First Divorce Related Court Session

It is July 8th 2014 and at 2pm is my first summons to court as my wife continues to pursue a divorce. I have not seen her since she came and visited me on a job site in her new car she had bought many weeks ago. That was a moment when she needed me to sign something, I think, and she also wanted to show me that I was still a man with passion. This kind of passion had been absent from our relationship for a long time but for those few minutes together it returned which brought joy to my heart and sent my blood rushing all over my body once more. After some four months or so on hormones one could wonder if I was able to respond as a man. I assure you I still could! Even to this day the Lord has blessed me like this. It may take a little longer, if you know what I mean, but I can, and still desire to be with my wife. The sad thing about that incident is that I think she was trying to show me that I am really a man and not female in any way so towards the end of this meeting together I picked up on that and got sad. She still does not understand that my sexuality has not changed and that I am passionately in love with her and want and need her. That it is my soul, my mind, my brain that identifies as mostly female. I pray she will one day realize this in a nonjudgmental way because then the way is open for us to reconcile if she can love me beyond my surface appearance and expression and not care about the opinions and judgments of others.

  I travelled into Tulsa downtown with my transgender attorney. She is a mtf transgender person and had just got her legal name change completed and had it changed on the bar, so she was now recognized in court as female. She was still getting used to the change and was taking it slowly with regards to her presentation which is why she wore female attire, but it was more subtle than my clear display of my gender. She was wise, I think, as she is forging new territory by being the first transgender male to female attorney in Tulsa.

  After passing through the security check point we went up to the first floor and paid for a court recorder to be present. My attorney wanted the session to be recorded just in case the issue of being transgender was going to be raised against me. My attorney had also arranged to have a medical doctor specialist attend the session to explain the truth about being transgender and to show that what I was doing was perfectly acceptable in my situation. However, my attorney decided to ask my wife's attorney to agree with some of the legal medical stance and they agreed to a stipulation as follows:

To clarify, here is the stipulation I propose:

"The parties stipulate that it is reasonable and necessary for any person who has been diagnosed with Gender Dysphoria pursuant to the DSM-V to seek treatment under the standards of care prepared by the World Professional Association for Transgender Healthcare which has been approved by the American Medical Association. Further, it is reasonable and often necessary to this treatment for any person so diagnosed to take hormones, if prescribed by their doctor, and to present to the public in a manner consistent with their gender identity."

Her attorney agreed to this stipulation so we did not call our specialist doctor to court. Our specialist doctor, by the way, is also a mtf transgender lady.

I arrived into the small court room about ten minutes before the start time of 2pm. Nearly all the single row of back seats were taken but I got a seat close to the entry door. My wife was not there. The room was full of attorneys sitting in the middle court section with just members of the public on the back row. I managed to take a couple of quick snap shots:

At just before 2pm the door opened and my wife started to come in and then straight away turned around and left. I know she saw me so I guess she waited outside as I was inside. It was then that I found out who her attorney was, as my attorney observed what happened and introduced herself to him. He was a short man, mature, but not old in age, and had a warm countenance yet I sensed he was good at using that approach in order to help achieve his goals. My attorney was most experienced at seeing these things and how to handle them, I was pleased to discover as the afternoon progressed.

After a role call session in court we were asked to negotiate together to see if we could come to a resolution before we were to be called into the courtroom. As I walked out of the room there was my wife, Prisci sitting on a chair right in front of me just a few feet away. She made a point of not looking at me. My heart went out to her, she looked drawn, tired, sad and broken. My heart cried to her as I bent down to look into her eyes as I said,
"Prisci."
She would not look at me and did all she could to look away from me, treating me like I was not there. She said nothing. A painful shot of rejection like an arrow pierced my heart, but my love for her was far greater to allow that to stay. My attorney who had exited the court room before me looked back and called to me to her. I left Prisci sitting there. I

was so sad to see her that way. Why was she doing this, surely she knows that the peace of the Lord is not in what she is doing. Has the Lord told her to divorce me or is this all her doing as she believes and feels that it is the only thing to do based on my actions? God always makes a way when we just let Him do the work. I do not believe that this course of action will bring her peace to her heart at all. I certainly know that it won't mine. My heart pines, weeps for her. Things would have been so different for botH of us and financially if I had not been judged and rejected.

We found a small room that my attorney and I could use. Then began two hours of interactions where her attorney did most of the walking between my wife and ourselves to try to resolve things prior to being called into court. My wife, as I had predicted, had our daughter Bianca, and our younger son Jacob and his wife Christy there for support. I think that Jeremy, the eldest son, was also there too as I heard his voice call out to her when she first started to enter the court room, but I never saw him. There was another young lady there but the two brief times I saw them, her back was to me and I did not recognize her. As I passed to go to the bathrooms once, my son Jacob saw me as he was talking and looked at me for a brief second then returned to his group. Bianca and I made a few seconds eye contact at the very end of the day and all I could pick up from her was anger in her eyes at what I was doing to them all. I did not say anything but wanted to at least mime that I loved her, but restrained myself from doing so as it might have instigated a bad response.

It became clear from Prisci's attorney that our children were all pushing Prisci to get all that she could from me. They were clearly against me and probably thought that I was lying about my income and situation. They probably thought that this 'lifestyle that I had chosen' was something that I need not have done. They probably also believe that it is false, a lie, and wrong and that I needed to be the man that they all knew before. They saw their mother hurting and naturally went to support her, leaving me as the bad person, on my own.

A few things did disappoint me during these negotiations. They had gone through the household and business bank statements from 2011 onwards and come up with these outrageous figures that were far inflated from the accurate tax returns. For example, the gross income for our business in 2011 was approximately $114,000, but the person who was supposed to be a book keeping specialist came up with $214,000, an additional $100,000! So much for their accuracy, even if most of that additional sum was categorized as 'non-business income'. When we got all the data before us we found many inherent errors. Firstly it looked like they 'double dipped' income as it was transferred between accounts. They also included cash withdraw and same cash deposits with no understanding of any recirculated cash flow between accounts. There was no link given from the individual items on the bank statements to the Excel spread sheet totals that they were representing and they had no idea what the checks written on either the business or personal account were for! It was a mess. As a certified Six Sigma Black Belt I would have thrown this out and had them do it all over, accurately. Still, if they persist to try and present this at the hearing, it will not take much to tear it down. Their figures also suggest that my previous year's tax returns are fraudulent which they are not.

Then I got accused of spending $200 a few times on herbal medicines a couple of years ago with the implication that I was feminizing my body with them. What! I simply truthfully denied it to her attorney. So far, I have not had one truthful and sensible comment, question or action come out from her camp and her attorney I think is getting a little tired of it. The 'advise' she is getting is poor indeed and they do not seem to want to acknowledge the reality of the current situation. It seems that revenge and perceived justice is on the agenda, not love, mercy and forgiveness. Fear, anger and self-protection seem to be the motivating forces. Now I love these people with all my heart and it tears me up to see them this way. Will someone please give them some real godly counsel and wisdom. Things would have been far, far better for all of us if Prisci had not taken this down the legal path and done what she did just before the divorce papers were served on me.

If indeed the Lord is with me and to my own shock, He has indeed called me to be and do as I have mentioned, then who is my wife and family coming against here? If I am indeed being truthful with my heart, words and actions, then who are they all trying to get some victory over? Me or God? Who has peace here? Did God tell my wife to start the divorce or did she do it because something just 'snapped' inside of her? Who is walking this out in love, both of us? Who has rejected whom here in the marriage covenant? Does she realize that she is coming against the head of her household irrespective whether I am living there or not as my motive was to spare her as much as I could?

If my wife is trying to apply any kind of 'displacement' theology that a wife supersedes her husband when he is acting in a supposedly ungodly manner, then that is just that, a theory that you will not find in scripture, and what if that so called 'ungodly' behavior is not ungodly at all but perfectly acceptable before the Lord for the purpose of His Kingdom? And where did unconditional love disappear to?

Is Prisci claiming that I 'abandoned' her? That could be no further from the truth at all. Not only did I fully support her until she filed divorce against me but she also knows that I would be back there with her in less than half an hour if she wants me back. I only left the physical house to spare her what she would not accept in me. No, if there is any abandoning going on here, it is by her rejecting who I am. And I do feel rejected and abandoned by her and the rest of my family, with the exception of Jacob my youngest son. If I was earning plenty now, I would still support her even though she is acting this way.

Was I deceiving to Prisci, knowing full well even before we were married that it was going to end up this way? I can answer that one, NO. This is as much a shock to me as it is to her. We were both blinded by the false belief that being transgender is a sin, an immoral sexual sin of some kind. And the truth is, is that it is not.

Did God know before we even got married that this was going to be the setup after the twenty year refining period? And also before we even got married? Yes, He did and He also knew that I was going to spend all these years fighting against it too and He used that to purge my heart. My frustration now is that I do not know the future for us at all. All I have to go on is this five years that the Lord keeps reminding me of and that He upholds His covenant if I call out to Him for help. However, I have no idea what that five years means and I have long learnt not to put my own desires and interpretation to it, but rather just wait on the Lord. I know my wife loves the Lord too, so I am counting on the Lord to see us through.

Back to the court hearing and 4pm was fast approaching and we had not been called. Prisci had not accepted any offer from us and was asking for a minimum that I just was not earning now. Well, time was moving on and we did not have enough time now within the normal business hours to be heard, so the two attorneys agreed to visit with the judge and postpone, which Prisci's attorney went and arranged. A new date of Friday July 25th was set.

July 25th was fifteen days after my facial surgery (see next chapter) so I was going to look a real mess I thought. How was the Lord going to help me through this now? I would not be in bandages by that time but I fully expected my face to still be swollen and bruised.

The day arrived and my attorney finally got to calling me to go through some details and vet me once more. Amazingly, my face was actually looking pretty good. Lips and end of my nose still a little swollen but only a few light patches of bruising to my face that makeup would hide well. I was healing at a rapid rate indeed. Thank you Lord.

Then, I started to get call backs from my attorney that the other party had put together a reasonable proposal. I reviewed the details. Basically, it amounted to my calculating the business net income for me to present each month. With that figure I would then pay out my agreed monthly personal expenses, then pay out up to a total of $1,500 each month to Prisci by the 10th of the following month. I also offered to continue to pay the mortgage and property taxes irrespective of my own means, as I had been since we separated and this amount would come out of the $1,500. This was a good and reasonable plan that should work well if I made the income level required to fulfill it all. If I made more, then I would keep the difference for business or personal use. This was agreed with the judge and an order made for a three month trial and review. Also added to the order was for Prisci to return the business use truck and trailer, together with the power washer, and my old violin which was still in her home.

    I hope that this works out; if a straight court order is granted by the judge for a set amount with no consideration to how much I actually earn in a particular month, then I could find myself in a tough situation. If I don't pay some business commitments like insurance or rent, or not pay some personal living commitments, and pay the court order, then the business and my life fall behind. But, if I don't manage to pay all of the court order then I will be in contempt of court and could be sent to jail. That would be a most interesting and challenging situation indeed for I would be taken to a male jailhouse, which would also affect my ability to earn of course.

    On a happier note…

Time for Surgery!

It is a transgender person's dream to be able to change some of their visual and even functional features of their body to the gender that they identify with. Often a controversial subject, especially coming from the church if you are a believer. I have already had things said to me like,
"God does not want you to mutilate your body," and,
"God made it to be the way that it is," or evening insinuating that,
"It is the devil that changed your brain to think that way." And just about every variation of these themes that you can think of.
Well, dearest people that hold to these kind of statements and beliefs, may I politely remind you, that doing alterations and 'mutilations' as you so call it, can be perfectly acceptable to the Lord as previously argued in an earlier chapter. It all depends on the reason that the change is to be made.

    If someone is born with a deformed hand and we have the skill and tools to correct it, do we not correct it? And if a person later in life gets cancer do we not poison the body with radiation to destroy those (as well as many other) cells in the hope to remove it? And if a person is in serious conflict with their gender and all the mind and soul counseling work etc. results in the same condition, then why should not that person be able to correct the body that is out of alignment? Of course we should be able to do so, and, praise God, many to this day are, again thanks to the same doctors and nurses that heal us from a deformed hand or from cancer. And maybe we should not forget those eunuchs of biblical times that chose to have themselves castrated! Then, look at all those believers and non-believers across the globe that have from minor to major cosmetic work done, just for appearance sake! Are they all to be condemned?

So, with me having satisfied myself that it is acceptable to do things to my body for the sake of peace of mind and having obtained inner peace with the Lord about this, then it's the green light for me, and here I go! The Lord told me to make myself as pretty as I can over the next two years and that He would be with me on this.

Now, for me, inner peace with God is paramount, absolutely vital. And I have sought the Lord on all the options that I know are available to me for surgery. I have peace about working on my facial features to remove, undo or improve my looks. Remove: to remove some of the effects of what testosterone did to me. Undo: to undo, or reverse what testosterone did to me. Improve: to improve on existing features that are okay but could be better.

However, I have no peace to have SRS, Sex Reassignment Surgery. No peace at all on this. I really do not believe that the Lord made a mistake when He designed my body sex organs as male and my soul, my brain mostly female. That might sound like an odd statement for me to make, especially if you are one of those people that can only think in terms of the male or female categories with no variation (though it baffles me how you could have read so far into this book and not even consider a broader spectrum by now). I have no issue with this at all for God can do anything He wants and it is our joy in Him to discover our own path in life toward Him. I am in His will and have peace about this. Now, if, for some crazy reason I went ahead and did SRS of my own accord, then I would be in rebellion to God and I would pay a price for that, as He has made clear NOT to do that. Besides, I don't need female parts down there as my sexuality is still male and the sheer thought of doing that would indicate to me that I wanted a man to come to me. That, *for me,* is the nastiest, grossest thing I can think of!

The question then is, what will I be looking to have done? Some things are easy to answer for me as you look once again at my facial features:

- Large hooked nose
- Large distance between upper lip and base of nose
- Thin upper lip
- Large Adams Apple

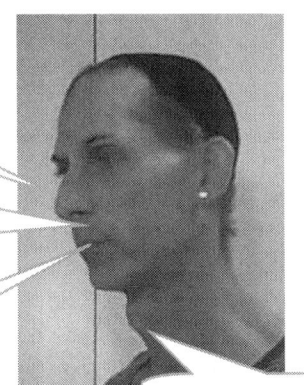

Well, for sure that Adams Apple has to go! So does that nose, just look at it! These are the first two priorities for me. Another thing that would really make a difference is a full face and neck lift together with a brow lift, and upper eye lid work due to aging. Even as a man in my earlier years, I had some excess facial skin and of course add that to aging a little and I would really benefit from soft tissue work to cover me through the next twenty years or so. Another area for improvement would be fuller lips and at the same time reduce the long distance between my nose and top lip. These were my initial goals.

Now I could also look to have cheek implants, brow contouring, jaw contouring, chin contouring or implants, pin those ears back a little and lower my forehead hair line. These changes would really give me more the best feminine look possible but you know what, I do not think that I am going to do these. The last thing I want to look like is some perfectly proportioned woman. That is not me for I am a transgender lady, not some kind of female model (not that there is anything wrong at all for those that desire to be that way. That's just not my desire). I really just want to remove those obvious male features that I have never really liked but put up with all my years. With regards to the soft skin tissue work that I would like to have done, that is simply to allow the other jobs to my face become noticeable without excess skin flopping around!

Then I believe I will be fully satisfied if my breasts do make it to a 'B' cup over the next year or so. I am already a good 'A' now after just six months of hormone therapy and they are still growing so I hope that they do continue to grow to a 'B'. My desire is that I will not need any surgery there at all which would be really great. Of course my laser and electrolysis work will have to continue until my face, neck and chest are free and clear.

Yes, this kind of specialized surgery costs, which brings me on to the next question. Where do I go to have the surgery and to what extent, if any, do I take into consideration the cost? Thank the Lord for the Internet, an amazing resource from which to get recommendations and to investigate various centers around the world. And this is exactly what I did. I conducted a systematic search in different countries and to different facilities within those countries. Then I contacted them sending them the required pictures of myself to gain opinions and estimates. I then factored in the cost of travel, food, accommodation and any other related expenses such as pre-op costs. I also rated how long they had been doing this specialized work and I looked for testimonies inside their own websites and also outside if I could find any. I then had to estimate the risk value with regard to any work that might have to be corrected and the cost to get that done. Finally, I made a judgment rating for the chance of risks based on the impact of long distance travelling verses staying local and also the risks involved in the different surgery techniques used.

Through the Tulsa transgender support group I was given a few places in the US to look into. The first was the Zukowski Center in Chicago, then one in Boston, two in California, and one in Florida. Peru, Mexico, Brazil, Spain, England, and Thailand were the other countries I researched.

Although maybe the largest number of FFS (Facial Feminization Surgeries) and SRS (Sex Reassignment Surgeries) surgeries seem to be carried out in Thailand, the overall cost worked out not much less than here in the US for the FFS. The risk factor due to travelling distance to a foreign country made that not a good option for me. Later, I came across Americans that had travelled there and had experienced complications, so that sealed it for me not to look at that anymore.

Peru seemed a good option and just over half the cost overall compared to the US. Reputation for this one particular center called FemLife seemed very good, but their techniques were more traditional and this meant the increased risk for complications such as loss of nerves and possible sinus issues. There would also be a longer recovery period involved.

Spain was a good option as I knew the country and had even been very close to the city where the surgery was located when on holiday during my first marriage to Karen. The center was called FacialTeam and is located in Marbella. Reputation was very good and I liked the idea that they had a team of doctors that would collectively come to the best solution for each individual. Cost seemed fair but there was a high European tax to apply, so overall it was not cheap at all. Shame, because I could have flown to my dad in England to recover before returning to the US. I kept Spain still as an option though at first. The center had also developed a faster recovery system it seemed; a facial mask of some kind kept the whole face at an optimum temperature to reduce swelling and promote recovery. The center in Spain also had a center in Brazil, but the Brazilian location did not do all the surgeries so may not be so well equipped.

England seemed to be an obvious possible choice for me. They seemed to be quite advanced in helping transgender people. On the National Health Service they have gender centers that you can go to. These centers help assess that you are transgender and to what degree. They will also put you on hormone therapy and after I think about two years you can get free SRS and FFS! I still had my UK passport and of course could stay with my dad, so that seemed a very plausible option indeed. The only thing I did not like was that you were assigned a surgeon to do the work and this bothered me as I soon came to realize that both SRS and FFS are specialized jobs that required both great skill but also a lot of experience and creativity. As far as I was aware, I would not be free to research each doctor and choose the one I wanted to work on my face. I would also have to reside back in the UK for at least three years to go through their schedule. Neither of these two last factors were acceptable to me. It would have been great though to have spent some time with my dad.

My dad, by the way has fully accepted me as being transgender and has told me that it is not uncommon to see transgender people out and about now. He sent me this wonderful birthday card for my birthday on June 25th of this year (2014):

Mexico was a no-show for me. The center I looked at was called TransOp and is located in Gauadalajara. Although the facility seemed reputable, their website seemed more like you were going to a grocery store to purchase what you wanted and they would do it for you. Also, I could not find any outside testimonies. (Post-surgery I did find a documentary of someone that went there and I was glad that I did not go!)

This left me with the US, so I spent much time finding out more about outside testimonies (patients not from the surgery center's own websites) and it became clear that the very first center in Chicago, the Zukowski Center, was the place to go. Cost was higher than abroad and just a little higher than some of the other locations in the US. Other than that I found what they were offering far outweighed anyone else in my opinion. Firstly I managed to locate many patients that Dr. Mark Zukowski had operated on and most were very impressed not only with the end results but also with the high level of care and preparation they were given from start to finish and also post-surgery. The facility was excellent, very professional and fully accredited. Dr. Zukowski's level of experience as a plastic surgeon is highly impressive, having worked in the US Navy as a staff plastic Surgeon, then head of the Naval Plastic Surgery center, including a top command consultancy position before setting up his own practice. He also attained the position of a terminal rank commander in the US Naval Reserve with full honorable discharge in 1997. He is well respected in the profession and is called on for advice and to speak in conferences. His compassion to help the Transgender community is inspiring and I was convinced that he was most genuine in this. I understand that about 65% of his patients are transgender. He only specializes in FFS (facial feminization surgery), not SRS (sex reassignment surgery) and has developed state of the art procedures using endoscopic techniques to minimize soft tissue damage and greatly reduced the possibility of permanent nerve damage and sinus problems.

So The Zukowski Center for me was my clear first choice. I told a close transgender friend here in Tulsa who had also looked and had made her mind up to go there too. She had decided to fly up there and do a face to face meeting with the surgeon and look over the facility. She returned very impressed. She went ahead and had the full facial work done to completely feminize her face. My budget didn't cover that amount of work and the Lord doesn't want me to go that far anyway. Her desire and goal is to be female and pass solely as female. God wants me to be a transgender lady and to be seen and recognized as one so my goal is a little less dramatic.

After forwarding the required pictures and a video, I had a phone consultation with Dr. Zukowski. At first I looked into all the procedures but I knew I would need to narrow it all down not only for budget reasons but also for not over feminizing myself as previously mentioned. I also have other responsibilities as I was then fully supporting my wife Prisci, as well as taking care of myself alone. The consultation went well and was the most in depth discussion, matching only the center in Spain. I was sent an official written breakdown of his recommendations and all related issues to going there. I was very impressed. I already had the finances together to go for the items I was looking to have done for now. However, the divorce situation caused me to withdraw a few thousand dollars but I also had a little reserve cash from late 2013 and I knew that the Lord would provide, and He did. My dad sent me some funds and I got another refund that I did not expect to receive. I also had to increase my credit card limit a little but I can get that down again.

So on my list for surgery was a tracheal shave (Adams Apple), a full nose job (Rhinoplasty and Septoplasty) and while the surgeon was right there he would raise and turn out my upper lip to make it more prominent and reduce the distance from the lip top to the base of my new nose. He also would try to locate some fat on me and inject it into my upper lip (good luck to him!). This fat grafting as it is called was at no additional cost so I was fine with that.

I have to say that the preparation before surgery was excellent. Starting maybe almost three months prior to surgery, I was getting material to review including a DVD that covered pre, the operation, and all the post-operative information that you needed. Phone calls to me from the surgeon, the administration, the nurse, the caregiver and the anesthesiologist all made sure I was fully prepared. This gave me more peace both about this center and what was going to happen.

With all the excellent communications and materials that I was sent to prepare me, the operation date was set for July 10th (just two days after my court hearing!). Thankfully, the Lord has really kept me fit and healthy and even youthful so I was a good candidate for this surgery. Pre-op face to face meeting with the doctor was on the afternoon of the ninth so I flew up in the morning. Taxi, hotel, and meetings were all in place. All went well and time flew by so before I knew it I was going under general anesthetic. I was totally at peace with all that was going on.

Surgery time was about three and a half hours. The Lord was good to me in recovery. Firstly Dr. Zukowski was kind enough to say to the caregiver nurse (that I was paying separately for) to charge him until she left the facility with myself. I could only afford her for seven hours so she would take me back to my hotel and get me all set up there, go off to get me some groceries as I had no transport of my own, then take care of me up to about 8pm. I am quite sure that Dr. Zukowski had calculated that if he covered her expense until I left his facility, then I would be able to have care from her virtually until I went to bed. What a kind and gracious thing for him to do to help me.

The caregiver, Milena, was very sweet and caring and showed me all that I had to do before she left. She would also continue to call me throughout the week to make sure I was okay. I truly wished that Prisci, my wife had been here as well. We should be sharing this together. Sorry reader, just got sad for a moment.

Pictures of me at the center and back at the hotel:

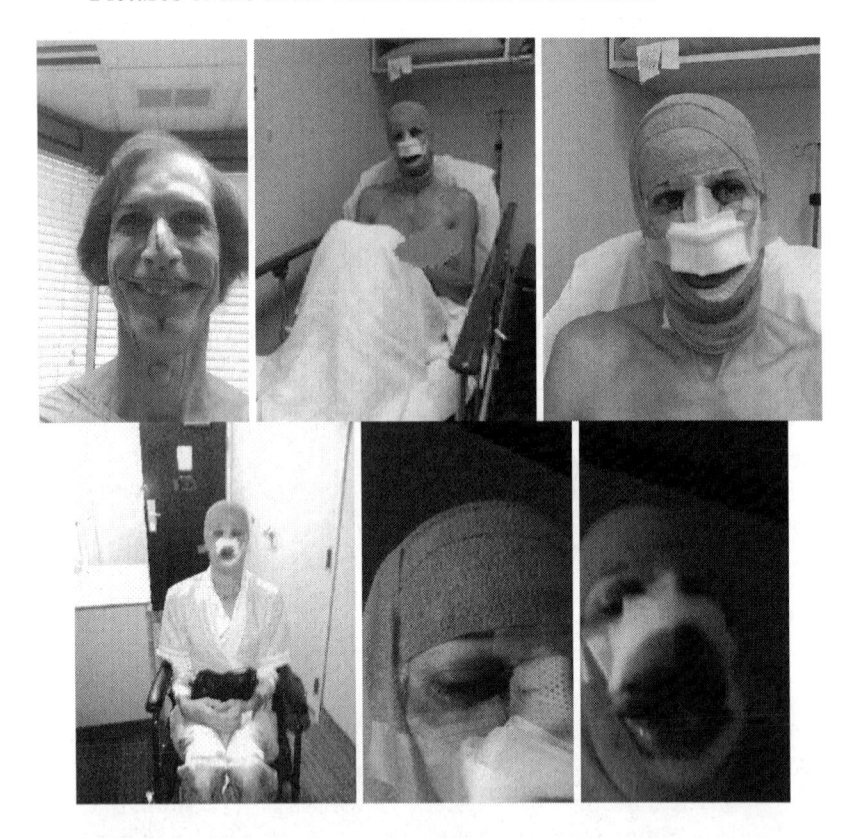

Not exactly too endearing are they! My throat hurts just a little from the breathing tube I had inside me there, My upper lip swollen to three times its size and now I know what it feels like to have a broken nose repaired! Of course, my nose job was somewhat more extensive and the doctor did a septoplasty that opens up the airways for easier breathing followed by a feminizing rhinoplasty which for me included, narrowing the bridge bone, slightly concaving my nose top arch, and balancing up my nostril as one was larger than the other. I had never even noticed that about my nostrils!

The shaving of my Adams Apple, the tracheal shave, went really well the doctor said. Other surgeons had told me that they may not be able to remove the entire Adams Apple as the vocal chords were situated very close, but Dr. Zukowski was able to remove it completely. He also pinned some of my throat skin and other things to my neck more to reduce the amount of skin that could go floppy on me around my neck.

This just left my upper lip which he did a few things to. He reduced its overall length, raised it up, and turned it out a little. He had also pointed out that my smile was uneven due to my left end lip side being lower than my right, something else I had never paid attention to. He fixed that too.

Finally he managed to locate enough fat from my belly to inject into my upper lip and to the sides of my lower lip to make them fuller. Fat grafting is semi-permanent in the lips and you can expect about 50% to remain and the rest to dissolve away over time.

To me, Dr. Mark Zukowski is at the peak of his work and after having a few discussions with him, I am honored for him to have worked on me. Not only is his work ethic impeccable but he really has a true heart to help genuine transgender people, I am totally convinced that he is doing just that in more ways than I think he realizes. He even came and visited me every day at my hotel room to make sure all was well.

The Zukowski Center in Chicago:

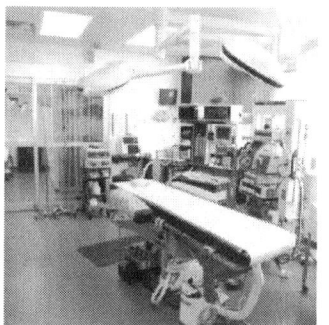

Right now it is late at night on the day of the surgery and I really want to make it clear that the level of care and attention that the Zukowski Center offers is most excellent. I am very impressed and I assure you for me to say it in this manner is unusual for me. Once I am fully recovered and the Lord blesses me with more finances one day, I hope to return here for sure to do a little more to my face which will probably consist of soft tissue work like eye lids, eye brow, face and neck lift.

My recovery from surgery was incredible. The first thing that was unusual, I did not even know about until that evening when back in my hotel room. Apparently, according to my nurse caregiver, Milena, I woke up out of general anesthetic almost two hours early and just 'snapped' out of the effect of it fully alert. Not only that but I could talk straight away and only had a really minor throat irritation. She told me all this and said that in ten years of working with Dr. Zukowski's patients they had never once seen that happen. Well, praise the Lord I say! Dr. Zukowski had also arranged for his two daughters to play their violins to me which they did while I was in the recovery room. It was wonderful to hear them both.

I drank liquids for those first two days but was healing so fast that on day three I was up and about eating solids at the Ruby Tuesday restaurant:

I also was able to take my first full shower on the third day. When I did so, nearly all my bandages just started falling off my face! I took pictures and texted my surgeon who said that if they were coming off then take them off! Okay! Off they came. Even the head bandage that you can see in the picture above I only wore for a few days as I had no excessive swelling at all. Although I had a whole course of pain killers, including valium, after only taking a few of the former, I never took them. I had zero pain! Praise the Lord, for He is good to me!

Crossing the Gender Line

Now here is a short chapter about something that I had no idea was going to happen at all. Crossing the gender line is about how the general public perceive me. Up to the point of having surgery, to many I was looking pretty good. Remember these pics taken in June 2014:

Now come on, not too bad for a fifty year old only six months after starting transition don't you think? But, and it's a big BUT, always when out in public people, a significant number of people would see me, stare once and often a second time and then, if I was still around just would not seem able to resist taking an occasional look at me. Now I had pretty much got used to it and because the Lord had delivered me from the fear of man, it no longer made me act any differently, but I still noticed them. After a while you get used to it as the norm and think no more about it. That is until…

Until I came out of surgery. I first noticed something different at the airport while waiting in the lounge before boarding my plane. Here I am on the left before surgery in the Tulsa International Airport, then at the Chicago airport to return home:

I would have thought that people would have paid more attention to me in the post-surgery state than when I flew out. Even if it was out of sympathy for my surgeries (they would not know what exactly and why I had surgeries). Nope, I found myself having very little attention toward me at all.

Having arrived safely back in Tulsa I noticed that only a few people paid attention to me as we filed off the plane. This is odd, I remember thinking. I was not seeking attention, I had just got used to people seeing me and processing what they saw.

Back in Tulsa I went to Ollie's, one of my local diners where all the staff know me well. Again the same phenomena. Same at my regular Starbucks, Chinese and Village Inn Restaurants. Something had clearly happened. Today, July 19th, nine days post-surgery, and my good friend Jackie and I were invited out for a meal with another friend. Here I am at the nine day timeline, then at the Royal Dragon Chinese about day fourteen (still a little swollen!):

And still people barely looked at me. I HAD SWITCHED SIDES on the whole. I thought at first it might just be because I was so bruised that people did not want to offend me and stare (kind of interesting if that were true as that would indicate that people felt that they have the right to stare more if gender expression is in question), but this is definitely not the case, at least now. In the eyes of the majority of the public, simply by re-shaping my nose, raising my upper lip and shaving off my Adams Apple made all the difference to how I am perceived. I still think that a good number still see me as male but it has become less offensive and less obvious so that they don't feel the need to continually look at me. Very odd things us humans are we not!?

Just to make it clear, I did not have these surgeries just so the public might notice me less in some way. I did it because the outward expression of who I am inside conflicted. Removing the maleness in my facial appearance delights my soul and I rejoice to the Lord my God that He has given me a way to do this, as He promised me He would in spite of all the other things that are happening in my life right now. For me, to say that God is good is an understatement!

A Letter to My Wife Prisci

My darling Prisci,

It may seem odd for me to write directly to you in a book, but I am doing so for a reason. I am not ashamed of who you are and all that you have thought, said and done since I met you in the prayer tower at the Oral Roberts University in 1993, and I want the whole world to know that I love you with all my heart, soul and strength. You have ALWAYS been good to me and always sought to ask forgiveness when your hurts and emotions have caused you to do otherwise. You are a true person, full of love and compassion, and you have exposed your heart to me over and over again, in spite of my weaknesses and sin. A man could ask for nothing more. I love you, spirit, soul, and body; you are beautiful to me in all ways.

I beg you my dear, do not pursue divorce but if you insist on doing so, please do so with the peace of the Lord telling you to do so. I am not going to stop loving you and in loving you that automatically means living together so that I can show you my love. Please find it in yourself to accept me as I am. I really am the same person inside. Nevertheless, do what God Himself tells you to do, for it is better you do His will and not mine.

I think about you every day and every night. I keep myself for you, my love. I desire no other. We can get through this together if you are willing. Seek the Lord as I am sure you already are. Wait until you clearly hear from Him before acting.

I am here waiting for you, waiting to hopefully come home to my baby, my Prisci, you, the love of my life. I know I do not deserve you and that is the truth. I am who I am Baby, so please do not reject me and break covenant. You are too good a person to do that and the Lord loves you too much. Be patient and trust in Him. I go to sleep thinking of you lying by my side and I can smell your scent and give you those little kisses to tell you I love you as you are. I was in church just this past Sunday and saw a lady rubbing her husband's back like you did mine, and I started crying. Don't you miss me too?

I am truly doing all I can with everything that has happened over these past six months or so. I want to help support you so please do not do things to prevent me from doing so to the best of my current ability. I gave you my word that I would take care of things but you took that out of my hands and we are both suffering because of this. I am doing my best, my love.

There is a passion that has been released inside of me for you like never before, so please do not harden your heart towards me my darling. I know you can look beyond mere appearances and behavior. Our love has been tested before, more than once, and we both know that we will have no peace being separated from each other. Being who I am is not a hardening of my heart baby, it is the opposite so please do not wait on me to change back as it were. I am who I am. Can you love and be with me for who I am? I wait on you.

My love, please forgive me for all I have ever done wrong to you. I love you, I love you, *I love you.*

Your loving, and still your husband, and sexually still your man,

Robbie

July 2014

I write this here to declare to all that read it that my love for you is true and that I want you and I want us to be together till death us depart as we so vowed.

The Current End of This Book!

I get up every day thanking the Lord my God that I can just be me. I am overwhelmed at this reality in my life. I thought that this would diminish as time went by, but the reverse seems to be true. There is a huge part of my soul that is increasingly amazed, and grateful with all joy that I am just being myself. The greatest of reasons for this I know is because God has given me great inner peace and that it is *He* who has orchestrated this in my life, and *He* who sustains me.

I still have regular times when I place my life before Him and give Him full acknowledgement that if He wants to change me in any way from being transgender, as long as it is by His hand, then please do it, but do it completely.

Without a shadow of doubt, it is not a sin before God to be transgender. This is a truth that all transgender people need to embrace. Like all people though, it is what we do with our lives that counts.

I have to end this book sometime, otherwise I am just going to continue to give you more stories of the grace of God on my life! Maybe I will write a sequel in a year or two! Actually, maybe sooner as new events are unfolding almost daily!

Questions like the following need to be answered: What will happen to my marriage? What doors to others will open? What kind of challenges await me in the church? What will I be doing in my life over the next few years? Will any of my family reconcile? Will I still be doing the handy-lady and remodeling jobs? Will my friend Art have a change of heart? Will I travel? To what extent will my worshipping the Lord on my violin be put to good use? Where and when will I be performing? How will everyone react to this book? Will it be well received? Will new doors open up for me to help educate others about being transgender? Will truth and love overcome the judgments of man? Will the church hide and keep silent? Will they open up and learn the truth? Will they react strongly against me? How will the newly forming business referral club work out? Lots of questions.

Already new events are piling up, including having the police and police detectives involved. More antics too with the business referral club! But, I will tell of all of this and more in my next book.

Before ending I am going to now do a summary and comments to the various people that I hope will get to read this book, so if you fit into one or more of these categories then please do take it personally:

To the transgender people out there:

Whether you see yourself as what I have defined holistically as a 'true' or a 'false' transgender person, or indeed if you are not sure which, or even if you are transgender, then I am speaking to you, my fellow human. I say human as that is a genderless reference and how wonderful this world would be for us if gender never was an issue for anyone. Reality is different and for us it is a journey that we have to navigate in our lives in order to become whole and at peace with ourselves. Stress, conflicts, and depressions, I think you might agree, happen every time we do not accept ourselves as we are. Many of us (probably all of us) have experienced this stress of being in conflict. But please remember, we experience this conflict due to the boundaries, rules if you were that society, the church impose on us and that we allow to influence us, as well as those things we impose on ourselves. This is where the lie is, not in who we are.

The great news is that more and more people are finally recognizing that we are genuine people, not some immoral, lust driven, rebellious to God and society bunch of freaks. So, whether you are at the beginning or at the end of transitioning in whatever form that looks like for you, may I invite you to shine for who you are. You are special my friend. You are unique and have an insight into life that goes beyond most.

If you are struggling emotionally, in your heart and conscience, then I applaud you to go get some wise counselling with someone that can help you discover *for yourself* who you are. Don't go to a person who is all for transgender people and who will just build you up and reassure you that all is well and to continue on the transgender path. Nor go to the opposite camp like the old school traditional church that insists you are what sex you were born as and so we will change your brain by the power and the Word of God! Go to someone non-judgmental and who is fine whether you discover that you are a 'true' or 'false' transgender person. If you truly are finding out that you are not transgender, then whether you believe in God or not, it would be a very good time just to raise your hands up to heaven and say "thank you God" because you have saved yourself years of tests and trials and you can go in peace. Do not go on what others tell you that you are. Don't be persuaded either way but find out for yourself whether you are or not. You have to get to the truth for yourself. My heart is that you get this answered for sure before you either start or continue to transform yourself. Inner peace is vital if you are on this path in life.

To the true transgender I say let's all stick together the best we can. There are hundreds of thousands of us here in the US alone. What I am saying is that you are NOT alone. If you are isolated, whether by your own actions and choice or not, may I really encourage you to step out just a little and find some good friends that are either transgender themselves or are very supportive and non-judgmental. Take it one step at a time. Try online and see where your nearest Equality transgender support group is. Find some wise transgender people online. Start to build relationships. I tell you the truth, you cannot transition without support, unless you want to go through many pains and trials that might otherwise have either been avoided or greatly reduced. I am a member of the Tulsa Transgender Support group at the Tulsa Equality center and they have all really helped me and come along side of me when I have needed someone to. In return I try to help others too. My friend, get involved a little bit, okay.

Finally, I want to let you know the truth about life being a transgender as a spirit being that you are, so here it is; Gods accepts the real you for who you are. He loves you passionately. Seek Him, find Him and hold Him in your heart. Live your life with integrity. I have told you where and how to find Him in this book. DO NOT get religious but stay at peace in your heart. Jesus is the door into Gods House my friend.

<u>To the body of Christ Jesus and the churches of today:</u>

Please be humble enough to take correction and question and revisit your values if you are judging transgender people as sinners because they are not conforming to their birth genital gender. Understand that gender and sexuality (sexual behaviors) are two different issues. Understand too that gender is not defined by your sex organs but by the brain which usually confirms that it identifies with the genitals, but not always this is so. Ever since the fall of Adam and Eve, the perfect male and female there are present every kind of body variation that you can think of. This includes the formation of the brain with regards to gender so don't pawn us off as having been deceived. Just because you may have a church doctrine that excludes true transgender people does not make it right. If you harden your heart to this truth, then you become the deceived ones before our Lord and I don't want that to continue in the body of Christ. Thankfully, more and more churches are gaining some knowledge and are both understanding and accepting of us now. May their reward in the final day be great.

    To those churches and bodies that insist on judging us and excluding us as we are, even though some of us are in the Kingdom of God, then the Lord's judgment be against you until you repent, but we pray mercy for you all. Please do not be ignorant of what being transgender is. Embrace us and many will either return back to, or come to the Lord. As a reminder, if you are part of a large church then it is very likely that you already have transgender people that attend, you just don't know it. Don't call them out and expose them, get educated, love them and let them know it is a safe place, a sanctuary, for them too and judge them not. And neither let their gifts and calling go to waste.

    If you have read this book and decide to turn a blind eye to this whole issue and just continue as you have been (after all, that's easier that way, right?), then know this: The Lord knows you have done that and He will judge you accordingly my friend. So please, DO something and make a difference. Be a part of reducing the transgender suicide rate and depressions that are currently rampant through the lack of love and acceptance. Shed the love of God that you have received into the hearts of lost transgender folk and find the lost sheep that have been sorely misjudged and condemned, so that they may be welcomed home. Be a healing arm that reaches out <u>and do not deny</u> them in the church to minister according to their calling and gifts.

    If you would like to communicate with me directly, then please refer to the contact information in appendix 2. I will be more than happy to talk over the phone or visit if appropriate. It is my heart's passion to reveal the truth in this matter I will do all I can to do my part in this for the sake of the Kingdom of God, our Lord and savior Jesus Christ.

To the counselors, doctors and surgeons that participate in helping transgender people:

God bless you all for doing your part to the best of your abilities. From all the transgender people that you are helping, with all our hearts we thank you. Help us please to educate others that being transgender is real and acceptable in our lives, in society, and in church. I know that some of you get morally questioned or challenged, even threatened because you help us. Thank you for being willing to take the heat and continue to help us all. We all thank you for all you do and please continue to help us all including educating others about this reality.

To the general public:

Thank you so much for reading this book. Whether you already knew about being transgender or not, I hope that the information has helped you in some way. I also personally hope that if you have never turned to your maker, then you will make a heart choice to turn to the Kingdom of God through the correct doorway, that is Jesus Christ and that you may dwell with peace in your heart that God will give you. Please feel free to contact me with any questions or sincere comments. Thank you.

To my family:

I guess I should know how you all would react based upon your stance on how my life has impacted you and other family members. So, I expect negative responses due to that, but if you are able to look beyond all that and see me for who I am and the message freely offered, then it is my hope that you will find it in your hearts not only to forgive me for all my wrongs, but to also reconcile us all together. I guess it all depends on your judgments towards me, and the desire or maybe ability to accept change, even a dramatic change as I have gone through.

With all my heart, and twenty years of working to support you, I love you all very much and if there is even a possibility that we could all be together as we all are, then my joy would be complete as at present there is a hole in my heart that only you all can fill. Prisci, I love you my darling, please forgive me for being me. Bianca, please somehow find a different judgment that allows me into your life. Jeremy, we are so alike in many ways, please use that wonderful gift you have to forgive me and let us at least stay in touch together. Jacob, you who will put all your efforts and heart into helping us, thank you and know I love you and Christy.

Charlotte and Jemma, I love you two girls, now ladies, and I bless you in the Lord with hope that one day you will both love me for who I am too. You know how to get in contact with me if you want to. I am waiting.

    I miss you all dearly. Please don't judge me until you are perfect. Please don't ostracize me nor do that disowning thing. I love you all. Please look beyond my presentation and ways and you will still see me, can you not do that and just accept me who I am and let me be me? Do I have to really lose you all if I am going to be real?

Appendix 1 – Online Documentaries and Articles

Transgender documentaries:

Please note that if you wish to view the video at YouTube.com then you can search for the title if you cannot use the link.

This first one is an HBO production that covers many aspects of being transgender. I would like to particularly mention the research that was done at the Free University Hospital in Amsterdam that went on to discover that the brains of transsexual male to female was found to be like that of a woman's, not a man's in construction:

Real Evidence (Transsexual-Transgender Brain Research)
https://youtu.be/W_655Vt6LKA

A Transgender HBO Biography Special - Middle Sexes
https://www.youtube.com/watch?v=ZFoe_0_gThw&feature=player_detailpage

Gender Change - Full Episode
https://www.youtube.com/watch?v=0hjIeg1tE68&feature=player_detailpage

Transgender and Christian
https://www.youtube.com/watch?v=ybffUHxSKI4&feature=player_detailpage

A more physiological medical approach:
Gender Dysphoria Treatment
https://www.youtube.com/watch?v=0tqil7Audws&feature=player_detailpage

Me My Sex And I : BBC Documentary
http://www.youtube.com/watch?v=7ZRD1OdHBA4&sns=em

The Transgender Taboo
https://www.youtube.com/watch?feature=player_detailpage&v=s76j6KxBwiI

I am a Transgender Woman and Proud of it -part 1:
http://youtu.be/zOWszwzO7CY

Our America with Lisa Ling - Transgender Child: A...:
http://youtu.be/S5P9kUz0yO0

Other related material on the internet:

An audio recording
https://soundcloud.com/rightwingwatch/harvey-satan-behind-transgender-rights-movement?utm_source=soundcloud&utm_campaign=share&utm_medium=email
Being Transgender in America | Larry King Now
http://youtu.be/4ZeTYZT2ESo

'I used to think being me would be a barrier': transgender woman honored
http://globalnews.ca/news/1720163/i-used-to-think-being-me-would-be-a-barrier-transgender-edmonton-woman-honoured/

Transgender and Christian:
http://youtu.be/ybffUHxSKI4

On the lighter side a little, here are a bunch of musicians from my home city in England that are all men that have to pass as performing women in concert.

Boys Who Wear Dresses: Gender Fluid, Nonconformin...:
http://youtu.be/WBblBjk_5js

Boys Who Wear Dresses #2: How You Can Help Your G...:
http://youtu.be/zKlU9EqeeDM

Intersexed documentaries:

Here is a most excellent BBC Documentary about the inter-sexed
Me My Sex And I
http://www.youtube.com/watch?v=7ZRD1OdHBA4&sns=em

Growing up intersex Part 1
https://www.youtube.com/watch?feature=player_detailpage&v=I9a1rXOpIuc

ig up intersex Part 2
://www.youtube.com/watch?feature=player_detailpage&v=vFd-_ikaQ3k

Intersex Advocate Hida Viloria In-Depth Interview By Jeff 4 Justice
https://www.youtube.com/watch?feature=player_detailpage&v=DmDP238ltHk

Documentaries concerning transgender children are quite common. Here are just a few:

Real Life: Transgender Children
https://www.youtube.com/watch?feature=player_detailpage&v=R0BmtInLGt8

Living a Transgender Childhood
https://www.youtube.com/watch?v=oYOY1CIyd_0&feature=player_detailpage

Diagnostic Criteria of Gender Identity disorder
https://www.youtube.com/watch?feature=player_detailpage&v=txd4Ycjl5ys

An Indian documentary:
'I'dentity - A documentary on Gender Identity Disorder (GID)
https://www.youtube.com/watch?feature=player_detailpage&v=V60lYY41slg

Barbara Walters has done quite a few documentaries about transgender children. Here is one that she did for 20/20:

20/20 A Story of Transgender Children
https://www.youtube.com/watch?v=YfqmEYC_rMI&feature=player_detailpage

I am Jazz
https://www.youtube.com/watch?v=Bk_YlBM5JAE&feature=player_detailpage

Here is one that is closer to home for me as I live in Tulsa, Oklahoma. The true story of Katie Rain Hill. She was the first transgender person that seemed to appear in the public eye right here in the middle of the Bible belt as a high school student. I understand that Katie was the first known transgender student to graduate from high school in the state. I know that she had some really testing times. I was fortunate to meet a friend of hers that attended the same school as Katie and she told me stories of how she had to encourage her while under masses of rejection which I fear was from conservative legalistic Christians that believed that they were right and somehow this gave them the right to act according to their own convictions. I hope Katie is doing well and that the actions of the so called Christians have not turned her heart away from the Lord for good. There are a few shorter videos but these seem to be the longest that tells her story:

Katie 19 and Arin 17 Teen Transgender Couple:
http://www.youtube.com/watch?v=Du_FdwIkzpE&sns=em

A Girl who was a boy fell in love with a boy who was a girl:
http://www.youtube.com/watch?v=6e6fpiqpxX4&sns=em

Update July 2014: I got to meet Katie and she is doing great. Totally at peace with who she is. She has just published a book about her life called 'Rethinking Normal' published by Simon and Schuster. I have read the book and thoroughly enjoyed it. An good book for people to read to help someone understand what a teenage transgender person goes through particularly with regards to young relationships. Here I am with her. Isn't she fabulous!

ly read another excellent book, a memoir by Chaz Bono, the ~~daughter~~ son of Sonny and Cher Bono. There are many very good truths in ~~his~~ book. One that I want to point out is how he came to a wrong conclusion that he must be a lesbian as he was clearly attracted to females and always acted the male role in that kind of relationship. It was only years later that he truly discovered why, that she is a he, a transgender man. Called, TRANSITION, it is published by Dutton, part of the Penguin Group, ISBN #978-0-525-95214-5

Here is a link to an interview with Chaz:

Nightline - Chaz Bono On Transitioning From Female
http://youtu.be/l-BHPl0-rsw

Here are some online articles and videos that discuss the physical development of a transgender person. Both sex organs and brain development differences are explained:

The Gender Puzzle:
https://www.youtube.com/watch?v=XPY28QW4T4E&feature=player_detailpage

Secrets of the Sexes - Episode 1: Brainsex (Documentary)
https://www.youtube.com/watch?v=uKk-VAMOsLk&feature=player_detailpage

Transas City:
http://transascity.org/the-transgender-brain/

A.E. Brain has various links for more research:
http://aebrain.blogspot.com/p/transsexual-and-intersex-gender-identity.html

Neuroscience of sex differences:
http://en.m.wikipedia.org/wiki/Neuroscience_of_sex_differences

Is there any scientific evidence to support that people can be born transgender?
https://answers.yahoo.com/question/index?qid=20110422202859AAD76tM

NewScientist: Transsexual differences caught on brain scan
http://www.newscientist.com/article/dn20032-transsexual-differences-caught-on-brain-scan.html#.VA9hUYd0yM8

PHYSICAL EVIDENCE FOR BEING TRANSGENDER. Article: Do Your Homework, Dr. Ablow
http://m.huffpost.com/us/entry/4616722

The above article references fifteen completed studies that I list independently here for you:

1) Sex Differentiation: Organizing Effects of Sex Hormones; Focus on Sexuality Research, 2014
http://link.springer.com/chapter/10.1007/978-1-4614-7441-8_1

2) Duisburg birth cohort study we studied associations of prenatal exposure to PCDD/Fs and PCBs with parent reported sexually dimorphic behavior in children: Environmental health perspectives, 2013
http://ehp.niehs.nih.gov/wp-content/uploads/121/11/ehp.1306533.pdf

3) European Journal of Physiology, 2013n (Starting at the intro)
http://www.cakeworld.info/transsexualism/sexual-identity-intro

4) Neuroscience in the 21st century, 2013
http://link.springer.com/referenceworkentry/10.1007/978-1-4614-1997-6_115

5) Journal of the Turkish-German Gynecological Association, 2013
http://www.journalagent.com/z4/download_fulltext.asp?pdir=jtgga&plng=tur&un=JTGGA-86836

6) The Journal of Neuroscience, 2012
http://www.jneurosci.org/content/32/2/674.abstract

7) Hormones and Behavior, 2012
http://www.sciencedirect.com/science/article/pii/S0018506X1200044X

8) The Journal of Sexual Medicine, 2012
http://www.ncbi.nlm.nih.gov/pubmed/22738413

Annual review of neuroscience, 2011
www.ncbi.nlm.nih.gov/pubmed/21438685

10) Journal of Pediatric Endocrinology and Metabolism, 2010
http://www.degruyter.com/view/j/jpem.2010.23.issue-6/jpem.2010.095/jpem.2010.095.xml

11) Faculty of Medicine, Universiteit Utrecht, 2010
http://dspace.library.uu.nl/handle/1874/182733

12) Paper prepared for the International Behavioral Development Symposium, 2005
http://www.shb-info.org/sitebuildercontent/sitebuilderfiles/desexposedhbs.pdf

13) Psychoneuroendocrinology, 2004
http://www.ncbi.nlm.nih.gov/pubmed/15177706

14) University of Amsterdam, 2004
http://dare.uva.nl/document/75961

15) University of Gothenburg, 1999
https://gupea.ub.gu.se/handle/2077/12418

The 15 studies listed above is a very small, partial list. V.S. Ramachandran has published a number of studies showing transgender individuals are wired to physically experience bodies of the opposite sex as well.
http://cbc.ucsd.edu/ramabio.html

Human Chromosomal Abnormalities: Sex Chromosome Abnormalities
http://anthro.palomar.edu/abnormal/abnormal_5.htm

Movies

I do have a list of movies but have decided just to include this one film as it is a true story:

A Girl Like Me The Gwen Araujo Story
https://www.youtube.com/watch?v=6jk_lxpW654&feature=player_detailpage

Appendix 2 – Contact Information

Name: Ms. Robbie Dee Ewens
Born: In England, UK June 25th 1962
Gender: Female
(Transgender, so please use female pro-nouns. Thank you.)

Address location: Tulsa, Oklahoma, USA
Email address: msrobbieewens@gmail.com
Facebook name: Robbie Dee Ewens
(all pages are public for viewing)

Acknowledgements

I would like to thank many, many people and organizations that have given up their time and resources to help me. So many people that are now personal friends have contributed in ways that they are not even aware of. I thank you all. I list them in no particular order. Being that so many people have directly or indirectly encouraged and supported me to find out what being transgender is all about, please forgive me if I do not mention you directly:

- Tulsa Equality Center, OKEQ which is just a building but has many amazing people working there and visiting there.
- The Wednesday transgender support group that is held at the OKEQ where I have made numerous friends during my first year that have all supported me in various ways. Thank you all.
- Individual conversations with other transgender people who have opened up their hearts and life stories to me.
- My doctor, Dr. J. Block for taking care of my body as I transition. A most caring and skilled person. Wonderful staff too!
- Counselor Ms. Jo Ann Howse who did a great job of listening and confirming who I am.
- Vicki Sue, my laser and electrolysis specialist.
- Dr. Mark Zukowski, for his amazing ethics, caring approach and impeccable skill who performed some facial work for me. I thank you and your staff.
- My close brother and sister in the Lord, Jackie Meeks, for continually supporting me when I really needed help.
- The staff and waitresses at the following places:
- Big Red Restaurant at Park Hill, near Tahlequah
- Village Inn 27th and Harvard, Tulsa
- Ollie's railway Restaurant, Tulsa
- Starbucks 51st and Harvard, Tulsa
- Gypsy Coffee House, Downtown Tulsa
- Royal Dragon Chinese Restaurant, Tulsa
- 95% of the general public here in Tulsa who, to my great surprise openly help and never came against me. I have had so, so many amazing conversations that I could fill this whole book with.

- Hundreds of transgender people online through Facebook.
- My proof readers and critics, Ms Carol Drummond, Lance Eames and a few others that want to remain anonymous.
- All my customers for not only accepting me, even if some do not understand, but are fully supportive as I reach out to help others.
- The organizers of the events at Guthrie Green for allowing me to freely perform there and hopefully touch the lives of other people.
- The wonderful staff at First Tulsa Federal Credit Union here in Tulsa for their support.
- To my friends that knew me prior to my transitioning and did not judge me and many who supported me. Thank you with all my heart.
- To the Lord my God through Christ Jesus, who not only gives me courage and strength but protects and guides me at all times. Great is His favor towards me, great is His mercy on my life. Thank you for making me whole.

Made in the USA
San Bernardino, CA
28 March 2017